FINANCIAL PROVISION ON DIVORCE AND DISSOLUTION OF CIVIL PARTNERSHIPS

AUSTRALIA
Law Book Co.
Sydney

CANADA and USA
Carswell
Toronto

HONG KONG
Sweet & Maxwell Asia

NEW ZEALAND
Brookers
Wellington

SINGAPORE and MALAYSIA
Sweet & Maxwell Asia
Singapore and Kuala Lumpur

FINANCIAL PROVISION ON DIVORCE AND DISSOLUTION OF CIVIL PARTNERSHIPS

Alan Bayley
Solicitor, Stodarts

THOMSON

★ ™

W. GREEN

Published in 2008 by
W. Green & Son Ltd
21 Alva Street
Edinburgh EH2 4PS

www.wgreen.thomson.com

Typeset by LBJ Typesetting Ltd, Kingsclere
Printed and bound in Great Britain by MPG Books Ltd.

No natural forests were destroyed to make this product;
only farmed timber was used and replanted

A CIP catalogue record for this book is available from
the British Library.

ISBN 978-0-414-01629-3

ACKNOWLEDGEMENTS

My particular thanks are due to Ruth Leonard for her detailed research and administrative support. It would simply have been impossible to complete this book without her assistance. My demands on her time have been unreasonable, but despite this she has retained her typical composure and good humour. I suspect she must punch cushions when she gets home at night.

Special thanks also go to my sister, Jan Bayley, for many hours spent proof-reading the text, generally late at night when sensible people should know better. I am also grateful to Lyndsey Clark, Joanne Nicoll, Keith Elrick and Gillian McLean for their assistance in this task. I choose not to believe that they simply had nothing better to do, and instead count myself lucky to have family, friends and colleagues who are so generous and talented.

I would also like to express my gratitude to everyone at Stodarts, Solicitors in Hamilton for their help and encouragement. In particular, my partner Grant Wood's expert guidance on child support was invaluable, and my secretary Annette Duff's high speed transcription of my nonsensical dictation nothing short of miraculous.

My good friend Adrian Stalker has a magnificent shoulder to whinge on.

My wife, Shirley Ann, has been both supportive and patient throughout this project (and, now that I come to think of it, with me more generally). I now look forward to spending more time with her, and with Roslyn and Jonathan. I'm not yet sure how they feel about this.

This also seems an opportune time to thank my mum and dad, Yuille and Meg Bayley, for their constant support, guidance and love. I dedicate this book to my mum. I have been lucky—marriage and family were everything to her.

CONTENTS

TABLE OF CASES

TABLE OF STATUTES

Acts of the Scottish Parliament

TABLE OF STATUTORY INSTRUMENTS

CHAPTER 1

INTRODUCTION

Background

The Family Law (Scotland) Act 1985 ("the Act") sets out the **1–01** legislative framework for financial provision on divorce and dissolution of civil partnerships in Scotland. The Act was introduced following extensive consultation and research by The Scottish Law Commission,[1] and the new rules on financial provision replaced a simpler, discretion-based system provided in the previous statute.[2] The previous system had been criticised because it failed to provide any certainty for couples facing the stressful business of dividing property on divorce. The Act aims to address this by setting out five principles and various other factors which provide a framework within which the courts must operate when deciding how to make financial provision for separating parties. The court still has a considerable discretion, but this must be exercised within the framework of the Act.

In many cases prior to the Act, the courts made awards against one spouse (usually the ex-husband) ordering them to pay periodical allowance to the other (usually the ex-wife). These awards were often to last until the death or re-marriage of the spouse receiving the support. The Act moved away from this reliance on continuing support and introduced a system where a clean break was encouraged. As far as possible, the courts will now seek to make orders for financial provision which finally dispose of all financial matters without the need for any on-going payments by one party to the other after decree. Periodical allowance remains an option, but only if a clean break is not possible, and usually only for a limited period.

The Civil Partnership Act 2004 introduced civil partnerships to Scotland. The rules for financial provision under the Act have been amended so that they now cover not only married couples who are divorcing, but also couples who are dissolving a civil partnership. The rules for financial provision are the same in both situations. It should also be noted that the law on financial provision under the Act applies equally to nullity,[3] although throughout this book the terms "divorce" and "dissolution" will be used.

Scope of this book

The rules introduced in the Act apply in relation to actions com- **1–02** menced on or after September 1, 1986, and this book deals with financial provision on divorce or dissolution of civil partnerships in actions raised

---

[1] See *Aliment and Financial Provision*, Scot. Law Com. No.67 (1981).
[2] The Divorce (Scotland) Act 1976.
[3] s.17.

after that date. It does not deal with cases raised before that date.[4] This book does not deal with actions for aliment of spouses or civil partners, although the provision of interim aliment for a spouse or civil partner pending divorce or dissolution is discussed. Issues relating to financial support of children are not covered. The book deals with the rules for financial provision set up in the Act, but does not discuss how parties might seek to regulate matters between themselves through separation agreements.

Some context

1–03   Most married couples and civil partners who break up do not go to court to settle the financial issues arising from their separation. For the most part, parties are able to resolve matters themselves or with assistance from solicitors and mediators. This is encouraging—whilst the Act provides rules and techniques which can be used (and imposed) if settlement is not achieved, it is by no means a perfect instrument. The biggest problem is one of uncertainty. In some cases the award which a court is likely to make—using the provisions of the Act—can be predicted with reasonable accuracy. However, more often than not, even experienced family lawyers will be unable to predict exactly how a court will split resources. Some uncertainties are created simply because certain assets (such as businesses) are difficult to value and wide discrepancies can be found in valuations produced by well-intentioned (and often expensive) experts. Other uncertainties arise because in many cases the courts will have quite a wide discretion, both in relation to the amount each party is to receive on decree, and in relation to the particular orders to be used to effect the final financial split. This uncertainty means that often all that an adviser will be able to do is to suggest a range of possible results to a client, all of which would be within the discretion of the court to order. If a court reaches a decision which is properly within its sphere of discretion, an appeal will not be successful. Unfortunately, this means that clients and their advisers are often left in a situation where there are no clear answers.

This problem of uncertainty can sometimes present an opportunity. It is a mistake for separating parties and their advisers to imagine that the rules set out in the Act provide the only mechanism which they can use to resolve financial issues. The Act only provides a limited range of options and techniques for clients who cannot agree matters. There may be other solutions which are right for some families but which a court would be unlikely to consider if working within the confines of the Act. For example, the Act stresses the importance of a clean break, but there are many couples who opt quite successfully for a more organic approach to the separation of their finances. Equally, the structure of the Act may not provide enough detail for some couples, and issues which might be very important for them might be ignored altogether by the courts: who is to pay for the school trip and what about the cost of music lessons or a birthday party? Still less does the Act take into account

---

[4] As a useful starting point for research on such cases see E.M. Clive, *The Law of Husband and Wife in Scotland*, 4th edn, (Edinburgh: W.Green, 1997), para.24.009.

emotional considerations and the important matter of maintaining a civil relationship for the sake of young children.

Of course, all of this is not to say that practitioners working in the field of family law do not need to have a sound knowledge of the Act and the way it works. They must be able to advise clients on their rights, obligations and the court procedures which may be used to protect their interests. Indeed, professional self-preservation dictates that solicitors must clearly warn clients if they give up valuable rights in a deal which falls short of the division of finances which they might achieve through the courts. However, no-one should lose sight of the fact that it is not just the matters raised by the Act which will be important to clients. In many ways the Act is a rather blunt instrument for hammering out a split of finances where all else has failed. Clients and their advisers who think creatively may well be able to find solutions which work very well for them, but which are radically different from terms which might be imposed by a court.

CHAPTER 2

AN OVERVIEW OF FINANCIAL PROVISION

Introduction

2–01   The Family Law (Scotland) Act 1985 ("the Act") provides a frame-work for courts when making decisions relating to financial provision on divorce and dissolution of civil partnerships. It is useful to have a working knowledge of the structure of the Act. The following are the most important sections of the Act for the purposes of financial provision:

Section 6	sets out provisions for interim aliment pending inter alia decree of divorce or dissolution.
Section 8	(along with s.8A) sets out the orders available to the court when making an award of financial provision.
Section 9	sets out five principles which the court is to use to calculate entitlement to financial provision. The most important is set out in s.9(1)(a) which provides for "fair sharing" of matrimonial and partnership property. Other principles are set out in s.9(1)(b)–(e).
Section 10	expands on the principle set out in s.9(1)(a) which provides for "fair sharing" of matrimonial and partnership property. Fair sharing will normally be equal sharing but the court can depart from this if "special circumstances" exist.
Section 11	expands on the principles set out in s.9(1)(b)–(e).
Sections 12–15	(including s.12A) give detailed rules regarding how the orders set up in s.8 are to work.
Section 16	makes provision for how agreements between the parties relating to financial provision may be varied or set aside by the court in certain circumstances.
Section 18	contains provisions allowing the court to vary or set aside certain transactions designed to avoid claims for financial provision.
Section 27	provides key definitions.

The interrelated principles, orders and other factors set out in the Act can be complex in the way that they apply in any particular case, but they are drawn up reasonably concisely within a few sections of the Act. The remainder of this chapter aims to give a brief outline of the statutory provisions which have a bearing on financial provision.

The orders

In an action of divorce or dissolution of a civil partnership, either **2–02** party may apply to the court for various orders. These are known as orders for financial provision[1] and they are listed in s.8(1) of the Act. They are dealt with in greater detail in Ch.3 but, in summary, the orders are:

(1) An order for payment of a *capital sum*.[2] The capital sum may be payable immediately on decree of divorce or dissolution, or it may be deferred to a specified future date. The court also has power to order that payment of the capital sum is made in instalments. It may be appropriate for interest to be paid on the capital sum.

(2) An order for a *transfer of property*.[3] These orders allow ownership of particular assets to be transferred from one party to the other as part of the overall order for financial provision. The transfer may be ordered immediately after decree of divorce or dissolution, or alternatively at a specified future date. There are protections for the rights of third parties with an interest in the assets to be transferred.

(3) An order for payment of a *periodical allowance*.[4] These are orders requiring one party to make a regular payment of income to the other. Periodical allowance may only be ordered: (a) if it is justified under particular principles of the Act; and (b) if the court is unable to dispose of the action in a way that creates a clean break between the parties.[5] Orders for periodical allowance will generally be for a limited period of time, although in certain fairly narrow circumstances the order may be without limit of time. It is open to parties to apply for a variation of an order for a periodical allowance if there is a material change of circumstances at a later date.

(4) A *pension sharing order*.[6] These orders allow the court to transfer some (or all) of the pension rights of one spouse or civil partner to the other. This will give the transferee their own pension fund.

(5) A *pension lump sum order* (commonly called an *earmarking order*).[7] These allow the court to provide for a capital sum to be

---

[1] s.8(3).
[2] s.8(1)(a).
[3] s.8(1)(aa).
[4] s.8(1)(b).
[5] s.13(2); see para.2–07 below.
[6] s.8(1)(baa).
[7] s.8(1)(ba) which refers to the terms of s.12A.

paid by one party ("the liable person") to the other out of any lump sum to be paid at a future date under the liable person's pension scheme.

(6) Various *incidental orders*.[8] The Act lists a wide variety of these facilitative orders.

A two-stage test

2–03   There is a two-stage test which must be satisfied before the court should grant any orders for financial provision.[9] First, the court is only to make such s.8 orders as are justified by the principles set out in s.9 of the Act. These principles are discussed briefly later in this chapter and in more detail in Ch.4. Secondly, any orders must be reasonable having regard to the resources of the parties. The term "resources" includes the present and foreseeable resources of the parties.[10] This provision provides a safety net for parties where, by the time of a proof, their resources have diminished to a point where they simply cannot afford to meet orders which would otherwise be justified in terms of the s.9 principles. This two-stage test is examined in detail at paras 3–02 to 3–08 of this book. Whilst the Act provides this useful safety net, it should always be kept in mind that s.8 sets out a wide range of potential orders. Even if one party has little money available at the time of the proof and cannot afford to pay a capital sum to the other party immediately, they might still be able to meet an award in favour of the other party through other s.8 orders such as a capital sum payable in instalments, payment of periodical allowance or through pension sharing.

The section 9 principles

2–04   As already mentioned, the court should only make an order for financial provision if it is justified under the five principles set out in s.9(1) of the Act. These principles are discussed in detail in Ch.4, but for the purposes of this introduction there follows a brief overview.

Fair sharing of matrimonial or partnership property

2–05   The first (and the most important) of the s.9 principles is set out in s.9(1)(a). This provides that the net value of the "matrimonial property" or "partnership property" is to be shared fairly between the parties.[11] There is a presumption that fair sharing will be equal sharing unless the court finds there are "special circumstances".[12] Section 9(1)(a) cannot be used to justify payment of a periodical allowance.[13]

It is the "matrimonial property" or "partnership property" which is owned by the parties at the "relevant date" which is to be shared on divorce or dissolution. The definition of the term "relevant date" is

---

[8] s.8(1)(c).
[9] s.8(2).
[10] s.27(1).
[11] s.9(1)(a).
[12] s.10(1).
[13] s.13(2).

important and is dealt with in detail in Ch.5 of this book. Speaking broadly for now, it will generally be the date that the parties finally separate.[14] The matrimonial property and partnership property will be all of the property belonging to the parties at the relevant date which was acquired by them or either of them (otherwise than by way of gift or succession) during the marriage or civil partnership but before the relevant date.[15] Property acquired before the marriage or civil partnership for use as a family home or as furniture or plenishings for that home will also be matrimonial or partnership property.[16] As it is the *net value* of the matrimonial or partnership property which is to be shared, any appropriate debts of the parties at the relevant date will also fall to be taken into account in establishing the value to be shared.[17] There is a more detailed examination of matrimonial and partnership property in Ch.6 of this book.

The value of property will change from time to time, so the precise date that the matrimonial or partnership property is to be valued is important. Generally, it is to be valued at the relevant date.[18] There is one important exception to this rule: where an item of property is to be transferred from one party to the other as part of the order for financial provision, then that item will be valued at a date to be agreed between the parties, or failing agreement, at the date of transfer (or in exceptional circumstances at a date as near as may be to the date of transfer as the court may determine).[19]

Although there is a presumption that fair sharing means equal sharing, the court may depart from this if it finds that there are special circumstances.[20] Special circumstances are considered in detail in Ch.7 and they allow the court to have regard to a wide range of factors. For example, the court may take into account the terms of any agreement between the parties, the fact that matrimonial or partnership property was acquired using funds belonging exclusively to one of the parties, or circumstances where it is unreasonable to realise an asset because (for example) it is needed for young children of the family.

The other section 9 principles

Although fair sharing of matrimonial property or partnership property **2–06** under s.9(1)(a) is the most important of the s.9 principles, there are four other principles which need to be considered. They are set out in s.9(1)(b)–(e). It is important to realise that an award under any of these four principles does not rely on a split of the matrimonial or partnership property. The principles are quite independent of s.9(1)(a) and of special circumstances arguments (which bear only on the division of matrimonial and partnership property). So, for example, the court might order that a payment justified under any of the principles set out in s.9(1)(b)–

---

[14] s.10(3) but subject to the provisions of s.10(7).
[15] s.10(2).
[16] s.10(4) and 10(4A).
[17] s.10(2).
[18] s.10(2).
[19] s.10(3A).
[20] s.10(6).

(e) is made by one party to the other even where there is no matrimonial or partnership property.

Section 9(1)(b) states that fair account is to be taken of any economic advantage derived by either person from the contributions of the other, and of any economic disadvantage suffered by either person in the interests of the other or of the family. So, for example, if one party (often the wife) with good career prospects gives up work in order to raise a young family and her career prospects are damaged, s.9(1)(b) might be used to redress any economic disadvantage suffered by her. Like s.9(1)(a), this section cannot be used to justify payment of a periodical allowance.

Section 9(1)(c) provides that any economic burden of caring after divorce or dissolution for a child of the family under the age of 16 should be shared fairly between the parties. This allows the court to recognise that fair sharing of matrimonial or partnership property may require that the party with the principal burden of caring for the children should receive something more than aliment or child support for the children. This principle may be used to justify any of the s.8 orders including payment of a periodical allowance.

Under s.9(1)(d), a person who has been dependent to a substantial degree on the financial support of the other person should be awarded such financial provision as is reasonable to enable him to adjust, over a period of not more than three years after decree, to the loss of that support. So, in circumstances where one party has developed a substantial financial dependency on the other during the course of the marriage or civil partnership, the court can recognise this in the orders for financial provision by making an award which will allow them to adjust to their new circumstances. This principle may be used to justify any of the s.8 orders including an award of periodical allowance for up to three years.

Under s.9(1)(e), a person who at the time of divorce or dissolution seems likely to suffer serious financial hardship as a result of the divorce or dissolution should be awarded such financial provision as is reasonable to relieve him of hardship over a reasonable period. Sometimes, even after the other principles are taken into account, it is clear that one party will be left in a position of serious financial hardship as a result of the divorce or dissolution, and s.9(1)(e) provides them with a safety net. Whilst it is possible for the court to use the provision to justify an enhanced "one off" award (e.g. an extra capital sum, or the transfer of an asset), the court more often uses this provision to justify an award of periodical allowance, sometimes for an indefinite period of time.

Clean breaks encouraged

2-07   The Act allows for on-going support after the divorce or dissolution in the form of periodical allowance, which is an order requiring one party to pay a regular sum to the other following the divorce or dissolution. However, the Act discourages this by stating that periodical allowance is only to be paid if an order for payment of a capital sum, transfer of property or pension sharing is inappropriate or insufficient.[21] Further, a

---

[21] s.13(2)(b).

periodical allowance is only to be paid if it is justified under the principles set out in s.9(1)(c), (d) or (e)—s.9(1)(a) and (b) alone (and these are the most commonly used principles) cannot justify payment of a periodical allowance.[22] In this way the Act is said to encourage a "clean break". Therefore, the court should first determine whether financial provision can be effected through an order that disposes of all financial matters without the need for on-going periodical allowance. Only if this cannot be achieved should periodical allowance be considered. Periodical allowance is examined in more detail at paras 3–32 to 3–45.

Conduct

The court is not to take into account the conduct of the parties unless **2–08** (a) the conduct has adversely affected the financial resources of the parties, or (b) in relation to the principles set out in s.9(1)(d) and (e), it would be manifestly inequitable to leave the conduct out of account.[23] Conduct is considered in more detail at paras 4–12 to 4–14.

Interim aliment

In an action for divorce or dissolution of a civil partnership, either **2–09** party may apply for interim aliment pending final disposal of the case.[24] Interim aliment is designed to provide an income for a party in need until longer-term financial provision is made upon decree of divorce or dissolution. Interim aliment is dealt with in more detail in Ch.8 of this book.

A discretionary approach

Although the rules set out in the Act establish a framework within **2–10** which the court is to operate, they do not impose a rigid formula. Even if matrimonial or partnership property is established and valued with clarity, this does not allow an accurate prediction of how the courts will make financial provision. The courts have discretion in many key areas, for example: which s.9 principles to apply and the weight to be given to those principles; whether there are special circumstances and whether (and to what extent) they might justify a departure from equal sharing; and which orders to apply when finally making financial provision for the parties upon divorce or dissolution. Provided that the court does not make an error in law, or a material error of fact and does not exercise the discretion in a wholly unreasonable way, its decision will not be interfered with on appeal.

---

[22] s.13(2)(a).
[23] s.11(7).
[24] s.6.

CHAPTER 3

SECTION 8—ORDERS FOR FINANCIAL PROVISION

INTRODUCTION TO SECTION 8 ORDERS

General discussion

3–01   Section 8(1) of the Family Law (Scotland) Act 1985 ("the Act") sets out the particular orders which are available to the court when making an overall order for financial provision. The section provides:

> "In an action for divorce, either party to the marriage and in an action for dissolution of a civil partnership, either partner may apply to the court for one or more of the following orders—
>
> > (a) an order for the payment of a capital sum to him by the other party to the action;
> > (aa) an order for the transfer of property to him by the other party to the action;
> > (b) an order for the making of a periodical allowance to him by the other party to the action;
> > (baa) a pension sharing order;
> > (ba) an order under section 12A(2) or (3) of this Act;
> > (c) an incidental order within the meaning of section 14(2) of this Act."

To break this down into slightly simpler terms, there are six available orders (defined in the Act as "orders for financial provision"[1]).

- An order for payment of a **capital sum**.[2]
- An order for the **transfer of property**.[3]
- An order for payment of a **periodical allowance**.[4]
- A **pension sharing order**.[5]
- A **pension lump sum order** (commonly known as an **earmarking order**).[6]
- Various **incidental orders**.[7]

---

[1] s.8(3).
[2] s.8(1)(a).
[3] s.8(1)(aa).
[4] s.8(1)(b).
[5] s.8(1)(baa).
[6] s.8(1)(ba) which refers to the terms of s.12A.
[7] s.8(1)(c).

These are the individual tools which the court can use to make its overall order for financial provision. Each of the available orders is dealt with individually in more detail later in this chapter. An application for an order for financial provision is generally made by a crave in the initial writ or defences.[8] However, an application for an incidental order in a depending action may be made by motion (unless the sheriff considers that the application should properly be made by a crave in the initial writ or defences).[9] The court cannot competently make any particular order unless the order has been craved.[10] A combination of orders will often be used.[11] Any combination is competent with one exception: the court is not, in the same proceedings, to make both a pension sharing order and an earmarking order in relation to the same pension arrangement.[12] Where several different s.8 orders are craved by the parties, the choice of which particular orders to use will be a matter for the proper exercise of the discretion of the court.[13]

Section 8(2)—a two-stage test

Criteria for making orders for financial provision

Section 8(2) is a key provision of the Act. It provides that (subject to **3–02** ss.12–15 of the Act[14]) the court shall make such an order, if any, as is: (a) justified by the principles set out in s.9 of the Act; and (b) reasonable having regard to the resources of the parties. So, there are two criteria which must be fulfilled before the court can make any order.[15] First, the court must carefully consider the s.9 principles to determine which s.8 orders (if any) are justified. These principles are discussed in detail in Ch.4 of this book. However, even if an order is justified under the s.9 principles, s.8(2)(b) provides the parties with a safety net—if it is unreasonable to expect a party to meet that order having regard to the present and foreseeable resources of the parties *at the time of the decree*,[16] then the order should not be made.

---

[8] Act of Sederunt (Sheriff Court Ordinary Cause Rules) 1993 No.1956 ("O.C.R.") r.33.48. If the application is made in the defences, the defender must include in his defences: craves, averments in support of the craves and appropriate pleas-in-law—O.C.R., r.33.34(2). If the application is made by a person other than the pursuer or the defender, the application is by minute in the action—O.C.R. r.33.48(1)(b).

[9] O.C.R. r.33.49(1)

[10] *Muir v Muir*, 1994 S.C.L.R. 178. However, a crave for an order will probably include by implication incidental orders relating to that order, even if those incidental orders are not specifically craved—see *Macdonald v Macdonald*, 1995 S.L.T. 72. Obiter comments in *Macdonald* also suggest that it may be equitable in some circumstances to allow a party to introduce craves by amendment even at a very late stage.

[11] See e.g. *Wallis v Wallis*, 1993 S.C. (H.L.) 49.

[12] s.8(4). See also s.8(5).

[13] See e.g. *Christie v Christie*, 2004 S.L.T. (Sh Ct) 95 at p.99.

[14] ss.12–15 set out more detailed provisions on how each of the orders is to work.

[15] For an excellent introduction to the two stages set out in s.8(2) see Joe Thomson, "The Law of Financial Provision on Divorce: An Overview and Update" S.L.G. 1992, 60(3), 99–102.

[16] Because the term "resources" is defined in s.27(1) as meaning both present and foreseeable resources—it is not confined to resources at the relevant date.

Definition of "resources"

3–03   The definition of the term "resources" used in s.8(2)(b) is important. Section 27(1) defines resources as "present and foreseeable resources". This definition is very wide. The term "resources" includes resources both of an income and of a capital nature.[17] The definition does not limit resources to matrimonial or partnership property. Non-matrimonial or non-partnership property will still be a resource. For example, one party may have inherited funds during the marriage or civil partnership. These will not fall to be divided between the parties on divorce or dissolution in terms of s.9(1)(a) (which provides for fair sharing of matrimonial and partnership property) because the Act provides that inherited funds are not matrimonial or partnership property.[18] However, those funds will be a resource within the meaning of s.8(2)(b), which can be used to assess the reasonableness of any order justified under the s.9 principles. Indeed, those resources (even though they do not form part of the matrimonial or partnership property) may be used to *fund* any award of financial provision.[19] It follows from all of this that sometimes the value of particular resources at the time of the proof will be important. In *Demarco v Demarco*, 1990 S.C.L.R. 635, Lord Cameron of Lochbroom responded to the defender's suggestion that it was unnecessary to obtain a valuation of the defender's shareholdings at a date later than the date of separation as follows[20]:

> "This in my view overlooks the fact that such information may be necessary to establish not only the value of the defender's shareholdings at the date of separation but, since the defender still holds them and may do when the court comes to make any order under section 8(1)(a), will also constitute part of his resources for the purposes of section 8(2)(b)."

As to "foreseeable" resources, the case of *Cunniff v Cunniff*, 1999 S.L.T. 992 is illustrative. In that case, Lord McCluskey commented[21]:

> "Section 27(1) contains the provision: '"resources" means present and foreseeable resources'. Having regard to the natural meaning of these words I should have no difficulty in holding that if a person, albeit unemployed, has an early prospect of earning a substantial income there are 'resources' within the meaning of the Act for the purposes of s.8."[22]

---

[17] See e.g. *Demarco v Demarco*, 1990 S.C.L.R. 635 and *Cunniff v Cunniff*, 1999 S.L.T. 992.

[18] s.10(4) and (4A).

[19] See para.3–04.

[20] At p.637.

[21] At pp.998–9, and see also p.1000. See also e.g. *Little v Little*, 1989 S.C.L.R. 613.

[22] Although see Lord Milligan at p.1001 where he reserves judgement on the question ". . . as to how far the mere hope of employment can, or should, be regarded as a 'resource' or even 'future resource' within the meaning of ss.8(2) and 27(1) of the Act". The issue is probably one of weight.

The effect of an increase in resources after the relevant date

Resources might increase between the relevant date and the date of **3–04** divorce or dissolution. Such an increase might expand the range of options available to the court. So, if we imagine that A and B are divorcing: the matrimonial property is straightforward and consists only of A's pension rights which have a value for the purposes of financial provision of £100,000. If, at the time of the divorce, this remains the position then it might be difficult for the court to insist on A paying a capital sum to B under s.8(1)(a) because A has no resources to make such a payment immediately. The court might have to consider options such as deferring payment of a capital sum, a pension sharing order or an earmarking order. However, if A wins the lottery between the relevant date and the date of decree, then the lottery winnings will not be matrimonial property falling to be divided between the parties, but they will be a resource within the meaning of s.8(2), and might allow the court to order immediate payment of a capital sum, thus allowing a clean break.

So, if an award is justified under the s.9 principles, s.8(2)(b) allows the court to use non-matrimonial or non-partnership assets as a resource to fund the award.[23] However, it is clear that the maximum award which can be made is the one which is justified by the s.9 principles in terms of s.8(2)(a). Section 8(2)(b) simply protects a party against an award which, although justified under the five principles, the party cannot afford at the time of the order. Section 8(2) should not be used to make an award which can be funded having regard to the resources available at the date of decree, but which is not justified under the s.9 principles.[24] This point was clearly made by Lord Marnoch in *Latter v Latter*, 1990 S.L.T. 805. Counsel had argued that under s.8(2)(b) the court could increase any capital sum beyond what it considered justified by the principles set out in s.9 of the Act. The argument was rejected[25]:

"In my view this proposition deprives the word 'and' of its plain conjunctive meaning . . . I am clear that I can do no such thing and that s.8(2)(b) can only operate to cut down any sum, otherwise justified, having regard to the current resources of the parties."

The effect of a decrease in resources after the relevant date

Another possibility, of course, is that the available resources might **3–05** decrease between the relevant date and the date of the proof. In some cases this might mean that an award which is justified under the s.9 principles should not be made simply because the party against whom the order is being sought cannot afford it.[26] There is a useful example of

---

[23] See the discussion about *Vance v Vance*, 1997 S.L.T. (Sh Ct) 71 in Joe Thomson, "Swings and Roundabouts?" S.L.G. 1998, 66(4), 202–3.
[24] See for example the critique of *Dawson v Dawson* in Joe Thomson, "The Law of Financial Provision on Divorce: An Overview and Update" S.L.G. 1992, 60(3), 99–102.
[25] At p.807.
[26] See e.g. *Shand v Shand*, 1994 S.L.T. 387; and *Welsh v Welsh*, 1994 S.L.T. 828 at p.836 discussed below.

the way that s.8(2)(b) can operate to reduce an award otherwise justified under the s.9 principles in *Crockett v Crockett*, 1992 S.C.L.R. 591. In that case, a large element of the value of the matrimonial property at the relevant date was the value of a business. However, the value of the business fell substantially between the relevant date and the date of the proof. Lord McCluskey held that, applying the s.9 principles, the wife would have been entitled to an award of £53,000, but s.8(2)(b) applied and, having regard to the resources of the parties at the time of the proof, it was not reasonable to make an award in excess of £17,500.

The following comments from *Wallis v Wallis*, 1993 S.C. (H.L.) 49[27] summarise the way that s.8(2)(b) works when the value of resources has fallen after the relevant date:

> ". . . if the matrimonial home, being held in the sole name of one of the parties, were to be destroyed by fire uninsured after the relevant date but before the date of the proof, the party who owned the property might be required to pay the other half its value at the relevant date if his or her total resources at the date of the proof were sufficient to make it reasonable for such payment to be made, but not if the party in question had no significant resources. Similar considerations could apply where the property in question consisted in a block of shares which had fallen dramatically in value."

If resources decline after the relevant date, s.8(2)(b) does not only operate to limit capital sum orders: it applies in relation to all of the s.8 orders. For example in *Millar v Millar*, 1990 S.C.L.R. 666, Sheriff Principal Nicholson commented on how s.8(2)(b) might serve to reduce an award of periodical allowance[28]:

> ". . . in my opinion I do not consider that an award of periodical allowance would be reasonable in this case having regard to the resources of the parties (see section 8(2)(b) of the Act) . . . Looking at the available resources of the parties, it is clear that neither of them is well off. The defender's income is greater than that of the pursuer, but so are his outlays."

A practical approach to section 8(2)

3–06   A logical way of dealing with s.8(2) is, first, to assess which orders are justified under the s.9 principles (s.8(2)(a)), and then to move on to assess whether this award is reasonable having regard to the resources of the parties (s.8(2)(b)). If an award is justified under s.9 principles, but is not reasonable having regard to the resources of the parties, then it may be reduced or dispensed with altogether.[29] This two-stage approach was adopted in *Macdonald v Macdonald*, 1993 S.C.L.R. 132 where Lord

---

[27] Lord Keith at pp.55–6.
[28] At p.672.
[29] See e.g. *Rodgers v Rodgers (No.2)*, 1994 G.W.D. 31–1869; *Rodgers* is also interesting because it makes it clear that the court should look at the resources of *both* of the parties in reaching its decision.

Caplan considered that the s.9 principles probably justified the transfer of the matrimonial home to the wife. However, he then had to consider the reasonableness of this order in the light of s.8(2)(b)[30]:

> "However, I consider that the pursuer would acquire an exceptional and unreasonable advantage if she were permitted to retain the whole of the matrimonial property at Danube Street. I am also obliged, in terms of section 8(2)(b), to have regard to the resources of the parties. At the moment the resources of the [*wife*] are stronger than those of the [*husband*]. The [*husband*] has a substantial overdraft . . . I think it would be rather unfair if he was left with nothing at all out of the matrimonial venture."

Sometimes, however, the court may not need to be quite so rigorous in adopting this two-stage process. Occasionally the resources available at the proof will be so low that the court may not have to look particularly closely at the first stage. There will be cases where it is clear from the outset that one party's (or indeed both parties') resources are so restricted at the time of the proof that an award justified by the s.9 principles is beyond them. Only a lesser award, or in some cases no award at all, is reasonable. The following passage from *McVinnie v McVinnie (No. 2)*, 1997 S.L.T. (Sh Ct) 12 illustrates[31]:

> "I can see a certain attractiveness in the first main submission advanced by counsel for the defender, namely that the test set out in s.8(2) of the Act is a two stage one which requires a court, first, to consider whether an award is justified and thereafter to pass on to a consideration of the reasonableness test only if the first part of the test has been satisfied. In practice this may well be the way in which a court will approach the matter in certain circumstances. However, the subsection is not in fact expressed in that way. What it does is to set out two criteria, each of which must be satisfied before an award can be made, but it does not in terms direct a court to consider one of those criteria in advance of, or in isolation from, the other. Indeed, it is not difficult to imagine circumstances where a court may, *ab ante*,[32] have regard to a party's resources and conclude that, even if an award of a capital sum[33] were otherwise to be justified, it would not be reasonable to make any award. It could not, I think, be suggested that in such a case the court had erred by not first addressing the criterion which is contained in s.8(2)(a). It would, of course, be wrong in my opinion for a court to seek to determine the outcome of the balancing exercise which is required by ss.9(1)(b) and 11(2) by reference to the resources of the parties at the time of

---

[30] At p.135.

[31] Sheriff Principal Nicholson at p.14.

[32] For those (like the author) with no Latin, the phrase means "in advance".

[33] This is not quite correct—the court does not only have the award of a capital sum at its disposal. The court would need to be clear that the resources of the parties were sufficiently spartan that other orders such as pension sharing, earmarking, deferred payment of a capital sum and the like were not reasonable.

a proof but, subject to that, I do not consider that a court can be faulted if an eye is kept, as it were, on both heads of s.8(2) at the stage when the whole question is being addressed."

Consider all available section 8 orders

3–07   Section 8(2)(b) provides protection for parties with limited resources at the time the order for financial provision is made. As Lord Osborne put it in *Welsh v Welsh*, 1994 S.L.T. 828[34]:

> "It appears to me that the purpose of [s.8(2)(b)], is to protect a party who might require to pay a capital sum which he or she could not afford, assuming an equal division, as a result of a diminution of the value of items of matrimonial property between the relevant date and the date of the divorce."

However, the emphasis in the foregoing passage may be a little misleading. Some cases, such as *McVinnie* and *Welsh* seem to stress the importance of s.8(2)(b) in reducing an award *of a capital sum* (otherwise justified by the s.9 principles) because there are insufficient capital resources available to make the payment at the time the order is to be made. However, it must always be kept in mind that s.8 sets out a broad range of orders—not simply orders for immediate payment of a capital sum by one party to the other. If the court finds that an award should be made to one party under the s.9 principles, but the other party only has very limited capital available at the time of the proof, this does not necessarily mean that an award cannot be made.[35] While cases like *Welsh* and *McVinnie* may well be correctly decided on their particular facts, remember that there are various orders available in the Act: although it may not be possible to achieve an award by way of the immediate payment of a capital sum, it may be possible to achieve financial provision through the creative use of other orders, for example, by deferring payment of a capital sum to a later date; by ordering payment of a capital sum by instalments over a period of time;[36] by ordering periodical allowance;[37] or perhaps by using pension sharing or earmarking.[38] Resources include both present and foreseeable resources.[39]

"Resources"—pleadings and evidence

3–08   The question of which resources will be available to a party at the date of proof is one of fact. A party seeking to establish that their available resources have dwindled, or that the other party has substantial

---

[34] At p.835.

[35] See the critique of *McKenna v McKenna* (Sheriff Court, February 11, 1992) in Joe Thomson, "The Law of Financial Provision on Divorce: An Overview and Update" S.L.G. 1992, 60(3), 99–102.

[36] See e.g. *Sweeney v Sweeney (No.2)*, 2005 S.L.T. 1141 at 1148; *Little v Little*, 1989 S.C.L.R. 613.

[37] An award of periodical allowance may be particularly useful in some circumstances—it allows an award to be made out of income. Even if only a nominal sum is awarded this it allows an award to be made out of income. Even if only a nominal sum is awarded this could be varied after divorce or dissolution to take account of a change of circumstances.

[38] Remember that a number of the decisions relating to resources and s.8(2)(b) predate the amendments to the 1985 Act introducing earmarking and pension sharing.

[39] s.27(1).

resources at the date of the proof, will need to aver this and establish it in evidence.[40] In *Fulton v Fulton*, 1998 S.L.T. 1262, Lord Nimmo Smith commented[41]:

> "I propose to deal at this stage with the question of the resources of the parties. The only averments on record about these resources are directed to the pursuer's conclusion for a periodical allowance . . . and nothing at all is said about the parties' capital resources. When an attempt was made to lead evidence about the defender's resources, counsel for the pursuer objected to the line of evidence on the ground that there was no record for it. Counsel for the defender submitted that I was bound to have regard to the question of resources and accordingly was bound to admit evidence on this matter even without a foundation on record . . . I formally sustained the objection. I shall now give my reasons for doing so. While a party who seeks an order for the making of a periodical allowance might readily be expected to lead evidence about the resources of the parties, which evidence in turn would require a foundation on record, the same considerations do not arise in connection with a conclusion for payment of a capital sum. Obviously such a conclusion must be supported by averments about the matrimonial property at the relevant date. Once the nature and value of the assets comprised in the matrimonial property at that date have been established, it seems reasonable to assume that they remain substantially the same at the date of the proof unless the contrary is proved. If it is desired to prove the contrary, fair notice requires to be given on record so that the matter can be properly investigated and thereafter tested at proof. There may of course be situations in which the value of assets has changed materially, but in my opinion if this is to be established there must be a foundation for it on record."

In addition to making averments, the party seeking to rely on them will also need to lead persuasive evidence about these matters at the proof. So, in *Fraser v Fraser*, 2002 Fam. L.R. 53, the wife sought to argue that the husband had an interest in heritable property at the date of the proof. She failed to establish this in evidence, and therefore the court declined to regard it as an available resource.[42]

SECTION 8(1)(A)—ORDERS FOR PAYMENT OF A CAPITAL SUM

General discussion

Under s.8(1)(a) of the Act, in an action of divorce or in an action for **3–09** dissolution of a civil partnership, either party may apply to the court for:

---

[40] In addition to the cases discussed see also e.g. *Shand v Shand*, 1994 S.L.T. 387.
[41] At p.1263.
[42] See also *Sweeney v Sweeney (No.2)*, 2005 S.L.T. 1141 at p.1147.

"an order for the payment of a capital sum to him by the other party to the action;".

Before granting an order for payment of a capital sum, the court must be satisfied that the order (along with any other orders being granted at the time of decree) is: (a) justified by the principles set out in s.9 of the Act; and (b) reasonable having regard to the resources of the parties.[43]

When the Act came into force, there was initially some doubt about whether the court could award both a capital sum and a transfer of property in the same action.[44] This doubt was cleared up by amendment to s.8(1) separating the orders for payment of a capital sum under para.(a) and for transfer of property under para.(aa). It is now clear that both orders may be made in the same action.

Any order for payment of a capital sum will be justified using the s.9 principles and this will include reference to the value of the matrimonial or partnership property. However, any capital sum ordered need not be paid out of matrimonial or partnership property.[45] It might be paid from non-matrimonial or non-partnership resources belonging solely to one of the parties,[46] or the court might order payment by instalments from income.[47]

Section 12(1)(b)—Deferred decisions

General discussion

3–10   Section 12(1) provides that an order for payment of a capital sum or transfer of property can be made either: (a) on granting decree of divorce or of dissolution of a civil partnership; or (b) within such period as the court on granting the decree may specify. In most cases the court will make the order for payment of a capital sum or transfer of property at the same time as the divorce or dissolution. However, s.12(1)(b) allows the court to grant the divorce or dissolution immediately, but to defer its *decision* in relation to the payment of a capital sum (or transfer of property) until a later time. This is quite different from an order made at the time of the divorce or dissolution deferring *payment*. Deferred payments are dealt with in s.12(2).[48]

The court might choose to defer the decision on the financial aspects of the case until after decree of divorce or dissolution for various reasons. For example, it might be appropriate to allow a divorce or dissolution to be granted where there is some pressing compassionate need for this (e.g. if one party wishes to re-marry or enter into a new civil partnership), with questions of financial provision reserved until later.[49] On some occasions it might be appropriate to allow decree of

---

[43] s.8(2). See paras 3–02 to 3–08.

[44] *Little v Little*, 1990 S.L.T. 230 and 1990 S.L.T. 785; *Walker v Walker*, 1991 S.L.T. 157.

[45] See para.3–04.

[46] See *Ranaldi v Ranaldi*, 1992 G.W.D. 26–1486.

[47] In some cases instalment payments may be necessary if justice is to be done—*Bell v Bell*, 1988 S.C.L.R. 457.

[48] See paras 3–12 to 3–15.

[49] See E.M. Clive, *The Law of Husband and Wife in Scotland*, 4th edn at para.24.092.

divorce or dissolution to be granted, but to continue financial aspects of the case for further discussion to ensure a fair result for the parties.[50]

Deferred decisions—some potential problems

Deferred decisions under s.12(1)(b) are very unusual. They should not **3–11** be used except where there is a pressing need to grant the decree of divorce or dissolution at the earliest possible opportunity. There are several potential problems.

If s.12(1)(b) is to be used to defer decisions on financial matters, the court must specifically reserve the decision *at the time decree of divorce or dissolution is made*. In *Leaper v Leaper*, 1998 S.L.T. 659, the pursuer raised an action in the sheriff court, and craved payment of a capital sum. The defender withdrew his defences but lodged a minute disputing the capital sum only (under an old procedure known as a Rule 34 Minute). A hearing under the minute on the financial matters was assigned, but prior to the hearing the pursuer lodged a minute for decree which resulted in decree of divorce being granted. The hearing under the minute (which was to deal with financial matters) then called but the sheriff reluctantly concluded that he was no longer able to deal with the financial matters because the court had not (when granting decree of divorce) reserved the decision regarding the crave for a capital sum. In subsequent Court of Session proceedings for reduction of the decree of divorce Lord Hamilton confirmed that the sheriff's decision was correct—the financial aspects had not been reserved *when the decree of divorce was pronounced*, therefore it was incompetent to consider these at a later stage. So, if it is proposed to defer a decision on financial matters to a later date, it is essential to ensure that the interlocutor granting divorce or dissolution makes specific reference to the reserved matters.

If the court grants divorce or dissolution, and uses s.12(1)(b) to continue consideration of a crave for a capital sum, the order has to be made within "such period as the court on granting the decree may specify". Normally, the court will simply defer this decision to a proof on the financial aspects of the separation. It has been argued unsuccessfully that, if this subsequent proof is itself adjourned, then the court is barred from making financial orders at any postponed proof. In *Mackin v Mackin*, 1991 S.L.T. (Sh Ct) 22, the court granted decree of divorce and continued consideration of the financial matters to a proof. A date was assigned for that proof. The proof on financial matters was later adjourned, and the court fixed a new diet of proof. At the later diet, the court made awards of a capital sum and periodical allowance. On appeal, the defender argued that these orders were incompetent because they had not been made within "such period as the court on granting decree of divorce may specify"[51] as required in terms of s.12(1)(b). The sheriff principal (not surprisingly) did not lose much time in rejecting this argument and held that the adjournment made no difference—the orders made at the final diet were competent.

---

[50] See e.g. *Muir v Muir*, 1993 G.W.D. 21–1297 and 1993 G.W.D. 39–2593.
[51] The wording of the sub-section has been amended slightly since the decision.

The court might defer the decision on the financial aspects of the case for a particular specified period. So, in *Lindsay v Lindsay*, 2007 Fam. L.R. 18, the sheriff deferred the decision on financial matters for a period of 12 months. The wife applied for this period to be extended. This was held to be competent. Even though the Act does not have any specific provision allowing an extension of time, it was held by the sheriff principal that the court has an inherent jurisdiction to grant this.

Another problem which might arise if the decision on financial matters is deferred concerns what is to happen if one of the parties dies before the order for financial provision is made. In these circumstances it may be impossible for the other party to obtain an order (there is, after all, no opponent). This danger is particularly acute because the surviving party will also have lost the option of claiming prior and legal rights from the estate of the other party—these rights will be lost on divorce or dissolution.

Yet another pitfall is that, once decree of divorce or dissolution is granted, it may be incompetent to seek to amend the craves or to introduce counterclaims to seek new orders. The argument here is that only the craves specifically reserved at the point of decree of divorce or dissolution are open for consideration. In *Christie v Christie*, 2003 S.L.T. (Sh Ct) 115, the court granted decree of divorce and then continued the cause to a proof to consider questions of financial provision. Prior to this proof (but after the divorce) the defender sought by amendment to introduce a counterclaim for a capital sum. The pursuer argued that this was incompetent. The sheriff agreed[52]:

> "... I require to determine what issues were reserved for further determination, by virtue of the interlocutors [granting divorce and allowing proof on financial matters]. It is clear that the proof originally assigned ... was 'a proof of their respective averments solely on the financial aspects of the case.' At that time, the only financial aspects existing before the court were those raised by the pursuer. As Sheriff Principal Ireland states, in *Mackin*, at 1991 S.L.T. (Sh Ct) 22 at p.23, in relation to s.12(1)(b): 'The obvious purpose of the provision was to enable the court, where appropriate, to grant decree of divorce immediately, but to allow time for inquiry into the craves for financial provision. The language of the Act must be read against the existing background of sheriff court procedure. If the interlocutor had simply specified a period, such as three months, within which the order was to be made ... it would have led to no practical result whatever. The only way in which the court can give effect to the Act is to order a proof on a specified day'.[53]
>
> The only craves for financial provision into which the court could have allowed time for inquiry were those in existence at the material

---

[52] Sheriff Small at pp.118–19.

[53] Although see *Lindsay v Lindsay*, 2007 Fam. L.R. 18. Further, it is difficult to square this decision with O.C.R. r.33.51(1)(a)(ii) which allows an application after final decree for payment of a capital sum or transfer of property to be made by minute in the original process. If the only orders which can competently be argued are those reserved at the time divorce or dissolution is granted (which will already have been craved), then what is the purpose of this rule?

time. That was the 'existing background'. I do not consider that the purpose of s.12(1)(b) was to allow a defender who had no counterclaim in process at the time of granting of decree of divorce to introduce a claim for a substantial capital payment almost two years after the decree of divorce was granted."

Section 12(2)—Postponed payment of a capital sum

General discussion

Section 12(2) provides that the court, on making an order for payment **3–12** of a capital sum or property transfer order, may stipulate that it shall come into effect at a specified future date. This might be useful where the party with the obligation to pay has little available capital at the time decree of divorce or dissolution is granted, but there is a reasonable expectation that they will come into some funds at a date after the decree. For example, in *Symon v Symon*, 1991 S.C.L.R. 414 Sheriff Russell deferred capital payments until a house was sold, and in *Shand v Shand*, 1994 S.L.T. 387, Lord Coulsfield deferred payment to the date when the husband was likely to be discharged from bankruptcy. In *Little v Little*, 1989 S.C.L.R. 613,[54] the court held that, as part of the overall order for financial provision, the defender should pay a substantial capital sum to the pursuer, but deferred payment of part of this commenting[55]:

> ". . . having regard to the limited amount of the defender's capital assets at present but having regard to his expectancy, first, of a further substantial capital sum upon retirement, and some additional capital sum in the event of the maturing of the remaining endowment policies, I consider it reasonable that payment of part of this sum only be ordered now and that the remaining part be deferred until 1995."

Does the "specified date" need to be a fixed date?

Cases are divided on the issue of whether the court needs to specify a **3–13** fixed date for payment (i.e. a particular date in the calendar) or, alternatively, whether it is competent for payment to be deferred until the happening of a particular event. In *Geddes v Geddes*, 1991 G.W.D. 16–990 Sheriff Principal Bennett ruled that s.12(2) could not be triggered by the husband acquiring possession of a farm on his uncle's death, as this was not a "specified future date". This seems unnecessarily restrictive. A different interpretation was adopted by the sheriff in *Symon v Symon*, 1991 S.C.L.R. 414, who made an order for the sale of the matrimonial home, and deferred payment of part of a capital sum until a date one month after the house was sold. Similarly, in *Collins v Collins*, 1997 Fam. L.R. 50 Sheriff Smith deferred payment of a capital sum until the death of the husband and commented[56]:

---

[54] Outer House, Lord Cameron of Lochbroom.
[55] At p.620.
[56] At para.10–13.

"Questions have arisen in the past as to whether the words 'specified future date' mean specified exclusively by reference to the calendar. That is not the view of the author in Clive, *Husband and Wife* (3rd ed.) p.497. I adopt his view. Indeed he instances a date of death as an example of such a date in a s.12(2) order."

Security for deferred payments

3–14   If a capital sum is to be deferred until some future date, the party awaiting payment will need to consider carefully the issue of security for that payment. Much may change between the date of decree and the date when the payment is to be made under s.12(2), and in some circumstances the order might ultimately prove difficult or impossible to enforce. The issue of security for the payment will be particularly important if the party who is to make payment has a history of trying to avoid obligations, or if they have a poor track record with money management. The court has power to deal with this by ordering that a security be granted over heritage,[57] and this may be a pragmatic solution in some cases. The court has power to order such a security even if there is no specific crave or conclusion requesting this. In *Macdonald v Macdonald*, 1995 S.L.T. 72 Lord Caplan commented[58]:

"A further question arises as to the provision of security for the pursuer's entitlement to the said capital payment . . . It was suggested by the pursuer's counsel that the defender is in considerable debt to his bankers so that once the house is sold his share of the price may be attached to his creditors, leaving the pursuer unable to recover her capital entitlement. She contended that it is critical not only to the pursuer but to her children that she should receive her [capital sum] so that she can be in a position to buy a new house. Counsel for the defender resisted this suggestion. He contended that the pursuer had no conclusion which would enable her to obtain an order under s.14 of the 1986 (*sic*) Act for the provision of security. He also argued that if a security right was imposed on the defender's share of the realisation price, his bank would be disturbed and might take immediate steps which would destabilise the defender's position. In my view the pursuer's conclusion for a capital payment would cover incidental orders relating to it. It may well be difficult for a party to anticipate which particular incidental orders will be appropriate until it is clear what financial arrangements are to be granted by the court. In any event the pursuer's counsel offered to add to the pursuer's 11th conclusion the words 'and to make such other incidental orders as to the court seem appropriate'. If such a formal addition to the conclusions were required, I would have no hesitation in granting leave to amend. The defender has had ample notice of the pursuer's intention to move that her capital sum be secured since the matter was raised [at a prior hearing]. I have no doubt that such an incidental order is

---

[57] By granting an incidental order under s.14(2)(f).
[58] At p.74.

appropriate. It is a matter of concern that the defender's share of the house sale proceeds might be claimed by his bankers. The decision that the pursuer should have a capital sum (rather say than a property transfer order or occupation rights) was based on the view that it would be preferable that she should have a share of the house proceeds to assist her in replacing the family home. I shall accordingly grant decree for [a capital sum in favour of the pursuer] but make the sum payable on the date when the prospective purchaser obtains entry to that property."

The court went on to make an incidental order requiring the defender to grant a standard security over the property in favour of the pursuer. Sensibly, the court provided that if the defender did not execute the deed then the Clerk of Session was authorised to sign it in his place.

On a practical note, parties seeking security over heritage should check whether there are any pre-ranking securities or diligences, in the same way that any other prudent security holder would.

Interest on deferred payments

If payment of a capital sum or transfer of property is to be deferred, it **3–15** may be appropriate to order that interest is paid.[59]

Section 12(3)—Instalment payments

General discussion

Section 12(3) provides that the court, on making an order under s.8(2) **3–16** for payment of a capital sum, may order that the capital sum shall be payable by instalments. Instalment payments may be appropriate where the party ordered to make the payment does not have the ability to fund the order immediately but has a regular income.[60] So, for example, in *Bell v Bell*, 1988 S.C.L.R. 457, Sheriff Jardine ordered a capital sum to be paid by instalments[61]:

"Although the defender plainly enjoys a good income, I am satisfied that his purchase of a house (for which he has a substantial loan commitment over a comparatively short term) at this stage will mean that he now has virtually no further capital readily available from which to pay this sum, nor would I assume that he would necessarily find it easy to borrow such a further sum in the circumstances. For these reasons, I have concluded that this is a case in which it would be entirely appropriate to order payment of the capital sum by instalments of say £200 per month, as provided for in s.12(3) of the Act."

---

[59] The question of interest is discussed in more detail at paras 3–20 and 3–90. Interest will not always be appropriate—see e.g. the comments in *Collins v Collins*, 1997 Fam. L.R. 50 at para.10–14.

[60] It appears that a capital sum payable by instalments might still be appropriate in some cases even where the payer's income is restricted to state benefits—see *Gray v Gray*, 1999 G.W.D. 38–1852.

[61] At p.464.

If the court is considering ordering payment of a capital sum by instalments, it may be important to consider whether interest should be paid. Interest might be payable on the principal sum from a specified date, or on the instalments from the date they fall due, or both.[62] Equally, it might be appropriate in some cases to seek security for the instalment payments.[63]

Instalment payments or deferred payment?

3–17   In circumstances where the court feels that a capital sum should be paid but cannot be paid immediately, it will be a matter of judgement for the court to decide whether the capital sum should be paid by instalments,[64] or whether it may be better to defer payment of the whole capital sum to some specified date in the future.[65] In *Dorrian v Dorrian*, 1991 S.C.L.R. 661, the parties were agreed on the amount of a capital sum to be paid, but could not agree on how it was to be paid. The only source available for payment was the defender's pension scheme.[66] The defender would not be entitled to his pension until about 10 years after the divorce, and at that time he would be able to claim both a lump sum and a regular payment. The pursuer suggested that the capital sum to which she was entitled should be paid by instalments following the divorce, but the court preferred to defer payment.

Contrast with periodical allowance

3–18   A court can order both a capital sum payable by instalments and an award of periodical allowance in the same action,[67] but there are important distinctions between the two types of order. The main differences are:

- Where a capital sum is to be paid by instalments, the capital sum is for a defined amount, and payments will cease once the principal has been paid. Periodical allowance is for a specified regular payment of money with no reference to any principal amount (although the payments will often only be for a particular period of time).
- Periodical allowance can only be ordered if it is justified by one of the principles in s.9(1)(c), (d) or (e).[68] A payment of a capital sum by instalments can be ordered using any of the s.9 principles as justification.
- An order for payment of a capital sum can be varied in terms of s.12(4) but only in relation to the date or method of payment *not* the quantum.[69] The quantum specified in an order for periodical allowance is open to review in terms of s.13(4).[70]

---

[62] See paras 3–20 and 3–90.
[63] See para.3–14.
[64] Under s.12(3).
[65] Using s.12(2).
[66] Note that this decision was reached before the introduction of pension sharing orders and pension lump sum orders into the scheme of the Act.
[67] See e.g. *Kelly v Kelly*, 1992 G.W.D. 36–2130.
[68] See s.13(2).
[69] See para.3–19.
[70] See paras 3–40 to 3–44.

Section 12(4)—Variation of the date or method of payment

Section 12(4) provides that where an order for payment of a capital **3–19** sum or transfer of property is made the court may, on an application by either party, vary the date or method of payment of the capital sum or the date of transfer of property.[71] In relation to orders for payment of a capital sum, it is important to note that s.12(4) only allows variation in the *date or method of payment*. So, the court might use this provision to substitute a deferred payment of a capital sum under s.12(2) for an instalment payment under s.12(3). However, the *amount* of the capital sum cannot be changed. This is different from the provisions of the Act relating to variation of periodical allowance, where the quantum can be varied and may even be reduced to nil.[72]

Interest on capital sums

The court can make an award of interest on a capital sum, either at **3–20** the judicial rate or at such other rate as the court considers appropriate. There is a specific power in the Act giving the court discretion as to the date from when interest is to run.[73] Interest can be extremely important. The court has a wide discretion in relation to this matter, and there will be a number of important questions which need to be addressed in any given case.

First, the court will need to consider whether the principles of the Act justify any award of interest at all. This will depend on the circumstances of each case. Although it may appear at first glance that there are imbalances which should be corrected by an award of interest, it should be remembered that the 1985 Act is a web of interrelated provisions. These imbalances may already have been corrected by other awards. For example, the court might (rather than award interest) make a higher award of capital using s.9(1)(b) as its justification.

Next the court will need to consider what rate of interest is appropriate. Interest may run on the outstanding capital sum at the prevailing judicial rate or at such other rate as the court considers appropriate. Advisers should always consider whether the judicial rate is appropriate in any given case. If an asset is producing income at a rate considerably higher than the judicial rate then a higher rate may be justified; if the asset is performing poorly (or produces no income at all) a rate lower than the judicial rate or no interest at all may be appropriate.[74]

The rate of interest payable might vary from one asset to another in any given case. So, in *Savage v Savage*, 1993 G.W.D. 28–1779, Lord Sutherland decided not to award any interest on sums awarded in relation to a business because the business made a very poor return during the period concerned. In relation to certain bank accounts, the court did not make an award at any particular rate at all, but seems to have used a "broad brush" and capitalised the interest on the bank accounts at a figure of £2,500.

---

[71] An application for such an order would be made by minute in the original process—O.C.R. r.33.51.

[72] See s.13(4); See paras 3–40 to 3–44.

[73] s.14(2)(j). See para.3–90.

[74] See *Savage v Savage*, 1993 G.W.D. 28–1779.

It is not competent to grant interest on a sum greater than the capital sum actually awarded.[75]

Pension lump sum orders ("earmarking orders")

3–21   If the court makes an order for payment of a capital sum, and the matrimonial or partnership property includes rights or interests in benefits under a pension arrangement of the payer, and those benefits include the right to a lump sum (whether payable to the person or on his death), then the court can order that the capital sum payable under s.8(a) is paid (or partly paid) out of the pension lump sum.[76] Such an order is known as a pension lump sum order or (more colloquially) as an earmarking order. Earmarking orders are rife with problems and pitfalls.[77]

SECTION 8(1)(aa)—TRANSFER OF PROPERTY ORDERS

General discussion

3–22   Under s.8(1)(aa) of the Act, in an action for divorce or dissolution of a civil partnership, either party may apply to the court for:

> "an order for the transfer of property to him by the other party to the action;".

Before granting an order for transfer of property, the court must be satisfied that the order (along with any other orders granted at the time of decree) is: (a) justified by the principles set out in s.9 of the Act; and (b) reasonable having regard to the resources of the parties.[78] The second part of this test will often be particularly important in relation to claims for transfer of the family home—it may be desirable to transfer this asset to one party, but if this causes injustice to the other, the order may be inappropriate.[79]

When the Act was introduced, there was initially some doubt about whether the court could award both a capital sum and a transfer of property in the same action.[80] This doubt was resolved by amendment to s.8 separating the orders for payment of a capital sum under para.(a) and for transfer of property under para.(aa). It is now clear that both orders may be made in the same action. An action for divorce or dissolution may (and often does) contain applications for both a capital

---

[75] *Ogg v Ogg*, 2003 G.W.D. 10–281.

[76] ss.8(1)(ba) and 12A(1).

[77] See paras 3–68 to 3–79.

[78] s.8(2). See paras 3–02 to 3–08.

[79] See *Murley v Murley*, 1995 S.C.L.R. 1138 where Lord MacLean was convinced that the matrimonial home should be transferred to the wife (and thus retained for the benefit of the children) but for the imbalance that this would create in favour of the wife. The court used a creative solution: the house was transferred to the wife, but subject to a standard security in favour of the husband to be repaid when the house was sold or when the child reached the age of 16, whichever was the earlier.

[80] *Little v Little*, 1990 S.L.T. 230 and 1990 S.L.T. 785; *Walker v Walker*, 1991 S.L.T. 157.

sum and for a transfer of property order, and a combination of orders may be used by the court to make financial provision which is justified by the s.9 principles.

The effect of a property transfer order is to require one party to transfer his or her interest in a particular asset to the other. The asset to be transferred may be owned exclusively by one party or jointly by the parties. The order does not actually transfer the asset; it simply directs one party to transfer ownership to the other. After the order is granted the transfer itself still needs to be carried through. So, for example, a heritable property will need to be conveyed, a life policy will need to be assigned and so on.

Can non-matrimonial/non-partnership property be transferred?

Most orders under s.8(1)(aa) will involve the transfer of matrimonial **3–23** or partnership property. However, the Act does not state that the provision is limited to ordering the transfer of matrimonial or part-nership property. Section 8(1)(aa) simply states that the court may make an order for *the transfer of property*, without limiting the category of that property. It seems at least theoretically possible that an order could be made for the transfer of a non-matrimonial or non-partnership asset.[81] By analogy, the Act is quite clear in stating that the payment of a capital sum can be deferred (thus allowing the capital sum to be paid out of non-matrimonial or non-partnership capital).[82] There seems to be no reason that, in the same way, non-matrimonial or non-partnership assets could not be subject to a property transfer order. The order is simply a mechanism for effecting financial provision which is justified by the s.9 principles and which is reasonable having regard to the resources of the parties.

Deferred decisions

Section 12(1) provides that an order for payment of a capital sum or **3–24** transfer of property can be made: (a) on granting decree of divorce or of dissolution of a civil partnership; or (b) within such period as the court on granting the decree may specify. Normally the order will be granted at the same time as the divorce or dissolution, but sometimes there may be sound reasons for granting the divorce or dissolution before the court considers financial matters. There are dangers in this approach.[83]

Postponed orders

Section 12(2) provides that the court, on making an order for the **3–25** transfer of property, may stipulate that it shall come into effect at a specified future date. In some circumstances it may be appropriate to defer the order until some later date or event. For a detailed discussion see paras 3–12 to 3–15. In an order for transfer of heritable property it

---

[81] See E.M. Clive, *The Law of Husband and Wife in Scotland*, 4th edn at para.24.089 for a persuasive argument. See also *Ranaldi v Ranaldi*, 1992 G.W.D. 26–1486 (opinion reserved on this point).

[82] See paras 3–12 to 3–15.

[83] See paras 3–10 to 3–11.

may often be appropriate to delay the transfer for a short period to allow conveyancing formalities to be carried out. If a transfer of property is to be deferred, it will be important to consider whether the party who is to wait should be awarded interest pending the transfer.[84] That party may also wish to consider whether they should seek some form of security to protect them against unforeseen problems such as the bankruptcy of the transferor.

Variation of date of transfer of property

3–26   Section 12(4) provides that, where an order for transfer of property is made, the court may, on an application by either party on a material change of circumstances, vary the date of transfer of property.[85] Section 12(4) only allows variation in the date of transfer; it does not allow any variation of the items of property which are to be transferred. Timing may be varied, but quantum is not to be affected.[86]

Implementation of the order

3–27   If one party is ordered to transfer property to the other but refuses to do so, the court has power to order the clerk of court to execute the necessary documentation required to effect the transfer.[87]

Rights of third parties

3–28   A party may seek an order for the transfer of property in which a third party has an interest. The most common example will be a heritable property which is subject to a standard security. If a party seeks transfer of an asset under s.8(1)(aa), s.15 of the Act protects the rights of third parties with an interest in the asset in two ways:

- section 15(1) provides that the court shall not make a property transfer order if the consent of any third party which is necessary under any obligation, enactment or rule of law has not been obtained; and
- section 15(2) provides that the court shall not make a property transfer order in relation to property which is the subject of a security without the consent of the creditor unless the creditor has been given the opportunity to be heard by the court.

---

[84] See para.3–15.

[85] An application for such an order would be made by minute in the original process—O.C.R. r.33.51.

[86] See para.3–19.

[87] The Sheriff Courts (Scotland) Act 1907 s.5A; 1985 Act s.14(2)(ja); See also *Clokie v Clokie*, 1993 G.W.D. 16–1059; *MacDonald v MacDonald*, 1995 S.L.T. 72; and *Wallis v Wallis*, 1991 S.C.L.R. 192 where the interlocutor which sparked 15 years of debate read— ". . . ordains the defender within three months of the date hereof and on payment to her of the capital sum hereinafter decerned for, to transfer to the pursuer All and Whole her one-half share in the subjects situated at and known as 10 Rosebank Avenue, Falkirk, failing which, grants authority to the sheriff clerk at Falkirk on production to him of satisfactory evidence of payment of the said capital sum to execute all documentation required to effect the said transfer on the defender's behalf. . ."

The distinction between subss.(1) and (2) was explored in *MacNaught v MacNaught*, 1997 S.L.T. (Sh Ct) 60, where the wife sought a transfer of her husband's interest in the matrimonial home. The matrimonial home was in joint names, and was subject to a standard security in favour of a building society. It was a condition of the security that neither party could transfer their interest in the property without the consent of the building society. Sheriff Principal Risk commented[88]:

> "In my opinion s.15(1) clearly applies to a contractual obligation. In this case the parties have a contract with the building society in terms of which they are forbidden to transfer the property without the consent of the building society . . . I agree with the solicitor for the defender that the court's power to order a transfer does not exceed the owner's power to grant a transfer. What that means in this case is that the court cannot grant decree [for the transfer] unless it is satisfied that the consent of the building society has been obtained.[89]
>
> Section 15(2) of the 1985 Act is worded in such a way as to apply to a security which does not include a condition requiring the consent of the security holder to a transfer of property. It confers upon such a security holder a right, which he would not otherwise have, to appear and be heard by the court in divorce proceedings. It also allows the court, having afforded such an opportunity to the security holder, to make a transfer order even without his consent.[90] The contrast between the two subsections is this: under s.15(1) the obligor has the right to withhold his consent and that right cannot be overridden by an order of the court, whereas under s.15(2) the security holder has no legal right to withhold his consent, but he is entitled to tell the court why he objects to a transfer and the court, having considered any such objection, may grant or refuse the order sought."

Where the consent of a third party is required, intimation of the proposed order must be made on the third party or creditor.[91] Accordingly, whenever craving a property transfer order, agents should consider whether the property concerned is subject to third party rights.

Description of the property

The property which is to be transferred should be clearly specified in **3–29** any interlocutor (and in the crave seeking the interlocutor). This will be particularly important in cases where heritable property is to be transferred. In *Walker v Walker*, 1991 S.L.T. 157, the First Division discussed the way in which interlocutors should be worded where heritage is to be transferred[92]:

---

[88] At p.61.

[89] So, if consent of the type specified under s.15(1) is required, the court has no power to make the order without such consent . . .

[90] . . . but, if the circumstances set out in s.15(2) apply, the court may override the objection of a third party.

[91] O.C.R. r.33.7(i).

[92] Opinion of the court at pp.159—60.

"There is no doubt that a sufficiently detailed description of the lands must be included in any disposition which is to be presented to the keeper of the registers for recording in the Register of Sasines, and the requirements where the title is to be or has been registered are no less exacting. The point is discussed in Halliday's *Conveyancing Law and Practice*, Vol. II at paras 18–06, 18–64 and 18–74.

. . . an inadequate description at the outset can lead to much confusion when attempts are made to put the order into effect. So a sufficient description of the property should be included in the order which is made under s.12(1) to satisfy the requirement of the common law, which is to distinguish the subjects from all other lands. In most cases a brief description will be all that is needed. In more complex cases it may be necessary for a more detailed description to be given. The court will expect to be provided with sufficient information by the party who seeks the order to enable this to be done."

In practice, it would seem sensible for a party seeking the transfer of heritage to include a proper conveyancing description of the land concerned in the crave seeking the transfer. If the transfer order is granted, the description in the interlocutor will allow a conveyancer to clearly identify the land.

Co-owned property after divorce or dissolution

3–30   In most divorces or dissolutions, property owned jointly by the parties will be dealt with by an order for sale or a property transfer order. This means that there will be no co-owned property after the action is disposed of. Generally, this will be desirable as it will result in a clean break for the parties. However, what happens if the couple co-own property, but this is not dealt with in the divorce or dissolution? In these circumstances, the property simply remains co-owned property, and the normal law relating to such property will apply. For example either party can apply for division and sale of jointly owned heritable property. Any special destination will effectively be revoked by the divorce or dissolution, unless the parties have specifically stated that the destination is to endure after decree.[93]

After divorce or dissolution, the rules on financial provision set out in the Act no longer have any part to play in relation to jointly owned property. In *Burrows v Burrows*, 1996 S.L.T. 1313, the husband and wife had entered into a separation agreement, under which it was agreed that the husband would retain a one-third interest in the former matrimonial home and two-thirds would be transferred to the wife. It was agreed that the husband would not seek to force a sale for five years following the date of divorce. The wife was to be entitled to stay in occupation of the house so long as it remained unsold. The parties divorced, and after five

---

[93] The Family Law (Scotland) Act 2006 s.19; the Civil Partnership Act 2004 s.124A. Third parties acquiring property which was subject to a special destination are protected if they acquire in good faith and for value.

years the husband sought division and sale of the property. The wife sought to postpone the sale and argued, amongst other things, that the sheriff at first instance had failed to take into account equitable factors in that the husband had a degree of financial security whilst the wife had no means to purchase her husband's reversionary interest in the property. Perhaps not surprisingly the Court of Session rejected this argument, pointing out that, once decree of divorce has passed, there can be no question of further adjustment of financial provision[94]:

> "In the present case the pursuer has an absolute right to insist in his action. While he was prevented by his agreement not to do so for the five years from the date of the divorce, that period has expired and his right is now unqualified. Counsel for the defender argued that it was *pars iudicis* to have regard to the hardship his client would suffer on a division and sale, but no authority was given to us for the suggestion that the right to insist on a division and sale is subject to such a consideration."

Practical considerations

It is often the case that one party will wish to retain some part of the **3–31** matrimonial or partnership property after divorce or dissolution. Commonly one party (or both) will wish to retain the family home. There can be strong emotional and practical ties, particularly if the property is the family home of young children. However, advisers should be careful to fully explore whether the party seeking to retain the property can really afford to do so; if they cannot, then the party will be ill-advised to spend time and money on prolonged proceedings requesting a transfer that is simply unrealistic. It is a sad fact that, after the separation, both parties will generally require to adjust to tighter financial circumstances. The comments of Sheriff Thomson in *Shipton v Shipton*, 1992 S.C.L.R. 23[95] are instructive:

> "Clearly the parties are both in a very unfortunate position. It is impossible to avoid sympathy for the pursuer. She is not well and although her spirits will no doubt benefit from having the children with her, the physical burden of caring for them is unlikely to improve her health. She enjoyed a good standard of living in a handsome house in Eddleston and her wish to continue to live in Eddleston, if only so that the children could remain at school there, where they appeared to be particularly happily settled, was readily understandable. But it will simply not be possible for them to continue to live in the former matrimonial home. There is no money to pay the mortgage and it will soon be repossessed."

The sheriff went on to explain that he also had some measure of sympathy for the defender but pointed out that the stark reality is that for the court[96]:

---

[94] Opinion of the court at p.1314.
[95] At pp.26—7.
[96] At p.27.

"The question, however, is not one of balancing sympathy but of seeking to divide the property fairly in terms of the Act."

SECTION 8(1)(b)—PERIODICAL ALLOWANCE

General discussion

3–32   In an action for divorce or dissolution of a civil partnership a party may apply to the court under s.8(1)(b) for:

"an order for the making of a periodical allowance to him by the other party to the action;".

Periodical allowance is an order against one party to pay a regular income to the other after divorce or dissolution. As with all types of order for financial provision, before granting an order the court must be satisfied that the order (in conjunction with any other orders being granted) is: (a) justified by the principles set out in s.9 of the Act; and (b) reasonable having regard to the resources of the parties.[97] Leaving this general requirement aside, s.13(2) of the Act sets out two over-arching requirements which must be met before an award of periodical allowance can be made. These are now considered in turn.

1.   Justified under section 9(1)(c), (d) or (e)

3–33   Section 13(2)(a) provides that an award for periodical allowance may only be made if it is justified under the principles in:

- s.9(1)(c)—economic burden of caring for a child;
- s.9(1)(d)—adjustment to loss of support; and
- s.9(1)(e)—relief of serious financial hardship.

There is a more detailed discussion of these principles in Ch.4. It is important to appreciate that periodical allowance should not be awarded if the purported justification is under either of the other two s.9 principles:

- s.9(1)(a)—fair sharing; or
- s.9(1)(b)—economic advantage/disadvantage.[98]

Why is there this split? The logic appears to be that s.9(1)(c), (d) and (e) largely look to the future—the *future* burden of childcare; adjustment to loss of support *after divorce or dissolution*; and serious financial hardship *as a result of the divorce or dissolution*. On the other hand, s.9(1)(a) and (b) essentially look to the past (fair sharing of matrimonial/partnership property and adjustment for economic advantage/disadvantage). Periodical allowance is an award which can provide a party with an income to cater for certain prospective financial needs.

---

[97] s.8(2). See paras 3–02 to 3–08. See e.g. *Millar v Millar*, 1990 S.C.L.R. 666 for a case where the court felt that an award of periodical allowance was not reasonable having regard to the resources of the parties.

[98] s.13(2).

2. Clean break

Under s.13(2)(b), the court is not to make an order for periodical **3–34** allowance unless it is satisfied that an order for payment of a capital sum or for transfer of property, or a pension sharing order,[99] would be inappropriate or insufficient to satisfy the requirements of s.8(2).[100] In *Petrie v Petrie*, 1988 S.C.L.R. 390, Sheriff Risk discussed how s.13(2) operates[101]:

> ". . . my understanding of s.13(2) of the 1985 Act is that an award of periodical allowance should only be considered if the financial rights of the parties cannot be regulated in a capital context, and then only if it can be justified by one out of three of the principles set out in s.9(1)."[102]

This is often referred to as the "clean break" principle. The phrase is used explicitly in *Johnstone v Johnstone*, 1990 S.L.T. (Sh Ct) 79, by the Sheriff Principal (Ireland)[103]:

> "By s.13(2) of the Family Law (Scotland) Act 1985 an order for periodical allowance can be made only if the court is satisfied that an order for payment of a capital sum is inappropriate or insufficient . . . One of the principles embodied in the 1985 Act is that in ordinary circumstances it should be possible for the parties to make a clean break, so that one spouse should not be entitled to lifelong support from the other . . ."

So, before awarding periodical allowance, the court should carefully consider whether any of the other s.8 orders can be used to achieve fair division of matrimonial or partnership property; only if they cannot will periodical allowance be appropriate.[104] The court firstly has to rule out the possibility of achieving financial provision through capital means.[105] Notice how Sheriff McInnes points out that a clean break order is insufficient and *therefore* periodical allowance is justified in the following passage from *Gribb v Gribb*, 1994 S.L.T. (Sh Ct) 43[106]:

---

[99] It is worth pointing out that many of the authorities relating to periodical allowance were decided before pension sharing orders were an option. The problem (prior to the introduction of pension sharing) was that often much of the matrimonial property was locked up within a large pension scheme. Accordingly, much of the matrimonial capital was illiquid, making periodical allowance the only reasonable option. See e.g. *Kelly v Kelly*, 1992 G.W.D. 36–2130.

[100] i.e. that any order for financial provision must be (a) justified by the s.9 principles, and (b) reasonable having regard to the resources of the parties. See e.g. *Savage v Savage*, 1993 G.W.D. 28–1779.

[101] At p.392.

[102] See also e.g. *Tyrrell v Tyrrell*, 1990 S.L.T. 406.

[103] At p.80.

[104] See e.g. *Atkinson v Atkinson*, 1988 S.C.L.R. 396.

[105] So, in a case such as *Morrison v Morrison*, 1989 S.C.L.R. 574, where an award under s.9(1)(c) was justified, periodical allowance was held not to be appropriate, because unequal division of capital assets could see justice done. However, in *Proctor v Proctor*, 1994 G.W.D. 30–1814, also argued under s.9(1)(c), periodical allowance was justified because a payment of a capital sum from the available resources would have been insufficient to redress the imbalance.

[106] At p.46.

> "In my opinion an order for the transfer of Mr Gribb's interest in 78 Burghmuir Road is insufficient having regard to the resources of the parties to secure the fair sharing of the net value of the matrimonial property and the avoidance of serious financial hardship for Mrs Gribb. I am of the opinion that the making of an order for a periodical allowance is justified by the principles set out in s9 of the 1985 Act and is reasonable having regard to the resources of Mr and Mrs Gribb."

The court should look at the overall package of awards which the party claiming periodical allowance will receive. If they are receiving substantial awards of capital, it may be difficult for them to maintain that periodical allowance is also justified under one of the principles set out in s.9(1)(c), (d) or (e). Alternatively, large awards of capital might mean that any award of periodical allowance which *is* justified should be restricted, either in terms of quantum or in terms of how long the periodical allowance should be paid. For example, in *McConnell v McConnell*, 1995 G.W.D. 3–145 at first instance[107] the court had awarded to the wife: (1) a transfer of property (which included a valuable development site); (2) a capital sum; and (3) a substantial periodical allowance (justified under s.9(1)(d)—adjustment to loss of support) for three years. On appeal the Second Division held that the Lord Ordinary had not given proper weight to the transfer of property and the capital sum. Both of these were available to her to allow her to adjust to the loss of support. The court reduced the period for payment of periodical allowance to six months, to allow the development site to be sold.[108]

If a party wishes to claim periodical allowance, the clean break principle must be kept firmly in mind when preparing pleadings and when leading evidence.[109] The party must clearly show the court why a clean break will not be sufficient to implement the principles of the Act. In *Mackin v Mackin*, 1991 S.L.T. (Sh Ct) 22 Sheriff Principal Ireland stressed this point[110]:

> "If a pursuer seeks an award of periodical allowance she must aver and prove that the conditions laid down in s.13(2) are satisfied. If she does not do so, the principle of the 'clean break' embodied in the 1985 Act prevents the court from considering the question of periodical allowance at all. In the present case there was no material before the sheriff to justify his award."

The requirement to plead the case properly is stringent. In *Mackin*, there was no averment that capital would be insufficient, so the court held that periodical allowance could not be granted. Even in undefended actions failure to attend to these matters will carry a risk that the court will simply not consider the issue of periodical allowance,[111] as was the case in *Thirde v Thirde*, 1987 S.C.L.R. 335, where Sheriff Scott commented[112]:

---

[107] 1993 G.W.D. 145.

[108] See also *McKenzie v McKenzie*, 1991 S.L.T. 461.

[109] *Bairstow v Bairstow*, 2000 G.W.D. 17–688.

[110] At p.24.

[111] Although it appears that in undefended actions proof can be by way of affidavit evidence—*Main v Main*, 1988 G.W.D. 24–1036.

[112] At p.336.

"As I see it, there can never be any question of a party being 'entitled' to an award of periodical allowance. The court does have a discretion, a limited discretion, to make an award in certain circumstances.

In my opinion, before the court can be asked to make an award of a periodical allowance the attention of the court must be directed to the circumstances which in the applicant's submission justify the making of an award. The plea-in-law should refer to whichever of the principles contained in section 9(1)(c), (d) and (e) is founded upon. There should be averments and proof which make it clear that an order for payment of a capital sum or for transfer of property would be inappropriate or insufficient. There should be averments and proof covering the considerations in section 11(3), (4) and (5) as appropriate, to which the court has to have regard in considering whether any order for a periodical allowance is justified."

To summarise these comments, the pleadings and evidence of the party seeking a periodical allowance should:

- confirm that the conditions in s.13(2) are satisfied (i.e. that a "clean break" is not possible);[113]
- state which of the principles in s.9(1)(c), (d) or (e) of the Act is being founded upon. The plea-in-law should clearly refer to the appropriate section and there should be averments and proof in support of the relevant principle; and
- deal with the considerations set out in s.11(3), (4) and (5) (which expand on s.9(c), (d) and (e)).

Section 13(1)—When can an award of periodical allowance be made?

Section 13(1) of the Act sets out when an order for periodical **3–35** allowance can be made:

"An order under s.8(2) of this Act for a periodical allowance may be made—

(a) on granting decree of divorce or of dissolution of a civil partnership;
(b) within such period as the court on granting the decree may specify; or
(c) after such decree where—

　(i) no such order has been made previously;
　(ii) application for the order has been made after the date of decree; and
　(iii) since the date of decree there has been a change of circumstances."

Of course, most orders will be made at the point that divorce or dissolution is granted in terms of s.13(1)(a). However, s.13(1)(b) allows

---

[113] See *Mackin v Mackin* above.

the court to defer the decision to a later date. There are some dangers in this approach.[114]

In terms of s.13(1)(c), the court also has power to make an award of periodical allowance *after* the decree of divorce or dissolution provided the three criteria set out in the provision are met.[115] Any such order would also need to be justified under one of the three criteria set out in s.9(1)(c), (d) or (e).[116] It is fairly easy to envisage a change in circumstances under s.9(1)(c) relating to the economic burden of childcare (e.g. the child might be diagnosed with an illness requiring special care or accommodation). It is harder to see how s.13(1)(c) can be applied to s.9(1)(d) which relates to loss of support *on divorce or dissolution*, although perhaps this might occur if a party's income dropped unexpectedly.[117] It appears still more unlikely that s.9(1)(e) awards could be made after the decree, since they relate to serious financial hardship *on divorce or dissolution*—this, by definition, requires an analysis of financial circumstances at the point of the divorce or dissolution itself, and logically it is difficult to see how a change of circumstances after the divorce or dissolution could impinge on these conditions.

Quantum and period of the award

The court's discretion

3–36   When making an award of periodical allowance, the court must operate within the framework of the Act. Provided that it does so, the quantum of periodical allowance and (subject to the rules outlined below on maximum periods of payment) the period of payment are matters largely within the discretion of the court of first instance.[118] Appeal courts will be reluctant to interfere with awards. Sheriff Principal Nicholson pointed this out in *Hutchison v Hutchison*, 1990 S.C.L.R. 819[119]:

> ". . . in a matter of this sort, an appeal court is entitled to review the decision of a court of first instance only where the court has proceeded upon the basis of a material error of fact or where the court's discretion has been exercised in a wholly unreasonable manner . . ."[120]

The period of award

3–37   The three principles of s.9 which may be used to justify an award of periodical allowance all have different implicit or explicit provisions

---

[114] See paras 3–10 to 3–11.
[115] An application for such an order would be made by minute in the original process—O.C.R. r.33.51.
[116] *Murray v Murray*, 1990 S.C.L.R. 226.
[117] See the commentary to *Murray v Murray*, 1990 S.C.L.R. 226.
[118] See e.g. *Millar v Millar*, 1990 S.C.L.R. 666; *Sullivan v Sullivan*, 2003 Fam. L.R. 53.
[119] At p.820.
[120] See e.g. *Gray v Gray*, 1968 S.L.T. 254.

regarding the maximum length of time that an award of periodical allowance may run:

- s.9(1)(c) awards are to cater for the economic burden of caring for children under 16 and will generally only run until the child is 16;[121]
- s.9(1)(d) awards are to be for not more than three years;
- s.9(1)(e) awards are not subject to any particular time limit— they are to allow relief of hardship over a "reasonable period".

Subject to the particular provisions in s.9(1)(c), (d) and (e), s.13(3) provides that periodical allowance may be ordered for:

- a definite period;[122]
- an indefinite period;[123] or
- until the happening of a specified event.[124]

It may be possible to argue that the period should be restricted because substantial awards of capital are also being made.[125] A party may argue for a restricted time-limit for the award of periodical allowance even though the pleadings do not give advance notice of such an argument.[126]

Section 13(7) of the Act provides that the order shall cease to have effect[127] if the person receiving payment marries, enters into a civil partnership or dies. However, under s.13(7)(a) the death of the party with the obligation to pay periodical allowance does not end the obligation. Periodical allowance continues to be enforceable against the party's estate. However, in these circumstances, it may be appropriate for the estate to make an application for variation under s.13(4), perhaps with a view to capitalising the periodical allowance and clearing the obligation with a single payment.

Comparison with capital sums payable by instalments

The distinction between periodical allowance and an order for payment of a capital sum by instalments under s.12(3) is important. The distinction is explored at para.3–18. **3–38**

Relationship to aliment

Periodical allowance is payable after divorce or dissolution whereas aliment is payable up to the divorce or dissolution. There are different considerations and criteria for each order. In particular, the Act **3–39**

---

[121] Although, see *Monkman v Monkman*, 1988 S.L.T. (Sh Ct) 37, discussed at greater length at para.4–54.

[122] e.g. in *Stott v Stott*, 1987 G.W.D. 17–645 periodical allowance was awarded for three years under s.9(1)(d) and then a further four years under s.9(1)(e).

[123] See *Haugan v Haugan*, 1996 S.L.T. 321; 2002 S.C. 631 where the award was without limit of time.

[124] e.g. in *Galloway v Galloway*, 2003 Fam. L.R. 10 periodical allowance was awarded until sixtieth birthday, death or remarriage of spouse obtaining the award; or in *Bolton v Bolton*, 1995 G.W.D. 14–799, the award was only until the payment of the capital sum.

[125] See para.3–34.

[126] See *Robertson v Robertson*, 1989 S.C.L.R. 71.

[127] Although any arrears will still be recoverable.

encourages a clean break after the divorce or dissolution, and where periodical allowance is awarded it will usually (although not always) be for a restricted period. The comments of Sheriff Principal Nicholson in *Hutchison v Hutchison*, 1990 S.C.L.R. 819[128] are instructive:

> "While an award of aliment is intended to provide for a person's support and financial needs, that has never, so far as I am aware, been the purpose of an award of periodical allowance. Granted, the precise purpose of an award of periodical allowance was never made explicitly clear until the passing of the 1985 Act, but inasmuch as it replaced the old pre-1964 law which, on divorce, entitled a spouse to legal rights as if the other spouse had died, I think that it may be assumed that in general the purpose was not to provide continuing support but rather to effect an equitable distribution of wealth between the former parties to a marriage."

Variation of periodical allowance awarded by decree

3–40   This section deals with variation of awards of periodical allowance made under a court decree. Different rules apply to the variation of periodical allowance set up in separation agreements. These are discussed separately at paras 3–45 to 3–48. If the award of periodical allowance was made before the 1985 Act came into force, then the criteria for variation of an award of periodical allowance are different.[129]

Section 13(4) allows variation of an award of periodical allowance made by the court in some circumstances.[130] The section provides:

> "Where an order for a periodical allowance has been made under section 8(2) of this Act, and since the date of the order there has been a material change of circumstances, the court shall, on an application by or on behalf of either party to the marriage or his executor, or as the case may be either partner or his executor, have power by subsequent order—
>
> (a) to vary or recall the order for a periodical allowance;
> (b) to backdate such variation or recall to the date of the application therefore or, on cause shown, to an earlier date;
> (c) to convert the order into an order for payment of a capital sum or for a transfer of property."

These provisions are important because, amongst other things, they allow the court to revisit the quantum of the award of periodical allowance. This differs from the provisions of s.12(4) which deal with variation of awards of capital sums or transfers of property: in those cases, quantum cannot be varied; only the date or method of payment. Related to s.12(4), the court has power under s.13(1)(c), if no award of periodical allowance was made at the time of the divorce or dissolution,

---

[128] At p.822.
[129] See *Hutchison v Hutchison*, 1990 S.C.L.R. 819 as a useful starting point for research.
[130] An application for such an order would be made by minute in the original process— O.C.R. r.33.51.

to award periodical allowance if there is a change of circumstances after the date of the decree.[131] The remainder of this section looks at some of the questions which need to be addressed when considering variation of an award of periodical allowance.

1.   What is to be varied?

There are essentially three things which the court might vary: the **3–41** quantum of the award[132]; the period of the award[133]; and the nature of the award.[134] So far as quantum is concerned, it is competent to apply for either a reduction or an increase in the amount of the award. In relation to the period of the award, the party paying the periodical allowance can seek a reduction of the time period, but on the other hand, the party in receipt of the payment can apply for an extension.[135] However, it would not be possible to extend an award beyond the maximum periods envisaged by the Act. So, an award under s.9(1)(d) could not be extended beyond the maximum period of three years. It is competent to argue for restriction of quantum and the period for payment as alternatives.[136]

The third aspect of an award of periodical allowance which may be varied is the nature of the award itself. Section 13(4)(c) allows a party (or the executor of a party) to apply for the award of periodical allowance to be converted into a capital sum or property transfer order. This may be appropriate if the party paying the periodical allowance comes into some capital, perhaps by gift or inheritance. Further, the obligation to pay periodical allowance does not terminate with the death of the payer,[137] and s.13(4)(c) may be useful to allow the executors to capitalise payments.

2.   Has there been a material change of circumstances?

Before the court will entertain a variation in periodical allowance, **3–42** there has to be a *material* change in financial circumstances. The power to vary the award is not to be used for small adjustments where there have been minor changes in the financial circumstances of the parties. Rather, it is to be used where there have been significant changes, and if the court does not find there to be any material change in circumstances, then it should not vary the award of periodical allowance.[138] In *Macpherson v Macpherson*, 1989 S.L.T. 231, the sheriff at first instance had

---

[131] Interestingly, the word "material" is not used in s.13(1). Contrast with s.13(4). See para.3–35.

[132] See e.g. *Haugan v Haugan*, 2002 S.C. 631.

[133] See e.g. *Kerray v Kerray*, 1991 S.L.T. 613; *Hutchison v Hutchison*, 1990 S.C.L.R. 819 is a case decided under the provisions of the Divorce (Scotland) Act 1976, but contains some useful observations about some of the factors which might come into play if a party is seeking to restrict the period of an award of periodical allowance.

[134] s.13(4)(c).

[135] See *Macpherson v Macpherson*, 1989 S.L.T. 231—again a case decided under the Divorce (Scotland) Act 1976, but which provides a useful discussion of relevant factors when seeking to extend an award of periodical allowance.

[136] *Hutchison v Hutchison*, 1990 S.C.L.R. 819.

[137] s.13(7)(a).

[138] *Kerray v Kerray*, 1991 S.L.T. 613.

increased an award of periodical allowance on the application of the wife. The sheriff's note did not outline what he considered to be the change of circumstances, and the Inner House held that he had therefore failed to give proper reasons for his decision. The Inner House went on to note that the material changes in circumstances actually altered the husband's position for the worse and accordingly held that the sheriff could have had no justification for increasing the wife's award of periodical allowance, and refused the wife's application for an increase.

What changes are likely to be considered material? Significant changes in the financial position of one or both parties or changes in the number of dependants of a party may well justify variation. In addition, the Act itself explicitly provides under s.13(4A), without prejudice to the generality of s.13(4), that the making of a maintenance calculation with respect to a child who has his home with a person to whom the periodical allowance is made (if the person paying the periodical allowance has an obligation of aliment towards that child) is a material change of circumstances.

The alteration in circumstances must have a financial impact.[139] A change in personal circumstances which has no financial consequences will not be enough to justify variation. For example, the fact that one party starts to co-habit with another is not of itself enough to justify a variation.[140] When considering whether there has been a material change in circumstances, the court will look at all relevant changes, and importantly it should examine alterations to the financial circumstances of both parties. It is the totality of these circumstances that will have a bearing on whether variation of the order is appropriate.[141] In some cases, it may be difficult to determine whether there has been such a change simply because the financial circumstances of the parties at the time of the original order are unclear or difficult to prove. The onus will be on the party seeking to establish the variation.[142]

If the court at first instance made an award on the basis of incomplete or erroneous information, this will not be considered a material change in circumstances, and the court will not use s.13(4) to adjust periodical allowance. The legislation requires an actual rather than hypothetical change of circumstances.[143]

3.   What adjustment is justified?

3–43   If there has been a material change in the financial circumstances of the parties, how is the court to go about deciding how to adjust the periodical allowance (if at all)? There seem to be two ways the court

---

[139] *Gray v Gray*, 1991 G.W.D. 30–1797.

[140] See *Kavanagh v Kavanagh*, 1989 S.L.T. 134.

[141] *Macpherson v Macpherson*, 1989 S.L.T. 231.

[142] See *Haugan v Haugan*, 2002 S.C. 631 at 638; and *Macpherson v Macpherson*, 1989 S.L.T. 231.

[143] See *Bye v Bye*, 1999 G.W.D. 33–1591 (surely one of the more aptly named cases in legal history). See also *Stewart v Stewart*, 1987 S.L.T. 246 (a decision made under the Divorce (Scotland) Act 1976), *Walker v Walker*, 1995 S.L.T. 375 (a case dealing with variation of aliment) and *Ritchie v Ritchie*, 1987 S.L.T. (Sh Ct) 7.

might approach this. First, upon holding that there has been a material change of circumstances, the court might analyse the whole financial situation of new and make an award of periodical allowance based on the financial circumstances of the parties at the time of the application for variation.[144] However, this does not seem to bear close analysis; after all, the original award of periodical allowance was designed to effect financial provision *on divorce or dissolution*. The award will normally have been made as part of a package of orders for financial provision, and it does not seem correct to completely re-assess the award based on the financial position at the time of the application for variation.

A better approach[145] is simply to assume the initial award of periodical allowance was reasonable, and then decide how any material change in financial circumstances should skew the award (if at all). This approach was used in *Hutchison v Hutchison*, 1990 S.C.L.R. 819[146] the sheriff took as his starting point an assumption that the award of periodical allowance made at the time of the divorce was reasonable.[147] He then looked at how the material change in circumstances should affect the existing award. In *Hutchison* the wife was in receipt of periodical allowance. The husband later applied for a variation. At the time of the divorce the wife's annual income was substantially less than the husband's (allowing for the payment of periodical allowance by the husband to the wife). At the time of the application for variation, the situation had reversed—if the order continued without variation, then the wife would have considerably more annual income than the husband. This amounted to a material change in circumstances, and the court reduced the amount of periodical allowance.

4. Should the variation be backdated?

The court can backdate the order for variation of periodical **3-44** allowance.[148] If the court backdates an order, then it has power to order that sums overpaid (in the light of backdating) should be repaid.[149] The fact that there is little prospect of recovery of arrears of periodical allowance is not grounds for varying periodical allowance to nil and backdating this. In *Haugan v Haugan*, 2002 S.C. 631, the Inner House commented[150]:

> "It is a matter for the pursuer whether she seeks to enforce, with or without success, any order to which she is properly entitled. It is the

---

[144] See e.g. *Sutherland v Sutherland*, 1988 S.C.L.R. 346.

[145] See e.g. *Macpherson v Macpherson*, 1989 S.L.T. 231 (decided in relation to the provisions for periodical allowance under the Divorce (Scotland) Act 1976); *Haugan v Haugan*, 2002 S.C. 631.

[146] Note that this is a case which relates to variation of a pre-1985 award of periodical allowance, but the arguments seem sound for post-1985 variations too.

[147] See p.822; see also *Macpherson v Macpherson*, 1989 S.L.T. 231 at 235.

[148] s.13(4)(b); and see *Laws v Laws*, 1991 G.W.D. 11–664. The court cannot backdate if the order for periodical allowance was made prior to the Act coming into force—see *Wilson v Wilson*, 1992 S.L.T. 664. An application backdating periodical allowance would be made by minute in the original process—O.C.R. r.33.51.

[149] s.13(6).

[150] At p.637.

function of the court, having regard to the provisions of the Act, to determine what is her entitlement."

Separation agreements and periodical allowance

3–45　　Parties may enter into a separation agreement which contains provisions that periodical allowance is to be paid after divorce or dissolution. If they do so, care should be taken to ensure that the agreement of the parties is correctly reflected, and in particular the agreement should be crystal clear about: (a) the amount of periodical allowance; (b) the period of payment (and events that trigger cessation of payment, such as death, remarriage or entering into a new civil partnership); and (c) if, when and how the provisions may be varied. The terminology used within the agreement will be particularly important. Agreements which contain such provisions may be set aside or varied by the courts in certain circumstances. There are three ways that such a review may be carried out.

1.　*General rule*

3–46　　Agreements containing provisions about periodical allowance are subject to the same rules as agreements containing provisions on capital payments and transfers of property. They can be set aside because they are not fair and reasonable at the time they were entered into.[151]

2.　*Variation under section 16(1)(a)*

3–47　　The Act also contains specific provisions which apply to the variation or setting aside of agreements containing provisions for periodical allowance. Section 16(1)(a) of the Act provides that, where the parties have entered into an agreement regarding financial provision, the court may make an order setting aside or varying any term of the agreement relating to a periodical allowance where the agreement expressly provides for the subsequent setting aside or variation by the court of that term. Such an order can be made at any time after the granting of decree of divorce or dissolution.[152] If the agreement gives the court power to consider setting aside or varying a term in the separation agreement relating to periodical allowance, then the court will have a wide discretion in applying the power.[153]

If the wording of s.16(1)(a) is examined it is clear that, if the parties wish the court to have power to vary the periodical allowance provided within the agreement, then the agreement itself should grant the court power to vary or set aside the payments. Generally agreements will specify that this power of variation will come into play on a material change of circumstances. However, if the power of variation is not mentioned then the court will have no power to review the term of the agreement dealing with periodical allowance. In *Drummond v Drum-*

---

[151] s.16(1)(b). See paras 9–05 to 9–08. Note that it is not possible to contract out of s.16(1)(b)—see s.16(4).

[152] s.16(2)(a).

[153] See the comments of Lord Cameron of Lochbroom in *McAfee v McAfee*, 1990 S.C.L.R. 805.

mond, 1996 S.L.T. 386, the couple entered into a separation agreement which (amongst other things) provided that the husband was to pay a monthly sum. These payments were described as "aliment" in the agreement but were to continue after the divorce. The agreement also stated that these payments were in full and final satisfaction of the wife's claims to "aliment and periodical allowance" before and after the divorce. The agreement did not contain any clause allowing variation on a material change of circumstances. The parties divorced, and some years later the husband sought a variation of the provisions, relying on s.7(2) of the 1985 Act which allows the court to entertain variations where "a person owes an obligation of aliment to the other". The First Division upheld the wife's argument that s.7(2) could not be used because, at the point of the application for variation, there was no obligation of aliment (the parties were now divorced). Equally, because the agreement did not contain provisions allowing variation of the post-divorce support, the court had no power to interfere with the payments.[154] The action was dismissed and the husband had to continue to pay.

Drummond is also a reminder to agents to use clear language in drafting separation agreements. If the power of variation set out in s.16(1)(a) is to be reserved to the court, the term "periodical allowance" should be used to define the payment which is to be subject to review.

It also seems that, if s.16(1)(a) is to be relied upon to give the courts power to set aside or vary the order, then the agreement has to spell out that *the court* is to have this power. In *Ellerby v Ellerby*, 1991 S.C.L.R. 608 the parties entered into a separation agreement a few months before the divorce. It provided for payment of periodical allowance after the divorce and a clause in the following terms was included[155]:

> "In the event of a material change in circumstances of either party, the sum payable in terms of articles second and third hereof, shall be subject to variation."

Importantly, the clause did not say how that variation was to be carried out. Sheriff Bell held that, in these circumstances, he was not able to deal with an application for variation of the provision within the agreement for periodical allowance[156]:

> "The point is an extremely narrow and difficult one. The wording of section 16 and in particular subsection (1)(a) is such as to persuade me that it is only where the agreement expressly provides for the subsequent setting aside or variation *by the court*[157] that the court may make an order setting aside or varying the term. The agreement does provide that the sum payable shall be subject to variation. It is difficult to see any meaning to that provision . . . Had

---

[154] See *Jackson v Jackson*, 2003 G.W.D. 941 for a discussion of the position where there is such a clause.
[155] At p.609.
[156] At p.611.
[157] Emphasis added.

it not been for the presence of the word 'expressly' in subsection
1(a) of section 16, I would have held that [the clause allowing
variation] must be read with an implication that the variation may
be done by the court. Subsection 1(a) does not, however, allow me
to imply anything into the agreement, because the court is only
given power to make the order if the term of the agreement
expressly provides for the subsequent setting aside or variation by
the court of that term. That makes it clear that unless there is an
express provision in those terms and in particular unless it is
expressly provided that the variation is to be by the court, then the
court may not make such an order. I think this is an unfortunate
result, but if I am to give meaning to the word 'expressly' in the
subsection, then I cannot see how I can imply into the relative term
of the agreement that variation is to be by the court."

Unfortunate indeed for Mr Ellerby—if the court cannot vary the
agreement, and the parties could not reach a compromise, then he was
bound to continue the payments without any hope of variation.[158]

*3. Variation under section 16(3)—bankruptcy, child support assessment
etc.*

3–48   Under s.16(3) of the Act, if the parties have entered into an
agreement containing provisions for periodical allowance then the court
will have power to vary the agreement in four circumstances:

(a) the estate of the person by whom any periodical allowance is
payable under the agreement has, since the date when the
agreement was entered into, been sequestrated, the award of
sequestration has not been recalled and the person has not
been discharged;
(b) a remedy analogous to sequestration[159] has, since that date,
come into force and remains in force in respect of the payer's
estate;
(c) the payer's estate is subject to a trust deed for the benefit of
creditors (or an analogous arrangement); or
(d) by virtue of the making of a maintenance calculation, child
support maintenance has become payable by either party to the
agreement with respect to a child to whom or for whose benefit
periodical allowance is paid under the agreement.

Section 16(4) makes it clear that it is not possible to contract out of
these provisions.

---

[158] Unless perhaps he could argue that the agreement could be struck at common law on
grounds of error, fraud, force or fear—see *McAfee v McAfee*, 1990 S.C.L.R. 805.
[159] See the Bankruptcy (Scotland) Act 1985 s.10(5).

SECTION 8(1)(baa)—PENSION SHARING ORDERS (AND PENSION SHARING BY AGREEMENT)

General discussion

Pensions are often a problem for parties who separate. They are **3–49** valuable assets, but the value cannot be released for use by the parties until retirement of the pensioner. Even then, the party who retires will generally not be able to take the whole capital value of the asset. In the early days of the Act there were difficulties because the Act did not include any mechanism to allow sharing of the value of pensions. This meant that, where a significant proportion of the matrimonial property was locked up in a pension, the party with the right to the pension was obliged to retain this. Often there was insufficient capital to make a balancing payment to the other party.

To take an extreme example, suppose that the only item of matrimonial property is a pension in name of the husband with a cash equivalent transfer value[160] at the relevant date of £100,000. The husband cannot draw down the pension until he reaches retirement age. Even then he will not normally be entitled to take the whole capital sum of £100,000—he will be entitled to a smaller lump sum plus regular income from the pension. If we assume that equal sharing of the matrimonial property is justified, the husband will be due to make a balancing payment to the wife of £50,000. However, at the point of the divorce it may be difficult or impossible for him to fund this payment. A deferred payment may be unattractive to the wife for a number of reasons. For example, the husband might die before he draws down the pension or he might disappear making the deferred payment impossible to enforce.

To help combat this problem the concept of pension sharing was introduced by the Welfare Reform and Pensions Act 1999 ("the 1999 Act"), and implemented in Scotland by amendments to the 1985 Act. Pension sharing may be used in actions commenced on or after December 1, 2000. Pension sharing provides a mechanism to transfer some (or all) of the pension rights from one spouse or civil partner to the other. There are now ways in which pension sharing can be effected. First, under s.8(1)(baa) of the Act, in an action for divorce, or for dissolution of a civil partnership, either party may apply to the court for a *pension sharing order*. Secondly, pension sharing can arise as a result of a *qualifying agreement*. The result will be the same, but the procedures and rules for each method are different.

Pension sharing has been used fairly sparingly since its introduction, perhaps because in many cases a fair division of matrimonial or partnership property can be achieved by one party retaining their pension assets, and the other becoming sole owner of other assets (often the family home). This is generally referred to as offsetting.[161] There has

---

[160] See paras 6–15 to 6–16.

[161] Although offsetting assets against the pension is often used when there are sufficient available assets, it may not always the best solution. For example, if one party is in poor health, pension sharing may provide a solution which is of benefit to both parties with the pension provider suffering financially—see John Buchanan, "Apportioning and sharing" J.L.S.S., May 2006, p.28.

been little authority on pension sharing orders to date. In *Galloway v Galloway*, 2003 Fam. L.R. 10, an Outer House decision of Temporary Judge Coutts, the husband held interests in two pension funds worth about £500,000. He also had other valuable assets in his name, including the family home, a shareholding in a business and other heritable property. The husband did not want to realise either of the houses or his interest in the business, and the parties were agreed that a pension sharing order should be used.

What types of pension can be shared?

3–50   The 1999 Act states that two types of pensions can be shared: (a) shareable rights under a specified pension arrangement;[162] and (b) shareable state scheme rights.[163] Between them, these categories encompass most types of pension including private pensions, state earning related pensions schemes ("SERPS") and pensions in payment. A very limited category of pensions and pension rights is excepted from pension sharing,[164] and pension sharing is not available for the basic state pension.[165] Section 8(4) of the 1985 Act provides that the court cannot in the same proceedings make a pension sharing order and a pension lump sum order (earmarking order) in relation to the same pension arrangement. Equally, if there is already in force a pension lump sum order which relates to a person's benefits or future benefits under a pension arrangement, the court cannot make a pension sharing order in respect of those rights.[166] Pension sharing is not available in respect of compensation paid under Ch.3 of Pt 2 of the Pensions Act 2004.[167]

Effect of pension sharing

3–51   The effect of pension sharing is to subject the shareable pension rights of the party with the pension to a debit of the appropriate amount or percentage, and gives the other party to the divorce or dissolution a credit of the same amount or percentage against the managers of the pension arrangement.[168] The debit/credit may be either a specified amount of money or a percentage of the value of the pension rights. If the pension sharing order specifies a particular amount of money to be transferred, then that is the amount that will be transferred. If the order specifies a percentage, then the amount to be transferred will be the cash equivalent of that percentage calculated on the "valuation day".[169] The

---

[162] Chapter I of Pt IV of the 1999 Act. The 1999 Act and the Family Law (Scotland) Act 1985 both use the term "pension arrangement". Almost all non-state pension schemes will fall within this definition.

[163] Chapter II of Pt IV of the 1999 Act.

[164] s.27(1) of the 1999 Act states that pension sharing under Chapter 1 of Pt IV of the 1999 Act is available under any pension arrangement other than an "excepted public service pension scheme". Section 27(2) provides that any rights under a pension arrangement may be shared other than rights specified in regulations made by the Secretary of State; see also the Pension Sharing (Valuation) Regulations 2000, SI 2000/1052 reg.2.

[165] s.47 of the 1999 Act.

[166] 1985 Act s.8(6).

[167] 1985 Act s.8(4A).

[168] 1999 Act s.29(1).

[169] 1999 Act s.29(2).

valuation day will be a day specified by the pension provider within the "implementation period".[170] The implementation period will generally be four months from the date that the appropriate documents are intimated to the pension provider.[171]

Once a pension sharing order has been made, the transferee's options will be determined by the rules of the scheme. They may or may not be able to leave the credit in the pension scheme, and they may or may not be able to transfer it to another scheme. For example, many public sector pension schemes are unfunded and will not allow transfers out. Whichever option is chosen or available, the transferee will be entitled to a pension in his or her own right when he or she fulfils the requirements of the scheme—generally when they reach retirement age. It is worth noting that, in cases where pensions are shared on a 50/50 basis, this will not mean that both parties will receive the same amount of pension. The actual pension received by each party will depend on various actuarial factors such as mortality rates and, if the parties have some way to go before retirement, each of their new pension funds will perform differently over the years to when the pension is taken.[172]

Pension sharing by order and agreement

Pension sharing can be triggered in two ways. First, a *pension sharing* **3–52** *order* can be made by the court as one of the orders for financial provision. Secondly, pension sharing can arise as a result of a *qualifying agreement*. The result will be the same, but the procedures and rules for each method are different. This section briefly explores the distinction.

Pension sharing orders

A pension sharing order is one of the orders which can be made by **3–53** the court in making financial provision on divorce or dissolution, so a party seeking such an order should include a crave to that effect. An application for a pension sharing order has to be intimated to the pension arrangement, who may enter the process, so there should also be a crave for intimation on the pension arrangement.[173] It may also be appropriate to crave interest, particularly if the crave requests that a particular amount of money (rather than a percentage) is to be the subject of pension sharing (although see the comments below at para.3–67). The purpose of a pension sharing order is not simply to split pension rights, but to form part of the overall financial provision in terms of the 1985 Act. As with all types of order for financial provision, before granting an order the court must be satisfied that it (in conjunction with any other orders being granted) is: (a) justified by the principles set out in s.9 of the Act; and (b) reasonable having regard to the resources of the parties.[174] If a pension is being shared, it will still be

---

[170] 1999 Act s.29(7).
[171] 1999 Act s.34(1).
[172] See Harry Smith, "Pension Sharing: The Law of Unintended Consequences" 2004 Fam. L.B. 2–5.
[173] O.C.R. r. 33.7(m).
[174] See paras 3–02 to 3–08.

valued at the relevant date for the purposes of establishing the net value of the matrimonial or partnership property.[175] However, the value of the pension at the time of the order may be highly relevant from a practical point of view (e.g. if the order is to specify a percentage of the rights to be transferred).

Qualifying agreements

3–54   If the parties want to reach agreement on pension sharing, rather than having the agreement imposed on them by the court, then this must be done under a "qualifying agreement". The following rules apply to any qualifying agreement.

- It must be entered into under relevant regulations.[176]
- It must be registered in the Books of Council and Session.[177]
- There must not be a pension lump sum order (earmarking order) in relation to the benefits or future benefits to which the transferor is entitled under the pension arrangement which is the subject of the agreement.[178]
- It must be in prescribed form[179] and the specific provisions for pension sharing must be contained in an annex to (which is separable from) the qualifying agreement.[180] In relation to private (rather than state) schemes, the annex must set out:

  (a) in relation to the transferor: (i) all names by which they have been known; (ii) their date of birth; (iii) their address; (iv) their national insurance number; (v) the name and address of the pension arrangement concerned; and (vi) the transferor's membership number or policy number in the pension arrangement;

  (b) in relation to the transferee, the following information is required: (i) all names by which they have been known; (ii) their date of birth; (iii) their address; (iv) their national

---

[175] *Burnside v Burnside*, 2007 G.W.D. 24–404, discussed at 2007 Fam. L.B. 89–3.

[176] 1999 Act ss.28(3) and 48(3). Regulation 3 of the Pensions on Divorce etc. (Pension Sharing) (Scotland) Regulations 2000 (SI 2000/1051) provides that "A qualifying agreement is, for the purposes of section 28(1)(f) of the 1999 Act, one which the transferor and transferee have entered into in order to determine the financial settlement on divorce or dissolution of a civil partnership and in respect of which the transferor has intimated to the person responsible for a pension arrangement prior to the making of the agreement the intention to have the transferor's pension rights under the pension arrangement shared with the transferee." Under reg.5, there is a similar provision for shareable state scheme rights, but with one important difference in that the parties must "have received confirmation from the Secretary of State that shareable state scheme rights are held in the name of the transferor".

[177] 1999 Act ss.28(3) and 48(3).

[178] 1999 Act s.28(6).

[179] 1999 Act ss.28(1)(f)(ii) and 48(1)(f)(ii); regs 2 and 4 of the Pensions on Divorce etc. (Pension Sharing) (Scotland) Regulations 2000 (SI 2000/1051). For a style of agreement see e.g. Division F of *Butterworth Scottish Family Law Service* and particularly note that slightly different styles will be required for agreements relating to private and state schemes.

[180] It is probably useful to have the agreement in a separable annex anyway, since it means that the annex only can be exhibited to the pension provider, thus keeping the other parts of the separation agreement confidential.

insurance number; and (v) if the transferee is already a member of the pension arrangement from which a credit is derived, their membership number;

(c) details of the amount or percentage share to be transferred to the transferee;

(d) where the transferee has consented[181] to the payment of the pension credit to another pension arrangement, (i) the full name of the arrangement; (ii) its address; (iii) if known, the transferee's membership number or policy number in the arrangement; and (iv) the name or title, business address, business telephone number and (where available) the fax and e-mail of a person who may be contacted in respect of the discharge of the liability for the credit;

(e) details of the provision of apportionment (if any) made between the parties in respect of any charges;

(f) confirmation by the transferor that he has intimated to the pension arrangement his intention with respect to pension sharing and that the pension arrangement has acknowledged receipt of the intimation.

- Similar but slightly different procedures are to be adopted when state scheme rights are to be shared.[182]
- It must take effect on the grant of decree of divorce or dissolution of a civil partnership.[183]
- The agreement on pension sharing will only become effective following the divorce or dissolution provided that the proper post-decree procedure is followed. These procedures are considered at para.3–56 below.

Administration charges

It is likely that the pension administrator will impose charges as a **3–55** result of pension sharing. These might be charged as an outlay, or might be applied as a debit to the scheme. In any agreement the parties should agree how the charges are to be paid, and any decree for pension sharing should deal with this matter. The court may include in the order provision regarding the apportionment of these charges between the parties.[184]

Procedural rules—post-decree

In order that pension sharing is carried through after the divorce or **3–56** dissolution, a strict series of procedural rules require to be followed. These will apply whether the pension sharing has been triggered by a pension sharing order or a qualifying agreement coming into effect upon a decree of divorce or dissolution. The main steps are set out in s.28(7),

---

[181] In accordance with paras 1(3)(c), 3(3)(c), or 4(2)(c) of Sch.5 to the 1999 Act.
[182] See reg.4 of the Pensions on Divorce etc. (Pension Sharing) (Scotland) Regulations 2000 (SI 2000/1051).
[183] 1999 Act s.28(1)(f)(iii).
[184] 1985 Act s.8A.

(8) and (9) (for private schemes) and s.48 (for state schemes) of the 1999 Act. The following is a summary, but the relevant sections should be consulted for the comprehensive rules.

> (1) The person responsible for the relevant pension arrangement (or, in the case of state schemes, the Secretary of State) must receive before the end of a period of two months[185] of the date of decree of divorce (or dissolution of a civil partnership):
>
>> (a) the relevant documents which will be either: (i) for a pension sharing order a copy of the pension sharing order and the decree of divorce or dissolution; or (ii) in the case of a provision made under a qualifying agreement, a copy of the provision, a copy of the decree of divorce or dissolution, and documentary evidence that the agreement is in prescribed form;[186]
>> (b) such information relating to the transferor and the transferee as the Secretary of State may prescribe.[187]
>
> (2) After the documentation at (1) above has been intimated, the pension arrangement has four months to implement the transfer.[188]

Need for expert advice

3–57   It cannot be stressed highly enough to both clients and agents, that expert advice will be needed by both parties if they are considering pension sharing. This will be the case whether they are seeking an order from the court, or whether they are seeking pension sharing through a qualifying agreement. Pension sharing cannot be looked at in isolation. It is, after all, a provision which will affect both parties' retirement planning and must be looked at in the context of their overall (individual) financial circumstances, just as they would take advice when making any alterations to their own pensions. It should be remembered that, although solicitors tend to look at pension sharing as part of the division of matrimonial or partnership property, it may be more important for the parties to consider the *effect* of pension sharing (i.e. when can they draw the pension, and how much are they likely to receive). Generally actuaries will have the best experience in providing advice on pension sharing, but some input from an independent financial adviser may be useful. Remember that the Law Society of Scotland imposes rules on financial matters which solicitors can and cannot advise upon.[189]

The parties must consider whether pension sharing is appropriate at all. It may be better (for one or both parties) to leave the pension undisturbed and simply to transfer other assets to the non-pension

---

[185] The two-month period can be extended by the sheriff on the application of a person having an interest—1999 Act ss.28(10) and 48(9).

[186] 1999 Act ss.28(9) and 48(8).

[187] 1999 Act ss.28(7) and 48(6); reg.5 of the Pensions on Divorce etc. (Provision of Information) Regulations 2000 (SI 2000/1048).

[188] 1999 Act s.34(1).

[189] See "Guidance on Pension Sharing on Divorce", J.L.S.S., June 2001, p.9.

holder to offset the value. This will certainly avoid the charges which are likely to be levied by the pension arrangement as part of the pension sharing process (and may avoid the need to incur the expenses of an actuary). In addition, there may have been significant events after the relevant date which might materially affect the decision about whether it is wise for the parties to consider pension sharing. Some events which might have significant effects on the pension rights are: changes in the scheme itself; transfer of funds into or out of the pension; the retirement of the scheme member; the death of either party; changes to the scheme member's salary; and changes in health of the scheme member.

If the parties are convinced that pension sharing is the right way to proceed, expert advice will be required to consider the best way to effect the transfer. Where the transferor has more than one pension scheme, the decision about which scheme or schemes to use to effect pension sharing, and to what extent, are very important.[190] In the case of the transferee, it will be important to establish whether they are permitted to remain a member of the scheme after the transfer. If there is an option to transfer out of the scheme, expert advice will be required to assess which option will be best.

Consultation with the pension arrangement

If a party is seeking pension sharing, it is crucial that the pension **3–58** arrangement (or the state scheme) is contacted at the earliest possible opportunity to ensure that the suggested sharing is workable within the terms of the scheme. In practice, the party seeking sharing should contact the arrangement and request that they provide the information which the scheme is obliged to provide in terms of reg.4 of the Pensions on Divorce etc. (Provision of Information) Regulations 2000.[191] Under this regulation the pension arrangement has to provide certain information within 21 days of notification. Some of the information is practical (such as the name and address of the person to whom intimation should be given that pension sharing is to be activated) whilst other information is highly technical and will be of importance to the financial advisers and/or actuaries who are giving advice to the client. Obtaining this information is crucial, and will allow parties' advisers to check whether the proposed transfer can be carried through in the way that the parties wish.[192]

What should be transferred?

The statutory rules on pension sharing allow either a percentage or a **3–59** specific amount to be transferred. The problem of how much to transfer is a rather difficult one. The Act provides that it is the value of the matrimonial or partnership property at the relevant date which is to be shared.[193] However, the pension will fluctuate in value between the

---

[190] See Harry Smith, "The reality of pension sharing", J.L.S.S., April 2003, p.21.

[191] SI 2000/1048.

[192] For an excellent summary of information to seek from the scheme see Fiona Sasan, "Pension sharing tips on divorce", J.L.S.S., May 2007, p.40.

[193] Subject to s.10(3A) which does not apply to the valuation of pension rights which are to be shared; see *Burnside v Burnside*, 2007 G.W.D. 24–404 and discussed at 2007 Fam. L.B. 89–3.

relevant date and the date of decree (and remember also that pension sharing whether under an order or a qualifying agreement will not take effect until after the decree). A long period of time can elapse between these dates, sometimes several years. During this time extremely significant events might take place which would have a radical effect on the pension.

Strictly, it would be correct to transfer a specified amount (rather than a percentage) to the transferee to compensate them for the appropriate amount required to share matrimonial or partnership property fairly at the relevant date. However, this might be disastrous in certain circumstances. Imagine that the only matrimonial asset in a separation is a pension in name of the wife with a value at the relevant date of £200,000. If pension sharing is agreed and is calculated with reference to the value of the pension on the relevant date, the appropriate amount to transfer to the husband is £100,000 (on the assumption that the matrimonial property is to be shared equally between the parties). Imagine now that the parties enter into a qualifying agreement providing that £100,000 is to be transferred under pension sharing. Time elapses during negotiations, and further time passes before decree is sought and granted. After decree it takes still further time for the transfer to be implemented by the pension administrator. At the time the debit is made from the fund, imagine that the value of the pension has crashed and it is only worth £100,000. In order to satisfy the agreement the whole value of the fund will go to the husband leaving the wife with nothing. In an extreme case there might be insufficient funds in the scheme to satisfy the pension sharing order.[194]

It might be thought that the transfer of a percentage of the scheme is better, but this presents problems of uncertainty. From the point of view of the transferee they will not know how much of a credit they will receive until well after the agreement is entered into. Equally, the person with the pension will often have continued to contribute towards the scheme after the relevant date and up to the transfer. It seems unfair that the benefit of these contributions (or a percentage of them) should accrue to the other party.

There is no absolutely satisfactory answer to these problems. Clients must be advised of the risks. Once again, expert advice will help to identify the potential problems in any given set of circumstances. To minimise the chances of major fluctuations in the value of the rights under the scheme, it will generally be best to ensure that pension sharing is carried through as quickly as possible after it is ordered by the courts or the agreement is entered into. It might also be wise to build into any qualifying agreement a provision that the effect of the pension sharing is to be reviewed at around the time of the divorce or dissolution, perhaps with a provision for review of the agreement in the event of a material change in the CETV of the pension.[195] If a fixed amount (rather than a percentage) is to be transferred, then consideration should be given to a

---

[194] This does not appear to be a fanciful notion—see Harry Smith, "Pension Sharing: the Law of Unintended Consequences" 2004 69 Fam. L.B. 2–5.

[195] Although of course this would leave the parties with a degree of uncertainty that they might wish to avoid.

provision for interest from the relevant date to the date of decree, although see the potential problems out lined below at para.3–67.

Traps

The concept of pension sharing creates some traps for the unwary. **3–60** The following are almost certainly only a few of them.

Trap 1—Beware of simplified procedure

We have seen that pension sharing may be agreed through a qualifying **3–61** agreement, but the sharing will not be *effected* until divorce or dissolution. We have also seen that, in order for the pension sharing to come into effect, various procedures must be followed immediately after the decree is granted, otherwise the pension sharing cannot be carried through. It is not uncommon for parties to enter into a separation agreement and then, having finalised the difficult financial negotiations, to wait for some time before proceeding with the divorce or dissolution. They may wait until they can use simplified procedure to ensure that their costs are minimised. Anne Hall Dick and Tom Ballantine in *The Science of Family Law*[196] point out that there will be a serious problem if the parties enter into a qualifying agreement, and then later progress the divorce or dissolution personally (or indeed through agents) using simplified procedure. There is a significant danger that the parties (or agents) will forget to take the appropriate steps to ensure that the pension sharing is effected. The authors correctly point out that it is vital that the parties are very clearly advised at the time they enter into the agreement that steps must be taken within a strict timetable after the divorce or dissolution if the pension sharing is to be effected.[197]

Trap 2—Old separation agreements

This is really the same as Trap 1 but in a slightly different guise. It is **3–62** not uncommon for clients to appear in a solicitors' waiting room stating that they sorted out the financial aspects of the separation in an agreement some time ago, and now all they want is a divorce or dissolution. If there is an old separation agreement, this must be carefully checked. If the agreement contained a pension sharing agreement then the appropriate steps within the timetable must be taken to effect the agreement.

Trap 3—Death before implementation

There may be a problem where the transferor under a pension sharing **3–63** agreement dies before implementation; everything will depend on the terms of the agreement and the scheme's approach to the problem.[198] It would be well worth running the wording of any agreement past the pension administrator to ensure that, in the event of the death of the

---

[196] 1st edn, (Edinburgh: W. Green, 2001), Ch.4.

[197] If the timetable is not followed it is open to apply to the sheriff for an extension under ss.28(10) or 48(9) but it would be wise to avoid having to rely on this.

[198] See John Pollock, "Pensions", 2006 80 Fam. L.B. 1–4.

transferor, the transferee will still receive a credit of the appropriate amount or percentage.

Trap 4—Transfers out

3–64   The parties may agree pension sharing but, during the time which elapses between the date of the agreement and implementation of pension sharing, the transferor may transfer his pension interests out of the relevant scheme and into a new one. Any agreement must cover this possibility. Presumably it would be sensible to provide that such alterations will either void the agreement, or some form of penalty would apply.

Trap 5—Retirement

3–65   Time will elapse between the agreement itself and implementation of the pension sharing. What happens if during this period the party with the pension retires? The retirement will almost certainly result in a reduction in value of the fund. Again any agreement should contain specific provisions about what is to happen in these circumstances. The result may be particularly harsh to the transferee if they have elected to take a percentage of the fund rather than a specified sum.

Trap 6—Foreign divorces and dissolutions

3–66   Parties may enter into an agreement for pension sharing under the Scottish regulations. However, if subsequently the parties move to another jurisdiction (even within the UK), it might be that the Scottish pension sharing agreement will be difficult to activate upon decree of divorce or dissolution (or their equivalent) in the new jurisdiction.[199]

Practical advice

3–67   If considering pension sharing, then the following practical steps should be considered.

- Obtain a CETV at the relevant date (and value all of the other matrimonial or partnership property in the normal way).
- Obtain an up-to-date CETV (in addition to the relevant date valuation) to check whether there has been any significant rise or fall in the value of the pension.
- If pension sharing is contemplated, take expert financial advice.
- At an early stage request all information in terms of reg.4 of the Pensions on Divorce etc. (Provision of Information) Regulations 2000.[200] Further information not set out in the regulations might also be required—the expert adviser should provide guidance.
- Carefully consider alternatives to pension sharing (e.g. payment of a capital sum by instalments; offsetting other assets against the CETV of the pension).

---

[199] See Fiona Sasan and Lucia Clark, "Pension sharing agreements and foreign divorces", 2007 Fam. L.B. 89–2.
[200] SI 2000/1048.

- Decide whether the pension should be shared by use of a percentage or a specific amount.
- Establish whether the transferee can remain in the scheme, or whether there is an option to transfer out.
- Ascertain the charges to be imposed by the scheme, and how these are to be paid.
- If a specific amount is to be transferred, consider whether interest should be applied. It probably should, but there is a potential problem here—with interest accruing on a day-to-day basis, there is a danger that the pension providers might feel that it is impossible to accurately effect the transfer. The problem should be avoided if the proposed wording is pre-approved by the pension provider. Alternatively, the interest could be paid separately from the pension share.
- If pension sharing is dealt with under an agreement, consider carefully what would happen if one of the parties dies or retires. Make sure that any proposals are approved by the pension provider. Advise the client of any risks. Consider contingency clauses to cover what is to happen if pension sharing cannot be implemented.
- Send the proposed qualifying agreement (or details of the order craved) to the pension administrator to ensure that they are happy that it can be effected. It will be embarrassing and professionally dangerous to find out after the decree has been granted that, because of some problem with the wording of the agreement or order, the pension sharing simply cannot be effected for technical reasons.
- Establish what paperwork the scheme will require to carry through the transfer. Given the strict time limits imposed in the legislation, it will be important to ensure that all relevant documents are available and signed by both parties well in advance of the expiry of any time limits.
- If pension sharing is agreed under a qualifying agreement, it is probably best to proceed with the divorce or dissolution as quickly as possible after the agreement is entered into. This will minimise the possibility of large fluctuations in value of the pension leading to the problems outlined above.
- Once the decree is granted which either contains a pension sharing order or which triggers pension sharing under a qualifying agreement, carefully diarise the two-month timetable.
- Advise clients clearly on any risks inherent in the procedure.

Section 8(1)(ba)—Pension Lump Sum ("Earmarking") Orders

General discussion

Under s.8(1)(ba) of the Act, the court is empowered (rather cir- **3–68** cuitously) to make an order under s.12A(2) or (3) of the Act. These are termed pension lump sum orders in the Act, but are commonly known as earmarking orders. Essentially, a pension lump sum order allows the court to order that a capital sum is paid by one party to the other out of any lump sum released from their pension either on retirement or death. They are quite different from, and should not be confused with, pension sharing orders.

As with all types of order for financial provision, before granting a pension lump sum order, the court must be satisfied that the order (in conjunction with any other orders being granted) is: (a) justified by the principles set out in s.9 of the Act; and (b) reasonable having regard to the resources of the parties.[201] Apart from these general considerations, s.12A(1) of the Act provides that a pension lump sum order may be made where the court makes an order for payment of a capital sum by a party to the marriage or a partner in a civil partnership ("the liable person") in circumstances where: (a) the matrimonial property or the partnership property includes any rights or interests in benefits under a pension arrangement[202] which the liable party has or may have (whether such benefits are payable to him or in respect of his death); and (b) those benefits include a lump sum payable to him or in respect of his death. It is worth particularly noting that a pension lump sum order may only be granted if the court also grants an order for payment of a capital sum—the pension lump sum order is ancillary to the capital sum order. If the criteria in s.12A(1) are fulfilled then the court may make a pension lump sum order, and there are two distinct ways the order can be made. These will be examined in turn.

1. Lump sum payable to the liable person

3–69   Where the benefits under the pension scheme include a lump sum payable to the liable person then the court, on making the capital sum order, may make an order requiring the pension scheme to pay the whole or part of the lump sum to the other party when it becomes due.[203] The responsibility to make the payment is on the pension scheme rather than the liable person. In this way the pension lump sum order may be seen as more secure than relying on the party themselves to make the payment by, for example, a deferred payment of the capital sum.

2. Lump sum payable on death of the liable person

3–70   Where the benefits under the pension scheme include a lump sum payable on death of the liable person then the court has a number of options under s.12A(3): (a) if the person responsible for the pension arrangement[204] has power to determine to whom the sum (or any part of

---

[201] See paras 3–02 to 3–08.

[202] The Act uses the term "pension arrangement" rather than "pension scheme" and this is defined in s.27(1) as meaning: (a) any occupational scheme within the meaning of the Pension Schemes Act 1993; (b) a personal pension scheme within the meaning of that Act; (c) a retirement annuity contract; (d) an annuity or insurance policy purchased or transferred for the purpose of giving effect to rights under an occupational pension scheme or personal pension scheme; or (e) an annuity purchased or entered into for the purpose of discharging liability in respect of a pension credit under s.29(1)(b) of the Welfare Reform and Pensions Act 1999 or under corresponding Northern Ireland legislation.

[203] s.12A(2).

[204] The "person responsible for a pension arrangement" is defined in s.27(1) as being: (a) in the case of an occupational scheme or a personal pension scheme, the trustees or

it) is to be paid then the court can require the person responsible for the pension arrangement to pay the sum to the other party to the divorce or dissolution; (b) if the liable person has power to nominate the person to whom the lump sum (or any part of it) is to be paid, then the court can require the liable person to nominate the other party to the divorce or dissolution; or (c) in any other case, the court can require the person responsible for the pension arrangement to pay the lump sum (or any part of it) to the other party to the divorce or dissolution rather than to the person to whom it would otherwise have been paid.

Any payment under a pension lump sum order (whether the lump sum is payable to the liable person or on their death) will discharge the liability of the pension scheme to the liable person to the extent of the payment.[205] The payment under the pension lump sum order shall be treated for all purposes as a payment made by the liable person in or towards the discharge of his liability under the capital sum order.[206]

If the liable person discharges their liability under the capital sum order (in whole or in part) other than by a payment under the pension lump sum order, then the court may, on an application by any person having an interest, recall the pension lump sum order or vary the amount specified in the order, as appears to the court appropriate in the circumstances.[207] So, if the liable person comes into funds, they may find it convenient to settle the sums due under the capital sum order early, and then seek to have the pension lump sum order discharged or varied.

The liable person might transfer their pension credits from one scheme to another. In these circumstances, provided that the second pension scheme is given the appropriate notice,[208] the pension lump sum order will become effective against the new scheme.[209] Without prejudice to this, the court may, on an application by any person having an interest, vary a pension lump sum order transferring obligations from one scheme to another.[210]

If a pension scheme collapses its assets may be transferred to the Pension Protection Fund.[211] If the failed fund had an obligation to make

---

managers of the scheme; (b) in the case of a retirement annuity contract (falling within paras (d) or (e) of the definition of a "pension arrangement") the provider of the annuity; and (c) in the case of an insurance policy falling within para.(d) of that definition, the insurer.

[205] s.12A(4)(a).

[206] s.12A(4)(b).

[207] s.12A(5). An application for such an order is made by minute in the original process—O.C.R. r.33.51(3).

[208] Under s.12A(8) and regulations made under it. The Divorce etc. (Notification and Treatment of Pensions) (Scotland) Regulations (SI 2000/1050) reg.2 provides that the person responsible for the first pension scheme is to give notice to both the new pension scheme and the person entitled to payment under the pension lump sum order. Regulation 3 deals with subsequent transfers. If only some but not all of the accrued rights of the liable party are transferred, reg.4 provides that the pension scheme from which the transfer is being made is to give notice to the other person about various matters including the likely extent of the reduction in the benefits payable under the scheme as a result of the transfer; the name and address of the new pension scheme; the date of the transfer; and the fact that the court has power to vary the pension lump sum order.

[209] s.12A(6).

[210] s.12A(7). An application for such an order is made by minute in the original process—O.C.R. r.33.51(3).

[211] Created under the Pensions Act 2004.

a payment under a pension lump sum order, then the person entitled to payment under the order is given certain protections.[212]

If the person who is to receive payment under the pension lump sum order changes their name and address they are under an obligation to advise the pension scheme of this within 21 days.[213]

Problems with pension lump sum orders

3–71   The provisions for pension lump sum orders seem relatively straight-forward, and on the face of it provide a useful way of securing payment of a capital sum where there are limited resources available at the time of the divorce or dissolution. However, in practice pension lump sum orders are rarely used. There are several problems relating to the use of these orders which have made them unpopular with agents.[214] Clients should be clearly advised about the risks inherent in pension lump sum orders. The potential problems fall into several categories, and these are now considered.

Death of the liable person

3–72   What is to happen if the liable person dies before the payment is made? Many pension schemes will pay out only a relatively small sum on death. In these cases there may simply be insufficient funds to pay the sum due under the pension lump sum order on death. If the pension lump sum order was the only mechanism for recovering the capital sum, then the party who was to receive the benefit may, in fact, receive little or nothing. The way that the pension lump sum order is worded will be important.[215]

Commutation of capital sum on retirement

3–73   Another problem is that many pension schemes give the retiring party a choice regarding the amount of the lump sum they take on retirement. They may choose to take a smaller lump sum in return for a larger monthly payment. If they exercise this right to commute the capital sum to a considerable extent, then they might largely defeat the pension lump sum order. If the court order is framed in such a way that the pension lump sum order is the only way to enforce payment of the capital sum, then the order might prove to be of little real worth. Again, the way that the pension lump sum order is worded will be important.[216]

---

[212] s.12A(7ZA), (7ZB), (7ZC), (7A), (7B) and (7C).

[213] Divorce etc. (Notification and Treatment of Pensions) (Scotland) Regulations (SI 2000/1050) reg.5. Regulation 6 provides that, if the person entitled to payment under the pension lump sum order does not give this notice, and rights are transferred from one pension scheme to another, then if the person gives notice to the first scheme of the change within one year of the transfer, the first scheme is to send the notice to the new scheme, and is also to notify the person entitled to payment under the pension lump sum order of the transfer of pension rights in terms of reg.2.

[214] "Suffice to say that there are virtually no circumstances where [a pension lump sum order] would be better than a sharing order for the pension scheme member, and if a lawyer is considering using such an order, he/she would be well advised to take professional advice before doing so."—Harry Smith, "The reality of pension sharing", 2003 J.L.S.S. 48(4), 21–5.

[215] See para.3–79.

[216] See para.3–79.

Poorly performing pension schemes

Pension schemes may not perform as well as expected and may even **3–74** collapse altogether. As a result there may be insufficient funds paid out by the scheme to allow the pension lump sum order to be satisfied. Some protection is given if the assets of the collapsed pension fund are transferred into the Pension Protection Fund.[217]

Bankruptcy of liable person

Concerns have been expressed about what would happen if the liable **3–75** person becomes bankrupt before payment is made under the pension lump sum order.[218]

Administrative problems

There is a real worry that pension lump sum orders may fail because **3–76** of errors of administration on the part of the pension provider. At the time the order is made, the liable person may still have many years to work before they retire and take their pension. What would happen if the pension provider lost sight of the pension lump sum order on retirement of the liable person? There is a danger that they might simply pay the lump sum to the pensioner without implementing the pension lump sum order. The person due to benefit from the pension lump sum order may have a right to pursue the pension provider in these cases, but it will be cold comfort to find that the only way to secure the money is to raise expensive proceedings against a large financial institution with deep pockets. There are also potential problems if the beneficiary of the order fails to tell the pension administrator about changes of address.[219]

Transfer of pension interests

Pension interests may be transferred from one scheme to another. **3–77** Clearly the original pension administrator will not be able to implement the pension lump sum order in these circumstances. Although s.12A(6) and (7) give some protection,[220] they are not ideal. There is a very real concern that, after such a transfer, the paperwork relating to the pension lump sum order will be overlooked or improperly completed. This might leave the party entitled to payment under the pension lump sum order (and perhaps their advisers) in a rather precarious position.

Pension sharing or pension lump sum orders?

For the reasons outlined in the previous section, there are significant **3–78** problems with pension lump sum orders. Most of these problems relate to the fact that the payment due under a pension lump sum order will not actually be paid until some (and often many) years in the future. These problems are much less significant with pension sharing orders,

---

[217] See para.3–70.
[218] See e.g. Anne Hall Dick and Tom Ballantine, *The Science of Family Law*, 1st edn, Ch.5.
[219] See para.3–70.
[220] See para.3–70.

and for this reason pension sharing will often be the preferred route. It should be noted that the court cannot, in the same proceedings, make both a pension sharing order and a pension lump sum order in relation to the same pension arrangement.[221] Equally, if a pension lump sum order is already in place relating to the benefits or future benefits in a pension scheme, then the court cannot make a pension sharing order in relation to the rights under that pension scheme.[222] Pension lump sum orders are not available in respect of compensation paid under Ch.3 of Pt 2 of the Pensions Act 2004.[223]

Practical matters

3–79   If a pension lump sum order is being considered, it is important to consult the pension administrators at an early stage. They should be asked to check the proposed wording of the order and to confirm that the order can be implemented. It will also be prudent for the parties to take advice from a financial adviser regarding the implications of the order in relation to their own retirement planning. It will be important to know as much as possible about the way the scheme operates. Some of the questions to be considered are: whether the recipient has power to commute the lump sum to an income; how much (if anything) is payable on the death of the recipient; and whether the recipient can make decisions about the timing of the payment of the lump sum.

The person seeking the order must carefully consider the question of interest. If the capital sum is not to be paid under a pension lump sum order for many years, then it will generally be appropriate to ensure that interest is added.

If earmarking is sought, it will be sensible to make sure that the order clearly shows that the pension lump sum order is ancillary to the order for payment of a capital sum. That is to say, the order is really only one method of enforcing payment of the capital sum. The order sought should be framed widely enough to clearly state that, if the pension lump sum order fails completely or is insufficient to pay the capital sum due, then the capital sum is to be paid in some other way (perhaps by instalments or from other assets). It might also be possible to seek security for the sums due in some cases.

SECTION 8(1)(c)—INCIDENTAL ORDERS

General discussion

3–80   In terms of s.8(1)(c) of the Act, in an action for divorce or dissolution, either party may apply to the court for an incidental order within the meaning of s.14(2). Section 14(2) provides that an incidental order means one or more of the following orders:

"(a) an order for the sale of property;

---

[221] s.8(4).
[222] s.8(6).
[223] s.8(4A).

(b) an order for the valuation of property;
(c) an order determining any dispute between the parties to the marriage, or as the case may be the partners, as to their respective property rights by means of a declarator thereof or otherwise;
(d) an order regulating the occupation of—

(i) the matrimonial home, or
(ii) the family home of the partnership,

or the use of furniture and plenishings therein or excluding either person from such occupation;
(e) an order regulating liability, as between the persons, for outgoings in respect of—

(i) the matrimonial home, or
(ii) the family home of the partnership,

or furniture or plenishings therein;
(f) an order that security shall be given for any financial provision;
(g) an order that payments shall be made or property transferred to any curator bonis or trustee or other person for the benefit of the person by whom or on whose behalf application has been made under s.8(1) of this Act for an incidental order;
(h) an order setting aside or varying any term in an ante-nuptial or post-nuptial marriage settlement or in any corresponding settlement in respect of the civil partnership;
(j) an order as to the date from which any interest on any amount awarded shall run;
(ja) in relation to a deed relating to moveable property, an order dispensing with the execution of the deed by the grantor and directing the sheriff clerk to execute the deed;
(k) any ancillary order which is expedient to give effect to the principles set out in s.9 of this Act or to any order made under s.8(2) of this Act."

As with all types of order for financial provision, before granting an incidental order the court must be satisfied that the order (in conjunction with any other orders being granted) is: (a) justified by the principles set out in s.9 of the Act; and (b) reasonable having regard to the resources of the parties.[224] An incidental order is not to be used for matters which are unrelated to financial provision.[225]

Financial provision may be effected entirely through the use of an incidental order. For example, in *Reynolds v Reynolds*, 1991 S.C.L.R. 175 the couple's home was the only item of matrimonial property. The sheriff applied his mind first to the s.9 principles, and concluded that the matrimonial property would properly be shared in terms of those principles if the house was sold and the proceeds divided equally. In the circumstances, there was no need for him to grant an order for transfer of the property or for a capital sum. Fair division could be achieved by

---

[224] s.8(2). See paras 3–02 to 3–08.
[225] See *Reynolds v Reynolds*, 1991 S.C.L.R. 175.

granting an incidental order for the sale of the property and equal division of the proceeds.

In some cases incidental orders may be *essential* to give effect to the s.9 principles. In *Jacques v Jacques*, 1995 S.C. 327 the title to the matrimonial home was in joint names. At first instance the sheriff took the view that the principles of the Act would be served by leaving the house in joint names so that each party would be entitled to a one half share. He simply left it to the parties to sell the property in due course. On appeal, the Inner House took the view that it would not interfere with the sheriff's decision that the value of the matrimonial home should be shared equally, but it then considered whether the sheriff should have granted various incidental orders to ensure that the value of the house was actually realised (by incidental orders providing for the sale and the division of the proceeds)[226]:

> "We consider however that the sheriff can reasonably be criticised for not granting [the incidental orders] in order to give effect to his decision that the net value of the matrimonial property should be shared equally . . .
>
> In our opinion it would have been competent for the sheriff to make the orders which were sought by the pursuer as incidental orders in terms of sec 14(2)(a), (c) and (k) as an order for financial provision under sec 8(2) of the Act. They were the appropriate orders to make in order to give effect to his decision that the value of [the family home] was to be shared equally between the parties."

The Inner House pointed out that, by leaving the house in joint names, if either party wanted to realise their share of the property, they would require to resort to an action of division and sale. This would lead to unnecessary delay and expense—the proper course would have been to make an incidental order for the sale to give effect to the decision that the value of the property should be shared equally between the parties.

An application for an incidental order is generally made by a crave in the initial writ or defences.[227] However, an application for an incidental order in a depending action may be made by motion (unless the sheriff considers that the application should properly be made by a crave in the initial writ or defences).[228] Incidental orders can be varied or recalled by a subsequent order on cause shown.[229] However, the court will not allow variation or recall simply because a party regrets their decision to allow an incidental order to be granted.[230]

Rights of third parties

3–81   Section 15(3) of the Act provides specific protection for third parties in relation to incidental orders:

---

[226] At pp.332—3.

[227] O.C.R. r.33.48. If the application is made in the defences, the defender must include in his defences—craves, averments in support of the craves, averments in support of those craves and appropriate pleas-in-law—O.C.R. r.33.34(2). If the application is made by a person other than the pursuer or the defender, the application is by minute in the action—O.C.R. r.33.48(1)(b).

[228] O.C.R. r.33.49(1).

[229] s.14(4).

[230] *Clark v Clark (No.2)*, 2007 Fam. L.R. 34 at para.54.

"Neither an incidental order, nor any rights conferred by such an order, shall prejudice any rights of any third party insofar as those rights existed immediately before the making of the order."

When can an incidental order be made?

Orders under s.14(2)(d) (regulating occupation of the matrimonial or **3–82** family home) and s.14(2)(e) (regulating liability for outgoings for the matrimonial or family home) may only be made on or after the granting of decree of divorce or dissolution.[231] All other incidental orders may be made before, on or after the granting or refusal of decree of divorce or dissolution.[232]

Specific incidental orders

This section will examine in more detail some of the specific types of **3–83** incidental orders listed in s.14(2) of the Act.

Section 14(2)(a)—Orders for sale of property

This type of incidental order is not limited to the sale of heritable **3–84** property, although it is most commonly used for the sale of the matrimonial or family home. The order will not normally be made at an early stage in proceedings before full enquiry into the facts has been made.[233] However, it is competent to make such an order at an early stage if the parties consent to it, or if such consent may be inferred.[234] An incidental order of this type is not simply an alternative to an action of division and sale. It is an order for financial provision and must be justified by the s.9 principles. In *Reynolds v Reynolds*, 1991 S.C.L.R. 175, Sheriff Simpson stressed[235]:

"The obvious line to take in this situation is to order a sale of the house and declare that the net free proceeds of sale should be divided equally between the parties, on the basis that this would be the end result of an action of division and sale, and section 14(2)(a) and (c) of the 1985 Act makes a separate action of division and sale unnecessary in the circumstances. However, this course is open to the objection that the powers under section 14(2) arise in respect of section 8(1)(c). This section of the Act is headed 'Financial provision on divorce, etc.' and section 8 is headed 'Orders for financial provision'. Section 8(1) lists the orders which can be applied for by either party to the marriage 'in an action of divorce'. Accordingly, the incidental orders (for that is what are sought) require to be, at least principally, aimed at financial provision on divorce and the provisions of sections 9, 10 and 11 must come into play. I do not think that I can grant an incidental order just to save

---

[231] s.14(3).
[232] s.14(1). See e.g. *Jackson v Jackson*, 1999 Fam. L.R. 108; although see *Amin v Amin*, 2000 Fam. L.R. 114 (and the editor's comments on this decision).
[233] *McKeown v McKeown*, 1988 S.C.L.R. 355.
[234] *Clark v Clark (No.2)*, 2007 Fam. L.R. 34 at para.42.
[235] At p.175.

the pursuer the trouble of raising a separate action for division and sale."

So, the order must be justified in terms of the principles in the Act. However, in *Reynolds*, the court still decided that the order was appropriate. Why? After all, the property was in joint names, and the court decided that its value was to be shared equally. The answer is that leaving ownership in joint names may not always achieve a fair result in terms of the principles of the Act. It may be fairer to sell the property so that capital will be released. Without an incidental order for sale, one party may require to raise an action of division and sale. The incidental order may therefore save further litigation. In *Jacques v Jacques*, 1995 S.C. 327, the sheriff at first instance had decided that the family home which was in joint names should simply remain in joint names and did not grant an incidental order for sale. The Inner House criticised the decision[236]:

"We see no advantage, in that situation, in the sheriff's decision to leave it to the parties to resort to separate proceedings for a division and sale of the property if an agreed solution could not be worked out between them. It would have been preferable for [the sheriff] to give effect to the pursuer's crave for the necessary orders to be made in these proceedings, to avoid further expense and delay in the working out of his decision that the property should be shared between the parties equally."

Similarly in *Larkin v Larkin*, 1992 S.C.L.R. 130 Sheriff Stoddart commented[237]:

"[An incidental order for sale of a jointly owned property] is not the same as a crave for division and sale, which is declaratory in nature and in which a sale of the property is not an immediate outcome of a decree in favour of the pursuer. The procedure is tortuous and expensive; and the sale of the subjects may not even be ordered until after the intervention of a surveyor or other person of skill. Here, the defender seeks an immediate sale of the former matrimonial home . . ."

If the order for sale of jointly owned property is granted without any specification of how the proceeds are to be split, then the proceeds will be divided in terms of the parties' respective shares of ownership in terms of the title. So, in the most common case, where parties own the property in equal shares, they will each receive an equal share of the free proceeds.[238] It is open, however, to the court to order that the proceeds be divided in some way other than in terms of the title shares.[239]

---

[236] At p.333.
[237] At p.133.
[238] See the decision in *Symon v Symon*, 1991 S.C.L.R. 414 where the order granted avoids any ambiguity about division of the proceeds.
[239] See *Reynolds v Reynolds*, 1991 S.C.L.R. 175.

The order for sale can be postponed until after divorce or dissolution. So, for example, in *Thomson v Thomson*, 2003 Fam. L.R. 22 the sheriff postponed the sale of the family home until the summer when a child of the marriage was due to move from primary to secondary school. The order might be postponed until a specified time after the interlocutor to give the parties time to make any necessary arrangements.[240] In *Symon v Symon*, 1991 S.C.L.R. 414 the sheriff's order was for sale within such reasonable time as the parties might agree, but failing agreement, within six months of the date of decree.

On a practical level, the order craved should be full, covering all matters required to deal with the sale.[241] Having said this, the courts may take the view in some cases that it is better to avoid imposing rigid conditions on the parties, leaving some scope for discretion in the mechanics of sale.[242]

Section 14(2)(b)—Orders for valuation of property

Under this provision the court can order a valuation of property. An **3–85** incidental order of this nature may be useful where the party with control of the asset is reluctant to allow a valuation to take place. In one case, the court held that this order may only be used to value property owned by the couple and not property belonging to third parties. In *Demarco v Demarco*, 1990 S.C.L.R. 635 the wife sought an incidental order for the valuation of the heritable and moveable property belonging to two companies in which the defender had a shareholding. It was held by Lord Cameron that this was not competent[243]:

"I deal first with the part of the motion for an order for valuation so far as it seeks valuation of the heritable and moveable property of the two companies. It was submitted for the defender that the word 'property' in section 14 of the Family Law (Scotland) Act 1985 could only refer to such property as was property encompassed within the ambit of the Act, that was the property of one or other or both of the parties to the marriage. The pursuer here only avers that at best the defender's interest in each of the two companies extended to a shareholding in each of them and not to ownership of the heritable and moveable property of either company . . . If any order was made, it should accordingly be limited to valuation of the shareholdings. In my opinion, this submission is correct. The definition of 'property' in section 27 of the Act implies that it is limited to what is owned by one or both of the parties and this is fortified by the manner in which the word is used, for instance in

---

[240] *Jacques v Jacques*, 1995 S.C. 327.

[241] See "Division and sale of family homes" 1999 Fam. L.B. 37–6.

[242] See the closing comments in *Reynolds v Reynolds*, 1991 S.C.L.R. 175. The sheriff also pointed out that, if the flexible approach did not work, then it was open to the parties to apply for further incidental orders at a later date to regulate the sale. However, from a practical point of view, if parties have reached the point of litigating, it would probably be better in most cases for the order to be clear about as many specifics as possible (e.g. the appointment of estate agents and solicitors). This will probably speed the process and reduce the chances of further disagreement.

[243] At p.637.

section 8(1)(a), which could only refer to what is owned by one party so as to be transferred to the other. It is also consistent with the concept of 'matrimonial property' in section 10(4)."[244]

On a practical level, the party seeking an incidental order for valuation should be careful to ensure that the crave includes details of who is to carry out the valuation, and the date or dates to which the valuation is to be brought down.

Section 14(2)(d)—Orders regulating the occupation of the matrimonial or family home or the use of the furnishings and plenishings therein or excluding either party from such occupation

3–86   This is an important power. It can only be granted on or after the grant of decree, not before.[245] There may be circumstances where it is a reasonable application of the s.9 principles to allow one party to continue to occupy the matrimonial or family home after the divorce or dissolution, even if the property is jointly owned or owned by the other party. This incidental order may be useful if it is accepted that the house is to be sold, but it is appropriate to defer sale for a period, perhaps to allow the party in occupation to find alternative accommodation. An order under s.14(2)(d) might make it clear that the other party is not to interfere with the occupation during the period from date of decree until sale.

An argument under this paragraph may be particularly useful where the parties have young children and might allow the party with the main responsibility for their care to retain possession of the house for a period to minimise disruption for the children.[246] For example, in *Symon v Symon*, 1991 S.C.L.R. 414, an order was made by the sheriff for the sale of the family home within six months of the date of decree, but an order was made finding the wife and children entitled to occupation of the house until the property was sold. Similarly, in *Little v Little*, 1990 S.L.T. 785, when the case called before the Lord Ordinary he had explained that an order under s.14(2)(d) had been made[247]:

">. . . to protect the pursuer prior to the execution of the conveyance transferring a one-half share in it to her, and thereafter for a period to allow parties to determine how they wished to deal with the matrimonial home in joint ownership while recognising that the younger children still regard the house as the matrimonial home . . . As parties agreed that six months is a reasonable time to complete

---

[244] This may be a rather restrictive view. Sometimes, in order to value a shareholding (particularly in an unquoted privately owned company) it may be necessary to value the underlying assets of the company. See paras 6–30 to 6–32. Of course, if specific and relevant averments were made about the necessity of such valuations, it may be possible to use the more traditional approach of motion and specification to obtain the necessary information.

[245] See s.14(3). Until the grant of decree matters occupancy rights will be regulated by the Matrimonial Homes (Family Protection) (Scotland) Act 1981 and the Civil Partnership Act 2004.

[246] *Smart v Smart*, 1995 Fam. L.B. 14–9.

[247] See p.792.

the conveyance of the one-half share, I consider that the pursuer should be protected in her occupation for a period of one year from the date of decree which will permit of a further six months' protected occupancy to enable any adjustment between the parties to the new situation to be made."

If a person is granted a right to occupy the matrimonial or family home (or a right to use the furniture and plenishings thereof) under an incidental order, then s.14(5), (5A) and (5B) give that party two important protections. First, they are given general powers of management in relation to the property;[248] and secondly they have protection against certain arrangements intended to defeat their occupancy rights.[249] However, it has been pointed out that these provisions in themselves do not prevent the other party from selling their interest in the property notwithstanding the rights of occupancy created under the incidental order, and if there is any fear of a sale then interdict may be appropriate.[250]

Section 14(2)(e)—Orders regulating liability for outgoings in respect of the matrimonial or family home or the furniture or plenishings therein

Like the order in s.14(2)(d), this order may only be made on or after **3–87** the granting of decree of divorce or dissolution, and not before.[251] So, an incidental order of this type cannot be used to regulate the payment of outgoings during the difficult period between separation and divorce or dissolution. The position was made clear in *Macdonald v Macdonald*, 1995 S.L.T. 72, where Lord Caplan discussed an application for an incidental order under s.14(2)(e)[252]:

"The pursuer's counsel contended that the pursuer is presently paying mortgage instalments on the parties' joint mortgage at the monthly rate of £340 ... That being so she claimed that the defender should be found liable for his half share of the mortgage liability since the date of the proof and also in the future until the mortgage liability (which is a joint liability of the parties) should be discharged. The pursuer's counsel sought such an order under s.14(2)(e) of the Family Law (Scotland) Act 1985. However, I agree with counsel for the defender that an incidental order for payment by the defender to the pursuer of mortgage instalments due in respect of the past would not be competent. Subsection (3) of s.14 provides that an incidental order under subss.(2)(d) and (e) can only be made on or after the granting of decree of divorce. The scheme of legislation is that orders regulating outgoings which arise after divorce and which relate to the matrimonial home should be

---

[248] s.14(5)(a) which imports by reference the provisions of s.2(1), (2), (5)(a) and (9) of the Matrimonial Homes (Family Protection) (Scotland) Act 1981; and s.14(5A)(a) which imports by reference s.102(1), (2), (5a) and (9) of the Civil Partnership Act 2004.
[249] s.14(5)(b) and (5A)(b).
[250] See E.M. Clive, *The Law of Husband and Wife in Scotland*, 4th edn at para.24.119.
[251] s.14(3).
[252] At p.74.

made in terms of s.14(2)(e), whereas orders which regulate such outgoings before divorce should be made in terms of s.2 of the Matrimonial Homes (Family Protection) (Scotland) Act 1981."

However, the order can be used after divorce or dissolution, for example to make provision for payment of mortgage instalments or other outlays pending a sale or transfer.[253] The issue of who should meet mortgage payments and other household expenses pending the sale will depend very much on the facts and circumstances of any given case.[254]

Section 14(2)(f)—Orders for security for any financial provision

3–88   At the point of divorce or dissolution, the court may make orders which are not to be implemented until some later date. For example, the court might make an order for payment of a capital sum which is deferred until a later date (often to allow the family home or some other asset to be sold). Without any security, the party entitled to the payment is in a risky position, particularly if the liable party has financial difficulties or has a track record of avoiding their obligations. Section 14(2)(f) allows the court to protect the party who is entitled to the payment, by granting security.

In *Macdonald v Macdonald*, 1995 S.L.T. 72, Lord Caplan made an order for security. He ordered that a standard security be granted to protect the spouse who was to be entitled to a payment on the sale of a house. He discussed his reasons for making the order and the comments provide an excellent example of how the creative use of various overlapping incidental orders can assist in an overall decision on financial provision.[255] In *Murley v Murley*, 1995 S.C.L.R. 1138 Lord MacLean ordered a standard security be granted to secure a capital sum[256] which was to be paid on the earlier of the sale of the property or the eighteenth birthday of the younger child. In *Collins v Collins*, 1997 Fam. L.R. 50 the pursuer suffered from multiple sclerosis and it was felt by the sheriff to be essential that the defender's interest in the family home be transferred to the pursuer. However, he made an order for payment of a capital sum to the defender, but this was to be deferred until the death of the pursuer. In order to secure this, the pursuer was ordered to execute a standard security over the former matrimonial home.

Section 14(2)(h)—Orders setting aside or varying any term in an ante-nuptial or post-nuptial marriage settlement (or corresponding settlements between civil partners)

3–89   This type of incidental order allows the court to vary or set aside agreements made between the parties before or after marriage or registration of a civil partnership.[257] It seems that the agreement must

---

[253] See e.g. *McCormick v McCormick*, 1994 G.W.D. 35–2087.

[254] See e.g. *Macdonald v Macdonald*, 1995 S.L.T. 72 at p.75.

[255] See paras 3–14 to 3–87; and also comments at p.74 of the report.

[256] Although the justification used in the case seems to be s.14(2)(k) rather than (f). See the discussion of *Murley v Murley* in *Trotter v Trotter*, 2001 S.L.T. (Sh Ct) 42.

[257] Under s.14(6) of the 1985 Act, this includes settlements by way of a policy of assurance to which s.2 of the Married Women's Policies of Assurance (Scotland) Act 1880 relates.

clearly be of the nature of an ante-nuptial or post-nuptial agreement, rather than simply any agreement which might have a bearing on the way matrimonial or partnership property is to be divided. In *Robertson v Robertson*, 2003 S.L.T. 208, in an action of divorce the pursuer requested an incidental order under s.14(2)(h) varying a clause of a co-partnery contract between the parties which related to the disposal of assets on the dissolution of the partnership by the death or retirement of one of the parties. After referring to various English authorities Temporary Judge Coutts commented[258]:

> "It is not instantly apparent that a contract of copartnery could be a marriage settlement. It is a business arrangement. In the present case the parties have each contributed to the enterprise and each continue to run it as a business. It is independent of their marital status other than referring to the second party as wife of the first party in the pre-amble. There is no reason why the partnership should determine on divorce. Parties of full age have made a very specific provision about the situation which would arise on dissolution of their partnership by death or retiral. The conclusion effectively seeks to make the retiral of one of the partners possibly more advantageous to him than it was specially designed to be by each of the parties at the time of their contract . . .
>
> The contract of copartnery does not look like a marriage settlement. It has no distinctive features which would make it such, however wide an interpretation one gives to the words of the statute."

Section 14(2)(j)—Orders as to the date from which any interest on any amount awarded shall run

The question of interest generally is discussed at para.3–20. However, **3–90** often the most important question for the court to determine will be the date from which interest is to run. In terms of s.14(2)(j) the court has a wide range of options.[259] For example, interest might only be used as a penalty for late payment. This will commonly be appropriate where there is an on-going liability to make a payment out of income, say, for periodical allowance. So, for example, *Bell v Bell*, 1988 S.C.L.R. 457, the court awarded periodical allowance, but indicated that interest would run in the event of late payment.

However, if the award to be made is one of capital (either by way of a capital sum, transfer of property, or indeed pension sharing or earmarking), it may be appropriate to use interest not as compensation for late payment, but to compensate a party for loss of use of funds or assets. Therefore, it may be appropriate to order that interest is to run on the sum due (or the value of the asset) from a fixed date. Appropriate dates will depend on the circumstances of the case. Most commonly interest will be awarded from the date of decree, and interest will be particularly

---

[258] At p.210.
[259] See *Muir v Muir*, 1989 S.C.L.R. 445; *Savage v Savage*, 1993 G.W.D. 28–1779; *Bolton v Bolton*, 1995 G.W.D. 14–779; *Tahir v Tahir (No 2)*, 1995 S.L.T. 451.

important if payment of the capital sum is to be deferred or is to be paid by instalments.[260] In *Gulline v Gulline*, 1992 S.L.T. (Sh Ct) 71, the issue of interest in a case relating to a deferred payment was considered, and the court held that it was appropriate to award interest from the date of decree commenting[261]:

> "The justification for making such an award is that it would compensate the defender for the fact that her payment of the capital sum has to be postponed."

Sometimes the courts may go further and hold that it is appropriate to award interest from a date *before* the date of decree. For example, if one party has enjoyed the use of valuable matrimonial or partnership assets for a substantial period of time between the relevant date and the date of decree, it may be appropriate to compensate the other party through an award of interest. In *Geddes v Geddes*, 1993 S.L.T. 494 the Inner House held that s.14(2)(j) gave the court the power to award interest from a date *before* the date of decree.[262] Lord President Hope commented[263]:

> "I think it can be assumed that the purpose of including an order for interest among the list of incidental orders in s.14(2) was to give the court a power which it would not otherwise be able to exercise. There was no need to legislate on this matter if all that was intended was to allow the court to award interest from the date when payment was due in terms of the decree. The power to award interest from that date exists already at common law. It is inherent in the principle that interest may be recovered by virtue of the principal sum having been wrongfully withheld and not paid on the date when it ought to have been paid. The amount of the principal sum is fixed by the court's decree, and the date of the decree is, unless it states otherwise, the date when that sum ought to be paid. The award of interest follows naturally from the pronouncing of decree for payment of the principal sum. Furthermore, the fact that

---

[260] s.12(2) and (3). In either of these cases, it is important to note the distinction between interest for *late payment* and interest running from *the date of decree*. Imagine for example an award of a capital sum of £100,000 payable by 10 annual instalments. If interest is due only for *late payment* interest will only run on any particular instalment of £10,000 if the payer is late. However, if interest is running on the whole capital sum from the date of decree, this will be running on the declining capital sum (i.e. the declining balance of £100,000) throughout the 10–year period of payment. If a party is to wait for payment, it may be appropriate to compensate them for the delay through interest (although this will not always be the case—see *Collins v Collins*, 1997 Fam. L.R. 50). Any ambiguity in the order should be avoided—see *Nicol v Nicol*, 2004 Fam. L.B. 68–7.

[261] At p.74.

[262] See also *Ogg v Ogg*, 2003 G.W.D. 10–281 where interest was awarded from the date of commencement of proceedings until payment (although the appellate court suggests that it might have preferred an approach awarding interest from the relevant date in this particular case). Also note that the decision in *Kennedy v Kennedy*, 2004 Fam. L.R. 70 regarding the date from which interest may be awarded seems to be wrong in the light of the decision in *Geddes*.

[263] At p.499.

an order for interest is an incidental order, which, if made, must be made under s.8(2) of the Act, suggests that the provisions of that subsection will have some relevance to the question as to the date as from which any interest on any amount awarded should run. It is difficult to see what relevance that subsection could have to a decision to award interest, if the court was not to be entitled to award interest from a date other than the date of payment in terms of the decree.

For these reasons I think that it can be inferred that the purpose of s.14(2)(j) is to enable the court to award interest on the whole, or any part, of any amount awarded as a financial provision as from such date as it thinks appropriate, even although this may be a date earlier than the date of payment in terms of the decree."

Interestingly, later in the decision the Lord President indicated that, although he agreed that interest could be awarded from an earlier date than the date of decree, he did not agree with the sheriff at first instance in his reasoning for why interest should be awarded in this particular case. He said[264]:

"[The sheriff said that the award of interest was due] because the sum which he awarded as a capital sum was ex hypothesi due when the action was raised. It seems to me, however, that he based his decision on a misconception because, as was pointed out in *Carpenter*[265] and also by the sheriff in *Skarpaas*,[266] there is no right to payment of a capital sum until decree of divorce has been pronounced. Since a capital sum cannot be assumed to have been due for payment on any earlier date, some other basis must be found for awarding interest from a date before payment is due. In these circumstances it may be helpful for me to say something about the way in which I think s.14(2)(j) ought to be applied . . ."

The Lord President then explained that a claim for financial provision is unlike other more familiar categories of claim which attract interest from before the date of decree: the money has not been wrongfully withheld; it is not a claim in the nature of a debt; it is not a claim in the nature of damages. Rather, the claim is more akin to the rule that, where possession is given on the sale of land, interest is due from the date that possession is given.[267] The court held that it was not unreasonable to follow the guidance afforded in that rule in the exercise of the power under s.14(2)(j)[268]:

---

[264] At p.500.
[265] *Carpenter v Carpenter*, 1990 S.L.T. (Sh Ct) 68.
[266] *Skarpaas v Skarpaas*, 1991 S.L.T. (Sh Ct) 15.
[267] See the comments of Lord McLaren in *Greenock Harbour Trustees v Glasgow and South Western Railway Co* 1909 S.C. (H.L.) 49 at p.1441: "It is perhaps, as the law is so fixed, of no great importance to say upon what principle such a payment of interest falls to be awarded, but the way in which I can most easily represent the principle to my mind is that the interest is given in place of rent, because before the transaction has been completed by the payment of the price, the purchaser has been put in possession, and therefore he must pay interest as a substitute for rent, or as consideration for the possession he has had during this intermediate period."
[268] At p.500.

"There may be circumstances where a party who has had the sole use or possession of an asset since the relevant date, the whole or part of the value of which is to be shared with the other party on divorce, should be required to pay interest as consideration for the use or possession which he has had between the relevant date and the date of decree. An order for interest may, for example, be appropriate where the use or possession has resulted in a benefit which has not been taken into account in some other way in making the order for financial provision. It may also be appropriate where, as in *Gulline*[269] the amount of the principal sum is fixed by the decree but payment of it, in whole or in part, is postponed to a later date. Whether interest should be awarded on this basis, and if so on what part of the award, from what date and what the rate of interest should be is in the discretion of the court, bearing in mind that an incidental order for interest under s.14(2)(j) is an integral part of the order for financial provision under s.8(2) of the Act."

See also Lord Allanbridge's succinct comments[270]:

"In particular I agree that s.14(2)(j) of the 1985 Act is very wide in its terms and gives power to the court to award interest on any capital amount from any date considered appropriate either before, on or after the date of decree. I also agree that where, for example, one party has had the sole use of any part of the matrimonial property after the relevant date, then in appropriate cases compensation therefore by way interest awarded to the other party could be considered justified and reasonable in terms of s.8(2) of the Act."

Applying all of this to the case in issue, the court noted that the principal asset was a farm, of which the pursuer had sole possession since the date of separation. The court felt that it was appropriate that some interest should be awarded on the defender's share of that value, since the value of that share was fixed at the date of separation and the pursuer had the benefit of that share through possession of the farm. Interest was awarded from the date of citation.

An argument for payment of interest from a date before the date of decree must be justified in terms of the s.9 principles. So, for example, if one party has had sole use of the bulk of the capital since the relevant date, the other party can argue that they have been "deprived" of their capital since the date of separation, and that they should be compensated by an award of interest—because the other party has gained an economic advantage (in terms of s.9(1)(b)) as a result of the contribution of the other. In order to redress the balance, the court could award interest on the half share that the "disadvantaged" party was entitled to from the relevant date (or such other date as seems reasonable in the circumstances). This argument was clearly in focus in *Welsh v Welsh*, 1994 S.L.T. 828, where the husband had resided in the matrimonial

---

[269] *Gulline v Gulline*, 1992 S.L.T. (Sh Ct) 71.
[270] At p.501.

home since the relevant date, and Lord Osborne held that this had caused economic disadvantage to the wife in terms of s.9(1)(b)[271]:

> "It is my view that the defender has enjoyed the economic advantage of living rent free since the relevant date in a house of which the pursuer was beneficial owner to the extent of a one half share. That advantage appears to me to be the counterpart of the economic disadvantage suffered by the pursuer in respect that she has, during the period in question, enjoyed no return from her property in that respect. In my opinion, in these circumstances there is a clear imbalance as between the parties, which I ought to correct . . ."

To correct this imbalance the court awarded interest on the wife's share of the property from the relevant date (based on the value at the relevant date) to reflect the loss of use which she had suffered.

An argument for backdating interest will not always succeed. *Livie v Livie*, 1999 G.W.D. 34–1639 is another case where it was argued (along the lines of *Geddes*) that there should be an award of interest under s.14(2)(j) to the party who did not have occupation of the matrimonial home from the relevant date. Sheriff Davidson declined to do so pointing out that the court in *Geddes* indicated that it had a wide discretion, and there were factors in *Livie* mitigating against an award of interest including the facts that the party in occupation had: (a) successfully invoked s.19 of the Matrimonial Homes (Family Protection) (Scotland) Act 1981; and (b) had paid the mortgage and endowment policy payments since the relevant date.

Section 14(2)(ja)—In relation to a deed relating to moveable property, an order dispensing with the execution of the deed by the grantor and directing the sheriff clerk to execute the deed

The Sheriff Courts (Scotland) Act 1907, s.5A gives sheriff clerks **3–91** power to execute deeds relating to heritable property if this is necessary to give effect to an order for financial provision. Section 14(2)(ja) gives sheriff clerks the same power in relation to moveable property.

Section 14(2)(k)—Any ancillary order which is expedient to give effect to the section 9 principles or to any order made under section 8(2)

The discretion given is clearly wide. Orders have included: an order **3–92** for conveyancing expenses;[272] an order to grant a standard security;[273] an order requiring the defender to arrange for discharge of debt secured over the matrimonial home;[274] and an order remitting the matter to a conveyancer to prepare documents, or authorising the sheriff clerk to sign a conveyance if one party refused.[275]

---

[271] At p.836.
[272] *Little v Little*, 1990 S.L.T. 785.
[273] See *Murley v Murley*, 1995 S.C.L.R. 1138 and *Trotter v Trotter*, 2001 S.L.T. (Sh Ct) 42.
[274] *McConnell v McConnell*, 1993 G.W.D. 34–2185.
[275] See *Wallis v Wallis*, 1991 S.C.L.R. 192; *Macdonald v Macdonald*, 1995 S.L.T. 72.

CHAPTER 4

SECTION 9—PRINCIPLES FOR FINANCIAL PROVISION

INTRODUCTION

General discussion

4–01   When making an order for financial provision, s.8(2) of the Family Law (Scotland) Act 1985 ("the Act") provides that the court shall make such order as is: (a) justified by the principles set out in s.9 of the Act; and (b) reasonable having regard to the resources of the parties. So, there are two steps in the process. This chapter deals with the first step—establishing which orders (if any) are justified under the s.9 principles. The two step process in general, and the second part of the process in particular (establishing which orders are reasonable having regard to the resources of the parties), is discussed at paras 3–02 to 3–08.

Section 9(1) sets out five principles:

"The principles which the court shall apply in deciding what order for financial provision, if any, to make are that;

(a) the net value of the matrimonial property should be shared fairly between the parties to the marriage or as the case may be the net value of the partnership property should be so shared between the partners in the civil partnership;

(b) fair account should be taken of any economic advantage derived by either person from contributions by the other, and of any economic disadvantage suffered by either person in the interests of the other person or of the family;

(c) any economic burden of caring, should be shared fairly between the persons—

   (i) after divorce, for a child of the marriage under the age of 16 years;

   (ii) after dissolution of the civil partnership, for a child under that age who has been accepted by both partners as a child of the family.

(d) a person who has been dependent to a substantial degree on the financial support of the other person should be awarded such financial provision as is reasonable to enable him to adjust, over a period of not more than three years from—

   (i) the date of the decree of divorce, to the loss of that support on divorce;

    (ii) the date of the decree of dissolution of the civil partnership, to the loss of that support on dissolution.

  (e) a person who at the time of the divorce or of the dissolution of the civil partnership, seems likely to suffer serious financial hardship as a result of the divorce or dissolution should be awarded such financial provision as is reasonable to relieve him of hardship over a reasonable period."

Each of these five principles is considered in detail later in this chapter. For the sake of brevity it may be useful to classify the principles as follows:

Principle (a)—fair sharing of matrimonial/partnership property;
Principle (b)—fair account of economic advantages and disadvantages;
Principle (c)—fair sharing of economic burden of child care;
Principle (d)—adjustment to loss of financial support; and
Principle (e)—relief of serious financial hardship.

The s.9 principles have to be read alongside various other sections of the Act which expand on the principles and define certain key terms, and in particular:

- **Section 10** expands on the s.9(1)(a) principle. Section 10(1) is especially important, stating that matrimonial or partnership property will be shared fairly when it is shared equally or in such other proportions as are justified by "special circumstances";
- **Section 11** expands on the other four principles, and also states that the conduct of the parties is not to be taken into account in applying the s.9 principles unless (a) the conduct has affected the relevant resources of the parties, or (b) in the case of the principles set out in paras 9(1)(d) and (e) if it would be manifestly inequitable to leave the conduct out of account.

  Any order which is made by the court must be justified under one or more of the five s.9 principles. However, the principles do not set out a mathematical formula for the court to apply. They create a structure within which the court has to operate, but provided that it does so a great deal will be left to the court's discretion. A range of results may be justified in any given case. Any examination of reported decisions will show that the discretion of the court is rather wide, and it is difficult to predict how the court will apply the principles in any given case. In the simplest cases, it is true that an application of the s.9 principles would involve a calculation of the net matrimonial or partnership property followed by a straightforward equal division of this.[1] However, even in these circumstances, the court will still have a decision to make

---

[1] i.e. if the only principle to apply was principle 9(1)(a) (fair sharing) and there were no special circumstances under s.10(6) to justify a departure from the presumption of equal sharing in s.10(1).

regarding *how* the assets are to be divided. In reality, most cases are more complex than this, and will involve a balancing by the court of more than one of the s.9 principles, along perhaps with an analysis of whether a departure from equal sharing of matrimonial or partnership property is justified by any special circumstances under s.10(6). Some of these factors may tend to cancel one another out. Further, even if the court is persuaded that an order is justified by one or more of the s.9 principles, it still has the discretion not to make such an order if this is not reasonable having regard to the resources of the parties.[2]

A practical approach to the section 9 principles

4–02   The complex way in which the various parts of the Act relate to one another and the degree of discretion which the court has can be daunting. Anyone seeking to apply the s.9 principles to a particular set of circumstances will need to find a practical and systematic approach. The following steps might be helpful.

(1)   Ascertain the matrimonial/partnership assets and debts at the relevant date

4–03   The most important of the s.9 principles is s.9(1)(a) which states that upon divorce or dissolution the net value of "matrimonial property" or "partnership property" is to be shared fairly. Therefore a useful starting point in any case will be to establish what the matrimonial property or partnership property is. Chapter 6 deals with matrimonial and partnership property in detail, but in very broad terms, it will be all of the property belonging to the parties at "the relevant date"[3] which was acquired by them or either of them (otherwise than by way of gift or succession) during the marriage or partnership but before the relevant date. Property acquired before the marriage or registration for use as a family home (or as furniture or plenishings for that home) will also be matrimonial property or partnership property.[4] As it is the net value of the matrimonial or partnership property which is to be shared, any debts of the parties at the relevant date will also fall to be taken into account. Clear and full instructions will be needed. Parties may not be sure about the position and enquiries might need to be made with banks, insurance companies and so on. It may be necessary to make enquiries of the opponent. In some cases, where there are fears that the opponent is concealing assets or funds, an action may need to be raised and techniques used to force discovery of the assets.[5]

(2)   Value the matrimonial/partnership property and debts

4–04   The property and debts must be valued. They should initially be valued at the relevant date. However, the value at the date of any order may also be important for three reasons. First, if property is to be

---

[2] s.8(2).
[3] Broadly speaking this is the date of separation, but see s.10(3) and (7). See paras 5–02 to 5–05.
[4] s.10(4) and (4A).
[5] Using s.20 of the Act or perhaps commission and diligence.

transferred from one party to the other[6] then that property is generally to be valued at the date of the transfer.[7] Secondly, if pension sharing is to be considered, the value of the relevant pension interests at the date of the order might be important.[8] Thirdly, the Act provides that any order made must be justified and reasonable having regard to the resources of the parties,[9] and the term "resources" includes both present and foreseeable resources.[10] Therefore, the value of the resources at the time of the order may be important. A valuation at the precise date of the order is virtually impossible since, in the course of negotiations and litigation, one can never be sure of the exact date when the division of the resources will be made (at least until the very last minute). Nevertheless, the value of assets and debts as the case progresses is a highly relevant matter (particularly where property is likely to be transferred from one party to the other at the conclusion of the case). In practice, it will usually be apparent which assets are likely to be significantly changing in value, and clients will often have a good idea of how values are changing with time.

Expert advice may be needed in assessing the value of some assets such as heritage, business interests and unquoted shares. Advisers and clients will also need to weigh the advantages of obtaining expert advice, against the likely costs of the expert. The expert should be instructed to value the property at the relevant date (and in appropriate cases at the date of the valuation). It may also be crucial to remind the valuer that the asset should be valued in accordance with the principles in the Act and having regard to any relevant precedent.

(3)   Prepare a schedule of matrimonial/partnership assets and debts

As a solicitor carries out steps 1 and 2 above, it will be useful to **4–05** prepare a schedule of assets and debts, showing values at the relevant date (and if necessary at current values). The schedule can have notes appended to it for any issues which are unclear or which need further consideration. The schedule will serve as a useful *aide memoire* and can be updated as negotiations progress.

(4)   Apply section 9(1)(a) on the basis of equal sharing

Once all assets and debts have been valued, the next step is to work **4–06** out what an equal sharing of net property would be. The most important principle is s.9(1)(a) (fair sharing), and s.10(1) states that fair sharing means equal sharing unless special circumstances apply. So, the presumption is for equal sharing, and this gives a good baseline before considering any departure from this. In calculating equal sharing, if assets are to be transferred, it will be important to value those assets at their current value rather than at the relevant date.[11]

---

[6] Under s.8(1)(aa).
[7] Or the date upon which the parties agree—see s.10(3A). See para.5–06.
[8] See para.3–59.
[9] s.8(2).
[10] s.27(1).
[11] s.10(3A).

(5) Look for special circumstances

4–07   Section 10(1) provides that there may be a departure from equal sharing of matrimonial or partnership property if there are special circumstances. Special circumstances are considered in detail in Ch.7. It is therefore important to consider whether any special circumstances under s.10(6) apply to the case in question. If so, a careful examination of similar cases may help to assess the strength of the claim and its likely effect on the case. However, an adviser should always keep in mind that the scheme of rules for financial provision provided in the Act depends to a great extent on the discretion of the sheriff. His views (and those of the opponent) may differ from those of the adviser. Generally the best that can be done is to advise clients that special circumstances *may* apply and that this will produce *a range of possible results*. Bear in mind that other special circumstances may benefit the opponent. Sometimes arguments will tend to cancel one another out.

(6) Look at the principle in section 9(1)(b)—economic advantage/ disadvantage

4–08   The next step might be to consider whether there have been any economic advantages or disadvantages for either party which have not been balanced by other factors.[12] Section 9(1)(b) bears quite a close relationship to "special circumstances". Some circumstances can be argued on both bases. It is important to realise that s.9(1)(b) represents a s.9 principle in its own right which the court can use to make an award of financial provision *irrespective of the extent of the matrimonial or partnership property*. This differs from special circumstances arguments which can only ever have a bearing on the way that matrimonial or partnership property is to be divided.[13]

(7) Look at principles in section 9(1)(c), (d) and (e)

4–09   Do any of the principles in s.9(1)(c) (economic burden of child care), (d) (loss of support) or (e) (serious financial hardship) apply to the case in question? If so, again assess the strengths of the argument and consider the range of possible results. If these sections apply then periodical allowance may be appropriate, but remember that the Act directs a clean break where possible.[14] These principles are looked at in detail at paras 4–50 to 4–86, and periodical allowance is considered in detail at paras 3–32 to 3–48. Like awards under s.9(b), awards under s.9(1)(c), (d) and (e) do not rely on a split of matrimonial or partnership property.[15]

(8) Which section 8 orders might achieve the desired result?

4–10   The next step may be to explore which orders are appropriate under s.8 to achieve the desired (and fair) result. Here, instructions from the client are of high importance. For example, the client may place a very

---

[12] ss.9(1)(b) and 11(2). See paras 4–21 to 4–49.
[13] See para.4–26.
[14] See para.3–34.
[15] See para.4–26.

high priority on retaining the family home, or alternatively they may see it as key that they have a reasonable pension to provide for retirement. These goals and aspirations will be crucial in any negotiations and also in relation to the orders which will be craved if the case proceeds to court.

(9) Consider whether the orders sought are reasonable

Section 8(2) provides that any orders must be reasonable having **4–11** regard to the resources of the parties. The term "resources" in this context includes present and foreseeable resources.[16] It is therefore important to consider whether the result sought is reasonable to *both* parties. An order justified under the principles of the Act may still be refused if it produces a result which is simply unfair to the other party.

Conduct of the parties

Section 11(7) of the Act states that: **4–12**

"In applying the principles set out in section 9 of this Act, the court shall not take account of the conduct of either party to the marriage or as the case may be of either partner unless:

(a) the conduct has adversely affected the financial resources which are relevant to the decision of the court on a claim for financial provision; or

(b) in relation to section 9(1)(d) or (e), it would be manifestly inequitable to leave the conduct out of account."

The first point to note is that para.(a) above applies to all of the s.9 principles, whereas para.(b) applies only to s.9(1)(d) and (e). Paragraphs (a) and (b) are now considered in turn.

Section 11(7)(a)

Section 11(7)(a) allows the court to take the conduct of a party into **4–13** account only if that conduct has affected resources.[17] It should be recalled that the term "resources" in the Act is not restricted to the resources at the relevant date, but encompasses "present and foreseeable resources".[18] The law is clear that (subject to the limited exception provided in s.11(7)(b)) even if a party has behaved in an entirely unacceptable way over the course of the marriage or partnership, he or she is entitled to equitable financial provision under the Act, unless their conduct has affected the resources of the parties. It follows from this that a party seeking to rely on s.11(7)(a) to justify a departure from equal sharing will need to carefully aver and prove the adverse effect that the conduct has had on the resources of the parties.[19]

---

[16] s.27(1).

[17] This differs from s.11(7)(b) where moral considerations can come into play in certain limited circumstances.

[18] s.27(1).

[19] See e.g. the differing opinions of Lord McCluskey and Lord Milligan in *Cunniff v Cunniff*, 1999 S.C. 537. See also the comments of Sheriff Principal Risk in *Bremner v Bremner*, 2000 S.C.L.R. 912.

Conduct can influence resources in a variety of ways. On the simplest level, a party could destroy an asset, and that would clearly reduce the resources. On a slightly more indirect level, a party could squander resources on gambling, drink or drugs.[20] In both of these examples there is a direct and immediate effect on resources. It seems fairly clear that this conduct could fall within the type of conduct envisaged by s.11(7)(a). However, what if the conduct concerned is more remote from the adverse effect on the resources? For example, what happens if one party's appalling behaviour leads to the other becoming depressed with the result that they cannot work, thus reducing resources? There is clearly more than one link in the causal chain. This type of situation was considered in *Bremner v Bremner*, 2000 S.C.L.R. 912 where, over a period of some years, the wife associated with other men, abused and taunted her husband, and regularly drank to excess. Her conduct was the principal cause of a depressive illness in her husband which resulted in him requiring to leave employment. The fact that the husband had given up his job resulted in a substantial drop in income, and the sheriff treated this as a special circumstance justifying unequal division of matrimonial property. Sheriff Principal Risk affirmed the decision[21]:

> "Section 27(1) of the 1985 Act defines 'resources' as meaning 'present and foreseeable resources'. That definition directs the court's attention to the resources which exist at the time when the order is made or which are likely to exist thereafter. Where s.11(7)(a) refers to 'the financial resources which are relevant to the decision of the court' it must refer to resources as so defined. Accordingly, if the resources available as at the date of proof have been adversely affected by the conduct of a party, that is a matter to which the court is entitled to have regard in applying any of the principles set out in s.9. In particular, when considering the principle under s.9(1)(a) it is open to the court to regard conduct adversely affecting resources as a special circumstance under s.10(6) justifying a division in other than equal proportions under s.10(1). The Act does not say that, in order to be relevant, the conduct must have affected the value of the matrimonial property at the relevant date. It does not seem to me that it is either necessary or desirable to read into the statute a requirement that the conduct in question must have been intended to reduce the resources available, or even that it should have been reasonably foreseeable by the party whose conduct is in question that it would reduce the resources."

The sheriff principal also commented[22] that it is not necessary that the conduct itself involves direct dealing with the resources, although it appears that there needs to be a "chain of causation" between the conduct and the adverse effect on the resources.[23] It is interesting to note

---

[20] See *Skarpaas v Skarpaas*, 1991 S.L.T. (Sh Ct) 15.
[21] At p.916.
[22] At pp.915—16.
[23] The court referred to a passage in E.M. Clive, *The Law of Husband and Wife in Scotland* 4th edn, para.24.045 where the author suggests that the court cannot take into account conduct such as adultery, cruelty or desertion. The sheriff principal suggested that the author was directing his comments at adultery, cruelty or desertion without financial consequences and not at a situation where such conduct had economically adverse consequences.

that it was observed that there was no requirement that the conduct had to have been intended to have such an adverse effect, or even that the effect was reasonably foreseeable. However, it appears that losses which result from bad luck or judgement in business are probably not financial misconduct within the meaning of s.11(7)(a).[24]

In *Gray v Gray*, 2001 S.C.L.R. 681, it was held that conduct after the relevant date can have an adverse effect on resources which may be relevant under s.11(7)(a). As a result of the husband's reluctance to pay aliment or mortgage payments after the separation, the wife had to borrow money from her family. In relation to this conduct Sheriff Stewart commented[25]:

> "I accept that 'conduct' in the context of this subsection usually refers to the conduct of a party during the subsistence of the marriage, but I see no reason why it should not also refer to the conduct of a party affecting financial resources *after* the parties have separated. In the present case I am satisfied that the defender's conduct . . . is something which has adversely affected the pursuer's financial position and is therefore a factor of which I am entitled to take account in applying the principles set out in section 9 of the Act, especially the principle that the net value of the matrimonial property should be shared fairly between the parties."

Another case which deals with conduct after the relevant date is *Collins v Collins*, 1997 Fam. L.R. 50. Here the wife had been offered a significant sum during the course of negotiations. The husband made arrangements to obtain a substantial loan, with a view to paying a capital sum to the wife, and in return she was to convey her interest in the matrimonial property to him. A draft minute of agreement was prepared, but it took quite some time to arrange the loan and to deal with the conveyancing work. When the loan was ultimately made available, the wife refused to accept payment of the capital sum "on principle" claiming that she had understood payment was to have been made within four weeks of the original settlement proposal. Had she accepted the deal, she would have achieved settlement on terms which were highly advantageous to her. By the time of the proof the loan funds were no longer available and the husband had no access to this resource to assist in making financial provision. Sheriff Smith found that the wife's actions were conduct which adversely affected the resources available to the parties, commenting rather tersely[26]:

> "Put bluntly, if the defender regards what has happened as unfair it is her own fault."

Section 11(7)(b)

Section 11(7)(b) allows conduct to be taken into account in relation to **4–14** the application of the principles in s.9(1)(d) and (e) if it would be manifestly inequitable to leave it out of account. Only in these circum-

---

[24] See *Russell v Russell*, 1996 Fam. L.B. 21–5, where the wife had lost heavily on business ventures in Turkey after the separation—this was held not to fall within the ambit of s.11(7)(a).
[25] At p.684.
[26] At para.10–14.

stances can the court take into account conduct which had no adverse economic effect. This is one of the few areas within the Act where issues of morality may be relevant. In *Bremner v Bremner*, 2000 S.C.L.R. 912 the sheriff principal commented[27]:

> "Sub-paragraph (b) of s.11(7) is concerned with the moral question of equity and may indeed involve a consideration of the intention and foresight of a party . . ."

However, it is important to realise that such conduct will not be considered routinely. Section 9(1)(d) and (e) (which respectively deal with adjustment to the divorce or dissolution and serious hardship) deal with quite narrow situations, and even then the court is restricted to circumstances where it would be "manifestly inequitable" to leave non-economic conduct out of account.

PRINCIPLE (A)—FAIR SHARING OF MATRIMONIAL AND PARTNERSHIP PROPERTY

General discussion

4–15   Section 9(1)(a) requires that the net value of the matrimonial or partnership property should be shared fairly between the parties. This is the most important of the s.9 principles. The section states:

> "the net value of the matrimonial property should be shared fairly between the parties to the marriage or as the case may be the net value of the partnership property should be so shared between the partners in the civil partnership;".

An order justified by s.9(1)(a) cannot be effected through payment of periodical allowance, as periodical allowance may only be justified under s.9(1)(c), (d) or (e).[28] Section 11(7) of the Act provides that, in applying the principle set out in s.9(1)(a), the court is not to take account of the conduct of either party unless the conduct has adversely affected the financial resources which are relevant to the decision of the court in a claim for financial provision.[29]

Section 10 of the Act then expands on s.9(1)(a). Section 10 contains several key concepts. The remainder of this section is a brief guide to the most important provisions of s.10. This is expanded in Ch.5 ("The Relevant Date"), Ch.6 ("Matrimonial and Partnership Property") and Ch.7 ("Special Circumstances").

Fair sharing means equal sharing unless there are special circumstances

4–16   Section 9(1)(a) provides that matrimonial and partnership property is to be shared "fairly". Section 10(1) provides that in applying this principle, the net value of the matrimonial property or partnership

---

[27] At p.916.
[28] s.13(2).
[29] See paras 4–12 to 4–14.

property shall be taken to be shared fairly when it is shared equally or in such other proportions as are justified by "special circumstances". So, there is a presumption for equal sharing unless there are special circumstances.[30] This presumption does not mean that ownership of each and every asset is split between the parties. Rather, the court establishes the net value of the matrimonial property or partnership property, and then seeks to share this value between the parties equally: some assets will go to one party, some to the other, and sometimes a balancing payment will be required. Often the way that the property is shared can be very important, especially if both parties wish to retain a particular asset.

The court may depart from the presumption of equal sharing if there are "special circumstances". Section 10(6) gives five examples of special circumstances: (a) the terms of any agreement between the parties on the ownership or division of any of the matrimonial or partnership property; (b) the source of the funds or the assets used to acquire any of the matrimonial or partnership property where those funds or assets were not derived from the income or efforts of the parties during the marriage or partnership; (c) any destruction, dissipation or alienation of property by either person; (d) the nature of the family property or partnership property, the use made of it (including use for business purposes or as a family home) and the extent to which it is reasonable to expect it to be realised or divided or used as security; and (e) the actual or prospective liability for any expenses of valuation or transfer of property in connection with the divorce or dissolution. However, these five examples are without prejudice to the generality of the words "special circumstances"—there are situations outside the five examples which may constitute special circumstances.

To summarise, one party may argue that they should receive more than half of the matrimonial or partnership property if there are special circumstances. Special circumstances, and how they may sometimes be used to depart from the norm of equal sharing, are considered in detail in Ch.7.

The relevant date

There is a detailed examination of the term "relevant date" in Ch.5. **4–17** For the purpose of this introduction, it is important to point out that it is only the matrimonial or partnership property which is owned on the "relevant date" which is to be shared between the parties.[31] In many cases the nature of the matrimonial and partnership property and its value may change quite substantially between the relevant date and the date of proof or settlement of the action. What the Act does is to require the court to take a "snapshot" of the matrimonial or partnership property at the relevant date—it is this which is to be shared under the principle set out in s.9(1)(a).

---

[30] See e.g. *McCaskill v McCaskill*, 2004 Fam. L.R. 123. See also *Robertson v Robertson (No.1)*, 2000 Fam. L.R. 43, where the sheriff principal held that the broad policy underlying s.9(1)(a) and s.10 of the Act was that in principle an equal division should apply to the fruits of the economic efforts of the parties during the marriage.

[31] s.10(4) and (4A).

The relevant date will be the earlier of: (a) the date on which the parties ceased to co-habit;[32] and (b) the date of service of the summons in the action.[33] Situation (b) will be rare, and generally the relevant date will be the date that the couple cease to co-habit. For the purposes of the Act a couple are deemed to be co-habiting only when they are in fact living together as man and wife.[34] This is important because it means that the couple may, for the purposes of the Act, be deemed to have ceased to co-habit even though they are still living under the same roof.

Matrimonial and partnership property

4–18   Chapter 6 of this book looks at the definitions of matrimonial property and partnership property in greater detail. However, for the purposes of this initial discussion, it is worth briefly outlining these definitions. In terms of s.10(4) and (4A) the matrimonial or partnership property is all property belonging to the parties, or either of them, at the relevant date, which was acquired by the parties (otherwise than by way of gift or succession from a third party): (a) before the marriage or partnership for use by them as a family home or as furniture or plenishings for that home; or (b) during the marriage or partnership but before the relevant date.

It is crucial to understand that it is only matrimonial property or partnership property which is to be shared by the parties in terms of s.9(1)(a). Property owned by the parties which does not fall within the definition of matrimonial or partnership property is not to be divided under the principle. It can be seen from the foregoing definition that matrimonial and partnership property will not include (a) inherited property, (b) gifts, (c) property acquired by a spouse or civil partner before the marriage or registration (except property acquired by them for use as a family home or as furniture or plenishings for that home), and (d) property acquired by a spouse or partner after the relevant date.[35] Resources which do not fall within the matrimonial or partnership property will still be relevant as any order justified under the s.9 principles (including s.9(1)(a)) must be reasonable having regard to the resources of the parties.[36]

Valuation of matrimonial or partnership property

4–19   In terms of s.9(1)(a), it is the *net value* of the matrimonial or partnership property which is to be shared. In terms of s.10(2) this (subject to an exception provided in s.10(3A) discussed in the next paragraph) will be the value of the property at the relevant date after deduction of any debts outstanding at that date incurred by one or both of the parties (a) before the marriage so far as they relate to matrimonial property or before registration so far as they relate to partnership property, and (b) during the marriage or partnership.

---

[32] Subject to the provisions of s.10(7) which provide detailed rules on how the relevant date is to be established where there have been periods where the parties resume co-habitation after an initial separation. See para.5–05.

[33] See s.10(3).

[34] s.27(2). See para.5–04.

[35] See paras 6–58 to 6–64.

[36] See paras 3–02 to 3–08.

Section 10(3A) (which is discussed in more detail elsewhere in this book[37]) provides that, if property is to be transferred from one party to the other using a property transfer order,[38] then it is to be valued not at the relevant date, but at the "appropriate valuation date" (which will generally be a date agreed by the parties or the date of transfer).

The proportion of the value of any pensions or life policies accumulated between the date of marriage or registration and the relevant date will be included within the matrimonial or partnership property, even though the investment was started before marriage or registration.[39]

Method of division of matrimonial or partnership property

In terms of s.9(1)(a), fair division will, in the absence of special **4–20** circumstances, be equal division. In many cases, the net value of the matrimonial or partnership property may already have been shared more or less equally at the relevant date. In such cases it may be that no order at all is required.[40] More usually, however, there will be a number of available methods of dividing the matrimonial or partnership property all of which will achieve equal division. For example, in a simple case where A and B separate and their only matrimonial or partnership property is a house worth £100,000, any of the following options would achieve equal division: (1) A keeps the house and pays a balancing payment of £50,000 to B; (2) B keeps the house and pays a balancing payment of £50,000 to A; or (3) the court orders that the house is sold and the proceeds split equally. Although each option results in equal division, the practical effects will be quite different in each case. How then is a court to approach a case where both parties are seeking an equal division of assets, but want to achieve this in quite different ways? There is no clear answer—the court has a wide discretion. In *Christie v Christie*, 2004 S.L.T. (Sh Ct) 95 Sheriff Principal Kerr stated[41]:

> ". . . various kinds of financial provision may be made to achieve the object of sharing the net value of the matrimonial property fairly . . . The choice to be made among the various methods in any given case is essentially a matter for the exercise by the sheriff of a discretion or (perhaps more accurately) of a judgment on the facts presented to or found by him and with that exercise of discretionary judgement an appellate court cannot in my opinion readily interfere."

In *Christie* it was held that, in exercising that discretion, the court has to state a reason for preferring one method of division over another, but provided a sufficient reason is given, an appellate court will not interfere with the exercise of the discretion. The appellate court would only interfere if (1) there was no sufficient reason, (2) there was legal

---

[37] See para.5–06.
[38] Under s.8(1)(a).
[39] s.10(5).
[40] *Goldie v Goldie*, 1992 G.W.D. 21–1225.
[41] At p.99.

misdirection at first instance, or (3) an irrelevant factor was relied upon.[42]

Principle (b)—Fair Account of Economic Advantages and Disadvantages

Key statutory provisions

4–21   Section 9(1)(b) of the 1985 Act provides that one of the principles to be applied in deciding which orders for financial provision might be appropriate is that:

> "fair account should be taken of any economic advantage derived by either person from contributions by the other, and of any economic disadvantage suffered by either person in the interests of the other person or of the family;".

This principle needs to be read with s.9(2) which defines two key terms:

(1) "economic advantage" means advantage gained whether before or during the marriage or civil partnership and includes gains in capital, in income and in earning capacity, and "economic disadvantage" shall be construed accordingly; and

(2) "contributions" means contributions made whether before or during the marriage or civil partnership; and includes indirect and non-financial contributions and, in particular, any such contribution made by looking after the family home or caring for the family.

Section 11(2) provides that for the purposes of s.9(1)(b) of the Act, the court shall have regard to the extent to which: (a) the economic advantages or disadvantages sustained by either person have been balanced by the economic advantages or disadvantages sustained by the other person; and (b) any resulting imbalance has been or will be corrected by a sharing of the value of matrimonial or partnership property or otherwise.

An order justified by s.9(1)(b) cannot be effected through payment of periodical allowance, as periodical allowance may only be justified under s.9(1)(c), (d) or (e).[43] Section 11(7) of the Act provides that, in applying the principle set out in s.9(1)(b), the court is not to take account of the conduct of either party unless it has adversely affected the financial resources which are relevant to the decision of the court on a claim for financial provision.[44]

---

[42] In *Christie* the wife, at first instance, had the husband's interest in the matrimonial home transferred to her. The husband argued at appeal that this led to unfairness, requested that the order be set aside, and an order for sale of the house (with other related orders) be granted. On appeal, the sheriff principal pointed out that the sheriff had, in his decision, alluded to several factors which he considered supportive of the appropriateness of making the property transfer orders in favour of the pursuer. The sheriff principal was not prepared to interfere with the exercise of the sheriff's discretion.

[43] s.13(2).

[44] See paras 4–12 to 4–14.

General discussion

Some examples

In a marriage or civil partnership, circumstances can arise where one **4–22**
party gains a considerable economic advantage from the contributions of
the other. Section 9(1)(b) allows the court to take these economic
imbalances into account when making orders for financial provision.
There is a more detailed examination of the types of situation where
s.9(1)(b) has been argued at paras 4–32 to 4–49 below, but for the
purposes of this introduction examples could include:

- one civil partner works to support the other while she obtains
  qualifications which ultimately improve her earning capacity;
- a house owned by the wife (and not forming part of the
  matrimonial property) might be improved, and increased in
  value, by the efforts of the husband;
- a wife's contributions during the marriage might have helped a
  business brought into the marriage by the husband (which was
  not itself matrimonial property) to grow and become more
  valuable[45];
- one spouse might put money or labour into the (non-
  matrimonial) business of the other spouse[46]; and
- money belonging to one spouse might be given to the other
  during the marriage.[47]

Equally, one spouse or civil partner might suffer economic disadvantage
in the interests of the other party or the family. Examples could include:

- a wife with good career prospects gives up work in order to
  raise a young family, resulting in her earning capacity being
  reduced (and perhaps her ability to build up pension rights)[48];
- a business owned by the wife may have suffered because of her
  need to look after her husband after an accident[49]; and
- both spouses may have come into the marriage with property;
  one party might have used their property to support the family
  whilst the other retained theirs.[50]

When does the advantage/disadvantage arise?

Economic advantage means advantage gained whether before or **4–23**
during the marriage or civil partnership, and can include gains in capital,
income or earning capacity. The term economic disadvantage is construed accordingly.[51] So, advantages and disadvantages arising whether
before or during the marriage or civil partnership may be taken into

---

[45] *De Winton v De Winton*, 1996 G.W.D. 29–1752.
[46] *Vance v Vance*, 1997 S.L.T. (Sh Ct) 71.
[47] *Davidson v Davidson*, 1994 S.L.T. 506.
[48] *Luckwell v Luckwell*, 1992 G.W.D. 34—2005; *Kelly v Kelly*, 1992 G.W.D. 36–2130.
[49] *Skarpaas v Skarpaas*, 1991 S.L.T. (Sh Ct) 15.
[50] *McVinnie v McVinnie (No. 2)*, 1997 S.L.T. (Sh Ct) 12.
[51] s.9(2).

account. It is implicit in this definition that there are three distinct periods to consider.

First, the principle in s.9(1)(b) can compensate for advantages or disadvantages arising *before* the marriage or registration. Therefore circumstances prior to the marriage or registration might be important and will need investigation in some cases.

Secondly, the principle can compensate for economic advantages and disadvantages arising during the marriage or civil partnership. This seems straightforward enough. However, note that the wording in s.9(2) does not confine the operation of the principle in s.9(1)(b) to the period leading up to the relevant date. Rather, it refers to the whole period of the marriage or civil partnership. This includes the period after the relevant date but before the divorce or dissolution.[52]

The third period to consider is the period after the divorce or dissolution. Section 9(2) excludes this period and it is clear that the consequence of a court order for financial provision in itself cannot be regarded as an economic disadvantage or advantage. On a strict construction s.9(2) requires that there can be no compensation for an economic advantage/disadvantage arising after the divorce or dissolution. On this reading of the provision, Sheriff Morrison is correct in *Dougan v Dougan*, 1998 S.L.T. (Sh Ct) 27 when he says[53]:

"In my opinion the pursuer's loss of income and any need to support the child after the marriage, that is to say after decree of divorce, although causally linked to an event which occurred before or during the marriage, are not economic disadvantages sustained before or during the marriage."

However, if one considers this more closely, there appears to be an inconsistency. Section 9(2) states that economic advantage can include gains in income and *earning capacity* and economic disadvantage is to be construed accordingly. However, surely a loss of earning capacity is a loss which will necessarily be suffered (in an on-going way) after the date of the divorce. As Sheriff Principal Bowen points out in *Cahill v Cahill*, 1998 S.L.T. (Sh Ct) 96[54]:

"Section 9(2) specifically refers to earning capacity and if earning capacity becomes disadvantaged in the course of the marriage I

---

[52] Although see the comments of Lord Sutherland in *Tyrrell v Tyrrell*, 1990 S.L.T. 406 at 408 where the court seems to accept the defender's argument that economic advantage/disadvantage arguments should be confined to looking at "any unusual situation during the course of the marriage, by which is meant the time during which the parties lived together . . ." This is not consistent with the wording of s.9(2). It is reasonable enough to say that the property needs to be valued at the relevant date in terms of s.9(1)(a), but s.9(1)(b) is a separate principle which needs to be looked at after s.9(1)(a) and it clearly can take account of imbalances arising after the separation but before divorce or dissolution. The court misses this in *Tyrrell* in the following passage—"I am quite satisfied that the proper method of valuation is to value the fund as at the date of separation and there are no special circumstances in the present case which would allow for any increase to be made." So far so good—but the court then needs to look at the other s.9 principles.
[53] At p.31.
[54] At p.99.

have difficulty in seeing how that loss can be evaluated except by reference to an extended period of time part of which may be after the dissolution of the marriage."

This seems convincing. Although the claim for loss of earning capacity cannot be stated with absolute accuracy, this does not mean that a proper estimate of the claim cannot be arrived at. This is precisely what happens in personal injuries claims where loss of future earnings is an issue—the court is asked to capitalise an on-going loss.

Contributions

Section 9(1)(b) refers to economic advantages derived from "contribu- **4–24** tions" of a party. Section 9(2) provides that the term "contributions":

(a) includes indirect and non-financial contributions, and in particular, any such contributions made by looking after the family home or caring for the family[55]; and
(b) encompasses contributions whether before or during the marriage or registration.

As a preliminary point, it is worth noting that, although the wording of s.9(1)(b) requires economic advantages to be the result of "contributions", there is no corresponding requirement for economic disadvantages. So far as economic disadvantages are concerned, the court may take into account "any economic disadvantage suffered by either person in the interests of the other person or of the family".

It must be stressed that if one party makes a contribution to the other, then before s.9(1)(b) can have any effect, the contribution must result in an *economic* advantage. Many contributions will not have any economic effect. So, for example, a party may look after the family home, but if this contribution does not economically advantage the other party (e.g. they may not have advanced their career any more quickly as a result of the contribution) then there is nothing to be redressed by an award under s.9(1)(b).[56] The section is only designed to correct economic imbalances; it is not in any way designed to pay or compensate a party for contributions which do not result in such an imbalance.[57]

If one party makes a financial contribution to the other who then goes bankrupt, the donor party can still claim an award under s.9(1)(b). The bankruptcy does not in any way wipe the slate clean for the purposes of an economic advantage/disadvantage argument.[58]

Contributions do not need to be made voluntarily. One party may demand or indeed take a contribution from the other.[59] So, for example, if one spouse forced the other to use their (non-matrimonial) property to support the couple during the marriage, then s.9(1)(b) could be used

---

[55] e.g. *Petrie v Petrie*, 1988 S.C.L.R. 390; *Jesner v Jesner*, 1992 S.L.T. 999. See paras 4–33 to 4–35.
[56] See *Petrie v Petrie*, 1988 S.C.L.R. 390.
[57] See also *Tyrrell v Tyrrell*, 1990 S.L.T. 406.
[58] *Symanski v Symanski (No.2)*, 2005 Fam. L.R. 2.
[59] *Tahir v Tahir (No. 2)*, 1995 S.L.T. 451 where the husband took jewellery belonging to the wife.

to redress the balance. However, the economic advantage must be conferred by some sort of contribution.[60]

A balancing exercise

4–25   Section 9(1)(b) allows the party who is economically disadvantaged to seek to redress the economic imbalance. Section 9(1)(b) (when read alongside ss.9(2) and 11(2)) requires the court to carry out a balancing exercise. The court may find that the various advantages and disadvantages of the parties cancel one another out. It is only if the scales do not balance that the court should make an order, using s.9(1)(b) to correct the imbalance.[61] *Welsh v Welsh*, 1994 S.L.T. 828 is a good example of this balancing act in operation. The wife suffered economic disadvantage by giving up well-paid employment to look after the children during the marriage. However, she gained certain economic advantages—she was maintained by her husband and her husband paid the mortgage for the jointly owned family home. Equal division was sufficient to achieve a fair division.[62] Lord Osborne explained[63]:

> "I have come to the conclusion, in the light of the facts which I have found and of the foregoing arguments, that the net value of the matrimonial property available in this case should be shared equally between the parties . . . While it is plain that the pursuer herself suffered an economic disadvantage in the interests of the defender and her children, insofar as she gave up quite well paid employment to look after her family, it appears to me to be equally plain that she enjoyed certain associated economic advantages in the same situation, in respect that she was subsequently maintained exclusively from the earnings of the defender during the period in which she had no employment. Furthermore in the allocation of matrimonial property which I propose to make she will enjoy the results of the mortgage payments made exclusively by the defender during the period of time in which she was not employed. It appears to me also that, in consequence of the pursuer giving up her paid employment, the defender himself sustained an economic disadvantage, in respect that he was thus rendered the sole breadwinner for the family, assuming the responsibility for maintaining, not only his children, but also the pursuer herself. In the whole circumstances I am unable to discern any significant imbalance in the situation of the parties in relation to economic advantages and disadvantages. In these circumstances I see no reason, based upon s.9(1)(b), to depart from an equal division."

So, the advantages and disadvantages may have been "accounted for" already. Another case where the court felt that advantages and disadvantages had been counterbalanced was *Petrie v Petrie*, 1988 S.C.L.R. 390

---

[60] See *Phillip v Phillip*, 1988 S.C.L.R. 427 discussed below at para.4–37.
[61] See e.g. *De Winton v De Winton*, 1996 G.W.D. 29–1752.
[62] See also the commentary to the report in *Toye v Toye*, 1992 S.C.L.R. 95.
[63] At p.835.

where Sheriff Risk weighed up economic advantages and disadvantages[64]:

> "[The defender's agent] submitted that by staying at home and keeping house for five years before the marriage and two years while the marriage subsisted, the wife had made a contribution in terms of s.9(2). With that I cannot quarrel. It is not, however, enough to entitle the wife to an order for financial provision in terms of section 9(1)(b). She would have to go on to show that her contribution enabled the husband to gain an economic advantage which was not balanced by an economic advantage sustained by herself in terms of section 11(2)(a). This she has failed to do; indeed her pleadings and her evidence do not seriously address the question. So far as I can tell, when the parties began to cohabit, the husband, far from gaining an economic advantage, sustained an economic disadvantage in respect that he continued in his job with the taxi firm but had to support the wife as well as himself. There is nothing to indicate that it was the presence of the wife in the home which enabled him, subsequently, to obtain better paid employment offshore, nor that he used his increased earnings for any purpose other than the support of the household which he shared with the wife. On the other hand, the wife, who prior to the start of cohabitation had been a single parent supporting her two children from her own earnings, was able to give up work and rely upon the husband for support which, at least while he was working offshore, was at a higher level than that to which she had been accustomed. In my opinion, therefore, the principle set out in section 9(1)(b) does not justify any award in favour of the wife."

Other examples where advantages and disadvantages might balance could be:

- if one party gives up work to let the other develop their career, they may have benefited from enhanced savings and pension rights built up during the marriage or civil partnership[65]; and
- if one party owns a business which is not matrimonial or partnership property, the other (non-owner) party might devote time to the business. As a result the business becomes more profitable and more valuable. The non-owner might try to rely on s.9(1)(b) to seek an award to reflect part of the increased value. However, the owner might argue that the non-owner has enjoyed balancing economic advantages during the marriage or civil partnership through a better lifestyle as a result of the enhanced profit.[66]

It is important that the balancing exercise is carried out by the court. If there are countervailing economic advantages and disadvantages

---

[64] At p.394.
[65] *Adams v Adams (No.1)*, 1997 S.L.T. 144—see para.4–35.
[66] The argument will be weaker if much of the profit has been retained in the business rather than used by the parties during the marriage—see *Wilson v Wilson*, 1999 S.L.T. 249.

brought out in evidence, then the court must weigh these in the scales created by s.11(2). A failure to do this may render a decision fundamentally flawed.[67] In *Kennedy v Kennedy*, 2004 S.L.T.(Sh Ct) 102 Sheriff Principal Kerr commented[68]:

> "The Act requires by s.11(2) that a balancing exercise should be carried out in the manner there set out for the purposes of applying s.9(1)(b), which means that any countervailing economic advantages or disadvantages sustained on the other side are to be weighed against those sustained on the one side. No doubt there will be cases in which there exist no countervailing economic advantages or disadvantages on the other side to be so balanced but this was not one such, as is clear from [the sheriff's note] where he summarises the pursuer's submission to him that she had in this marriage suffered an economic disadvantage of the classic type (giving up a better paid job). Here then was an alleged economic disadvantage clearly requiring to be weighed in a balancing exercise under s.11(2). There appears to have been no attempt on the pursuer's side to quantify the extent of this disadvantage . . . but there is no mention of this feature of the case by the sheriff in his opinion or in his findings in fact and I am driven to the conclusion that no balancing exercise of the type required by s.11(2) was embarked on or even contemplated. In these circumstances I regard the sheriff's approach to any application by him of the principle in s.9(1)(b) as fundamentally flawed . . ."

The relationship of section 9(1)(b) and special circumstances

4–26   It is important to bear in mind that s.9(1)(b) sets out a s.9 principle in its own right which the court can use to make an award for financial provision. This is quite different from a "special circumstances" argument under ss.9(1)(a) and 10(6). Any application of special circumstances can only result in an "unequal" division of such matrimonial or partnership property as may exist. The importance of this distinction is apparent if we imagine a situation where there is no matrimonial or partnership property, and how special circumstances and s.9(1)(b) arguments might apply:

- *special circumstances*—even if special circumstances exist, these can have no effect as there is no property to divide unequally;
- *s.9(1)(b)*—the position is different. It may still be appropriate to make an award under s.9(1)(b).

At this point one could be forgiven for asking how any s.9(1)(b) award could be made if there is no matrimonial or partnership property. The answer can be found in *De Winton v De Winton*, 1997 S.L.T. 1118,[69] where there was no matrimonial property but, crucially, each party had valuable non-matrimonial assets. The wife made substantial non-

---

[67] See e.g. *Pressley v Pressley*, 2002 S.C.L.R. 804.
[68] At p.108.
[69] Outer House, Lord Cameron of Lochbroom.

financial contributions to the husband's business which allowed it to prosper. Section 9(1)(b) was successfully used, and the wife obtained an award to compensate her for the economic advantage her husband was gaining by taking the valuable business.[70] Even if there are no non-matrimonial or non-partnership assets or savings, an award under s.9(1)(b) may still be made and serviced out of income by payment of a capital sum by way of instalments.[71] For example in *Dougan v Dougan*, 1998 S.L.T. (Sh Ct) 27 the pursuer acknowledged that there could be no award under s.9(1)(a) as there was no matrimonial property to be divided, and successfully relied solely on s.9(1)(b). In that case the award was largely to be paid by annual instalments.[72]

In one case at least it has been suggested that there is a more fundamental distinction between, on the one hand, special circumstances and s.9(1)(a) which can only have a bearing on division of matrimonial or partnership property and, on the other hand, the other principles set out in s.9(1)(b) to (e) which can be applied to make orders out of non-matrimonial or non-partnership property. In *Jackson v Jackson*, 2000 S.C.L.R. 81, the court, whilst not ruling out the use of s.9(1)(b) where it had a bearing on matrimonial property, felt that its application was better restricted to cases where it simply had a bearing on non-matrimonial property. In other words, if there is matrimonial property to be divided, and a party wishes this to be divided unequally, then they should rely on special circumstances arguments rather than s.9(1)(b). This does not seem convincing. Section 9(1)(b)[73] stands alone and covers matters which are distinct from the special circumstances provisions of s.10(6). Whilst no doubt there will be an overlap from time to time, it seems unnecessarily restrictive to limit the application of paras (b) to (e) to awards bearing on non-matrimonial or non-partnership property.

It also has to be said that the courts have not always grasped the distinction between s.9(1)(b) arguments and special circumstances arguments. Some cases confuse the two provisions, or the judgements simply do not clearly state which provision is being used to justify the decision.[74] This can make the preparation of cases difficult, and it will probably be prudent to argue many cases on both bases.[75]

Quantification

Sometimes the quantification of a s.9(1)(b) claim can be straightfor-　4–27 ward. For example, in *Tahir v Tahir (No.2)*, 1995 S.L.T. 451, the husband took jewellery belonging to the wife, which was not matrimonial

---

[70] See also *Ranaldi v Ranaldi*, 1994 S.L.T. (Sh Ct) 25 where an award under s.9(1)(b) was made where the only significant asset was non-matrimonial.

[71] s.12(3).

[72] See also *Buchan v Buchan*, 1993 G.W.D. 24–1515.

[73] And for that matter s.9(1)(c), (d) and (e).

[74] See the detailed comments on *Farrell v Farrell*, 1990 S.C.L.R. 717 below at para.4–39; see also the comments of Sir Stephen Young in *Pressley v Pressley*, 2002 S.C.L.R. 804; see also Professor Thomson's commentary to the S.C.L.R. report in *Shipton v Shipton*, 1992 S.C.L.R. 23.

[75] The fact that it is probably best to argue a case on any available bases is demonstrated by *Livie v Livie*, 1992 G.W.D. 34–1639 where the court observed that it was surprised that it had not been asked to consider a s.9(1)(b) argument. Of course no award was made because the argument had not been made. The implications of the comments are clear enough.

property. The quantum of the s.9(1)(b) award here was the market value of the jewellery, since that was clearly the extent to which the wife had been economically disadvantaged and the husband advantaged. However, in many (if not most) cases matters will not be so clear cut, and it will often be difficult to put a definitive value on a s.9(1)(b) claim. The difficulties might be broadly categorised as follows.

1. Balancing considerations

4–28   As discussed in more detail at para.4–25 above, s.11(2) requires a balancing exercise to be carried out before an award under s.9(1)(b) is made. The "counter" advantages/disadvantages may tend to cancel one another out making precise analysis of quantum difficult.

2. Relationship with other factors

4–29   As discussed above, many reported cases do not clearly state whether s.9(1)(b) or some other factor is being relied upon. Equally there may be several different factors (e.g. other s.9 principles and perhaps special circumstances arguments) that in combination lead to the court's ultimate decision. It is often impossible to determine what financial weighting the court has placed on any one factor.[76]

3. Inconsistency of judicial methods of quantifying awards

4–30   The courts have used different methods of calculating awards under s.9(1)(b). Sometimes the court will use the principle to award a quantifiable extra amount to a party.[77] In other cases the court will use the principle to justify a skewing of the percentage division of matrimonial property away from equal sharing.[78] Accordingly, it is often nearly impossible for parties and their advisers to predict with any accuracy how s.9(1)(b) will be applied by the courts (if at all) to a particular set of facts.

4. Evidential problems

4–31   It may be very difficult to prove how much a claim under this principle is worth. For example, how does one prove how much a loss of earning capacity is worth? The disadvantaged party may have given up their career 20 years ago to look after the children. How can one accurately establish what they would have been earning now if they had not made the sacrifice?[79] In many cases the cost of proving the loss (perhaps by way of expert evidence) may outweigh any financial benefit to the party advancing the argument. An examination of decided cases demonstrates that the courts have not applied a consistent approach in relation to their requirements for proof. Sometimes the courts require a detailed

---

[76] See for example *Davidson v Davidson*, 1994 S.L.T. 506, where a combination of factors including s.9(1)(b) led to unequal division; see also *Jesner v Jesner*, 1992 S.L.T. 999.

[77] e.g. *Dougan v Dougan*, 1998 S.L.T. (Sh Ct) 27.

[78] So in *Loudon v Loudon*, 1994 S.L.T. 381, the court shared the overall matrimonial property 55/45 per cent.

[79] See e.g. *Cunningham v Cunningham*, 2001 Fam. L.R. 12 at para 2–32.

calculation of the loss or gain, whereas at others they will allow a "broad brush" approach to be used. For example in *Cunniff v Cunniff*, 1999 S.L.T. 992 the Lord Ordinary had held that the pursuer had suffered an economic disadvantage in the interests of the defender. On appeal the defender argued that no evidence had been led to allow the court to conclude that the pursuer was at the relevant date in any worse position in the job market than she would have been had she not married the defender. The Extra Division approved the Lord Ordinary's approach which had been one of "common sense" and "stating the obvious". It was held that there was ample material to show that the wife gave up work shortly after the marriage and within a short time had two daughters to raise at home. As Lord McCluskey observed[80]:

> "The Lord Ordinary was plainly not in any position to quantify these matters with any precision but I consider that he was clearly entitled to conclude that on an overall view there was a resulting imbalance between the parties relevant to this principle . . ."

Similarly, Lord Milligan commented in *Loudon v Loudon*, 1994 S.L.T. 381[81]:

> "The difference between [the wife's] earning potential now and what she would probably have been earning but for her marriage to the defender cannot be calculated with any accuracy but I think it reasonable to conclude that the pursuer has suffered a material economic disadvantage in this connection."

However, the courts have not always been so relaxed.[82] Contrast the foregoing comments with those of Sheriff Bell in *Quinn v Quinn*, 2003 S.L.T. (Sh Ct) 5[83]:

> "I was . . . concerned about the argument that the defender alone had contributed to the upkeep of the matrimonial home during the separation. The problem is quantifying this. There does not appear to be any agreed quantification or any evidence on which I could come to a quantification of this. Had there been then that is a matter that I could certainly have taken into account."

This approach appears to be supported by the comments of Sheriff Principal Kerr in *Kennedy v Kennedy*, 2004 S.L.T. (Sh Ct) 102[84]:

> "An immediately apparent problem is that there seems to have been no attempt by the sheriff or anyone else to quantify at the proof or in the judgment the extent of the economic advantage . . . That I

---

[80] At p.997.
[81] At p.385.
[82] In addition to the cases discussed below see also *Cunningham v Cunningham*, 2001 Fam. L.R. 12 at para.2–32.
[83] At p.7.
[84] At p.107.

would regard as an essential ingredient, even if done in broad terms only, of any exercise purporting to be carried out in application of the principle set out in s.9(1)(b)."

Of course, this difference in approach leaves solicitors in a rather difficult position when preparing a case involving a s.9(1)(b) argument. The onus of proving the economic advantage or disadvantage will rest with the party who is arguing for the adjustment, and they will need to make efforts to discharge that onus. The safe course (bearing in mind the comments in *Quinn* and *Kennedy* above) will be to gather up as much evidence of the financial effect of the advantage/disadvantage as possible. Although it may not be possible to establish the quantum of the loss or gain with absolute accuracy, every effort should be made to do so.[85] The pleadings on this matter should be as clear as possible. Evidence from appropriate witnesses should be available. Whilst the courts may not insist on a high level of detail in every case, it seems clear that, by preparing an argument on quantum as fully as possible, the risk of the courts rejecting the argument altogether will be minimised.

Cases

4–32   In this section some cases where s.9(1)(b) has been argued are examined and are grouped into broad categories.

Interruption of career

4–33   This is probably the most common use of s.9(1)(b). The argument used is that one spouse or partner has interrupted their career (often to bring up children). Thus (they argue) they have been economically disadvantaged because they have lost opportunity and advancement in their career. Their earning potential and promotion prospects have diminished. On the other hand, the other party has generally been economically advantaged, as they have been able to pursue and advance their career. It is useful when considering the cases to split the cases into successful and unsuccessful arguments.

(a)   Successful arguments

4–34 When looking at cases of this type which have been successfully argued,[86] it seems generally that there is a very clear imbalance in the economic advantages and disadvantages between the parties as a result of one party interrupting their career. This imbalance was clear in *Loudon v Loudon*, 1994 S.L.T. 381 where the wife had looked after the home and a child rather than pursuing employment. The couple had been married

---

[85] See e.g. *W v W*, 2004 Fam. L.R. 54 at para.68.
[86] In addition to the cases mentioned in detail below, see also *Kelly v Kelly*, 1992 G.W.D. 36–2130; *Toye v Toye*, 1992 S.C.L.R. 95; *Khan v Khan*, 2003 Fam. L.B. 61–7; *Luckwell v Luckwell*, 1992 G.W.D. 34—2005; *Clokie v Clokie*, 1993 G.W.D. 16–1059 and 1994 G.W.D. 3–149; *R v R*, 2000 Fam. L.R. 43; *Carrol v Carrol*, 2003 Fam. L.R.108; *Buchan v Buchan*, 2001 Fam. L.R. 48; *Burnside v Burnside*, 2007 G.W.D. 24—404; *McCormick v McCormick*, 1994 S.C.L.R. 958.

and living together for 17 years, and the wife had not worked for most of that period. Lord Milligan stated[87]:

> "I am left in no doubt whatsoever that [there] should be an allocation in which, in the whole circumstances, the pursuer receives more than 50 per cent of the matrimonial property . . . I find that on the question of economic disadvantage the pursuer is left economically disadvantaged to a material extent . . . The pursuer worked before the marriage but did not do so during the marriage. That she did not do so was not, I accept, due to any absolute insistence on the part of the defender that she should not work, but I interpret the evidence as indicating that he was content for her not to work. The defender is now well launched on a business career where he can command a high salary . . . The pursuer, on the other hand, requires to retrain in order to get back, as she put it, on the employment ladder. This she requires to do at the age of 45 years, which may well be problematical, at least so far as ending up with a well paid job is concerned."

The court held that, in the circumstances of this case, it was appropriate to divide the matrimonial property unequally with 55 per cent going to the pursuer and 45 per cent going to the defender.

Another case where the argument was successfully advanced was *Walker v Walker (No.1)*, 1989 S.C.L.R. 625 where the couple had been married and co-habiting for about 26 years. The wife had not worked for most of that time, but had run the house and had the main burden of looking after the children as they grew up. The evidence was that, by the time of the proof, there was no real prospect of her returning to paid work. The husband on the other hand had been able to build up his business throughout the marriage, partly as a result of the contributions made by the wife. The businesses should continue to provide him with a reasonable income after the divorce. Lord Morton of Shuna said[88]:

> "[The husband] thus has an advantage and the pursuer a disadvantage in terms of future income arising from the business built up by the contributions both parties made during the marriage."

Similarly, in *Cunniff v Cunniff*, 1999 S.L.T. 992, Lord McCluskey commented on some of the factors that supported an award under s.9(1)(b).[89] It is important to note how the economic advantages and disadvantages are weighed up by the court:

> ". . . the pursuer gave up work shortly after the marriage and, within a year or two, had two daughters to raise at home . . . The defender, however, continued to work full time and to gain additional qualifications. He was able to work in different parts of the

---

[87] At p.384.
[88] At p.627.
[89] At p.997.

world and the condition of his doing so was plainly that the pursuer remained at home and could not acquire additional relevant experience or further qualifications to increase her earning capacity."

In all the cases discussed so far there was an imbalance between the parties as a result of the decision that the wife give up employment to look after the home and children. In each case the husband advanced his career, whilst the wife gave something up: the wife in *Loudon* was in a position where she would have to retrain to get back on the career ladder; in *Walker* the wife was of an age where it was unlikely she would find paid work after the divorce; and in *Cunniff* the wife had lost the opportunity to advance her career through experience and education. In each case there is both an economic advantage to the husband and an economic disadvantage to the wife. The decision to stay at home has resulted in an economic imbalance.[90] This can be compared with the unsuccessful cases below, where there was no such imbalance.

(b)   Unsuccessful arguments

4–35 Section 9(1)(b) when read alongside s.11(2) involves a balancing exercise, weighing up all economic advantages and disadvantages. It is only if there is an overall imbalance that an award will be made.[91] A party who stays at home and looks after the family may be making a contribution to the other party, but this might be balanced by certain economic advantages. In *Adams v Adams (No.1)*, 1997 S.L.T. 144, an Outer House decision, Lord Gill said[92]:

> "The pursuer next relies on s.9(1)(b) (as read with s.9(2) and s.11(2)). She argues that the defender has enjoyed an economic advantage in that he has been able to further his career whereas she has prejudiced hers by bringing up the children. I accept that the pursuer has suffered an economic disadvantage in this respect. On the other hand in all the years during which they lived together, the defender contributed more than the pursuer to the household finances and during the periods when she was out of employment, he supported the family on his own. It is not suggested that the defender ever failed to maintain the family in a good standard of living. In my view this is a counterbalancing consideration which I am entitled by s.11(2) to apply. The pursuer's economic disadvantage is not the worst that she could have suffered. She was able to return to her professional employment soon after the birth of each child and she has for some considerable time been in full time pensioned employment and making her own contributions to a top up pension. I distinguish this case from a case such as *Loudon v Loudon*[93] where the property was divided in the proportions 55/45

---

[90] See also *Shipton v Shipton*, 1992 S.C.L.R. 23; *Toye v Toye*, 1992 S.C.L.R. 95; see also the commentaries at the end of each of these cases at in the S.C.L.R. reports.
[91] See e.g. *Little v Little*, 1989 S.C.L.R. 613.
[92] At p.148.
[93] 1994 S.L.T. 381.

per cent in the pursuer's favour largely on the basis that the pursuer was untrained and had no pension and that there was a great disparity between her assets and those of the defender (at 1994 S.L.T., p385C). I distinguish this case also from *McCormick v McCormick*,[94] where the wife was at a disadvantage in that it would be difficult for her to gain employment at her age in her former profession . . .; and from *Cunniff v Cunniff*[95] where the wife who received a transfer order had not worked for over 20 years, had an earning power not remotely comparable with that of her husband and, if not given the matrimonial home, would not have been able to afford alternative accommodation . . . I conclude therefore that in this case an unequal division in the pursuer's favour is not justified by s.9(1)(b)."

Another example of a case where the economic advantages and disadvantages were held to have balanced is *Welsh v Welsh*, 1994 S.L.T. 828 where the wife sought to argue that she had given up work and brought up the children. This, she argued, conferred an economic advantage on the husband by allowing him to maintain his income from employment; she was disadvantaged by giving up a good job. However, in this case Lord Osborne held that there was no significant imbalance. While the wife had given up her job and had thus suffered an economic disadvantage, it was also true that she enjoyed certain economic advantages—she had enjoyed the benefit of being supported by her husband and her husband's salary had allowed mortgage payments to be made with the result that she would benefit from any increase in value of the house.

Again in *Petrie v Petrie*, 1988 S.C.L.R. 390, the sheriff rejected a s.9(1)(b) argument. The parties co-habited from 1979 until 1983 and then married, separating in 1985. It is worth noting that the period of marriage was relatively short in comparison to most of the cases which have been argued successfully. This seems logical. It will be more difficult to argue that a short interruption of career has caused significant economic disadvantage.

Cases like *Petrie* and *Welsh* strongly suggest that, if the "stay-at-home" spouse or partner is to successfully sustain a s.9(1)(b) argument, they should stress the disadvantage they have sustained in foregoing *career prospects*. If they take a different approach and concentrate on the advantage conferred on the "working" spouse or civil partner by having someone look after the house, this advantage will often be counterbalanced by the enjoyment of income. In *Cunningham v Cunningham*, 2001 Fam. L.R. 12,[96] the wife had given up her career to look after home and family, and Lord Macfadyen accepted that as a result the family income had been diminished during the marriage. However, this was not of itself an economic disadvantage to the pursuer. He pointed out that there would have been a stronger point to be made if the pursuer had established that, had she not taken out time out from her work, she would have been more advanced in her career. However, the evidence did not allow any quantification to be made on this point.

---

[94] 1994 S.C.L.R. 958.
[95] OH, Lord Abernethy, unreported, August 31, 1994.
[96] At para.2–32.

Coyle v Coyle, 2004 Fam. L.R. 2 reinforces the point. The wife had given up her career to run the house and look after the children. The husband had valuable business interests which increased in value substantially over the course of the marriage. Lady Smith pointed out[97]:

> "It is important to recognise that Parliament did not, in the 1985 Act, provide that whenever a couple divorce after a marriage in which one has been the breadwinner and one has been the homemaker, the latter must receive extra and compensatory financial provision on divorce. The section [s.9(1)(b)] is quite specific. Before the principle here relied on can be taken into account it must be established that there has been an identifiable economic advantage which derives from an identifiable contribution by the other spouse and it must appear fair to the court to take account of it . . .
>
> In this case there was evidence that the pursuer managed the house and the children leaving the defender free to work. The defender's working day usually started very early, as was inevitable from the nature of the business of wholesale fruit and vegetable dealers operating from the fruit market. Clearly, if the pursuer had not been available to run the house and care for the children, other help would have had to be employed. However, on the evidence, if the pursuer had not been available that would have been because she would have been pursuing her own career, earning a significant salary and thus bringing more income into the household, from which the cost of help could have been met. That seems to me to be the correct approach rather than to ask what would the defender's financial position have been if he had not married.
>
> It does not follow, in my opinion, that the defender's net financial position would have been any less by reason of the need to employ help. In all the circumstances, even if it is the case that the defender's financial position, including the value of his interest in the company improved over the course of the marriage, I do not see that it can properly be characterised as the sustaining of an economic advantage that was derived from a contribution of the pursuer's. I am not, accordingly, persuaded that it would be appropriate to take this principle into account."

Increase in value of matrimonial/partnership property after separation

4–36 In a number of cases it has been argued that an increase in the value of matrimonial property (particularly the family home) after the date of separation results in economic advantage/disadvantage if one party is to retain the property after divorce or dissolution.[98] *Wallis v Wallis*[99] holds that such a rise in value does not of itself found a successful s.9(1)(b) argument. In that case the sheriff at first instance had ordered the

---

[97] At para.37.
[98] See e.g. *Phillip v Phillip*, 1988 S.C.L.R. 427; *Muir v Muir*, 1989 S.C.L.R. 445; *Quinn v Quinn*, 2003 S.L.T. (Sh Ct) 5.
[99] 1993 S.C. (H.L.) 49 and 1993 S.L.T. 1348 (House of Lords decision); 1992 S.C. 455 and 1992 S.L.T. 676 (Inner House).

transfer of the wife's one half share of the matrimonial home to the husband, and in return he awarded the wife a payment which took into account the increase in value of the house after the relevant date. The decision was upheld on appeal by the sheriff principal. The case was appealed to the Court of Session. One of the arguments maintained by the wife was that the increase in value of the house resulted in an economic advantage to the husband and a corresponding economic disadvantage to her. This argument was rejected by Lord President Hope[100]:

> ". . . the only economic disadvantage to the defender which has been identified in this case is the loss to her, in consequence of the transfer order, of one-half of the increase in value of the house after the relevant date. In my opinion that cannot be regarded as an economic disadvantage for the purposes of sec. 9(1)(b), since that provision is concerned not with the consequences of an order for financial provision but with one of the principles to be applied in deciding what financial provision, if any, is to be made."

So, the court stated clearly that the rise in value after the relevant date could not result in a successful economic advantage/disadvantage argument. If the court felt that an order to transfer an asset to a spouse was justified, then the other spouse would receive credit for half of the value at the relevant date, not the date of transfer (normally the date of divorce in a contested action). The Lord President continued[101]:

> "Section 11(2)(b) requires the court, for the purposes of sec.9(1)(b), to have regard to the extent to which an imbalance of economic advantage and disadvantage between the parties has been or may be corrected by a sharing of the value of the matrimonial property or otherwise. The sharing of the value of the matrimonial property which this provision contemplates is a sharing of the net value of the matrimonial property at the relevant date, as defined in sec. 10(2). There is no room here for a further adjustment to take account of the changes in the value of particular items of matrimonial property after the relevant date. Changes in their value after the relevant date may be taken into account when regard is had to the resources of the parties under sec. 8(2)(b). But that is a different matter . . ."

The House of Lords upheld this decision. The problems which this created are discussed elsewhere in this book.[102] Many of these difficulties will now be removed by the insertion of s.10(3A) of the 1985 Act;[103] and there is a more detailed discussion of this at para.5–06. However, s.10(3A) only resolves the *Wallis* problem in cases where an asset is to be transferred from one party to the other. In circumstances where the asset

---

[100] 1992 S.C. 455 at 462.
[101] At p.462.
[102] See para.5–06.
[103] Introduced by the Family Law (Scotland) Act 2006.

is not to be transferred,[104] but is to remain in the name of one of the parties, *Wallis* is still authority for the proposition that any rise in value is not to be considered an economic advantage in terms of s.9(1)(b).

Enjoyment of assets following the separation

4–37   There is an argument that if one party exclusively enjoys the use of an asset—most often the matrimonial or family home—after the date of separation, they gain an economic advantage. It should always be kept in mind that s.9(1)(b) requires there to have been *economic* advantage or disadvantage. It is not enough to argue that there has been a practical or tactical advantage or disadvantage. This point was raised in *Phillip v Phillip*, 1988 S.C.L.R. 427, where the house was in the husband's name and he continued to occupy it after the separation. It rose in value substantially. The wife argued that he had accordingly enjoyed an economic advantage within the meaning of s.9(1)(b). Sheriff Bowen stated[105]:

> ". . . the principle contained in section 9(1)(b) does not appear to me to have any bearing on the present situation. That speaks of fair account being taken of any economic advantage 'derived by either party from contributions by the other' and I do not see how the fact that the defender may have occupied the matrimonial home since the parties' separation could be described as a 'contribution' even giving that word the widest possible meaning."

The reasoning here seems to be open to criticism. The house was purchased during the marriage and was clearly matrimonial property, notwithstanding the fact that it was in the husband's name. Both parties appear to have been working during the marriage. Is it not reasonable to suggest that the wife made "contributions" during the marriage which allowed the parties to buy the house? Was it not partly these contributions which allowed the husband to live in the property rent free? It is certainly difficult to reconcile the decision with the comments in *Welsh v Welsh*, 1994 S.L.T. 828, where Lord Osborne seems to take a rather more expansive view in a similar situation[106]:

> "It is my view that the defender has enjoyed the economic advantage of living rent free since the relevant date in a house of which the pursuer was beneficial owner to the extent of a one half share. That advantage appears to me to be the counterpart of the economic disadvantage suffered by the pursuer in respect that she has, during the period in question, enjoyed no return from her

---

[104] e.g. in a case like *Phillip v Phillip*, 1988 S.C.L.R. 427, where the asset already stands in the sole name of one party and is not to be transferred or sold; see also *Tyrrell v Tyrrell*, 1990 S.L.T. 406 where the asset which increased in value after the separation was the pension fund in name of the husband—a s.9(1)(b) argument to the effect that the value at the date of the proof should be used rather than the value at the relevant date was rejected.

[105] At p.429.

[106] At p.836.

property in that respect. In my opinion, in these circumstances there is a clear imbalance as between the parties, which I ought to correct . . ."[107]

Expenditure after the divorce or dissolution

In some cases, one party may spend more money than the other on **4–38** the family after the separation but before the divorce or dissolution. This may result in an economic disadvantage to the "spending" party, and a corresponding advantage to the other. In *Macdonald v Macdonald*, 1993 S.C.L.R. 132,[108] after the separation, the husband was extravagant with his finances. The wife, on the other hand, had used her earnings for the benefit of the family: she paid for domestic help to assist with the care of the parties' large family and she maintained the matrimonial home. She had, following the separation, clearly made a greater economic contribution to the family. Lord Caplan took account of this factor in the orders made for financial provision.

The argument here is closely related to, but still distinct from, the principle set out in s.9(1)(c). Under that provision the court can take account of the economic burden of caring for the family *after divorce or dissolution*. However, para.(c) cannot be relied upon where the imbalance occurs between the relevant date and the date of decree—in these circumstances para.(b) can be applied to redress the imbalance.[109]

Payment of secured loan after separation

Sometimes one spouse or civil partner will continue to pay a loan **4–39** secured over heritage after the date of separation. Section 9(1)(b) has sometimes been deployed to argue that the other party accordingly has derived an economic advantage as a result. In *Kennedy v Kennedy*, 2004 S.L.T. (Sh Ct) 102, Sheriff Principal Kerr said[110]:

"I have no real difficulty in accepting the idea that the pursuer's occupancy of the defender's house during those six years subsequent to the separation . . . constituted an economic advantage within the meaning of s.9(1)(b) derived by her from contributions by him (funding of the endowment mortgage) being an advantage gained

---

[107] Perhaps the decisions in *Welsh v Welsh* and *Phillip v Phillip* are really more readily distinguished by the arguments on how the imbalance should be reflected. In *Phillip* it appears to have been argued that the non-resident spouse should be entitled to half of the increase in the value of the property after the relevant date should be awarded, whereas in *Welsh*, the argument was used simply to justify an award of interest on the capital sum awarded. See particularly the comments in *Welsh* at p.428. The party seeking to rely on s.9(1)(b) should always attempt to quantify their loss. See also para.4–31.

[108] Upheld 1994 G.W.D. 7–404.

[109] In *Macdonald v Macdonald* the court recognised that s.9(1)(c) arguments were also applicable since the wife would, after divorce, be assuming the greater responsibility for childcare.

[110] At p.107.

during the currency of the marriage and representing in effect a gain in income or revenue to her."[111]

Similarly, in *Kerrigan v Kerrigan*, 1988 S.C.L.R. 603, a case involving a very brief marriage where the husband had committed himself to continuing to pay the mortgage after the separation, Sheriff Evans stated[112]:

> ". . . I am entitled to take into fair account the fact that it is the pursuer who has all along paid off the mortgage, thereby increasing the value of the defender's share in the matrimonial home to his economic disadvantage and to her economic advantage derived from his contributions. Such a resulting imbalance should, if possible, be corrected in the instant action (vide section 9(1)(b) and section 11(2))."

There is a problem in examining some of the reported cases where this argument is advanced because it is sometimes difficult to determine exactly which principle the court is using to make its decision. In *Farrell v Farrell*, 1990 S.C.L.R. 717 the parties separated in July 1986. From the date of separation until the house was sold in 1989, the pursuer made all of the mortgage payments. Sheriff Stoddart stated[113]:

> "I reject totally the argument by [the defender's agent] that the pursuer has not suffered economic disadvantage in the interests of the defender. He has been relieved of his contractual obligation to pay the mortgage and he has been advantaged by the freeing of his funds for other purposes."

Although the words "economic disadvantage" are expressly used by the sheriff, it appears that the decision is actually justified by a special circumstances argument under s.10(6) rather than s.9(1)(b). It may be that cases can often be argued under both provisions.

The strength of the argument that payments towards the secured loan constitute an economic disadvantage will vary from case to case, and it is difficult to draw any general principles from the reported decisions. One problem is that on-going payments of this type may be viewed as part of an obligation to aliment the other party or children who continue to occupy the property—if so, then it is unlikely that the court will accept that an economic disadvantage has been suffered by the non-resident

---

[111] Although in that case the sheriff principal held that, because there had been no attempt at first instance to quantify the extent of the economic advantage, even if only in broad terms, the application of s.9(1)(b) was not justified. See also *Muir v Muir*, 1989 S.L.T. (Sh Ct) 20 at p.21—in that case there was an argument regarding whether the equity in a house should be shared equally; the sheriff appears to reach the conclusion that the wife may have made some non-economic contributions to running the household during the marriage; this had allowed the parties to retain the asset; but balanced against this was the fact that she had made no economic contributions to the asset since the separation; he split the equity equally between them.

[112] At p.605.

[113] At p.727.

paying party. An example of a rejection of the argument can be found in *McKenzie v McKenzie*, 1991 S.L.T. 461. The parties separated in 1987. From the date of separation until the proof, the wife continued to stay in the matrimonial home with an adult child. During this period the husband paid the mortgage. The husband argued that this had conferred an economic advantage on the wife and an economic disadvantage on him. Lord Prosser rejected this contention[114]:

> ". . . the pursuer's past enjoyment of the house since separation, and the defender's payments in respect of the house over that period, are more properly to be seen as aspects of the interim regulation of aliment which will be necessary in cases such as this."[115]

Other expenditure on matrimonial/partnership assets after separation

This is closely related to the arguments set out in the previous section. **4–40** The absent party may expend money on items other than the mortgage (e.g. maintenance of property, insurance payments and the like). A party advancing the argument should have clear pleadings and evidence on the amount they have spent.[116]

Improvements to non-matrimonial/non-partnership heritable property

One party may own heritage that is not a matrimonial or partnership **4–41** asset. Examples might include houses inherited by or gifted to one party, or houses owned by one party prior to the marriage or registration. The non-owner might spend a considerable amount of time and labour improving the property and this might increase its value. On occasion non-owners have used s.9(1)(b) to try to claw back the economic advantage gained by the other.

In *Cahill v Cahill*, 1998 S.L.T. (Sh Ct) 96, the defender and her sister were joint owners of a cottage which had been inherited by them. The pursuer had devoted considerable time and effort to improving the cottage, which having been in a barely tenantable condition before these efforts, ultimately became an asset capable of producing a reasonable rent. After the separation, the husband ceased to receive any share of the rent. In upholding the sheriff's decision that this constituted an economic advantage to the wife, Sheriff Principal Bowen commented[117]:

> "There can be no doubt that advantage to the defender as joint owner of the property was gained when the pursuer carried out the improvements to the cottage. It may be that the benefit of that advantage has not been realised until a subsequent date, but it does not in my view detract from the fact that the advantage was gained.

---

[114] At p.462.
[115] See also the comments of Sheriff Bell in *Quinn v Quinn*, 2003 S.L.T. (Sh Ct) 5— "There is no economic disadvantage to the defender in providing accommodation for his daughters."
[116] *Quinn v Quinn*, 2003 S.L.T. (Sh Ct) 5—see para.4–31.
[117] At p.99.

To take any other view would result in ignoring the improvement which the sheriff in my view properly regarded as 'contributions' on the part of the pursuer within the meaning of s.9(1)(b). I accordingly interpret the word 'gained' as meaning 'obtained' rather than 'accrued' . . . the economic advantage is derived from the asset which produces the income, not the income itself."

Contribution to businesses

4–42　　Sometimes one spouse or civil partner will own a business which is not matrimonial or partnership property. During the course of the marriage or partnership, the non-owner may devote considerable time, labour and skill to the business. This may result in an increase in its value, but the business itself will still be excluded from the pool of matrimonial or partnership property.[118] It may be possible to use s.9(1)(b) to redress the economic advantage gained by the owner spouse or civil partner.[119] This is an important protection for the non-owner.

In *Vance v Vance*, 1997 S.L.T. (Sh Ct) 71 the wife claimed that profits earned by the husband's farming business had been retained within the business. It was accepted that the business itself was not matrimonial property as the husband had owned his interest in the business before the marriage. The wife stated that she had assisted with the business in various ways and that it was open to her to argue that this resulted in an economic advantage to her husband in that it had allowed the business to grow during the course of the marriage. The court held that an argument on this line was relevant and admitted the case to proof. Although the increase in the value of the business was not matrimonial property, it was a resource which was available to meet a claim under s.9(1)(b). Similarly, in *Ranaldi v Ranaldi*, 1994 S.L.T. (Sh Ct) 25, the husband owned a boarding house which was not matrimonial property. The wife helped to run it and brought up the children of the marriage. Here the wife was awarded one half of the enhancement in value of the property.

Clearly the extent of any contribution will be important,[120] and some care has to be taken here to consider whether there are any economic advantages to the non-owner which counter-balance the disadvantages. If the business has produced substantial income during the course of the marriage or civil partnership, it might be argued that the non-owner has had the economic advantage of that income which may have been used to buy matrimonial or partnership assets; to purchase investments; or even simply to improve the lifestyle of the parties. It might be argued that these advantages counterbalance any disadvantage suffered by the non-owner. This objection will be harder to maintain if the profits of the business have not been of much benefit to the parties during the marriage or civil partnership. In *Wilson v Wilson*, 1999 S.L.T. 249, the husband owned a farming business which was not a matrimonial asset.

---

[118] Unless there has been substantial restructuring—see para.6–28.

[119] See e.g. *De Winton v De Winton*, 1997 S.L.T. 1118.

[120] See e.g. *Johnston v Johnston*, 2004 Fam. L.B. 70–6; although sometimes a small contribution will be enough to justify a significant award—see *Marshall v Marshall*, 2007 Fam. L.R. 48.

The profits were retained in the business rather than used for funding the couple's lifestyle. In allowing a s.9(1)(b) argument Lord Marnoch commented[121]:

> "In the present case it seems to me self evident that the defender could not have run his farming enterprise as successfully as he did had the pursuer, for her part, not throughout looked after the family home and the two children of the marriage. No attempt was made, even had it been possible, to place a value on the pursuer's services as housekeeper and nanny but it cannot be doubted that, even in stark financial terms, the contribution made by the pursuer in these respects was very considerable indeed. And, although the pursuer made no complaint anent the adequacy of the financial support which she received from the defender during the 17 years of the marriage, there was no evidence to suggest that the parties' lifestyle was in any way affluent. But, therefore, for the defender's decision to retain or plough back in the company the profits in question I do not doubt that that lifestyle could have been substantially improved. In any event, and for whatever reason, the pursuer has been denied, up to now, any share in the profits in question."

It appears that the contributions of the non-owner do not need to be contributions directly related to the business.[122] In some cases indirect contributions which have allowed the business to prosper have been taken into account. In *Walker v Walker (No.1)*, 1989 S.C.L.R. 625, the wife gave up work early to look after home and family. This allowed her husband to build up his businesses. At the end of the marriage, the husband could command a reasonable income, whereas the wife had no real prospect of returning to work. Lord Morton of Shuna held that application of s.9(1)(b) was appropriate.

Sacrifice of business interests

In *Skarpaas v Skarpaas*, 1991 S.L.T. (Sh Ct) 15, the husband suffered **4–43** serious injuries in an accident. The wife had to give up her boarding house business to look after him. This resulted in an economic disadvantage to her which the sheriff took into account.

Conduct of the parties

In applying s.9(1)(b) the court is not to take into account the conduct **4–44** of either party unless the conduct has adversely affected the financial resources which are relevant to the decision of the court on a claim for

---

[121] At p.254.
[122] See e.g. *Marshall v Marshall*, 2007 Fam. L.R. 48. See also the discussion in Joe Thomson, "Swings and Roundabouts?", S.L.G. 1998 66(4) 202–3. It might be argued that the critical issue is not whether the contribution is linked to the business. Rather, one should firstly look at whether the contribution (be it directly to the business or otherwise) justifies an award in terms of s.9(1)(b). Non-economic contributions (e.g. by bringing up the family and allowing the other party to devote more time to building up the business) may have a significant economic benefit to the business. If this is the case, a s.9(1)(b) award can be justified. The business is a resource in terms of s.8(2)(b), and that resource can be used to fund the payment.

financial provision.[123] So, the general rule is that adverse conduct will not be taken into account. However, if the conduct adversely affects the resources of the parties then this will be a relevant consideration and s.9(1)(b) may well be the correct provision give redress. For example, in *Skarpaas v Skarpaas*, 1991 S.L.T. (Sh Ct) 15 the husband had regularly consumed alcohol to excess, thus depleting the parties' resources. Unequal division of the matrimonial property was justified in terms of s.9(1)(b).

Use of non-matrimonial/non-partnership assets or income

4–45   One party might exclusively own non-matrimonial or non-partnership assets, but these might be used for the benefit of the other party or the family. So, in *Boyes v Boyes*, 1996 Fam. L.B. 20–6 the wife inherited money. She spent this on the family. It was held by the sheriff that she had suffered an economic disadvantage and she obtained an award under s.9(1)(b) to compensate her. Similarly, in *Davidson v Davidson*, 1994 S.L.T. 506 (an Outer House decision) the wife had made two gifts to the husband of her own non-matrimonial property—£10,000 to acquire equipment for his business and £1,500 to buy a car. Lord Maclean said[124]:

> "It is possible to regard the sums of £10,000 and £1,500 which were contributed by the pursuer to the defender, as economic advantages gained by the defender in terms of s9(1)(b) and 9(2)."

Another way in which non-matrimonial or non-partnership assets could confer an economic advantage would be if they produce an income during the marriage or civil partnership.[125] Also if, after separation, the income of one party is used for the benefit of the other party, this might allow a successful s.9(1)(b) argument.[126]

Retention of property belonging to the other party

4–46   If one party retains non-matrimonial or non-partnership property belonging to the other and does not return this, this may allow a successful s.9(1)(b) argument.[127]

Alimentary obligations to third parties

4–47   If one party pays aliment to children of another relationship, the other party might argue that they have suffered an economic disadvantage as a result of the use of matrimonial or partnership funds for the benefit of a

---

[123] s.11(7). See paras 4–12 to 4–13.
[124] At p.508.
[125] See the comments of Sheriff Principal Nicholson in *McVinnie v McVinnie (No.2)*, 1997 S.L.T. (Sh Ct) 12 at p.14. However, it must be remembered that during the marriage or civil partnership both parties owe an obligation of aliment to one another. Income from non-matrimonial or non-partnership assets might, in many cases, be regarded as payments towards that alimentary obligation.
[126] See *Galloway v Galloway*, 2002 G.W.D. 40–1349 and 2003 Fam. L.R. 10.
[127] *Tahir v Tahir (No 2)*, 1995 S.L.T. 451.

third party. The courts have rejected this argument. In *Hunter v Hunter*, 1996 S.C.L.R. 329 the pursuer argued that she had suffered economic disadvantage during the marriage because her husband had been paying £15 per week to support his children by a previous marriage. Sheriff Principal Risk commented[128]:

> "I am sometimes unsure of Parliament's intention in certain sections of the 1985 Act,[129] but . . . it cannot have been Parliament's intention that the fulfilment of a father's alimentary obligation to his children should render him liable to a further financial claim at the instance of his wife . . . In my opinion, the situation at which s.9(1)(b) and (2) is principally aimed is that in which a wife has given up a promising career, or even just regular employment, in order to look after the house and the children and/or to support her husband's career, with the result that when divorce occurs in middle age all of the property appears to have been acquired by the husband. No doubt the sections will cover other less obvious situations, but in my opinion they cannot be stretched so far as to cover the situation in the instant case."

Higher earnings during the marriage or partnership

If one party earns more than the other during the marriage or **4–48** partnership, this is not in itself a justification for a s.9(1)(b) award. The appeal to the sheriff principal in the case of *Pressley v Pressley*, 2002 S.C.L.R. 804 illustrates this. At first instance the sheriff had commented[130]:

> "While it is undoubtedly the case that the pursuer was earning during the currency of the marriage . . . there is no evidence to demonstrate that the defender made an equal contribution to the marital resources, whether in money or in money's worth. Indeed, it seems to me that the greater contribution by far was made by the pursuer who, at the same time, was contributing to the payment of the defender's debts and other expenditure, for example, on cigarettes and alcohol while at the same time, making a financial contribution to the upkeep of their home and to the marriage.
>
> There is therefore no doubt in my mind that in terms of s.9(1)(b) the defender gained an economic advantage throughout his relationship with the pursuer from the financial and other contributions made by her. It would therefore follow that the pursuer suffered an economic disadvantage in that she was not able to save as much as she might have been able to do had she not been contributing to the upkeep of the defender directly and indirectly, directly by purchasing food etc, and indirectly by relieving him of at least some of his debt."

On appeal Sheriff Principal Sir Stephen Young confessed that he found this reasoning difficult to follow[131]:

---

[128] At p.330.
[129] Aren't we all?
[130] At p.810.
[131] At p.811.

"Even if it be true that the defender derived an economic advantage from the pursuer's contributions and that she suffered a corresponding disadvantage, it is not clear to me how it can be said that the sheriff carried out the balancing exercise required by s.11(2) of the Act . . . My impression is that the pursuer's earnings during the marriage were higher than those of the defender. If this be correct, then it seems to me only to be expected that she should have contributed more towards the upkeep of the family than the defender (to his corresponding economic advantage) and also that she should have saved more of her income than him, and it scarcely seems fair that she should on this account alone be found entitled on the breakdown of the marriage to a larger proportion of the matrimonial property than she might otherwise have had."

Inappropriate financial advice when separation foreseeable

4–49 In *Kelly v Kelly*, 1992 G.W.D. 36–2130 the wife had been employed for about 11 years prior to the marriage. She returned to part time work later in the marriage and was given the chance to buy back valuable pension rights. The husband at this point was in a position to foresee the breakdown of the marriage. He had also concealed debt from his wife. He dissuaded her from exercising these rights, and the sheriff held that the wife suffered economic disadvantage as a result.

PRINCIPLE (C)—ECONOMIC BURDEN OF CHILD CARE

Key statutory provisions

4–50 Section 9(1)(c) of the 1985 Act provides that one of the principles to be applied in deciding what order for financial provision may be appropriate is that:

"any economic burden of caring, should be shared fairly between the persons—

(i) after divorce, for a child of the marriage under the age of 16 years;
(ii) after dissolution of the civil partnership, for a child under that age who has been accepted by both partners as a child of the family."

This should be read alongside s.11(3) which provides:

"For the purposes of s.9(1)(c) of this Act, the court shall have regard to—

(a) any decree or arrangement for aliment for the child;
(b) any expenditure or loss of earning capacity caused by the need to care for the child;
(c) the need to provide suitable accommodation for the child;
(d) the age and health of the child;

(e) the educational, financial and other circumstances of the child;
(f) the availability and cost of suitable child-care facilities or services;
(g) the needs and resources of the persons;[132] and
(h) all the other circumstances of the case."

Section 27(1) defines the term "child" as including:

"a child whether or not his parents have ever been married to one another, and any reference to the child of a marriage (whether or not subsisting) includes a child (other than a child who has been boarded out with the parties, or one of them, by a local or other public authority or a voluntary organisation) who has been accepted by the parties as a child of the family;".

General discussion

Cases turn on their own facts

There are surprisingly few reported cases dealing with this principle in **4–51** any detail. Those that do tend to turn very much on their own facts and it is difficult to tease out any clear guidelines on the way that the courts will apply the principle. The comments of Sheriff Principal Nicholson in *Millar v Millar*, 1990 S.C.L.R. 666 are illustrative[133]:

"During the course of the hearing I was referred to a number of cases in which awards of periodical allowance were in issue. I think that it was recognised that each of them turned on its own facts, and I have not found it necessary to refer to any of them."

Relationship with other principles

Matters are further confused because the courts have not always been **4–52** clear as to whether an award has been made under this principle or using other provisions of the Act.[134] Even if the court is clear in stating that s.9(1)(c) applies, it may be the case that other principles are also operating and it is often impossible to determine what financial impact s.9(1)(c) has had on the quantum of the decision.[135] It may sometimes be possible to reach the same conclusion in a case using either s.9(1)(c) or a special circumstances argument under s.10(6).[136] It will often be sensible to plead a case using both arguments.

---

[132] s.27(1) defines "needs" as including present and foreseeable needs; and "resources" means present and foreseeable resources.

[133] At p.671.

[134] See e.g. *Shipton v Shipton*, 1992 S.C.L.R. 23 where the pursuer was awarded periodical allowance, but it is not clear whether this was under s.9(1)(c), (d) or (e).

[135] See *Davidson v Davidson*, 1994 S.L.T. 506.

[136] See the pursuer's arguments in *Peacock v Peacock*, 1993 S.C. 88; see also *Toye v Toye*, 1992 S.C.L.R. 95 and in particular Professor Thomson's commentary to the S.C.L.R. report.

Periodical allowance or a clean break?

4-53   If the court considers that an award under s.9(1)(c) is justified then the full range of orders is available to the court in terms of s.8(1). This includes, under s.13(2), the power to make an order for periodical allowance, provided that the court is satisfied that an order for payment of a capital sum, for transfer of property or a pension sharing order would be inappropriate or insufficient to satisfy the requirements of s.8(2) of the Act.[137] This is often referred to as the "clean break" principle.[138] Every time the court is applying s.9(1)(c), it should consider carefully whether a "clean break" order would satisfy the principle. So, in a case such as *Morrison v Morrison*, 1989 S.C.L.R. 574, where an award under s.9(1)(c) was justified, periodical allowance was held not to be appropriate because unequal division of capital assets could see justice done. However, in *Proctor v Proctor*, 1994 G.W.D. 30–1814 periodical allowance was justified because payment of a capital sum from the available resources would have been insufficient to redress the imbalance. The case of *Maclachlan v Maclachlan*, 1998 S.L.T. 693 quite strongly suggests that periodical allowance (which is essentially provision of income) will often now be inappropriate under s.9(1)(c) because of the impact of the Child Support Act, whereas capital awards may still be appropriate in certain circumstances.[139]

Age of the children

4-54   Section 9(1)(c) refers to children under the age of 16, so it might be thought that awards made under this section will generally continue to the date that the children become 16, but this is not necessarily the case. In *Monkman v Monkman*, 1988 S.L.T. (Sh Ct) 37 the sheriff at first instance made an award of periodical allowance which appears to have been justified on the grounds of s.9(1)(c). The periodical allowance was to continue for 10 years but the child concerned would have turned 16 some six years after the date of the award. On appeal Sheriff Principal Caplan said[140]:

> "As the parties' circumstances stand at the moment I should not be inclined to interfere with the award of periodical allowance which the sheriff proposes. I accept that the sheriff should not take into account expenditure incurred by the pursuer on the child after she attains sixteen years of age. However it is not clear that the sheriff has done this. He may well be of the view that if a higher level of accommodation were maintained until the daughter is 16, some years may reasonably be required thereafter for the pursuer to readjust her domestic arrangements. Moreover the defender has a limited income and no capital. It may therefore be in his own interest that any contribution he ought properly to make to the

---

[137] s.13(2); *Morrison v Morrison*, 1989 S.C.L.R. 574; *Maclachlan v Maclachlan*, 1997 G.W.D. 8–339; *Monkman v Monkman*, 1988 S.L.T. (Sh Ct) 37.

[138] See para.3–34.

[139] Discussed in more detail at paras 4–60 to 4–67 below.

[140] At pp.38–9.

pursuer's extra outlay while the child is under 16 should be somewhat deferred by being spread over a rather longer period than six years."

The order must be reasonable having regard to the parties' resources

Even if an award is justified in terms of s.9(1)(c), the court must **4–55** decide whether a particular order is reasonable having regard to the resources of the parties.[141] For example in *Millar v Millar*, 1990 S.C.L.R. 666 Sheriff Principal Nicholson declined to make an award of periodical allowance under s.9(1)(c) commenting[142]:

"... in my opinion I do not consider that an award of periodical allowance would be reasonable in this case having regard to the resources of the parties ... Looking at the available resources of the parties, it is clear that neither of them is well off. The defender's income is greater than that of the pursuer, but so are his outlays."

Even if the court feels that an award under s.9(1)(c) is justified, the requirement that the order must be reasonable may affect the *way* that the court structures its order. For example, in *Macdonald v Macdonald*, 1993 S.C.L.R. 132, Lord Caplan accepted that an award in favour of the wife was justified by s.9(1)(c), but he refused to grant the wife's crave to transfer the matrimonial home to her because this would give her an "exceptional and unreasonable advantage". So, instead he awarded her a higher capital sum than equal sharing would dictate, and ordered that the house be sold.[143]

The court has to look at the situation as a whole in assessing the reality of the economic burden of caring for the child. In *Millar v Millar*, 1990 S.C.L.R. 666 the sheriff at first instance acknowledged that the pursuer would bear a greater share of the economic burden of child care, but pointed out that any imbalance between the parties could largely be redressed by an appropriate award of aliment. On appeal Sheriff Principal Nicholson considered whether aliment for the child was an appropriate issue for the court to consider in assessing whether an award should be made under s.9(1)(c)[144]:

"... it would in my opinion be unreasonable to consider the principle without at the same time considering such other resources as there may be to alleviate the burden of caring for a child of the marriage. Such resources might come from, for example, a trust fund in the child's favour, or they might come, as in this case, from an alimentary provision enforceable against a former spouse. It is in my opinion the totality of the situation which must be looked at when considering the principle set out in s.9(1)(c)."

---

[141] Section 8(2). See paras 3–02 to 3–08.
[142] At p.672.
[143] There is a useful discussion of the balancing act which the court requires to perform in terms of s.8(2) at pp.134–5.
[144] At p.671.

If the principle is used to justify an award in favour of one party, then it is of course the case that the other party will have correspondingly fewer resources. It may be desirable to give one party a large award, but if the effect of this would create an injustice to the other party, then the award will be inappropriate. In *Murley v Murley*, 1995 S.C.L.R. 1138, Lord MacLean was convinced under the principle that, if possible, the matrimonial home should be transferred to the wife and thus retained for the benefit of the children but confessed[145]: "The difficulty I have is with the imbalance in favour of the pursuer." The court dealt with this imbalance in a creative and apparently very fair way. The approach Lord MacLean took was to transfer the husband's share of the house to the wife, but to order the wife to grant a standard security to the husband to the extent of £24,000 (which was the amount of the economic imbalance between the parties which the transfer caused). The sum of £24,000 was to be repaid when the house was sold or when the younger child of the marriage reached 18, whichever was earlier.[146]

If a party has responsibilities to a second family, then the court can take that into account when assessing a claim under s.9(1)(c), even if there is no legal obligation to provide aliment.[147]

A relative matter

4–56   The factors in s.11(3) will depend on the particular circumstances of any couple and any child. So, for one child in particular circumstances, it may be appropriate to use s.9(1)(c) to seek a substantial award designed to pay for private schooling,[148] or to allow a party to retain an expensive family home.[149] In other circumstances an award to cover such costs may be wholly inappropriate.

Payments under section 9(1)(c) may be alimentary in nature

4–57   Payments under s.9(1)(c) may be alimentary in nature, with the result that the party against whom payment is ordered may require to continue the payments notwithstanding their discharge from bankruptcy.[150] Even if the award under s.9(1)(c) was of a capital sum, it may be considered to be alimentary if the award was made to allow the sum to be invested so that an income is produced for the payee.[151]

Conduct

4–58   The court is not to take into account the conduct of either party unless the conduct has adversely affected the financial resources which are relevant to the decision of the court on a claim for financial provision.[152]

---

[145] At p.1139.
[146] In this case the court did not grant interest on the figure of £24,000 but in other cases this might be appropriate.
[147] s.11(6).
[148] See e.g. *Macdonald v Macdonald*, 1993 S.C.L.R. 132; *Maclachlan v Maclachlan*, 1998 S.L.T. 693.
[149] See e.g. *Murley v Murley*, 1995 S.C.L.R. 1138.
[150] *Lessani v Lessani*, 2007 Fam. L.R. 81 at para. 14.
[151] *Lessani v Lessani*, 2007 Fam. L.R. 81 at para. 14; *Van den Boogard v Laumen* [1997] QB 759, [1997] All E.R. (EC) 517; *AB v CD*, 2007 Fam L.R. 53 at para.25.
[152] s.11(7). See paras 4–12 to 4–14.

Quantification

It will often be difficult to quantify a claim under this provision. It may **4–59** be difficult to predict with accuracy the impact of the costs of child-care.[153] Further, s.9(1)(c) is sometimes applied by the court along with other s.9 principles and with special circumstances arguments. As a result, even when unequal division results, it is difficult to determine to what extent the court has relied on the principle (and the financial value placed on it).[154] In one case the court made an award of a capital sum under s.9(1)(c) and calculated this by applying a multiplier to the amount of interim aliment being paid immediately before the decree,[155] but this approach will not be appropriate in all cases.

However, the fact that the cases are often unclear on the precise financial effect of the application of s.9(1)(c), does not excuse agents from seeking to establish as clear an argument on quantum as they possibly can.[156] In *Maclachlan v Maclachlan*, 1998 S.L.T. 693, there was an argument made to the effect that there should be a s.9(1)(c) award to the wife to cover school fees. However the evidence regarding provision for the costs of these fees was "rather vague". Lord Macfadyen commented[157]:

> ". . . I do not regard the evidence of the cost of such provision as of a sufficiently reliable quality. I see no reason why a proper formal estimate could not have been obtained and lodged in process."

Section 9(1)(c)—Relationship with the Child Support Act 1991

An argument against the continued application of section 9(1)(c)

Section 9(1)(c) has been relied on considerably less since the Child **4–60** Support Act 1991 ("the 1991 Act") came into force. The intent of s.9(1)(c) was that the party with care of the children should be entitled to something above and beyond aliment—aliment was for the child, but an award under s.9(1)(c) was for the party with the main financial burden of caring for the child. However, the 1991 Act requires a non-resident parent to contribute to the maintenance of children. The 1991 Act provides a formula for calculating the maintenance payable. The original formula provided in the 1991 Act (used in what are colloquially known as "old rules" cases) included an element for maintenance of the child (what would have been thought of as aliment before the 1991 Act was introduced), *and* an element for the living expenses of the parent with care[158] (which traditionally would have been dealt with using s.9(1)(c)). Accordingly, after the 1991 Act came into force there was a strong

---

[153] See e.g. *Macdonald v Macdonald*, 1993 S.C.L.R. 132 where a combination of factors including s.9(1)(c) led Lord Caplan to the conclusion that it was impossible to estimate the financial impact of these on "a fine basis".

[154] See e.g. *Macdonald v Macdonald*, 1993 S.C.L.R. 132.

[155] *Lessani v Lessani*, 2007 Fam. L.R. 81 at para.15.

[156] See e.g. *Munro v Munro*, 2006 Fam. L.R. 50.

[157] At p.699.

[158] See e.g. the commentary by Edward Jacobs and Gillian Douglas to "Child Support: The Legislation", 1999 at p.158.

argument (set out in full by E.M Clive in *The Law of Husband and Wife in Scotland*[159]) that in many cases there was no longer justification for an award under s.9(1)(c) because the Child Support Agency's maintenance assessment included account of the factors which might justify such an award. The Child Support, Pensions and Social Security Act 2000 introduce a new method of calculation of child support, and cases under the new regime are generally referred to as "new rules" cases. Put simplistically, "new rules" cases calculate child support based on a straightforward percentage of the non-resident parent's income, whereas "old rules" cases used the rather more complex procedure referred to by Clive. Although it is difficult to find direct authority for the proposition in "new rules" cases, the ethos of the 1991 Act remains to provide a straightforward and comprehensive means of providing maintenance for children (the "new rules" simplified the method of calculation, not this underlying ethos) and Clive's comments appear to remain pertinent for "new rules" cases.

In some rare cases, aliment for a child can still be subject to the jurisdiction of the court rather than the Child Support Agency. However, following amendment to the Family Law (Scotland) Act 1985 s.4, the court can now, in making an award for aliment, include in the award reasonable provision for the expenses of the person with care.[160] So even in these cases, the application of s.9(1)(c) is likely to be limited.

Section 9(1)(c)—A continuing role

4–61   In spite of the arguments outlined above, the courts have continued to make awards justified under s.9(1)(c).[161] Some situations where an award may be appropriate are considered below.

(1) Parent with little income but substantial capital

4–62   Section 9(1)(c) may still have a role if the absent parent has significant capital assets at the date of divorce or dissolution, but an income insufficient to allow any significant contribution by way of child support. This was the position in *Khan v Khan*, 2002 G.W.D. 38–1259, where it was held that the economic burden of child care was likely to be met almost wholly by Mrs Khan for the foreseeable future.[162]

(2) Unusual burden of care

4–63   The Child Support Agency's maintenance calculation uses a mathematical formula. In some cases, this may not take account of especially costly provision which may need to be made for some children, particularly those with disabilities or other special needs. In *Proctor v Proctor*, 1994 G.W.D. 30–1814 the wife sought an award under s.9(1)(c).

---

[159] 4th edn, para.24.071.

[160] s.4(4).

[161] See e.g. *Russell v Russell*, 1996 Fam. L.B. 21–5; *W v W*, 2003 Fam. L.B. 63–6; 2003 G.W.D. 13–427.

[162] It should be noted that the sale of the property was not reasonable here—it would have disrupted the lives of the children, and Mrs Khan's share of the free proceeds would not have been enough to provide suitable alternative accommodation.

Sheriff Bell observed that, although his decision was complicated by the fact that the Child Support Agency had not by the time of the proof made an assessment, it remained clear that the wife would suffer unusual economic disadvantage in looking after the children. In particular, in that case it was held to be reasonable that the wife should give up work to look after one of the children who had a medical condition. A capital sum from the available resources was insufficient to redress the imbalance and periodical allowance was also ordered.[163]

(3) No realistic prospect of payment of child support

In some cases a party may have shown themselves to be very **4–64** unreliable in meeting obligations to the children. It may be clear from the evidence that there is little realistic prospect of the party paying child support. The case of *Gray v Gray*, 2001 S.C.L.R. 681 suggests that s.9(1)(c) arguments may be stronger in these circumstances. The decision is not entirely clear on the matter of which principle is being applied, but there is a discussion of s.9(1)(c). The pursuer accepted that the Child Support Agency was now responsible for securing support, but pointed out that the husband was a man who had consistently refused to honour his obligations—he had failed to pay money which the court had ordered that he pay, and he had failed to honour an undertaking that he gave to the court. Sheriff Stewart was satisfied that the wife would have the greatest difficulty in enforcing any payment ordered by the Child Support Agency.[164]

(4) No payments being made under the 1991 Act

In *Donoghue v Donoghue*, 2000 G.W.D. 15–608, the wife sought **4–65** unequal sharing through a transfer of various items of matrimonial property which amounted to about two-thirds of the agreed net value of the matrimonial property. There were three children under 16. At the time of the proof the husband was unemployed. The sheriff granted the orders sought by the wife and (in part) relied on s.9(1)(c) to justify the award. The sheriff found that, if the matrimonial home was to be sold, then it was difficult to see how the wife could provide a home that was adequate for the needs of the children using her share of matrimonial property. The current property was convenient for the children's school and had always been the family home. Sheriff Bell observed that the husband's argument that the impact of the Child Support Act 1991 had reduced the general importance of s.9(1)(c) was acceptable as a general proposition, but had no relevance to the current case because the husband had not paid anything under the 1991 Act.

However, the other side of this coin is that, if it seems likely that the absent parent will provide reasonable maintenance if they become

---

[163] See also E.M. Clive, *The Law of Husband and Wife in Scotland* 4th edn, at para.24.072.

[164] A s.9(1)(c) award might be easier to enforce than an obligation to pay child support. The court need not use s.9(1)(c) to order payment of a periodical allowance, but might instead order a transfer of property, or payment of a capital sum. These "one off" orders might be easier to enforce than on-going payments where the obligant is likely to default.

employed, then an award under s.9(1)(c) may well be inappropriate. In *Adams v Adams (No.1)*, 1997 S.L.T. 144 the wife sought to rely on s.9(1)(c) to argue that she should be entitled to more than half of the capital to take account of the burden of caring for the children after the divorce. She maintained that this burden included paying for the mortgage and the costs of feeding, clothing and educating the children. She argued that she should get as much capital as possible from the divorce to allow her to meet the housing needs of the children and free up as much income as possible to meet the ongoing financial needs of the children. Lord Gill rejected these arguments[165]:

> "On the evidence, I hold that it is more probable than not that the defender will resume employment reasonably soon. When he does, he will resume payment of aliment for the children. He has gone out of his way to aliment them whenever he could. With these considerations in mind, I see no good reason to apply ss.9(1)(c) and 11(3)(a) in the pursuer's favour on account of the defender's present failure to pay aliment. Since I consider that the defender will resume payment of aliment in the near future, the possible application of s.8 of the Child Support Act 1991, and its interaction with s.9(1)(c) of the 1985 Act, need not be an issue in this case."

(5)   Voluntary agreements as to maintenance

4–66   E.M. Clive in *The Law of Husband and Wife in Scotland*[166] suggests that where there is a voluntary agreement between the husband and wife for aliment of a child, and if this only takes into account the factors required for the maintenance of the child, but does not include an element for the living expenses or child care costs of the adult, then an award under s.9(1)(c) may still be appropriate.

(6)   Capital adjustment required

4–67   There is some authority for the proposition that the provisions of the Child Support Act are designed to calculate a fair provision for the income required by the parent with the principal burden of care. However (so the argument goes) the Child Support Act does not cover major capital re-adjustments which may be required to properly cater for the children following the divorce or dissolution (say to provide a family home).[167]

In *Maclachlan v Maclachlan*, 1998 S.L.T. 693 the pursuer made two separate but related arguments under the principle set out in s.9(1)(c). She argued that an extra capital sum (over and above equal sharing) was required by her: (1) to make provision to secure the continued payment of the children's school fees; and (2) to purchase a house which would provide appropriate accommodation for her and the children. The first

---

[165] At p.148.

[166] 4th edn, para 24.072.

[167] In addition to *Maclachlan v Maclachlan* discussed below, see also *R v R*, 2000 Fam. L.R. 43; *Woodhouse v Woodhouse*, 2006 Fam. L.B. 82–4; *Orr v Orr*, 2006 Fam. L.B. 83–5; and *C v C*, 2007 G.W.D. 08–148.

argument (relating to continued payment of school fees) went along the following lines: she could not afford to pay school fees out of her salary; she was not confident that the defender would obtain employment sufficiently well-paid to allow the payment of the school fees; therefore she should be awarded a capital sum sufficient to allow her to purchase an annuity to pay the fees. Dealing with the first argument in *Maclachlan*, Lord Macfadyen[168] firstly expressed some reservations about the fact that no formal estimate of the costs of the fees had been lodged. He went on:

> "In the second place, and more importantly, I am of opinion that school fees are in their nature a revenue expense. While I do not go as far as to exclude the possibility of its ever being appropriate to make a capital award to enable such future expenditure to be provided for, I am of opinion that the court should be slow to make capital provision for a revenue expense. The legislation which largely takes the regulation of maintenance payments in respect of children out of the jurisdiction of the courts reserves the courts' right to order payment inter alia of school fees (Child Support Act 1991, s.8(7)). If one parent seeks a contribution from the other to the cost of school fees, it is in my view under that provision rather than by way of a capital sum justified by reference to the s.9(1)(c) principle that such a contribution ought normally to be sought."

The pursuer sought to justify the capital approach, but the court was satisfied on the evidence that it was likely that the defender would return to reasonably well-paid work in the near future, and so this would allow both parents to contribute to school fees out of income.[169]

The second argument advanced in *Maclachlan* was that a capital sum should be awarded to allow the pursuer to buy a house suitable for herself and the children. The defender argued that the impact of the Child Support Act 1991 had greatly reduced the scope for reliance on s.9(1)(c)[170]. Lord McFadyen said[171]:

> "I accept the generality of that proposition, but, insofar as the process of assessment under the 1991 Act was explored before me, I was not persuaded that it could be said wholly to supersede the s.9(1)(c) principle, which was not repealed or amended when the 1991 Act was passed. The fact that one parent has to purchase a house large enough, not only to accommodate herself, but also to provide suitable accommodation for the children, seems to me to be an aspect of the economic burden of caring for the children after divorce. If an award of a capital sum would enable that burden to be

---

[168] At p.698.

[169] It is not clear whether the capital payment approach might be justified if the defender had been completely unable to work; see also *Woodhouse v Woodhouse*, 2006 Fam. L.B. 82–4.

[170] Under reference to E.M. Clive, *The Law of Husband and Wife in Scotland*, 3rd edn, at pp.489–90.

[171] At p.698.

more fairly shared, I see no reason why reliance cannot be placed on s.9(1)(c) as justifying such a capital sum."

<h2 align="center">PRINCIPLE (D)—ADJUSTMENT TO LOSS OF SUPPORT</h2>

Key statutory provisions

4–68   Section 9(1)(d) provides that one of the principles to be applied by the court when deciding which orders for financial provision to make is:

"a person who has been dependent to a substantial degree on the financial support of the other person should be awarded such financial provision as is reasonable to enable him to adjust, over a period of not more than three years from—

(i) the date of the decree of divorce, to the loss of that support on divorce;

(ii) the date of the decree of dissolution of the civil partnership, to the loss of that support on dissolution."

This needs to be read alongside s.11(4) which provides—

"For the purposes of s.9(1)(d) of this Act, the court shall have regard to—

(a) the age, health and earning capacity of the person who is claiming the financial provision;[172]

(b) the duration and extent of the dependence of that person prior to divorce or to the dissolution of the civil partnership;[173]

(c) any intention of that person to undertake a course of education or training;

(d) the needs and resources of the persons;[174] and

(e) all the other circumstances of the case."

General discussion

4–69   This principle allows a party who has been dependent to a substantial degree on the financial support of the other to seek an award of such financial provision as is reasonable to enable him to adjust, over a period

---

[172] See *Barclay v Barclay*, 1991 S.C.L.R. 205 where the pursuer was suffering from multiple sclerosis and this factor was particularly pertinent.

[173] Note that the relevant period runs to the date of divorce or dissolution *not* the date of separation. So, in *Dever v Dever*, 1988 S.C.L.R. 352, the sheriff principal noted that, although the wife had been substantially dependent on the husband for the six years they were married and co-habiting, she had managed for the 18–month period between the separation and the proof without any support from him at all. The court was entitled to take the 18–month period into account in its decision to award periodical allowance for a very limited period (of six months). Although, as discussed below, this decision and others now need to be treated carefully because of the decision in *Haugan v Haugan*, 2002 S.C. 631.

[174] See s.27(1) for definitions of the terms "needs" and "resources". See also *Barclay v Barclay*, 1991 S.C.L.R. 205.

of not more than three years from the date of the decree of divorce or dissolution, to the loss of that support on divorce or dissolution. This principle appears to be similar to the s.9(1)(b) principle which allows recognition for economic advantage/disadvantage, but in fact s.9(1)(d) deals with a distinct situation. There will be circumstances where one party will develop substantial financial dependency on the other during the course of the marriage or civil partnership, but no economic advantage/disadvantage arises within the meaning of s.9(1)(b).[175] Section 9(1)(d) allows the court to recognise that, in these circumstances, it may be just to make an award to allow that party to adjust to their new circumstances.

The court is not to take conduct of the parties into account unless: (a) the conduct has adversely affected the financial resources which are relevant to the decision of the court; or (b) it would be manifestly inequitable to leave the conduct out of account.[176]

Periodical allowance or a clean break?

If the court considers that an award under s.9(1)(d) is justified, then **4–70** the full range of orders is available in terms of s.8(1). This includes, under s.13(2), the power to make an order for periodical allowance, provided that the court is satisfied that an order for payment of a capital sum, for transfer of property or a pension sharing order would be inappropriate or insufficient to satisfy the requirements of s.8(2). This is often referred to as the "clean break" principle, and this is discussed in more detail at para.3–34.

So, each time the court is applying s.9(1)(d), it should consider carefully whether a "clean break" order would satisfy the principle.[177] Generally, if there is liquid capital available or if a pension sharing order is a realistic option, then the court should use the capital assets or the pension to satisfy any award which is justified under s.9(1)(d). In *Loudon v Loudon*, 1994 S.L.T. 381, Lord Milligan commented[178]:

> "For my own part, in a case where liquidity was no problem at all, I think it is within the letter as well as the general spirit of the 1985 Act provisions for allowance to be made for retraining of someone in the pursuer's position within the allocation of the matrimonial property, namely as part of the capital sum awarded."

Of course, each case will turn on its own facts, and if a clean break is not sufficient to satisfy the principle, then periodical allowance may be justified.[179] Examples of situations where periodical allowance might be appropriate are:

---

[175] Although, as we shall see, there may be an overlap of the two principles in some cases.

[176] s.11(7). See paras 4–12 to 4–14.

[177] See e.g. *Bairstow v Bairstow*, 2000 G.W.D. 17–688.

[178] At p.385.

[179] See e.g. Sheriff Principal Taylor's comments in *Atkinson v Atkinson*, 1988 S.C.L.R. 396: "In my view the court's power to award a periodical allowance was not excluded by s.13(2)(b) of the Act. The sheriff held that the defender did not have any significant free

- a party may be unable to pay an extra capital sum to satisfy the need for provision under s.9(1)(d), for example because much of the matrimonial or partnership capital is illiquid or at least difficult to realise[180];
- if there is no matrimonial or partnership property, an award of periodical allowance might be justified—thus allowing provision to be made out of income[181];
- it is tentatively suggested that, even if liquidity of assets is not a significant problem, an award of periodical allowance might still be made if the parties both favour periodical allowance over a clean break[182];
- if a party will not have access to the capital sum directly, because for example they need to invest the proceeds in a business, then periodical allowance might be appropriate[183];
- even where the payment of a capital sum should be sufficient to provide for a party in the longer term, it may still be appropriate for an award of periodical allowance under s.9(1)(d) to be made to smooth the loss of support following divorce or dissolution.[184]

A clear time limit for periodical allowance

4–71　　Section 9(1)(d) is clear in stating that, if periodical allowance is to be paid under this provision, the time limit for payment is absolutely limited to three years. So, when the sheriff at first instance in *Atkinson v Atkinson*, 1988 S.C.L.R. 396 made an order for periodical allowance without limit of time justified only by s.9(1)(d), it was held to be incompetent and the sheriff principal on appeal limited the period of payment to three years. Therefore, if a party wants to be paid periodical allowance for more than three years, they will have to rely on s.9(1)(e) (relief of serious financial hardship) or (more rarely nowadays) on s.9(1)(c) (economic burden of child care). An award may be made for three years under s.9(1)(d) and then extended for a longer period under s.9(1)(e).[185]

"Adjustment"

4–72　　The purpose of an award under s.9(1)(d) is to allow a party to adjust to a loss of support. Arguments for provision under this section should therefore focus on the following question: what amount over which

---

capital after the pursuer had received half of the price of the matrimonial home and £10,000 for her shares in the company, and her car." See also *Buckle v Buckle*, 1995 S.C.L.R. 590, where a capital award was not possible because much of the matrimonial property was tied up in the defender's pension (but note that the decision was reached before earmarking and pension sharing orders were available).

[180] See *Park v Park*, 1988 S.C.L.R. 584.

[181] See *Dever v Dever*, 1988 S.C.L.R. 352.

[182] See *Loudon v Loudon*, 1994 S.L.T. 381 at p.385, although some caution is required—in *Loudon*, the court does seem to accept that the husband's liquidity (or lack thereof) has some bearing on the decision.

[183] See e.g. *McKenzie v McKenzie*, 1991 S.L.T. 461.

[184] See e.g. *Tyrrell v Tyrrell*, 1990 S.L.T. 406.

[185] See e.g. *McKenzie v McKenzie*, 1991 S.L.T. 461.

period is necessary to allow the process of *adjustment* to loss of support following divorce or dissolution? The aim of s.9(1)(d) is to provide transitional relief for up to three years to cushion the financial blow of decree. It allows a party time to adjust to new circumstances where money will be tighter.[186] If the circumstances following the divorce or dissolution are going to be much the same as they were beforehand, then an award under s.9(1)(d) will not be appropriate.

The court needs to have regard to other sources of income which might mitigate the effects of the loss of support. So, if it is reasonable to expect the party claiming periodical allowance to return to work, then the claim may fail even if they choose not to work.[187] Alternatively, if it is reasonable to expect a party to make some return on the capital awarded to them following a divorce or dissolution, then the court may take that into account in assessing the need for periodical allowance.[188] Similarly, if the result of a divorce or dissolution is that a capital sum is to be paid by instalments over a long period, this will generally mitigate the requirement to adjust to the loss of support.[189] The principle set out in s.9(1)(d) cannot be looked at in isolation. It must be considered in the context of the overall award which is being made for financial provision.[190] In *Loudon v Loudon*, 1994 S.L.T. 381, when considering whether to make an award of periodical allowance, Lord Milligan commented[191]:

> "I propose to deal with this matter by making an award of periodical allowance for a shorter period than that sought by counsel for the pursuer . . . In fixing this award I do not suggest that the need for funds for such purpose will necessarily have terminated within the year which I have fixed but I have fixed this part of the award with the allocation of matrimonial property which I propose to make in mind, deeming the total financial package awarded as reasonable and appropriate in my opinion in terms of the 1985 Act."

Perhaps the classic application of s.9(1)(d) will be to allow a party to retrain so that they are able to earn a living on their own account. For

---

[186] The decision in *Park v Park* discussed in detail at para.4–75 is a particularly interesting one because the court seems to have had the issue of "adjustment" quite firmly in mind. In that case the court awarded periodical allowance on a sliding scale—as time went on the periodical allowance was to decline, thus allowing adjustment to the new circumstances.

[187] *Bairstow v Bairstow*, 2000 G.W.D. 17–688.

[188] See *Muir v Muir*, 1989 S.L.T. (Sh Ct) 20. Also see the comments in *Wilson v Wilson*, 1999 S.L.T. 249 (quoted at length below) where the court was prepared to take into account the income arising on the capital sum in assessing periodical allowance but did not regard it as reasonable to expect the wife to encroach on capital to support herself during a period of retraining.

[189] See e.g. *Buckle v Buckle*, 1995 S.C.L.R. 590; *Bell v Bell*, 1988 S.C.L.R. 457.

[190] So for example, if substantial assets are to be realised for the benefit of the person seeking payment of periodical allowance, this will tend to limit the quantum and period of the award—see e.g. *McKenzie v McKenzie*, 1991 S.L.T. 461 and also *McConnell v McConnell*, 1996 G.W.D. 3–145.

[191] At p.385.

example, in *Wilson v Wilson*, 1999 S.L.T. 249 the wife had some experience as a receptionist. There was evidence that, if she intended to get back on the career ladder, it would be useful for her to go to college for one or two years to obtain an HNC or HND qualification. Lord Marnoch said[192]:

> "As regards the claim for a periodical allowance in terms of the 'principle' enshrined in s.9(1)(d) of the Act, counsel for the pursuer invited me to award to the pursuer an allowance over two and a half years at the rate of £200 per week. This was on the basis that the defender's income was in the region of £100,000 per annum and that the pursuer could not be expected to find a job immediately following on her course of re-training. In this connection, there is, I think, no guarantee that the pursuer will be eligible for a grant during the period of re-training and, even if she were so eligible, there is no possibility that it would maintain her in the standard of life to which she has become accustomed while married to the defender. Furthermore, and in disagreement with a submission made by counsel for the defender, I do not consider that it would be reasonable for the pursuer to have to encroach on capital in order to maintain herself during the period in question. She will, of course, derive some income from the capital sum which I have awarded her but this was taken into account by counsel for the pursuer in seeking an award of only £200 per week as opposed to the figure of £400 per week which the pursuer is presently receiving from the defender [as interim aliment]. For these reasons I consider that a periodical allowance should be awarded in the terms sought by counsel for the pursuer."

It follows from this that, if the party seeking periodical allowance is likely to come into further funds or streams of income, then this will tend to limit the period for which the award is to run. So, for example:

- in a case like *Wilson v Wilson*, above, if a party is to undertake a course of retraining to get back on the career ladder, then an appropriate period for the payment of periodical allowance might be the duration of retraining, perhaps with a little allowance for a short spell to look for a job thereafter;
- in *Murray v Murray*, 1993 G.W.D. 16–1058,[193] the court noted that the wife (who was seeking periodical allowance) was due to retire in June 1995, at which point her income would increase to a level where no further award to cover the adjustment would be required. In a pragmatic judgment the court awarded periodical allowance to June 1995;
- in *Sweeney v Sweeney*, 2003 S.L.T. 892, Mrs Sweeney was awarded a substantial capital sum, which would in due course produce an income for her. However, not all of the capital sum was to be paid immediately, and Lord Kingarth noted that it

---

[192] At p.254.
[193] Outer House, Temporary Judge Aronson.

would therefore be some time before the wife would receive the full benefit of the income stream. In the circumstances, he awarded a periodical allowance for one year.

Of course, it is open to the party who is being asked to pay periodical allowance to point out these potential sources of income in an effort to limit the period of payment. So, for example, if the party seeking periodical allowance will be attending college for two years, then it might be reasonable to limit the award to that period. This would be a useful argument to deploy against a party seeking periodical allowance for the full three years permitted under s.9(1)(d).[194]

It is important to bear in mind that the wording of the Act is clear— **4–73** s.9(1)(d) awards are to allow for adjustment *after divorce or dissolution*, not after separation. The distinction may be important in some cases. Often a substantial period of time will elapse between separation and decree. During that time (particularly if the delay has been a long one) there may be an argument that the party seeking periodical allowance has already adjusted to the loss of support, particularly if no aliment was being paid. If aliment was being paid during this period, it might be argued that the loss of aliment on decree is loss of support.[195] It is not yet clear to what extent the courts will support this argument. In *Millar v Millar*, 1990 S.C.L.R. 666 Sheriff Principal Nicholson commented[196]:

"It is to be noted that [s.9(1)(d)] speaks of adjustment to loss of support 'on divorce', and not following upon separation. In the present case the parties ceased living together in December 1986,[197] and so, effectively, the pursuer has, for more than three years, had to adjust as best she can to the [loss of] support which she enjoyed when the parties were living together. The learned sheriff has found that, during that time, the pursuer has adjusted quite well. [The pursuer] submitted that he was wrong to have reached that conclusion but, whether that be so or not, it seems to me that the proper question which falls to be considered in relation to s.9(1)(d) of the Act is whether an award of financial provision is required to enable the pursuer to adjust to loss of support *on divorce*.

It may be that the 1985 Act is defective in not acknowledging (except, possibly, to a limited extent under s.11(4)(b)) the time gap which may occur between the loss of support arising on separation and the subsequent loss of support which may arise on divorce, but of course the Act must be applied in the terms in which it is expressed. Viewed in that light it seems to me that, in a consideration of s.9(1)(d), one must consider the level of support available to the pursuer prior to decree of divorce being granted, and ask whether an award of financial provision is desirable in order to enable the pursuer to adjust to that loss."

---

[194] However, see *Stott v Stott*, 1987 G.W.D. 17–645—it may not be sufficient for the party against whom payment is sought to pay to argue that the other party *could* retrain (and thus enhance their earning capacity)—there may have to be an averment (and evidence) that the other party *intends* to retrain.

[195] See e.g. *Sweeney v Sweeney*, 2003 S.L.T. 892.

[196] At p.670.

[197] About three years before the proof.

The sheriff principal went on to point out that in this case, following the separation but before the divorce, the defender had been paying to the pursuer a total of £25 per week, of which £15 was aliment for a child of the marriage and £10 was personal aliment for the pursuer. After the divorce the total sum payable was to be £20, all of which was aliment for the child. Thus there was going to be a reduction in income of £5 per week for the pursuer. He went on[198]:

> "I appreciate that for those in straitened circumstances even £5 per week can be a significant sum, but I would not be prepared to say that the loss of that sum is of itself sufficient to justify a further award in order to assist the pursuer's adjustment after divorce."[199]

Similarly, in *Tyrrell v Tyrrell*, 1990 S.L.T. 406, Lord Sutherland took into account a long period of separation in limiting the period of payment to one year under s.9(1)(d)[200]:

> "I am satisfied that the pursuer is dependent to a material degree on the financial support of the defender. On the other hand, it is now seven years since the date of separation and the pursuer has had ample time to adjust to living without receiving financial support from her husband. While on a long term basis I am satisfied that the order for payment of a capital sum should be sufficient to satisfy the requirements of s.8(2), I consider that a short period should be allowed to the pursuer to adjust to the new circumstances while still being supported to some extent by the defender."

However, the decisions in the above cases can be contrasted with the Outer House decision in *Thomson v Thomson*, 1991 S.L.T. 126, where the wife had been entirely dependent on the husband for the last five years of co-habitation during the marriage. She did not seek interim aliment until about six months before the proof some three years after the date of separation. However, the court noted that the defender was a man who had taken every opportunity to avoid his financial responsibilities since separation, and awarded periodical allowance for three years.

4–74   The argument in cases like *Millar* and *Tyrrell*, above now also need to be read alongside the decision in *Haugan v Haugan*, 2002 S.C. 631. In that case the Inner House examined a very similar argument in the context of s.9(1)(e). The wording of that section provides that a party who, at the time of the divorce or dissolution, seems likely to suffer serious financial hardship as a result of the divorce or dissolution, should be awarded such financial provision as is reasonable to relieve him of

---

[198] At p.670.
[199] For another case where there had been a long period of separation before the divorce see *Muir v Muir*, 1989 S.L.T. (Sh Ct) 20. In that case periodical allowance for a period of one year was allowed, although there was a more significant drop in personal aliment after the divorce.
[200] At p.409.

hardship over a reasonable period. At the time of the divorce in *Haugan* the wife had not (for a substantial period prior to the proof) been receiving any aliment from the husband. He argued that this meant that she would not be suffering financial hardship *as a result of the divorce.* Even if she was suffering serious financial hardship before the divorce (so the argument ran) then this would simply continue after decree—it was not caused by the divorce. The Inner House rejected this argument (in relation to s.9(1)(e) but the logic looks as if it could be applied to s.9(1)(d) too). The Opinion of the Court in relation to this matter was[201]:

> "The principles set out in sec 9(1) of the Act are those to be applied in deciding what order for financial provision, if any, the court should make. That set out in sec 9(1)(e) looks, as from the date of divorce, to the future—including in some cases to the longer term. It requires consideration of whether one party to the marriage now to be dissolved is likely in the future to suffer grave financial hardship as a result of the divorce. The issue is whether, viewing matters prospectively at the time of the divorce, the change of status of that party from that of a person married to the other party (with the right in relevant circumstances to enforce the latter's obligation to aliment the former) to a person not so married (and so without the benefit of that right) is likely to occasion hardship of the kind specified. While the pattern of actual support afforded prior to the divorce, including during any period of separation, is among the factors to be taken into account when assessing whether the loss of the right to aliment is likely to give rise to that hardship, the presence or absence of such actual support cannot be determinative of that matter. The factor that prior to divorce a spouse has failed to fulfil his or her obligation of support to the other cannot, even when active steps have not been taken to enforce it, exclude the making of financial provision in accordance with the principle set out in sec 9(1)(e); nor can the fact that at the date of the divorce the claiming party is already suffering such hardship."

The Inner House is very clear that, if the decree of divorce results in the loss of *the right to claim aliment*, then that in itself is enough to allow a s.9(1)(e) claim. The decision looks only at s.9(1)(e). It remains to be seen whether the Court of Session would apply the same reasoning to s.9(1)(d). It may still be reasonable for parties to argue that, if there has been *de facto* adjustment, then this will be a factor tending to limit a s.9(1)(d) claim, but at least one eye should be kept on the decision in *Haugan*.

A subjective claim

The level of award which a party needs to adjust to the loss of support **4–75** is not an objective matter. It will depend on the level of support which they enjoyed during the period of co-habitation. So, in a case where a

---

party received considerable financial support before the divorce or dissolution, the award will be higher than in a case where the level of support before the decree was modest.[202] Disparity in incomes will also be a factor. In *Park v Park*, 1988 S.C.L.R. 584, both parties were working at the date of the proof. Sheriff Kelbie, in considering a claim for periodical allowance commented[203]:

> "The only reason for allowing the pursuer periodical allowance is in terms of section 9(1)(d) of the Family Law (Scotland) Act 1985 in order to allow her to adjust, over a period of not more than three years from the date of decree of divorce, to the loss of support from the defender. At present, her earnings contribute one-fifth of [the parties'] joint income. That being so, it would appear to me not unreasonable for her to expect to rely upon one-third of the joint income for her support. She will have to adjust from that figure to her own one-fifth contribution. Bearing in mind the short duration of the marriage, the fact that there are no children and the fact that she is earning herself, it would appear to me not unreasonable to expect the pursuer to make that adjustment over a period of two years. The adjustment should be made in two stages, which I think would be amply allowed for by awarding a periodical allowance of £70 a week for the first year from the decree of divorce and thereafter at the rate of £35 per week for one further year."

Relationship with other principles

4–76   The principle in s.9(1)(d) is closely linked to other principles. So, a case might be capable of being argued under both this and other sections of the Act. There may sometimes be quite a close link with the principle in s.9(1)(e).[204] Periodical allowance under para.(d) might initially be justified to allow an adjustment to new circumstances, but even after three years have expired there might still be serious financial hardship in terms of para.(e).[205] In *McKenzie v McKenzie*, 1991 S.L.T. 461, Lord Prosser said[206]:

> ". . . I am satisfied that in the near future, and particularly if she uses her capital so as to provide a basis for future income from her business and taking in a lodger, the pursuer will be seriously short of money. I am satisfied that she was dependent to a substantial degree on the financial support of the defender, and should be awarded a reasonable financial provision for her to adjust to the loss of that support over the next three years. I do not find it easy to judge whether she will be able to arrange her affairs so as to produce something like an adequate income in the longer term. If she is not

---

[202] e.g. contrast the award of £4,000 per month in *Sweeney v Sweeney*, 2003 S.L.T. 892 with the much more modest award in *Barclay v Barclay*, 1991 S.C.L.R. 205.
[203] At p.584.
[204] See e.g. *Davidson v Davidson*, 1994 S.L.T. 506.
[205] See e.g. *Stott v Stott*, 1987 G.W.D. 17–645.
[206] At p.464.

able to do so, I think that it is reasonable to describe the results as serious financial hardship. Such an outcome would be a result of the divorce, and making the best judgement I can as to the possibilities and prospects, it seems on balance likely that this will indeed occur . . . [At this point the judge recounted the particular facts of this case] . . . in the circumstances I do not think it appropriate to limit [the award of periodical allowance] to the three year adjustment period, but would leave it open ended, with a view to relieving the pursuer of the hardship which I expect to continue beyond that period."

In *Toye v Toye*, 1992 S.C.L.R. 95 the sheriff seems to combine factors pertinent to s.9(1)(c) and (d) in its decision to award periodical allowance.[207]

If there are alternative arguments under different provisions of the Act, a prudent agent will plead the case on a belt and braces basis.

Table of cases

There are a relatively small number of reported cases where this **4–77** principle has been argued. The following table may be of some assistance to agents preparing for a s.9(1)(d) argument.

Case	Granted/ Refused	Length of periodical allowance	Relevant Facts
Stott v Stott, 1987 G.W.D. 17–645	Granted	Three years under s.9(1)(d) then four years under s.9(1)(e)	The couple had been married for 24 years. The husband earned about £190 per week. The wife earned about £7 per week. The wife was 42 years old. The wife was not well-educated. Periodical allowance was awarded for three years under s.9(1)(d) at £75 per week and at £55 per week for a further four years under s.9(1)(e).
Birnie v Birnie, (1988—Sheriff Fulton, Inverness) unreported but referred to in *Barclay v Barclay* below	Granted	Three years under s.9(1)(d) and then a further seven years under s.9(1)(e)	The parties were married for about 22 years. The wife suffered from epilepsy and was incapable of earning. The court awarded periodical allowance for three years under s.9(1)(d) and for a further seven years under principle (e). However, the sheriff did not think it fair and reasonable for the periodical allowance to be paid until death or remarriage (for reasons that are not entirely clear).

---

[207] See p.100 where the court seems to combine factors relating to the burden of childcare and adjustment to loss of support. See also the commentary at the end of the S.C.L.R. report. See also *C v C*, 2007 G.W.D. 08–148.

Dever v Dever, 1988 S.C.L.R. 352	Granted	Six months	The couple had been married and living together for about six years. The wife was 27 and in receipt of state benefits. It was common ground that during the marriage she had been financially dependent on her husband. The wife had not been paid any aliment from the date of separation to the date of the proof. In the circumstances the court held that she had shown a capacity to survive for a substantial period and limited the award to six months.
Petrie v Petrie, 1988 S.C.L.R. 390	Granted	One year	The wife was 42 and had been married for two years. There was one child. There had been a period of several years' co-habitation prior to the marriage. The wife was in receipt of state benefits, and had no skills or qualifications. She was fit for work. She had claimed no maintenance since the separation. She received one year's periodical allowance under s.9(1)(d).
Atkinson v Atkinson, 1988 S.C.L.R. 396	Granted	Three years (reduced on appeal from an incompetent indefinite award)	After separation the wife was earning a salary which was not sufficient for her to keep up the standard of living which she had been used to during the marriage. She had been dependent during the marriage to a substantial degree on the support of her husband. Periodical allowance of £2,500 per year awarded for three years.
Park v Park, 1988 S.C.L.R. 584	Granted	One year then a further year at a reduced amount	The couple were married and living together for about five years. There were no children. The husband had about £20,600 annual gross income and the wife had about £5,040 annual gross income. The court noted that her earnings were about one-fifth of joint income. It was not unreasonable for her to expect one-third of joint income, but she would need to adjust from that level to her own income. Bearing in mind that she was earning, the short period of the marriage and the fact that there were no children, it was reasonable for this adjustment to take place over two years. The court ordered periodical allowance in two stages—£70 per week for the first year and £35 per week for the second year.
Muir v Muir, 1989 S.L.T. (Sh Ct) 20	Granted	One year	The couple had been married and co-habiting for about 20 years. They separated about four years before the proof. The wife was 47 and suffered from an arthritic condition. Between the separation and the proof, the husband was paying the wife £35 per week as interim personal aliment. He had also been paying £25 per week as aliment for the daughter until she reached the age of 17 (the year before the proof). He had been meeting certain household costs. The wife hoped to resume part time work when

			her medical condition improved. Her grown up children made a small contribution to the household. The court ordered £45 per week periodical allowance and observed that she would also be able to get some return on her capital award.
Tyrrell v Tyrrell, 1990 S.L.T. 406	Granted	One year	The parties had been married and living together for about 18 years. There were no children. The couple had been separated for seven years by the time of the proof. The wife was dependent to a material degree on the support of the husband. The court appears to have taken into account the long period of separation in awarding periodical allowance for a limited period of time as the pursuer already had time to adjust by the date of the proof.
Millar v Millar, 1990 S.C.L.R. 666	Refused	n/a	The couple had been married and co-habiting for about 10 years. There was one child. The pursuer was employed part-time as a home help. In the period between sep-aration and divorce the pursuer had been receiving from the defender £15 per week as aliment for the child and £10 per week aliment for herself. After the divorce she was awarded £20 as aliment for the child and was therefore going to be £5 per week worse off. The sheriff principal stated that whilst the loss of £5 per week in straitened circumstances might be significant to a party, it was not sufficient to allow him to award periodical allowance following divorce under s.9(1)(d).
Sheret v Sheret, 1990 S.C.L.R. 799	Granted	13 weeks	The marriage had lasted two years. The wife was 42 and had no immediate employ-ment prospects. She had only received intermittent support from her husband. She received periodical allowance for 13 weeks from the date of decree.
Thomson v Thomson, 1991 S.L.T. 126	Granted	Three years	There were no children. The wife had been wholly dependent on the husband for about five years before the separation. The wife had not sought interim aliment for about three years after the separation but did so six months before the proof. However, the court noted that the evidence showed the defender had taken every opportunity to avoid his financial responsibilities and awarded periodical allowance at £75 per month for three years.
Barclay v Bar-clay, 1991 S.C.L.R. 205	Granted	Three years	The wife was 29. The husband was 28. The couple were married and co-habiting for just over three years. There were no child-ren. The wife suffered from multiple sclerosis. She was awarded periodical allowance of £15 per week for three years. Particular factors persuasive towards making an award were "the age, health and earning capacity" of the wife (s.11(4)(a)) and her "needs and resources" (s.11(4)(d)).

McKenzie v McKenzie, 1991 S.L.T. 461	Granted	Three years under s.9(1)(d) then indefinitely under s.9(1)(e)	The parties were married and co-habiting for about 10 years. By the time of the proof the wife was 59 and the defender 54. The wife had been dependent to a substantial degree on her husband. She was likely to be "seriously short of money" following the divorce. The court took account of the fact that it was likely that she would have to invest the capital sum awarded to her in her business. Periodical allowance was awarded under s.9(1)(d) for an initial period of three years and then indefinitely under s.9(1)(e).
Toye v Toye, 1992 S.C.L.R. 95	Granted	Three years	The wife was aged 48 and the husband aged 49 at the time of the proof. Since the marriage the wife had not worked (except for a little occasional work). She looked after the five children of the marriage. The youngest child was the only dependent child at the time of the proof. The husband was employed in the oil industry and earned about £3,200 per month after tax. The court awarded £1,200 per month for three years as periodical allowance. Note—the decision is not clear on whether the award was made under para.(c) or (d) of s.9(1).
Kelly v Kelly, 1992 G.W.D. 36–2130	Granted	Three years	The wife had a secure job and a reasonable salary but was nevertheless entitled to periodical allowance for three years. The court took into account the fact that equal sharing could not take place as much of the matrimonial property was locked up in the husband's pension fund.
Murray v Murray, 1993 G.W.D. 16–1058	Granted	Two years	The wife was aged 56. The husband had paid mortgage and insurance premiums following separation and in addition had paid a monthly payment to the wife of £350. The wife worked part time as a teacher for 1½ days per week. The wife had been dependent to a substantial degree on the husband for support, but the court noted that the amount of work she did was a matter of personal choice. An award of £250 per month was made for a period of about two years until she retired at which point her pension would give her sufficient income and no further support to cover the period of adjustment would be required.
McConnell v McConnell, 1993 G.W.D. 34–2185 (First Instance); 1995 G.W.D. 3–145 (Appeal)	Granted	Six months (reduced from three years on appeal)	The wife had given up work to look after the children. By the time of the proof she was totally dependent on her husband. At first instance an allowance of £1,200 per month was made for three years from the date of decree. On appeal it was held that the Lord Ordinary had not given sufficient weight to the transfer of property and capital sum being paid to the wife (which contributed to her ability to adjust to loss of support) and reduced the period to six months.

Loudon v Loudon, 1994 S.L.T. 381	Granted	One year	The husband and wife married at age 26. They lived together for 17 years. The wife had not worked for 17 years. Periodical allowance of £500 per month was awarded for one year to assist with retraining and costs incidental thereto. In fixing the periodical allowance the court had regard to the whole package of awards which the wife was receiving under the 1985 Act.
Buckle v Buckle, 1995 S.C.L.R. 590	Granted	One year	The parties were married for 30 years. At the time of the divorce the defender had an income of £1,169 per month compared to the pursuer's income of only about £260 per month. To allow the pursuer to adapt she was awarded £100 per month over a period of a year. Any financial hardship was mitigated by a capital award payable by instalments over five years.
Wilson v Wilson, 1999 S.L.T. 249	Granted	30 months	The couple were married and living together for about 17 years. The husband had income of about £100,000 per year. The wife would need to retrain to get back on the employment ladder, but this would not be unduly difficult as she had some training and experience as a receptionist. There was evidence that suitable training for her would be an HNC and perhaps HND at college lasting one or two years. There was no guarantee that she would be eligible for a grant. Periodical allowance of £200 per week granted for 30 months.
Bairstow v Bairstow, 2000 G.W.D. 17–688	Refused	n/a	The parties were married and living together for about eight years. The wife sought periodical allowance, arguing amongst other things, that she had certain health difficulties which prevented her returning to education. The court found on the evidence that the wife had no intention of returning to work for so long as there were ties with her husband; she could regularise her income by getting some light work; her pleadings and evidence did not deal adequately with her claim for periodical allowance; and in any event the husband's resources were such that payment of periodical allowance was unreasonable.
L v L, 2003 Fam. L.R. 101	Granted	Three years (or until capital sum paid whichever soonest)	The parties had been married and living together for about 13 years. The wife had a substantial degree of dependence on her husband. She was awarded a capital sum but was also awarded periodical allowance of £1,000 per month for three years or until the capital sum was paid whichever was sooner.

Sweeney v Sweeney, 2003 S.L.T. 892	Granted	One year	The parties were married and co-habiting for 17 years. For most of that period the wife had been "wholly dependent" on her husband's income. Substantial maintenance had been paid since the separation. The wife was awarded a large capital sum, but payment of part of this was to be deferred. The court noted that the capital sum would eventually produce an income stream for the wife, but since this was not all payable immediately, it was reasonable to award periodical allowance of £4,000 per month (the rate at which aliment was being paid) for one year under s.9(1)(d).
W v W, 2004 Fam. L.R. 54	Refused	n/a	The arguments are reported rather briefly, but the court took the view that there was no justification for an award under s.9(1)(d). Even if there had been justification, periodical allowance was inappropriate as an award could have been satisfied through payment of a capital sum or transfer of property.
C v C, 2007 G.W.D. 08–148	Granted	Two years	The order here was justified partly in terms of s.9(1)(d) and partly in terms of s.9(1)(c). The wife required time to adjust to new mortgage commitments and also to part time work.

PRINCIPLE (E)—SERIOUS FINANCIAL HARDSHIP

Key statutory provisions

4–78   Section 9(1)(e) provides:

"a person who at the time of the divorce or of the dissolution of the civil partnership, seems likely to suffer serious financial hardship as a result of the divorce or dissolution should be awarded such financial provision as is reasonable to relieve him of hardship over a reasonable period."

This needs to be read alongside s.11(5) which states:

"For the purposes of s.9(1)(e) of this Act, the Court shall have regard to—

(a) the age, health and earning capacity of the person who is claiming the financial provision;[208]
(b) the duration of the marriage or of the civil partnership;[209]

---

[208] See e.g. *CR or D v ARD*, 2005 Fam. L.B. 76–4.
[209] See e.g. *Barclay v Barclay*, 1991 S.C.L.R. 205, and in particular the comments at pp.206—7 distinguishing that case (involving a marriage of only three years) from two cases involving marriages of much longer periods—*Johnstone v Johnstone*, 1990 S.C.L.R. 358 and *Birnie v Birnie* (unreported but referred to in *Barclay v Barclay*).

(c) the standard of living of the persons during the marriage or
civil partnership;

(d) the needs and resources of the persons; and

(e) all the other circumstances of the case."

General discussion

Under s.9(1)(e) a party who, at the time of the divorce or dissolution, **4–79**
seems likely to suffer serious financial hardship as a result of the divorce
or dissolution, should be awarded such financial provision as is reasonable to relieve him of the hardship over a reasonable period. The
wording of the section requires that the court must do some judicial
crystal ball gazing. *At the time of the divorce or dissolution* the court has
to look at whether it *seems likely* that a party will suffer serious financial
hardship *in the future.* The court has to make a decision at the time of
the decree about the likelihood of future hardship. If no such hardship
seems likely, then no award will be made.

The court is not to take conduct of the parties into account unless the
conduct has adversely affected the financial resources which are relevant
to the decision of the court on a claim for financial provision; or it would
be manifestly inequitable to leave the conduct out of account.[210]

Periodical allowance or a clean break?

If the court considers that an award under s.9(1)(e) is appropriate, **4–80**
then the full range of orders is available to the court in terms of s.8(1).
This includes, under s.13(2), the power to make an order for periodical
allowance, provided that the court is satisfied that an order for payment
of a capital sum, for transfer of property or a pension sharing order
would be inappropriate or insufficient to satisfy the requirements of
s.8(2). This is often referred to as the "clean break" principle. Each time
the court is applying s.9(1)(e), it should consider carefully whether a
"clean break" order will be sufficient. The issue of the clean break
principle in relation to periodical allowance is examined in more detail
at para.3–34.

So, a generous split of capital in favour of a party may tend to mitigate
against an award of periodical allowance.[211] However, it has to be
recognised that most of the cases dealing with s.9(1)(e) involve awards of
periodical allowance, rather than adjustments of capital.[212] This is
probably because s.9(1)(e) tends to deal with situations where ongoing
hardship for an extended period seems likely, and periodical allowance is
particularly suited to relief of such hardship. The courts have recognised
that, in some cases, a clean break will not adequately cater for the needs
of a party who finds himself in serious financial difficulty. Section 9(1)(e)
can provide a safety net. In *Johnstone v Johnstone*, 1990 S.L.T. (Sh Ct) 79

---

[210] s.11(7). See paras 4–12 to 4–14.

[211] See e.g. *Savage v Savage*, 1993 G.W.D. 28–1779; *Tyrrell v Tyrrell*, 1990 S.L.T. 406 at
pp.408–9.

[212] But see *Davidson v Davidson*, 1994 S.L.T. 506, a complex case where s.9(1)(e) applied
(along with a host of other factors) but periodical allowance was not awarded; rather
s.9(1)(e) was one factor borne in mind in unequal division.

Sheriff Principal Ireland was asked to reconsider an award of periodical allowance made by the sheriff at first instance in favour of the wife. The award was to be paid until death or remarriage of the wife, who suffered from epilepsy and was unable to work. In affirming the sheriff's decision the sheriff principal commented[213]:

> "One of the principles embodied in the 1985 Act is that in ordinary circumstances it should be possible for the parties to make a clean break, so that one spouse should not be entitled to lifelong support from the other. That principle is however subject to qualification, including the provision in s.9(1)(e) that 'a party who at the time of the divorce seems likely to suffer serious financial hardship as a result of the divorce should be awarded such financial provision as is reasonable to relieve [her] of hardship over a reasonable period'. The sheriff has taken the view that that provision is applicable to the present case because the pursuer is unfit to work because of epilepsy. If the marriage had continued she would have been entitled to be maintained by the defender throughout her life, but after the determination her inability to work would mean that she would be totally dependent on state benefits and would therefore suffer serious financial hardship. This state of affairs would continue so long as the pursuer continues to be unfit to work through illness. The sheriff had in my opinion material on which he was entitled to come to that conclusion."

The sheriff principal is pointing out that s.9(1)(e) is designed to prevent ongoing serious financial hardship, and sometimes the principle can be used to cut across the clean break ethos of the Act. Section 9(1)(e) claims are particularly difficult to quantify in capital terms, which means that in practice the courts will often resort to the use of periodical allowance. The sheriff principal continued[214]:

> ". . . the illness from which the pursuer suffers is not a temporary one which will disappear within a predictable period of time, and support to relieve her of hardship will continue to be required so long as it persists. A 'reasonable period' may therefore in the circumstances of this case be interpreted as meaning a period not limited to a particular length of time. If of course there is an improvement either in the physical or in the financial condition of the pursuer, or a change in the position of the defender, it will be open to the defender to apply to the court for a variation order under s.13(4) of the Act."

"Reasonable having regard to the resources of the parties"

4–81   An award under s.9(1)(e) (like any award of financial provision under the Act) requires the court to be satisfied that the order is "reasonable having regard to the resources of the parties".[215] The term "resources"

---

[213] At p.80.
[214] At p.80.
[215] s.8(2)(b). See paras 3–02 to 3–08.

encompasses present and foreseeable resources.[216] This examination of resources is particularly important in the context of s.9(1)(e) because, when considering making an award, the court has to determine whether a party seems likely to suffer serious financial hardship following the divorce or dissolution. This involves an analysis of both current and (likely) future financial circumstances. So, for example, if the party seeking payment of the award is likely to receive a substantial capital sum which will prevent hardship, then this will be an argument against an award under s.9(1)(e).[217]

The financial circumstances which the dependent party finds themselves in after the divorce or dissolution will of course be a factor in determining whether there is serious financial hardship. In *Gribb v Gribb*, 1994 S.L.T. (Sh Ct) 43,[218] as part of the sharing of matrimonial property, the court ordered that the husband should transfer his one half interest in the former matrimonial home to the wife. In ordering periodical allowance in favour of the wife the sheriff said[219]:

> "Mrs Gribb intends to live at [the former matrimonial home]. That is a three bedroom house which requires to have money spent on its maintenance. While she will not have to meet the cost of a mortgage in respect of that property it seems to me that she would suffer serious financial hardship if she were to live there with only the income from the pensions to which she is entitled. Her health is not good. It is deteriorating. She is of an age when she would find it difficult to find reasonably well paid work for which she is fit.
>
> In my opinion an order for the transfer of [the former matrimonial home] is insufficient having regard to the resources of the parties to secure the fair sharing of the net value of the matrimonial property and the avoidance of serious financial hardship for Mrs Gribb."

However, it is not just the financial circumstances of the claimant which are important. The court also has to apply itself to the issue of what resources *both parties* may have available to them both now and in the future. Even if it is plain that a party will suffer serious financial hardship following the divorce or dissolution, the claim will fail if the other party has such limited resources (or foreseeable resources) that it would not be just and reasonable to make an order against them. So, in *Savage v Savage*, 1993 G.W.D. 28–1779 the wife's claim for periodical allowance under s.9(1)(e) was refused partly because the husband would have had substantial difficulty funding periodical allowance from his earnings because (a) he had various tax debts to pay, and (b) he would have to obtain finance to pay his wife a capital sum due to her on divorce.

---

[216] s.27(1).

[217] See e.g. *Savage v Savage*, 1993 G.W.D. 28–1779; *Atkinson v Atkinson*, 1988 S.C.L.R. 396; *Tyrrell v Tyrrell*, 1990 S.L.T. 406 at pp.408–9; although note that the award of a substantial capital sum is not necessarily a bar to an award under s.9(1)(e)—see e.g. *McKenzie v McKenzie*, 1991 S.L.T. 461.

[218] Affirmed in *Gribb v Gribb*, 1996 S.L.T. 719.

[219] At p.46.

Another case where the issue of the resources of the "paying" spouse was an important factor is *Haugan v Haugan*, 2002 S.C. 631. In that case the Inner House considered whether or not to reduce an award of periodical allowance payable by the husband to the wife. The husband argued that there had been a material change in circumstances justifying a variation. The Inner House noted[220] that the wife's financial position was not materially different to when the case had been considered by the Outer House, but it was satisfied that there had been a material change in the circumstances of the husband: he was earning much less; was several years older; and was closer to retirement than when the court first considered matters. The Inner House reduced the quantum of periodical allowance from £1,000 per month to £500 per month.

The period of the award

4–82   Unlike awards under s.9(1)(d), which are limited to a maximum of three years, an award of periodical allowance under s.9(1)(e) can be made without limit of time. This is subject to the terms of s.13(7)(b) which provides that an order for periodical allowance will cease to have effect on the person receiving payment marrying, entering into a civil partnership or dying. It is not possible to formulate detailed rules for the period of time that periodical allowance will be payable in any given case. Much is left to the discretion of the court at first instance and appeals will generally be difficult.[221] The period of time needed for periodical allowance to relieve hardship may not be determinable with precision.[222] However, if there is a material change of circumstances after an award of periodical allowance is made, a party has the option to apply to the court for variation. For a more detailed discussion on variations of awards of periodical allowance see paras 3–40 to 3–44.

If, at the time of the proof, it is reasonably foreseeable that there will be significant changes in the resources of either party at some point in the future, then that will be an important factor in determining the period of the award. For example, if the party who is ordered to pay periodical allowance will lose income at an identifiable point in the future, then this might limit the period of an award of periodical allowance. So, in *Bell v Bell*, 1988 S.C.L.R. 457, the husband was working at the time of the proof and could afford payment of periodical allowance from his earnings. However, he was due to retire at the age of 60, and at that point his income would be significantly reduced. The sheriff ordered that periodical allowance was to be paid under s.9(1)(e) only until he reached the age of 60 (or until the death or remarriage of the wife, whichever was earlier). The other side of this coin is that, if the party who is seeking an award is likely to come into money (capital or income) which will resolve any financial hardship, then this too will be an important factor in determining the period of the award. In *Bolton v Bolton*, 1995 G.W.D. 14–799, the wife had been financially dependent to a substantial degree on the husband during a marriage of over 30 years,

---

[220] At p.637.
[221] See e.g. *Gribb v Gribb*, 1996 S.L.T. 719.
[222] See *Johnstone v Johnstone*, above.

but the court awarded her a transfer of the matrimonial home and a substantial capital sum. Lord Abernethy was of the view that, once the capital sum had been paid the wife would be financially comfortable, and therefore awarded periodical allowance only until payment of the capital sum.[223] Similarly, serious financial hardship might evaporate if a substantial capital sum is to be paid by instalments.[224]

The arguments for an indefinite award of periodical allowance under s.9(1)(e) will be much more persuasive if there is no realistic chance of the party seeking payment obtaining employment.[225] In *Bell v Bell*, 1988 S.C.L.R. 457 the wife was 51 years old by the date of the proof. She had given up work as a primary school teacher early in the marriage to bring up the children, and this was an arrangement in which the defender husband had acquiesced. This meant that the wife, by the time of the proof, had effectively been out of work for 26 years. There was evidence that, at the time of the proof, there was a policy of school closure and a list of 2,000 teachers awaiting jobs in primary schools in the area. Sheriff Jardine observed[226]:

> "Against such levels of competition, such employment does not seem to me to be a realistic prospect for the pursuer. Perhaps, with some luck, she may secure a part-time job as say, a shop or reception assistant, but I do not think such jobs are easily found and the potential earnings are not likely to be high.
>
> At the present time, the pursuer has a nice house but, unless some provision is made, she will have no income after divorce. The defender, in some contrast, has a good salary and a car provided, a house loan on specially favourable terms and some assistance in meeting household costs from the earnings of [a third party]. In my opinion, the Act envisages that relief may have to be specially given in terms of the principle set out in section 9(1)(e) of the Act. I consider that the particular circumstances of this case fully justify the making of some such further provision."

"Serious financial hardship"—Relative nature of the claim

The Act requires that any hardship must be "serious". The comments **4–83** of Lord Sutherland in the Outer House decision of *Tyrrell v Tyrrell*, 1990 S.L.T. 406[227] are instructive:

> "As far as s.9(1)(e) is concerned, I cannot say that the pursuer in this case seems likely to suffer serious financial hardship as a result of the divorce. She has already received £45,000 or thereby at the time of the separation and will receive a further capital sum under this judgement of £27,532. She is in part time employment and owns her own home. If she ceases to receive the current aliment of £180

---

[223] The rate awarded mirrored the rate of interim aliment which the husband had been paying in the run up to the divorce.
[224] See *Buckle v Buckle*, 1995 S.C.L.R. 590.
[225] See e.g. *CR or D v ARD*, 2005 Fam. L.B. 76–4.
[226] At p.465.
[227] At p.408.

per month this may result in some financial hardship, but I cannot say that it could qualify as serious financial hardship, bearing in mind that she will be able to receive interest on the capital sum now awarded."

It might be thought that the term "serious financial hardship" is an objective one. It seems logical to argue that any party will need a certain identifiable level of capital and income to avoid such hardship, and if the threshold is exceeded no award under s.9(1)(e) should be made. However, this is not the way the courts have treated claims. In practice the courts will examine the standard of living of the claimant party before the divorce or dissolution and compare it to the anticipated standard of living after the divorce or dissolution.[228] In *Haugan v Haugan*, 1996 S.L.T. 321 this relativistic approach seems to employed by Lord Marnoch in the following passage[229]:

"I am, however, of opinion that this is clearly a case in which an award for an unlimited period under s.9(1)(e) of the Act would be appropriate. For the whole of her married life the pursuer has lived in reasonable comfort albeit I accept that there was seldom any money left over for luxuries. At one stage in the marriage the parties worked hard to restore a somewhat dilapidated house . . . and, just before the marriage came to an end, they had finally reached the stage of building a new and 'beautiful' house, as it was described in evidence, standing in its own grounds near Oslo. From that she had gone to a single bedroom flat in Portobello High Street[230] where, but for support from the defender, she would be entirely dependent on state benefit. In the foregoing circumstances I am quite satisfied that, without support from the defender, the pursuer would be likely to suffer serious financial hardship . . ."

Hardship *as a result of the divorce or dissolution*

4–84   The wording of s.9(1)(e) makes it clear that the serious financial hardship must arise *as a result of the divorce or dissolution*. If a party is likely to suffer serious financial hardship in the future, but that hardship is not a result of the divorce or dissolution, then a claim will not be appropriate. This distinction will be important in some cases. In *Barclay v Barclay*, 1991 S.C.L.R. 205, the parties had been married for only about three years before the separation. The wife suffered from multiple sclerosis, and it was clear that her financial position would be precarious after the divorce. Sheriff Cameron was asked to consider the wife's claim for periodical allowance under s.9(1)(e).[231] He held that the undoubted hardship which would be suffered by the wife after the divorce was not caused by the divorce. He commented[232]:

"[Section 9(1)(e)] applies only where the party claiming an award seems likely to suffer serious financial hardship as a result of the

---

[228] *Barclay v Barclay*, 1991 S.C.L.R. 205.
[229] At p.324.
[230] Obiter at least it would seem that Oslo is preferable to Portobello High Street.
[231] Having already ruled that an award under s.9(1)(d) was appropriate.
[232] At p.207.

divorce. The simple fact is that due to the sad deterioration of the pursuer's condition her weekly financial needs exceed the defender's weekly income by more than £100. This situation has come about because of the change in the pursuer's condition and not to any extent as a result of the parties' separation or in relation to their prospective divorce. In the absence of divorce the pursuer's greatly increased financial needs would have remained equally incapable of being met from the defender's income. In that hypothetical situation the pursuer would also have required substantial support from public funds. It is for this reason that I consider that the cases of *Johnstone* and *Birnie*,[233] supra fall to be distinguished on the facts. In each of these cases the pursuer evidently remained in the community and her financial needs were capable of being met from the defender's resources. I am not oblivious to the fact that any contribution which the defender may have to make towards the pursuer's maintenance would be reflected by a lessening of the burden on public funds. In my view, however, my decision as to the application of principle (e) in the particular circumstances of this case hinges on whether the pursuer seems likely to suffer serious financial hardship as a result of the divorce. If periodical allowance at the rate of £15 per week ceases three years after divorce,[234] she would sustain a reduction of only about five per centum of her total weekly income. Before a party can rely on principle (e) he or she must demonstrate not merely that financial hardship but serious financial hardship seems likely to result. I do not consider that the pursuer has established hardship of that nature . . ."

The fact that the section speaks of hardship *as a result of the divorce or dissolution* presents an interesting (if rather distasteful) logical argument that, if a party is already suffering serious financial hardship prior to the divorce or dissolution, then there can be no claim under this section. So, one party might stop paying aliment before the divorce or dissolution, thus causing financial hardship to the other party. The argument runs that any hardship continuing after the divorce or dissolution is not *caused by the divorce or dissolution*.[235] The Inner House considered this argument and rejected it in *Haugan v Haugan* 2002 S.C. 631.[236] However, s.9(1)(e) is not designed to create a situation where things continue for the claimant just as if divorce or dissolution had never taken place. The obligation to aliment ends on divorce or dissolution. Serious financial hardship must be established. In addition to the loss of the right to

---

[233] *Johnstone v Johnstone*, 1990 S.C.L.R. 358; *Birnie v Birnie* (Sheriff Fulton, Inverness, April 26, 1988; unreported). It should be noted that in terms of s.11(5) of the Act, one of the factors to be applied in considering whether an award under s.9(1)(e) is appropriate is the duration of the marriage or civil partnership. In *Barclay* the duration of the marriage was only about three years, whereas the cases which are distinguished both involved marriages of much longer duration.

[234] This being the amount and period of award under s.9(1)(d).

[235] See *Barclay v Barclay* above.

[236] See para.4–74. In short the Inner House held that the loss of the right to aliment may in itself be enough to constitute serious financial hardship in terms of the Act; actual loss is not needed.

interim aliment, all of the other financial factors of the case will need to be considered.[237]

Relationship with section 9(1)(d)

4-85   Parties facing a claim for periodical allowance under s.9(1)(e) will be aware that the award can be made without limit of time. It is therefore in their interests to argue that the claim should be awarded under s.9(1)(d) where the maximum period of payment is three years to allow a party to adjust to a loss of support on divorce or dissolution—an award limited to three years will save money. As Sheriff Jardine put it in *Bell v Bell*, 1988 S.C.L.R. 457[238]:

> "I have heard it suggested colloquially (if less than elegantly) that the principle embodied in section 9(1)(d) of the Act, which would normally limit the provision of periodical allowance to allow for adjustment to loss of support to a maximum period of three years from and after the date of divorce, fulfils the modern precept that marriage is no longer to be regarded as 'a meal ticket for life'."

The principles in s.9(1)(d) and (e) are clear and distinct. For example, an award may be justified under para.(d) but not under para.(e).[239] To allow an award under para.(e) there must be serious financial hardship, so a party who has a reasonable income and a secure job is unlikely to obtain an award, although they might be entitled to an award under para.(d) for a limited period if they need time to adjust to a loss of support.[240] The awards under paras (d) and (e) are not alternatives; both can apply in the same case. It is possible that an award under para.(e) (to relieve serious financial hardship) might not be enough to provide for the period of re-adjustment under para.(d). In these circumstances, it may be that an award under both principles will be justified.[241]

On a practical level, it seems sensible for a party seeking an award under s.9(1)(e) to be fully prepared to lead evidence about the difficulties that they will encounter in securing a further source of income. On the other hand, a party seeking to resist such a claim will want to lead evidence showing that there are suitable jobs available, even if some retraining is required. This would perhaps allow the focus of the claim to be moved to s.9(1)(d), with the consequent three-year time limit for periodical allowance.

Table of cases

4-86   There is a relatively small number of reported cases dealing with s.9(1)(e). An examination of the decided cases may be helpful in analysing potential claims. The following table may be of some assistance.

---

[237] See e.g. *Bell v Bell*, 1988 S.C.L.R. 457.

[238] At p.464.

[239] *Barclay v Barclay* above; *Kelly v Kelly*, 1992 G.W.D. 36–2130; *Murray v Murray*, 1993 G.W.D. 16–1058.

[240] See e.g. *Kelly v Kelly*, 1992 G.W.D. 36–2130.

[241] See e.g. *Stott v Stott*, 1987 G.W.D. 17–645; *McKenzie v McKenzie*, 1991 S.L.T. 461.

Case	Granted/ Refused	Period of Award	Relevant Facts
Stott v Stott, 1987 G.W.D. 17–645	Granted	Three years under s.9(1)(d) then four further years under s.9(1)(e)	The husband earned about £190 per week. The wife earned about £7 per week. The wife was 42 years old. The couple had been married and co-habiting for 24 years. The wife was not well-educated. Periodical allowance awarded for three years under s.9(1)(d) at £75 per week and at £55 per week for a further four years under s.9(1)(e).
Birnie v Birnie, (1988—Sheriff Fulton, Inverness) unreported but referred to *in Barclay v Barclay* below	Granted	Three years under s.9(1)(d) and then a further seven years under s.9(1)(e)	The parties were married for about 22 years. The wife suffered from epilepsy and was incapable of earning. The court awarded periodical allowance for three years under s.9(1)(d) and for a further seven years under s.9(1)(e). However, the sheriff did not think it fair and reasonable for the periodical allowance to be paid until death or remarriage (for reasons that are not entirely clear).
Petrie v Petrie, 1988 S.C.L.R. 390	Refused	n/a	The couple were married and co-habiting for about 2½ years. Having regard to the short duration of the marriage and the standard of living enjoyed by the parties during the marriage, the court was not persuaded that an award under s.9(1)(e) was appropriate.
Atkinson v Atkinson, 1988 S.C.L.R. 396	Refused	n/a	The couple were married and living together for about five years. There were no children. The husband had about £20,600 annual gross income and the wife had about £5,040 annual gross income. The court noted that her earnings were about one-fifth of joint income. It was not unreasonable for her to expect one-third of joint income, but she would need to adjust from that level to her own income. An award under s.9(1)(d) was made to allow her to adjust to the loss of support over two years but the wife had an income and substantial capital. Although she would not be able to maintain the same standard of living as she had enjoyed before the divorce, there was no evidence that she would suffer "serious financial hardship".
Bell v Bell, 1988 S.C.L.R. 457	Granted	Until husband's 60th birthday or wife's death or remarriage	The wife was aged 51. The husband was 53. The couple had been married and living together for about 26 years prior to the separation. They were separated for about two years before the case came to proof. The wife was trained as a primary school teacher but had given up work early in the marriage when she fell pregnant. Apart from a very short period she had not worked since. She had been almost entirely dependent on the defender for support. He had acquiesced in that arrangement. Following the separation the husband had been paying interim aliment, ultimately at £450 per month. The husband was due to retire at 60. Periodical allowance ordered at £300 per month until the husband reached 60 or until the death or remarriage of the wife, whichever was earliest.

Muir v Muir, 1989 S.L.T. (Sh Ct) 20	Refused	n/a	The couple had been married and co-habiting for about 20 years. They separated about four years before the proof. The wife was 47 and suffered from an arthritic condition. Between the separation and the proof, the husband was paying the wife £35 per week as interim personal aliment. He had also been paying £25 per week as aliment for the daughter until she reached the age of 17 (the year before the proof). He had been meeting certain household costs. The wife hoped to resume part-time work when her medical condition improved. Her grown up children made a small contribution to the household. The court ordered £45 per week periodical allowance for one year under s.9(1)(d), but it was held that no award under s.9(1)(e) was appropriate.
Tyrrell v Tyrrell, 1990 S.L.T. 406	Refused	n/a	The wife was married and living with her husband for 18 years. She was in part-time employment and in receipt of maintenance for seven years after separation until the date of the proof. She had received substantial capital on separation and further capital on divorce. An award of periodical allowance under s.9(1)(d) was made, but none was made under s.9(1)(e).
Johnstone v Johnstone, 1990 S.L.T. (Sh Ct) 79	Granted	Until death or remarriage of spouse entitled to the award	The parties were both aged 35. They had been married and co-habiting for about 13 years. The wife was epileptic and unfit for employment. The condition was not a temporary one which would disappear within a predictable period of time. The sheriff principal (affirming the sheriff) held that an award of periodical allowance was appropriate until the death or remarriage of the wife. It was observed that, if the wife's condition improved, then it would be open to the husband to apply to the court for a variation of the order.
McGuire v McGuire's CB, 1991 S.L.T.. (Sh Ct) 76	n/a	No periodical allowance, but s.9(1)(e) used to balance against other considerations in decision on payment of capital sum	The pursuer wife sought a payment of a capital sum from the defender's curator bonis. The defender had been injured in a criminal incident. He was incapacitated to the extent that he would need residential care for the rest of his life. The pursuer wife had the responsibility during the marriage of caring for eight children, had no possibility of secure employment, and had the defender not suffered the injury, she would have expected support from him until he was about 65. The court appears to have used s.9(1)(e) as one factor favouring the wife, but this seems to have been balanced against other factors favouring the husband.
Barclay v Barclay, 1991 S.C.L.R. 205	Refused	n/a	The wife was 29. The husband was 28. The couple were married and co-habiting for just over three years. There were no children. The wife's circumstances were that she suffered from multiple sclerosis. She was held to be entitled to an award of periodical allowance of £15 per week for three years under s.9(1)(d). However, when this payment stopped she would suffer only a five per cent drop in income. The sheriff concluded that this would not constitute serious financial hardship, and refused an award under s.9(1)(e).

McKenzie v McKenzie, 1991 S.L.T. 461	Granted	Three years under s.9(1)(d) then indef-initely under s.9(1)(e)	The parties were married and co-habiting for about 10 years. By the time of the proof the wife was 59 and the defender 54. The wife had been dependent to a substantial degree on her husband. She was likely to be "seriously short of money" following the divorce. The court took account of the fact that it was likely that she would have to invest the capital sum awarded to her in her business. Periodical allowance awarded under s.9(1)(d) for an initial period of three years and then indefinitely under s.9(1)(e). (NOTE—it has been suggested that this case might have been better decided under s.9(1): see the commentary to the S.C.L.R. report at 1991 S.C.L.R. 255).
Murray v Mur-ray, 1993 G.W.D. 16–1058	Refused	n/a	The wife was aged 56. The husband had paid mortgage and insurance premiums fol-lowing separation and in addition had paid a monthly payment to the wife of £350. The wife worked part time as a teacher for $1\frac{1}{2}$ days per week. The wife had been depend-ent to a substantial degree on the husband for support, but the court noted that the amount of work she undertook was a matter of personal choice. An award of £250 per month was made for a period of about two years under s.9(1)(d) until she retired at which point her pension would give her suf-ficient income and no further support to cover the period of adjustment would be required. An award under s.9(1)(e) was not made because the wife failed to establish she would suffer serious financial hardship.
Savage v Sav-age, 1993 G.W.D. 28–1779	Refused	n/a	The wife sought periodical allowance. She had been certified by her GP as unable to work as a result of neck and lower back pain. However, there appear to have been two main factors which led the court to refuse to award periodical allowance. First, as part of the division of the matrimonial property, the wife was to receive a substan-tial capital sum (based on equal division of the net value of the matrimonial property). Secondly, the husband's resources after the separation were likely to be stretched as a result of liability to pay tax debts and also to fund borrowing to pay a capital sum to the wife.
Kelly v Kelly, 1993 G.W.D. 36–2130	Refused	n/a	The wife was 56 years old. The couple had been married and living together for 26 years. The wife had a secure job and a reasonable salary and accordingly could not be said to be likely to suffer serious finan-cial hardship. However, she was entitled to periodical allowance for three years under s.9(1)(d).

Davidson v Davidson, 1994 S.L.T. 506	Periodical allowance not granted but s.9(1)(e) one factor in unequal sharing	n/a	The couple were married and co-habiting for about three years. There were two dependent children. The wife was going to be wholly responsible for the children after divorce. The husband was 46 at the date of proof, suffered mental health difficulties and had a very restricted earning capacity. The case was unusual because many factors in the 1985 Act were relevant. One of the factors which the court bore in mind was that the husband would suffer serious financial hardship as a result of the divorce in terms of s.9(1)(e). It is impossible to quantify the impact of s.9(1)(e) because of all of the other factors bearing on the case.
Gribb v Gribb, 1994 S.L.T. (Sh Ct) 43; 1996 S.L.T. 719	Granted	Death or remarriage of party obtaining the award	The couple were married and living together for nearly 40 years. The wife was 62 at the date of divorce. There were no dependent children. At the time of the divorce the wife had a total net income derived from her pensions of about £58 per week. The defender had total net income of about £168 net per week. The court at first instance noted that there was a marked disparity in incomes. The wife was to receive the matrimonial home in the settlement. Whilst there would be no mortgage, the court was of the view that she would suffer serious financial hardship were she to rely only on her pensions. She was not in good health. She was of an age where it would be difficult to get work. Periodical allowance was awarded until her death or remarriage.
Buckle v Buckle, 1995 S.C.L.R. 590	Refused	n/a	The parties had been married for 30 years. The brief report indicates that the wife sought long-term periodical allowance along the lines allowed in *Bell v Bell*, 1988 S.C.L.R. 457. The court ordered a relatively high capital sum to be paid by instalments over a five-year period, resulting in the wife being paid £250 per month by instalments over this period. Any financial hardship was mitigated by the capital award, but she was awarded periodical allowance of £100 per month (apparently under s.9(1)(d)).
Bolton v Bolton, 1995 G.W.D. 14–799	Granted	Only until payment of capital sum	The husband and wife were married for more than 33 years prior to their separation. The wife was aged 60. She had no earning capacity at all. They had enjoyed a comfortable but not an extravagant lifestyle during their marriage. They had worked together for the benefit of their family. The wife was dependent to a substantial degree on the husband. She was likely to suffer serious financial hardship as a result of the divorce. However, because of the substantial assets which the wife would receive after divorce, the court was of the view that she would have sufficient resources to live comfortably once the capital sum was paid. The court ordered payment of periodical allowance until payment of the capital sum (at the same rate as interim aliment had been paid in the run up to the divorce).

Haugan v Haugan, 1996 S.L.T. 321; 2002 S.C. 631	Granted	Without limit of time	The couple were married for 27 years. The wife was 51 years old and had been in employment for only short periods during the marriage. She had poor health, and would be unfit for employment altogether for at least two years following the separation. Her husband had a high income, and had a very substantial surplus of income over expenditure. At first instance the Inner House awarded periodical allowance at £1,000 per month without limit of time (reduced to £500 per month on the defender demonstrating a material change in circumstances).
Galloway v Galloway, 2003 Fam. L.R. 10	Granted	Until 60th birthday, death or remarriage of spouse obtaining the award	The wife was 55. There were no dependent children. The husband had substantial income and the wife a low income.
Sullivan v Sullivan, 2003 Fam. L.R. 58	Granted	Until death or remarriage	The report is rather unclear, and it appears that s.9(1)(c) and (e) may both have had a bearing on the decision. The capital sum paid to the wife was modest and there was a substantial discrepancy in earning power between the parties. Periodical allowance of £75 per week was ordered by the sheriff at first instance. On appeal the decision was described as "finely balanced" but Lord Elmslie refused to interfere with the exercise of the discretion of the sheriff.
W v W, 2004 Fam. L.R. 54	Refused	n/a	The arguments are reported rather briefly, but the court took the view that there was no justification for an award under s.9(1)(e) and even if there had been justification, periodical allowance was inappropriate as an award could have been satisfied through payment of a capital sum or transfer of property.
CR or D v ARD, 2005 Fam. L.B. 76-4.	Granted	Until death or remarriage	The couple were married and living together for about 17 years. The wife was 44, suffered from schizophrenia and was unlikely ever to earn her own living. The couple had a good standard of living during the marriage, but following the separation the wife had to rely on state benefits and an award of interim aliment to meet her modest outgoings. The husband had an income in excess of £100,000 per year.

Chapter 5

THE RELEVANT DATE

General discussion

5–01   Section 10(2) of the Family Law (Scotland) Act 1985 ("the Act") provides that (subject to one important caveat discussed at para.5–06 below) the net value of matrimonial or partnership property will be its value (after deduction of relevant debts) on the "relevant date". The relevant date is important for two principal reasons. First, the assets which make up matrimonial or partnership property will vary from day to day—on any given day one of the parties might win the lottery or write off the Rolls Royce. Secondly, the value of those assets will change over the course of time.

After the couple cease to co-habit, a long period may elapse before the couple (or the court) decide upon how the matrimonial or partnership property is to be divided. During that time the parties' financial situation may have changed considerably. The relevant date is the date when a snapshot of the matrimonial or partnership property is taken. The Act provides that it is the property owned and the debts due on that date which arc to bc valued for the purpose of division of the net value of the matrimonial or partnership property. Similarly, it is (subject to the exception to be discussed at para.5–06 below) the net value of the assets at the relevant date which is to be shared fairly between the parties on divorce or dissolution in terms of s.9(1)(a). Therefore, establishing the relevant date, and the value of assets and debts on that date, is of fundamental importance.

Establishing the relevant date

5–02   Under s.10(3) "the relevant date" is the earlier of:

(a) (subject to s.10(7)),[1] the date on which the persons ceased to co-habit; or

(b) the date of service of the summons in the action for divorce or for dissolution of the civil partnership.

The circumstances in which para.(b) will be the earlier of the two dates will be rare, but it is possible that the couple may still be co-habiting (within the meaning of the Act) at the time that the action of divorce or dissolution is raised and in those circumstances, the relevant date will be the date of service of the action.[2]

---

[1] Which deals with short periods of reconciliation after long periods of separation. See para.15–05.

[2] s.10(3).

Even when there is a disagreement between the parties about the precise relevant date, this will often make little practical difference if the value or composition of the matrimonial or partnership property has not changed significantly between the disputed dates. However, in some cases a dispute can be material. For example, if the husband maintains that the relevant date is July 1; and the wife claims it is August 1; and between those dates, on July 15, the husband won the pools; if the husband is correct, the winnings are his (he won them after the relevant date); if the wife is correct, then she is entitled to a fair share of the winnings in terms of s.9(1)(a) (they were acquired during the marriage and before the relevant date).

In some instances then, the issue of the correct "relevant date" is a live one. In such cases, care will need to be taken by solicitors to try to establish the correct relevant date at the earliest possible opportunity. If the wrong date is picked, this may mean that property is established and valued at the wrong date, resulting in a lot of wasted time, money and effort. If it is possible for parties to agree the relevant date, then this should be encouraged—it will mean that only one set of valuations will need to be obtained. If agreement cannot be reached, then the issue may need to be determined by the court. It may be appropriate to have a preliminary proof on the issue in some circumstances.[3] Generally three issues will be important and these are now considered.

1. The facts

The parties may present quite different accounts of the latter days of **5–03** the marriage or civil partnership (particularly if large sums of money are at stake depending on which relevant date is accepted), and pleadings and evidence will be important.[4]

2. When is co-habitation not co-habitation?

Section 27(2) provides a definition of when, for the purposes of the **5–04** Act, married couples cease to co-habit:

> "For the purposes of this Act, the parties to a marriage shall be held to co-habit with one another only when they are in fact living together as man and wife."

---

[3] See *Banks v Banks*, 2005 Fam. L.R. 116.

[4] See e.g. *Brown v Brown*, 1996 Fam. L.B. 23–9 and 1998 Fam. L.R. 81. In *Webster v Webster*, 2003 G.W.D. 5–118, the husband claimed that the relevant date was the date when he began an affair with a third party in 1997. He claimed that, although they were living under the same roof, the marriage was a sham from then on. The wife claimed that, after her husband admitted the affair, there was a reconciliation, and the relevant date did not actually occur until October 2000 when she moved out of the shared bedroom. The court preferred the evidence of the wife. In *Mayor v Mayor*, 1995 S.L.T. 1097, the wife claimed that she had not lived with the defender since 1983, and had only spent one night under his roof since that date. On the other hand the husband claimed that on January 11, 1992 the parties went through a "ceremony of reconciliation" and after that continued to live together until August 3, 1992 when the wife left to go to India, but when she returned in 1993 the couple resumed cohabitation until July 1994 when the wife told the husband that she had been instructed by her solicitors not to have anything more to do with him. Even if men really are from Mars, and women from Venus, the difference in the parties' recollections is remarkable. (Lord Marnoch at p.1099: "In the foregoing circumstances there is no escape from the fact that in this case someone is giving perjured evidence to a degree which I confess I have seldom before witnessed.")

So, for married couples (although not for civil partners) the Act provides that they are taken to cease to co-habit when they stop "in fact living together as man and wife". Importantly, this means that, for the purposes of establishing the relevant date, parties may have stopped co-habiting although they are still living in the same house.

What factors will the court look at when considering whether parties living under the same roof, in fact, ceased to live together as man and wife in terms of the Act? The issue is one of fact, and will depend on the circumstances of the case.[5] The issue is to be determined objectively and the intention of the parties is not determinative, although this may be an important consideration.[6] If the parties are not staying with one another overnight then it will be difficult to maintain that there is co-habitation, even if there are short daytime visits.[7] Significant changes in financial arrangements may be important in some cases.[8] Sleeping and eating arrangements may be material. In *Buczynska v Buczynski*, 1989 S.L.T. 558, the parties agreed that they had ceased to co-habit for the purposes of the Act, but they disagreed about when co-habitation had stopped. Unusually, even at the date of the proof they were still living together, Lord Morton of Shuna discussed the arguments[9]:

> "There was also some disagreement between counsel as to the 'relevant date' to be decided in applying the provision of s.10 provisions of the Family Law (Scotland) Act. Counsel for the pursuer argued for May 1987, being the date of the letter from the defender's solicitors to the pursuer requesting that she leave. Counsel for the defender contended for 1980 or 1981 being the date when the pursuer told the defender of her relationship with [a third party]. I consider that on the evidence the parties ceased to co-habit, in the sense of ceasing to share the same bedroom and the pursuer ceasing to cook for the defender, at about the date of the letter and I consider that the relevant date is May 1987."

Marital relations[10] are important.[11] Perhaps unsurprisingly, parties who are spending a significant time with one another, and who are sleeping with one another, will find it difficult to argue that they have ceased to live together as man and wife. In *Brown v Brown*, 2003 G.W.D. 19–588, the parties asked the Outer House for a determination on the issue of the relevant date. The husband claimed that they had not lived together as husband and wife since 1991 when he left to live with

---

[5] In *Banks v Banks*, 2005 Fam. L.R 116 (also discussed at 2005 Fam. L.B. 78–5) reference is made to E.M. Clive *The Law of Husband and Wife in Scotland*, 4th edn, at para.21–075 where illustrative factors are listed—the amount and nature of time spent together; sleeping together and having sexual relations; eating together and having a social life together; sharing resources and tasks; and being mutually supportive and affectionate.

[6] See *Banks v Banks*, 2005 Fam. L.R. 116 at paras 33 and 48.

[7] See *Banks v Banks*, 2005 Fam. L.R. 116 at para.47.

[8] See *Banks v Banks*, 2005 Fam. L.R. 116 at para.48.

[9] At p.560.

[10] Which one presumes means sex rather than arguing over the remote control.

[11] See e.g. *Webster v Webster*, 2003 G.W.D. 5–118.

another woman. He moved back into the matrimonial home in 1996, but denied that he had resumed co-habitation with his wife at that stage. The evidence was that, after 1996 the husband stayed irregularly at the house, but during these periods the husband and wife slept in the same room and were having "marital relations". Lord McCluskey held that, although the husband had been absent on many occasions (and was conducting an affair), the overwhelming evidence was that there had been a resumption of co-habitation.

However, each marriage and civil partnership is different. In some cases, the norm may be that one party is not often at home, and devotes little time to family life. The court will look carefully at changes occurring in the normal pattern of activity (whatever that may be for a particular couple).[12]

3. *Periods of reconciliation*

It is more difficult to establish the relevant date if there have been **5–05** periods of reconciliation. In practice, this is not unusual. The last stage of a marriage or partnership often includes periods of trial separation, holidays apart, short periods of reconciliation and so on. All of this can serve to cloud the determination of the relevant date. The difference can be very important, for it is often during this period that the value of the matrimonial and partnership property can change as the parties start to re-arrange their finances. Section 10(7) sets down the rules which govern this situation and bears repeating here:

> "For the purposes of section (3) above no account shall be taken of any cessation of cohabitation where the persons thereafter resumed cohabitation, except where the persons ceased to cohabit for a continuous period of 90 days or more before resuming cohabitation for a period or periods of less than 90 days in all."

This is not an easy paragraph to read,[13] but the effect is that, if there has been a long period of separation (at least 90 continuous days), followed by short reconciliations (totalling less than 90 days), then the earlier date of separation will be the relevant date. Otherwise the earlier date will be ignored and the date of the final split will be the relevant date.[14]

Valuation of property subject to property transfer orders

The general rule in the Act is that the net value of the matrimonial **5–06** or partnership property is its value on the relevant date.[15] However this is subject to one important caveat. The Family Law (Scotland) Act

---

[12] See *Banks v Banks*, 2005 Fam. L.R. 116.

[13] It is difficult not to sympathise with Sheriff Bell in *Pryde v Pryde*, 1991 S.L.T. (Sh Ct) 26 when he said: "What effect then does s.10(7) have on this? I find this section extremely difficult to understand."

[14] *Brown v Brown*, 2003 G.W.D. 19–588 is a useful case which shows how these rules operate in practice.

[15] s.10(2).

2006 inserted[16] s.10(3A) of the 1985 Act. This provision has a significant impact on the date when certain property is to be valued. Where the property to be valued (for the purposes of establishing the value of matrimonial or partnership property) is to be transferred under a property transfer order,[17] that property is not to be valued at the relevant date, but at the "appropriate valuation date" which will be on one of three possible dates:

(a) where the parties agree on a date, that date;
(b) where there is no such agreement, the date of the making of the property transfer order;
(c) if the court considers that, because of the exceptional circumstances of the case (b) above should not apply, the appropriate valuation date shall be such other date (being a date as near as may be to (b)) as the court may determine.

The introduction of this provision was designed to circumvent the significant injustices which sometimes occurred as a result of the decision in *Wallis v Wallis*, 1992 S.C. 455. Put briefly, *Wallis* held that, where the court decided that a transfer of property order should be granted in favour of one party, that property had to be valued at the relevant date for the purposes of division of matrimonial property, and no account was to be taken of any increase in the value after the relevant date. The injustice this might create can best be illustrated by an example.

Imagine a case where the couple jointly own a house which was worth £100,000 at the relevant date but, by the date of the proof its value has grown to £180,000. The court decides that it is reasonable to transfer the house to one of the parties on divorce or dissolution. In these circumstances, using the old rule established in *Wallis v Wallis*, the party who received the transfer of the house would be treated (for the purposes of calculating the division of matrimonial or partnership property) as having received an asset valued at £100,000 (i.e. the value at the relevant date), and (on the assumption of equal sharing) would have to make a balancing payment to the other party of £50,000. In reality, at the point of the proof, the party retaining the house obtained an asset worth £90,000 (one half of the value of the house) in return for a balancing payment of only £50,000. This was often referred to as a windfall in favour of the party who received the transfer.

Section 10(3A) is designed to combat this problem. If the property is to be transferred, it is to be valued either at an agreed date or the date of transfer.[18] So, in the above example, the balancing payment would be calculated based on the value of the property at the point of decree which would appear to produce a more equitable result.

---

[16] Under s.16.
[17] Under s.8(1)(aa).
[18] Or in exceptional circumstances at a date as near as may be to the date of making the order—s.10(3A).

Whilst s.10(3A) makes a significant contribution to solving the *Wallis* problem, it is not a radical overhaul of the law. The provision only applies where a property transfer order is made. So, if an asset which grows in value is in the sole name of one party and is to be retained by that party, there will be no property transfer order, and s.10(3A) will not apply. This may create injustices in certain situations. To explore one of the problems, consider another example:

The facts are as follows:

- H & W separate.
- At the relevant date the only matrimonial property is (a) a house in joint names worth £100,000, and (b) shares in the husband's name worth £150,000.
- The couple fail to agree a settlement and litigate.
- After proof the court decides that: (a) the husband's interest in the house is to be transferred to the wife; (b) the shares are to remain in the husband's name; and (c) matrimonial property is to be shared equally.
- By the date of decree the values of the two assets are as follows: (a) the house has risen in value to £200,000; and (b) the shares in the husband's name have risen in value to £250,000.

Consider now the difference in the way that these circumstances are treated, before and after the introduction of s.10(3A).

Before s.10(3A)—Wallis applied
The house is transferred to W. Both the house and the shares are valued at the relevant date for the purposes of financial provision. W is treated as having received an asset worth £100,000; H is treated as having received an asset worth £150,000. The Act requires a balancing payment of £25,000 from H to W to achieve equal sharing. This means that at the date of decree W receives assets with a value of £225,000 (the house worth £200,000 at the date of decree and the balancing payment of £25,000). On the other hand H also receives assets with a value of £225,000 (the share portfolio worth £250,000 by the date of decree less the balancing payment).

After s.10(3A)
Again the house is transferred to W. Now the law is that the house will be valued at the date of decree (because it is subject to a transfer order) but the portfolio is valued at the relevant date (if we assume it is not to be subject to a transfer order and simply retained by H). So, for the purposes of the Act W is treated as receiving an asset worth £200,000 (the value of the house at transfer date), but H is treated as having an asset worth £150,000 (relevant date value). Now a balancing payment of £25,000 is due by W to H. The effect is that W at the date of decree receives assets worth £175,000 (the house now worth £200,000 less the balancing payment of £25,000) whereas H receives assets worth

£275,000 (his portfolio now worth £250,000 plus the balancing payment of £25,000).

It is not yet clear how the courts will approach the situation outlined above, but it does seem that the new rules will not produce an equitable result in all situations.[19]

---

[19] It has been suggested that s.10(3A) might work in a different way. The argument is that only the half of the asset which is to be transferred under the property transfer order which is to be valued at the transfer date. So, in the above example, the value of the wife's share of the house would continue to be valued at the relevant date value (i.e. half of £100,00 = £50,000) whereas the husband's share would be valued at the transfer date (half of £200,000 = £100,000). For a critique of this approach see David Nichols, "The Wallis problem and s.16", 2006 80 Fam. L.B. 1–4.

CHAPTER 6

MATRIMONIAL PROPERTY AND PARTNERSHIP PROPERTY

General discussion

Section 10(4) of the Family Law (Scotland) Act 1985 ("the Act") **6–01** defines the term "matrimonial property":

> "Subject to subsections (5) and (5A) below,[1] in this section and in section 11 of this Act 'the matrimonial property' means all the property belonging to the parties or either of them at the relevant date which was acquired by them or him (otherwise than by way of gift or succession from a third party)—
>
> (a) before the marriage for use by them as a family home or as furniture or plenishings for such home; or
>
> (b) during the marriage but before the relevant date."

Section 10(4A) defines the partnership property of civil partners in similar terms.

If this definition is broken down, it can be seen that matrimonial property or partnership property will comprise:

(a) all of the property which the couple acquired after the marriage or registration but before the relevant date other than gifts or inheritances;

(b) any property (other than gifts or inheritances) acquired by them before the marriage or registration for use by them as a family home or furniture or plenishings for that home; and

(c) interests in pensions or life policies held at the relevant date (although the value of these will be apportioned if contributions started before the marriage or registration).

Putting this another way, the following categories of property are not matrimonial or partnership property:

(a) property acquired by either party before the marriage or registration (except (i) property acquired for use as a family

---

[1] s.10(5) deals with pensions and life policies. These are dealt with in greater detail later in this chapter, but essentially if a party has an interest in one of these assets at the relevant date, then it will be matrimonial or partnership property even if started before the date of marriage or registration. However, the value is to be apportioned, so that only the value for the period from the date of the marriage or registration up to the relevant date is to be included as matrimonial or partnership property. Section 10(5A) makes similar provision for compensation payable to a party under the Pension Protection Fund.

home and its contents, and (ii) interests in pensions and life policies started before marriage or registration);
(b) property gifted to the parties;
(c) inherited property; and
(d) property acquired after the relevant date.[2]

The definitions of "matrimonial property" and "partnership property" are amongst the most important concepts in the Act. If an asset falls within the categories of property set out in these definitions then it will fall to be shared fairly between the parties in terms of s.9(1)(a). If not, ownership will be determined by the normal principles of property law.

This does not mean that non-matrimonial or non-partnership property is entirely irrelevant for the purposes of the Act. First, fair sharing of matrimonial or partnership property under s.9(1)(a) is only one of the five principles set out in s.9. The other four principles set out in s.9(1)(b) to (e) do not refer in any way to matrimonial or partnership property, and can be used to justify awards of financial provision themselves.[3] Secondly, in making any order for financial provision (justified by any of the five s.9 principles), the court has to be satisfied that the order is reasonable having regard to the resources of the parties,[4] and the term "resources" includes present and foreseeable resources.[5] These resources will include all assets of the parties—not just matrimonial or partnership property. However, it must be clearly understood that non-matrimonial or non-partnership resources are not part of the pool of assets to be divided in terms of s.9(1)(a); they are simply resources which may be relevant to the *way* that an award of financial provision is to be funded.[6]

Valuation of matrimonial and partnership property

6–02   In general, matrimonial and partnership property will be valued at the relevant date.[7] However, any property which is to be subject to a property transfer order is to be valued at a date agreed by the parties or, in the absence of such agreement, at the date of the transfer (or a date as near as possible to this).[8] Parties should lead evidence about the value of property: if they do not there is a danger that the court may leave the item out of account.[9] The way that the courts approach the valuation of particular assets is dealt with in more detail later in this chapter. However, the general tenor of reported decisions is that the courts will try to establish the real value of the asset to the parties rather than a hypothetical value based on contingencies. If a party arranges or conceals his affairs in such a way as to make accurate valuation impossible, the court may draw an adverse inference from this and place a value on the property accordingly.[10]

---

[2] See paras 6–58 to 6–64.
[3] So, for example, if there is no matrimonial or partnership property at all, s.9(1)(b) to (e) could still justify an award of financial provision. See the more detailed discussion at para.4–26.
[4] s.8(2)(b).
[5] s.27(1).
[6] See paras 3–02 to 3–08.
[7] s.10(2).
[8] s.10(3A).
[9] See e.g. *George v George*, 1991 S.L.T. (Sh Ct) 8.
[10] *Berry v Berry*, 1991 S.L.T. 42; *AB v CD*, 2007 Fam. L.R. 53; *Ali v Ali (No.2)*, 2001 S.C. 618; 2001 S.L.T. 602.

What is "property" for the purposes of the Act?

The courts have interpreted the term "property" broadly. It includes **6–03** heritable and moveable property;[11] and corporeal and incorporeal property.[12] It includes obvious assets like houses, bank accounts and cars; and less obvious ones like pension rights, fishing quotas and claims for damages. The safe course is to assume that anything of financial value is likely to be construed as property. When preparing for proof, parties will need to carefully plead details of all assets and debts which they wish to be taken into account. A party seeking to challenge an opponent's averments about matrimonial or partnership property will need to lead evidence and cross-examine on the disputed matters.[13]

Paragraphs 6–04 to 6–50 which follow examine a number of different categories of assets which have been considered by the courts.

Heritable property

General

Heritable property acquired during the marriage or civil partnership **6–04** and before the relevant date will be matrimonial or partnership property. Whether parties own such property will be a matter of evidence.[14] It is also important to note that s.10(4) and (4A) allow one special category of heritage acquired before the marriage or registration to be treated as matrimonial or partnership property, namely that acquired for use as a family home. Sometimes title to a heritable property might stand in the name of one of the parties as an individual, but if it is established that it is truly held in trust for another person, then it will be excluded from the pool of matrimonial or partnership property notwithstanding the terms of the title.[15]

When considering whether a particular heritable property is part of the matrimonial or partnership property, it does not matter whether the property has been acquired in joint names or the sole name of either party. If it was acquired during the marriage or civil partnership and before the relevant date (or if it falls in the special category of family homes mentioned above) then it will be matrimonial or partnership property regardless of in whose name the title stands. It will be aggregated with the other matrimonial or partnership property and will be subject to fair sharing in terms of s.9(1)(a).

Valuation of heritage

Heritage is valued at its market value. This is not a precise art and a **6–05** range of values may be justifiable. Parties and agents should be prepared to negotiate within reasonable parameters. If a value cannot be agreed,

---

[11] *Petrie v Petrie*, 1988 S.C.L.R. 390; *Smith v Smith*, 1992 G.W.D. 23–1325.
[12] *Latter v Latter*, 1990 S.L.T. 805.
[13] *Berry v Berry*, 1991 S.L.T. 42.
[14] In *Smith v Smith*, 1992 G.W.D. 23–1325, the wife's father owned a property. A disposition in favour of the wife was found after his death. The husband argued that the property had been gifted to the wife, but the court held that, in the absence of evidence of proof of delivery or recording of the disposition, there was no inference of the gift.
[15] *Marshall v Marshall*, 2007 Fam. L.R. 48.

then both parties will need to appoint expert valuers. In most cases the appropriate expert will be a surveyor. Unusual categories of heritage such as farms or crofts should be valued by an expert with experience in dealing with assets of the appropriate type. In a case which goes to proof the quality of evidence from the expert will be important, and care should be taken over the choice of valuer. The value of heritage may be enhanced in certain circumstances as where planning permission is granted to develop land.[16]

Until the Family Law (Scotland) Act 2006 came into force, all matrimonial and partnership property had to be valued for the purposes of financial provision at the relevant date. *Wallis v Wallis*, 1993 S.C. (H.L.) 49 held that, if it was appropriate to transfer the family home to a spouse on divorce, then the value of the property for the purposes of financial provision under the Act was its value at the relevant date. This meant that, if the house had risen in value after the relevant date, the party retaining the property would receive a windfall of the rise in value.[17] However, matters have now changed. The 2006 Act introduced s.10(3A) of the 1985 Act which provides that, where a property is being transferred to one party under a property transfer order, it is not to be valued at the relevant date but (in the absence of agreement) at the date of transfer.[18] What this means in practice is that, if a party is seeking a property transfer order of heritable property (which tends to rise in value), it will generally be better for them to seek the transfer at the earliest possible opportunity. The more time that passes, the more that property prices will rise, and the more the transferee will need to pay to the other party as a balancing payment. Because of s.10(3A), where the property is to be transferred, the decision in *Wallis* is now negated. However, the new provisions of s.10(3A) only apply *where the property is to be transferred*. If the property already stands in the sole name of the party who is to retain it after divorce or dissolution, then it is still to be valued at the relevant date. Thus, that party might still receive a windfall.

Homes acquired before the marriage or registration

6–06   As mentioned already, a property acquired by one or both of the parties before the marriage or registration will be matrimonial or partnership property if it was acquired by one or both of them "for use by them as a family home".[19] The question of whether houses acquired before the marriage or civil partnership were or were not acquired *for use as a family home* will be one of fact. The wording in the Act does not state that the parties had to be contemplating marriage or civil part-

---

[16] See e.g. *L v L*, 2003 G.W.D. 25–715. If planning permission is granted after the relevant date the enhanced value may not be appropriate. However, note: (1) it may be open to argue that, if there is a reasonable expectation that planning will be granted, then presumably this of itself will enhance the value of the heritage—it will be a matter of evidence; and (2) as a result of the introduction of s.10(3A) of the 1985 Act, if the property is to be subject to a property transfer order in favour of a party, then the property will fall to be valued after the relevant date (generally at the date of transfer).

[17] See para.5–06.

[18] Or in exceptional circumstances, at a date as near as may be to the date of transfer—see s.10(3A).

[19] s.10(4) and (4A).

nership when the property was acquired—only that they intended to use the property as a "family home". The Act deliberately uses this term and not the terms "matrimonial home" or "partnership home". So, it is quite possible that a property acquired long before the couple contemplated marriage or civil partnership might have been bought for use as a family home, and will therefore be drawn into the pool of matrimonial or partnership property. At the point of acquisition, there must have been an intention that the property was to be used as a family home. If there was no such intention at that time, but the parties later use the property as a family home, it will not form part of the pool of matrimonial or partnership property.[20] The comments of Sheriff Craik in *Ranaldi v Ranaldi*, 1994 S.L.T. (Sh Ct) 25 are clear[21]:

> "In the present case, the matrimonial home was purchased years before the defender even started to cohabit with the pursuer, and in no way could it have been said to have been acquired by the pursuer for use as a family home with the defender and his second family. I thus conclude that the house is not 'matrimonial property' . . . ."

Mitchell v Mitchell, 1994 S.C. 601, is an unusual case, but it shows just how wide the definition of a family home can be. The couple married. They then divorced and later still they re-married. During the first marriage they bought a house together for use as a matrimonial home. After the first divorce, the husband retained the house and the wife received a capital sum. They then re-married, and used the original house (now in the name of the husband) as the family home. In the second divorce, the wife argued that it was matrimonial property—it had after all been acquired before the (current) marriage for use as a family home. The Inner House accepted that it was matrimonial property and quoted with approval a passage from an article by Professor Meston, "Matrimonial Property and the Family Home", 1993 S.L.T. (News) 602.[22] In the article the professor anticipated a situation analogous to that in *Mitchell* and commented:

> "The house was acquired for the purpose of the first marriage, and under the present rules would have counted as matrimonial property of that marriage. If, after the first divorce and before there was any question of re-marriage, the husband had sold the house and bought another, it clearly could not be said that house had been acquired by him for use by him and his wife in the second marriage. In *Maclellan v Maclellan*, 1988 S.C.L.R. 399 it was made clear that it is the intention at the time of acquisition which matters. If it was acquired before the marriage, but not for use by the future spouses as a family home, it is not 'matrimonial property' . . . The problem in the present case arose from the fact that this particular house was acquired for use by these spouses as a family home, even although it was for the previous marriage between them. It therefore fitted the

---

[20] See e.g. *Maclellan v Maclellan*, 1988 S.C.L.R. 399.
[21] At p.26.
[22] At p.605.

statutory definition and it seemed that it therefore fell to be taken into consideration as matrimonial property in the divorce settlement in the second marriage. It might seem ludicrous that the inclusion of a house should depend upon it being the same house as was occupied during a previous marriage between the parties, even although a literal interpretation of the statute produced that result. The Act has not provided expressly for this situation, but the answer seems to lie in the 'special circumstance' clause in section 10(1)".

In *Mitchell* the court approved the above passage, pointing out that for a house to be brought into the pool of matrimonial property under s.10(4)(a) three requirements needed to be satisfied: (a) it needed to be owned by one or both of the parties at the relevant date; (b) it must be shown to have been acquired by one of the parties or both of them; and (c) it must have been acquired before the marriage for use by the parties as a family home. On this straightforward literal interpretation, the house fell to be included as part of the matrimonial property. The injustice that this might create is clear. Imagine that, at the time of the first divorce, there were only two assets (a) a house worth £100,000, and (b) £100,000 in a bank account. If one assumes that equal sharing is appropriate, a fair division might be for the husband to take the house, and the wife the cash. However, on the second divorce, assuming the husband still owns the house, it is matrimonial property because of the decision in *Mitchell*, but the cash is not.[23] Accordingly, the house is drawn back into the equation. The answer to this injustice, as Professor Meston suggests, is probably to argue special circumstances under s.10(6).

Special circumstances and section 9 arguments relating to heritage

6–07   Heritable property is generally one of the most valuable assets in any separation. Parties and their advisers should therefore particularly bear in mind that, although an asset is matrimonial or partnership property, its value need not necessarily fall to be divided equally between the parties. There may be special circumstances which justify unequal sharing.[24] Further, sometimes arrangements relating to the heritable property may justify an award in favour of one party in terms of the principles set out in s.9(1)(b) to (e). The following are a few possible arguments for unequal sharing in certain circumstances.

- H owned a house before the marriage. It was not bought for use as a family home. After the marriage it is sold, and the proceeds used to fund the purchase of a new house. The new house is matrimonial property and will fall to be divided on divorce using the principles of the Act. However, a departure from equal sharing may be justified under s.10(6)(b) (source of funds not derived from the income or efforts of the parties during the marriage).
- Civil partners purchase property in *pro indiviso* shares with one partner owning 70 per cent and the other owning 30 per cent.

---

[23] s.10(4)(a) and (4A)(a) only apply to houses, furniture and plenishings.
[24] s.10(6).

Taking title in this way may be suggestive of an agreement between the parties regarding ownership. A special circumstances argument could be advanced under s.10(6)(a).

- H and W own the house jointly. They have a family, and after the separation the principles of the Act justify that the house should be transferred to W with whom the children are to reside. W has insufficient funds to make a balancing payment to H. Section 10(6)(d) may allow unequal sharing because of the nature of the property and its use as a family home.
- If one party enjoys exclusive occupation of the house after separation, it might be argued that they have enjoyed an economic advantage, and the other party has suffered a corresponding disadvantage in terms of s.9(1)(b).
- If one party pays the mortgage or other outgoings after the relevant date, it might be argued that they have suffered an economic disadvantage within the meaning of s.9(1)(b).
- In some limited circumstances, it may be that a fair application of s.9(1)(c) (which provides that the economic burden of childcare should be shared fairly between the parties) will justify the transfer of the family home to one party even though a corresponding balancing payment cannot be made to the other party.

Transfer of heritage—practical issues

The ownership of heritage—particularly the family home—can be a **6–08** sensitive matter. It is often the case that one party will have a strong wish to retain the family home. The transfer of the property to one of the parties might well be a sensible option—it will avoid the delay, uncertainty and expense of a sale. If there are children, it may be desirable to prevent the upset and disruption of a move. However, parties must not lose sight of practicalities. Where one party wishes to retain the family home, it is important to determine at the earliest possible time whether they can realistically afford this. There are numerous factors involved in any case, but some of the questions to be considered are:

- what level of mortgage can the party seeking the transfer obtain (and realistically afford) after the finances are split?
- is there likely to be any increase in income (e.g. through part time work or payment of child support by the other party)?
- what are the other matrimonial or partnership assets? Is it likely that a balancing payment will need to be made by one party to the other?

Of course, the answers to these questions cannot be stated with precision at the outset of any case, but it will often be possible at a fairly early stage to assess whether transfer of the asset is realistic. If it is not, then the best advice (to both parties) may be to explore other options such as sale. This will relieve the parties of mortgage payments, and free up income for child support. If this problem is tackled early, it may save unnecessary tension and allow a quicker resolution to financial matters.

Tenanted properties

If a property is tenanted this will have an effect on its value. In some **6–09** cases the value may be enhanced if, say, commercial premises have a secure tenant who will be in the property for a number of years. On the other hand, if the tenancy is on unfavourable terms (to the landlord) then this will depress the value. The court will have to look at the reality of the situation.[25]

Survivorship destinations

6–10   If a family home is co-owned, the title will often include a survivorship destination. The effect of this is to carry title automatically to the survivor on first death. Survivorship destinations are revoked automatically on divorce or dissolution, unless the parties have specifically stated that the destination is to endure.[26]

Household contents and other corporeal moveables

6–11   Household contents and other corporeal moveables acquired after the marriage or registration and before the relevant date form part of the matrimonial or partnership property. In addition, any items acquired by the parties *before the marriage or registration* for use by them as furniture or plenishings for the family home[27] will be matrimonial or partnership property.[28]

There are various ways to value moveable assets. In most cases it will not be worthwhile for parties to enter into extensive negotiation and litigation about these items—the legal and valuation costs will soon outweigh any financial advantage to be gained. However, it may be important to obtain valuations of particularly expensive assets. Unusual assets such as stamp collections, boats and so on may need to be valued by specialists. If a formal valuation does prove to be necessary, the items should be valued at second-hand value, not at replacement value.[29] However, this still leaves some room for argument as to the precise valuation. Some of the arguments were considered in *Latter v Latter*, 1990 S.L.T. 805 where the court preferred to use a willing buyer/willing seller basis of valuation, rather than a price based on an auction room sale. Lord Marnoch commented[30]:

> "The first disputed item which I propose to deal with concerns the furniture and contents of the former matrimonial home which are now in the possession of the pursuer. It was not, I think, in dispute that these constituted 'matrimonial property' but the parties were at odds as to whether they should be valued for the purposes of the Act at auction room prices (£6,300) or on a willing seller/willing

---

[25] See e.g. *Wilson v Wilson*, 1999 S.L.T. 249 (Outer House, Lord Marnoch) where the husband's pension valuation turned on whether heritable property forming part of the fund should be valued on the basis of vacant possession or subject to tenants' rights—the tenant was a company in which the husband owned nearly all the shares. It was held that, even though there was evidence that the tenant company would not readily give up the lease, it was wrong to view the tenancies as being at arm's length. Lord Marnoch held that a reasonable approach was to use a valuation midway between the two values. See p.251.

[26] Family Law (Scotland) Act 2006 s.19.

[27] Within the meaning of s.10(4) and (4A).

[28] s.10(4) and (4A); see e.g. *Pryde v Pryde*, 1991 S.L.T. (Sh Ct) 26.

[29] Insurance valuations will not be appropriate—see *McConnell v McConnell*, 1993 G.W.D. 34–2185.

[30] At p.808; see also *Bolton v Bolton*, 1995 G.W.D. 14–799.

buyer basis (£14,450). According to the evidence the difference lies in the fact that the former involve transport costs and are in any event considerably less than what would have to be paid by a purchaser of the same articles in a retail shop. The willing seller/ willing buyer basis was said to be more appropriate to a situation where a purchaser had an interest in the existing location of the subjects as, for example, where fitted carpets are purchased along with a house. In the present case the pursuer has had to move house and accordingly it seems to me that neither method of valuation is strictly apposite. However I consider that in this case, of the two methods of valuation, the willing seller/willing buyer basis comes closer to a fair valuation for purposes of the Act . . ."

Parties seeking to establish a value of these items for the purposes of including them in the matrimonial or partnership property will need to provide the court with evidence on the issue. In *Pryde v Pryde*, 1991 S.L.T. (Sh Ct) 26 Sheriff Bell commented[31]:

". . . a more fundamental objection to taking account of any of this furniture is the simple one that I was not provided with any valuation of this property nor was any method suggested to me by which I could value it. If I am not given any valuation of the property then I cannot include it in the total net value of the couple's matrimonial property at the relevant date."

Having said this, if neither party leads evidence then the court may, in some circumstances, be prepared to adopt a pragmatic approach. In *Fleming v Fleming*, 1993 G.W.D. 9–620, neither party led expert evidence on the value of the contents of the matrimonial property. The sheriff principal arrived at a value by making an "educated guess". There are several cases where the courts have been prepared to take a common sense approach and infer a value.[32]

Tenancies

The tenant's interest under a lease is an asset and will be matrimonial **6–12** or partnership property.[33] It may be necessary to obtain expert evidence of the value of the tenancy. In *MacLean v MacLean*, 1996 G.W.D. 22– 1278, the wife was the tenant of a grouse moor under a lease in her favour. However, on the evidence, the court held that the lease had no value—it could not be assigned and there was no evidence that the landlords wished to buy out the tenant's interest.

Pensions

Section 10(5)—General comments

The Act is very specific about rights and interests to pensions. Section **6–13** 10(5) states:

---

[31] At p.29.
[32] See e.g. *Berry v Berry*, 1991 S.L.T. 42; *Cochran v Cochran*, 1992 G.W.D. 27–1579.
[33] See *Budge v Budge (No.1)*, 1990 S.L.T. 319.

"The proportion of any rights or interests of either person . . . in any benefits under a pension arrangement which either person has or may have (including such benefits payable in respect of the death of either person), which is referable to the period to which subsections (4)(b) or (4A)(b) above refers[34] shall be taken to form part of the matrimonial property or partnership property."

This section includes several important terms which need to be considered:

(1) *"Proportion" of pension*—It is only the proportion of the value of the pension which is attributable to the period from the date of marriage or registration up to the relevant date which will be regarded as a matrimonial or partnership property. Therefore, if the pension was started before the marriage or registration, the value attributable to the period before the marriage or registration will be discounted. A simple time-based apportionment is used.[35]

(2) *"Pension arrangement"*—This term is broadly defined, and almost all pension schemes are included within the definition.[36]

(3) *"Benefits under a pension arrangement"*—This term is defined in s.27(1) and includes any benefits by way of pension, including relevant state scheme rights, whether under a pension arrangement or not. This wording sounds odd—how can a benefit by way of a pension be paid other than by way of a pension arrangement? The answer is that there may be some situations where a pension is payable contractually by an employer to a former employee, but where there is no pension scheme in the sense we might normally imagine.

(4) *"Benefits payable in respect of the death of either party"*—This wording ensures that widows' or widowers' benefits under a pension scheme are to be brought into account in valuing the pension.[37] Under many pension schemes, the pension contributions purchase both a pension for the contributor on retirement and also financial benefits for the contributor's spouse in the event of death of the contributor.

The importance of pensions (and a word of warning)

6–14   Often pension interests are one of the most valuable assets of the marriage or civil partnership. However, on separation, it is often the case that the parties do not consider the value of the pension to be particularly important. It may be many years before the pension is likely to be paid. The pension cannot be sold or exchanged for cash nor can it be assigned for value. It is not unusual for clients to instruct their

---

[34] i.e. the period from the date of the marriage or registration to the relevant date.
[35] See para.6–16.
[36] See footnote 42 below.
[37] The wording was inserted in the 1995 Act to reverse the line of authority in e.g. *Brooks v Brooks*, 1993 S.L.T 184 and *Welsh v Welsh*, 1994 S.L.T. 828 where such interests were not being taken into account by the courts.

solicitors that they do not wish to seek a share of the other party's pension. This is dangerous territory for the solicitor. The value of pensions for the purposes of financial provision can often be considerably higher than the parties realise. In *Darrie v Duncan*, 2001 S.L.T. 941, the former wife had (with the benefit of legal advice) settled with her husband on terms which had not taken into account the value of her husband's pension rights. She later sued her former solicitors. Lord McCluskey held that such a claim was competent, with the loss being suffered at the point when the minute of agreement settling financial matters became effective. So far as quantum was concerned, he commented[38]:

> "The way to measure her loss, the damnum, is to calculate the amount at which she could then have properly valued her claim and to deduct from that amount the amount that she in fact received for surrendering that claim. So the task is to put a value on what the claim was worth when she surrendered it."

Given that interests in pensions are often very valuable indeed, the dangers to solicitors are clear. It is important that clients are advised fully and clearly about the importance and the potential value of pensions. If a party insists on leaving a pension out of account, solicitors should be extremely careful to record the instructions and any advice they tender against this course of action.

Parties who have moved jobs may have pensions from previous employers. They may no longer be contributing to these schemes, but the pension will still have a value. Therefore it may be important to obtain an employment history for both parties. Further, any person who has been in employment since 1978 is likely to have some sort of pension rights. Even if they have no personal or employer scheme, there will generally be provision through the State Earnings Related Pension Scheme ("SERPS") or the State Second Pension ("S2P"). The values of SERPS and S2P are matrimonial or partnership property. It is thought that these schemes are often overlooked by parties. The rights can often be very valuable.[39]

Valuation of pensions

The valuation of pensions was for many years a matter of considerable **6–15** difficulty, because the correct method of valuation was not clear.[40] There was substantial litigation and disagreement amongst advisers, courts and actuaries. The different methods could produce widely different results, which made it difficult to advise clients with any certainty about their rights. Matters are now much clearer because a statutory method of valuation has been introduced. Section 10(8) of the Act provides that the

---

[38] At p.944.
[39] See Harry Smith, "The reality of pension sharing", J.L.S.S. 2003, 48(4), 21–5.
[40] The main arguments related to: (a) whether the valuation should be based on an assumption of the member continuing in service or the assumption that they were leaving service; and (b) whether the widow's/widower's element of the pensions should be included.

Secretary of State may make regulations to provide for the calculation and verification of valuation of pensions. The Divorce etc. (Pensions) (Scotland) Regulations 1996 were the first regulations to deal with this matter, but for actions commenced on or after December 1, 2000 a new set of regulations has been introduced: The Divorce etc. (Pensions) (Scotland) Regulations 2000.[41] The regulations provide that pensions are to be valued using the Cash Equivalent Transfer Value ("CETV"). The key provisions of the 2000 Regulations are:

(1) The value of any pension under a pension arrangement[42] for the purposes of the Act is to be in accordance with the 2000 Regulations.

(2) Regulation 3 provides detailed information for the benefit of the pension providers regarding how the CETV is to be calculated for various schemes and situations. The rules are highly technical, but happily, in most cases, solicitors do not need to know the detail of the regulations—it is enough to know that the CETV is prescribed, and that the rules tell the pension providers how to calculate the figure.[43]

(3) For the technically minded, detailed methods of valuation are given under reg.3 for the valuation of all manner of different pension arrangements including the interests of deferred members of occupational schemes;[44] active members of occupational schemes;[45] members of personal pension schemes and persons with rights under a retirement annuity;[46] parties with pension rights in payment, and parties with pension rights under annuities other than retirement annuity contracts.[47] This means that there is a clear formula for how different types of pension interest are to be valued on divorce or dissolution.

(4) Relevant state scheme rights are to be calculated and verified in a manner approved by the Government Actuary.[48]

(5) The value of the proportion of any rights which a party has or may have in a pension arrangement or relevant state scheme as at the relevant date is to be calculated using a very straightforward time based apportionment.[49]

---

[41] SI 2000/112.

[42] "Pension arrangement" is defined by reference to s.27(1) of the Act. The definition is very broad and means: (a) any occupational scheme within the meaning of the Pension Schemes Act 1993; (b) a personal pension scheme within the meaning of that Act; (c) a retirement annuity contract; (d) an annuity or insurance policy purchased or transferred for the purpose of giving effect to rights under an occupational pension scheme or personal pension scheme; (e) an annuity purchased or entered into for the purpose of discharging liability in respect of a pension credit under s.29(1)(b) of the Welfare Reform and Pensions Act 1999 or under corresponding Northern Ireland legislation.

[43] The CETV is in fact a familiar concept to pension managers. (Very) broadly speaking, it is the sum that they would give to another fund on any particular date, if the member changed schemes.

[44] reg.3(3).

[45] reg.3(4).

[46] reg.3(5) and (6).

[47] reg.3(7), (8) and (9).

[48] reg.3A.

[49] reg. 4. See para.6–16.

In short, what all of this means is that, for virtually all pensions, the CETV (or for state schemes a prescribed method of valuation) is to be used for the purposes of the Act. The single most significant advantage of the regulations is that they provide certainty. A mathematical formula is applied to value the interest in the pension, and this will be its value for inclusion in the pool of matrimonial or partnership property. This removes the uncertainty which existed before the regulations were introduced, and in many cases it will also remove the requirement to obtain expensive (and often conflicting) actuarial valuations. In practical terms, the solicitor or party with the pension interest simply writes to the pension provider requesting the CETV. The pension provider is under an obligation to provide this information.[50] Care should be taken to make sure that the CETV obtained shows the value at the relevant date, and not any other date. It is not unheard of for CETVs to be produced by fund managers brought down to the wrong date. The CETV should be apportioned if the pension started before marriage or registration.[51] It is not impossible for the CETV to be calculated wrongly by the pension administrator. For funds with a substantial value, it may be worth considering having the value checked by an actuary.

Apportionment of value of pension

In some cases a party may have started contributing to their pension **6–16** before the marriage or registration. In these cases it is only a proportion of the CETV which will fall into the pool of matrimonial or partnership property. Regulation 4 of the 2000 Regulations provides a simple and clear method for apportioning the value of the pension for the period of the marriage:

> "The value of the proportion of any rights or interests which a party has or may have in any benefits under a pension arrangement or in relevant state scheme rights as at the relevant date and which forms part of the matrimonial property by virtue of s.10(5) shall be calculated in accordance with the following formula—
>
> $$A \times \frac{B}{C}$$
>
> Where—
>
> A is the value of these rights or interests . . . [calculated in accordance with the 2000 Regulations] . . .
>
> B is the period of C which falls within the period of the marriage of the parties before the relevant date and, if there is no such period, the amount shall be zero; and
>
> C is the period of the membership of that party in the pension arrangement before the relevant date or, as the case may be,

---

[50] See the Pensions on Divorce etc. (Provision of Information) Regulations 2000, SI 2000/1048. The regulations prescribe time limits for provision of the information. The spouse or civil partner of the member of the scheme is not entitled to a valuation (although they are entitled to some basic information—see reg.2).

[51] See para.6–16.

the period during which that party has held relevant state scheme rights before the relevant date."

The advantage of this formula is its simplicity. It is a straightforward time-based apportionment. Having said this, it will not always produce a fair result.[52] This will only be the case if throughout the period of membership the level of contributions is steady, and the pension grows at a steady rate. However, the formula will produce unfair results if substantial lump sums are introduced into pensions, or if the amount of contributions changes materially after marriage or registration. This can perhaps best be illustrated through an example.

Example

H is employed from 1987 to 1997. He is single throughout this period and his employer makes regular contributions to a pension scheme. In 1997 he changes employer, and £90,000 is transferred by his previous pension scheme into a scheme operated by his new employer. H marries W in 2000 but they separate in 2002 when the CETV of the rights in A's pension scheme has risen to £100,000. In this example, the formula in reg.4 can be fleshed out as follows:

A is £100,000

B is two years (2000–2002)

C is five years (1997–2002)

Therefore the proportion of the pension attributable to the period of the marriage is:

£100,000 × 2/5 = £40,000

This would appear to be unfair since the bulk of the pension was derived from contributions made before the marriage. Indeed, the rise in value of the pension after the marriage was only £10,000.

One further word of warning: check that the CETV produced by the pension provider has not already been apportioned by the fund manager. Some schemes do this. Care should be taken not to apportion the CETV twice.

Challenges to the CETV and its apportionment

6–17   The CETV is not a perfectly fair mode of valuation. It will produce results that are reasonably fair in many cases, but it has been pointed out that the regulations will produce an unfair result in a number of situations.[53] For example, actuaries might argue that the CETV of certain pension schemes, where the normal retirement age is before the age of 60 (e.g. police, fire brigade and armed forces pensions), does not produce a fair result because the CETV makes certain assumptions

---

[52] For a critique see Harry Smith, "The reality of pension sharing" (cited above).
[53] See e.g. 1996 Fam. L.B. 23–3; 1999 Fam. L.B. 38–3; See also Harry Smith, "Fairness and the Division of Pension Rights on Divorce", 2001 Fam. L.B. 53–2.

which are not appropriate. Equally, the CETV may not take into account valuable discretionary benefits which are available under some schemes. In addition, as illustrated in para.6–16, the method of apportioning the value of the pension attributable to the period of the marriage or partnership may not produce fair results in every case.

Given that the use of the CETV can produce unfair results in a number of situations, it is not surprising that there have been several cases which have challenged its use and the formula for apportioning it. To date, sheriff court cases have held that the CETV is prescriptive and must be used; the court cannot use other methods of valuation (e.g. actuarial valuations), nor can the courts use a different mechanism than that provided by the regulations to apportion the pension rights to the relevant period.[54] The courts have also, so far, been reluctant to accept special circumstances arguments[55] which were aimed at a departure from equal sharing of the pension.

In *Stewart v Stewart*, 2001 S.L.T. (Sh Ct) 114, the wife claimed that an actuarial valuation of the husband's pension should be preferred over the CETV. The husband argued that the use of the CETV was the only acceptable mode of valuation. The issue was important—based on the wife's actuarial method of valuation, the pension would have been worth about £97,000, whereas the CETV was about £57,500. The wife made two alternative arguments: (1) ss.9(1)(a) and 10(1) of the Act indicate that the concept of fairness was fundamental in division of matrimonial property, and the only fair way to value the asset was to use the actuarial valuation; and (2) if the CETV was the value to be included in the matrimonial property, then the lack of fairness in that valuation was a special circumstance allowing the court to depart from equal sharing. In rejecting the first argument the sheriff indicated that reg.3 of the 1996 Regulations[56] was clear in stating that pension schemes were to be valued in a particular way for the purposes of the Act. If the pension concerned falls within the ambit of the regulations[57] then the CETV must be used. The regulations[58] use the words "shall be taken to be" when introducing detailed rules for valuing pension rights and interests. The court regarded those words as prescriptive. So far as the secondary "special circumstances" argument was concerned, Sheriff Young commented[59]:

> "Turning to the alternative argument of counsel for the pursuer, I do not consider that the unfairness which, so it is claimed, would

---

[54] In addition to the cases discussed below see also *Webster v Webster*, 2003 G.W.D. 5–118; and *Logan v Logan*, 2002 Fam. L.B. 55–4. In *Logan* the decision in *Stewart v Stewart* below was followed. The argument related to the husband's army pension. Sheriff Bickett held that the CETV was mandatory. He refused a special circumstances argument based on the fact that the actuarial valuation was much higher than the CETV, pointing out that the actuarial valuation would only be enjoyed by the husband if he remained in service for a period after the relevant date.

[55] Under s.10(6).

[56] The Divorce etc. (Pensions) (Scotland) Regulations 1996 which are now superseded, but the argument will hold good for the Divorce etc. (Pensions) (Scotland) Regulations 2000.

[57] Almost all pension rights and benefits will now fall within the ambit of the 2000 Regulations.

[58] Both the 1996 and the 2000 Regulations (reg.3 in both cases).

[59] At p.118.

result from taking the cash equivalent transfer value of the defender's interest in the Strathclyde Fire Brigade pension scheme can be said to amount to a special circumstance within the meaning of s.10(6) of the Act which would justify an unequal sharing of the matrimonial property in terms of s.10(1). I say this because Parliament has provided in s.10(8) that the Secretary of State may by regulations make provision about calculation and verification in relation to the valuation for the purposes of the Act of benefits under a pension arrangement or relevant state scheme rights. In other words, Parliament has left it to the Secretary of State to provide how the value of benefits under a pension scheme are to be calculated, and this of course is what has been done in the 1996 Regulations. In my opinion it is incorrect to suggest that Parliament having conferred this power upon the Secretary of State, should simultaneously have provided that a party, who is dissatisfied with the result of a calculation properly carried out in terms of the regulations made by the Secretary of State, may side step these regulations by the device of relying upon the perceived unfairness of such a calculation as a special circumstance for the purposes of s.10(1). To allow this would effectively mean that the aggrieved party could drive a proverbial coach and horses through regulations made by the Secretary of State under the authority of Parliament. That in my opinion cannot be right."

Is this entirely persuasive? All that the regulations do is provide a formula for arriving at a valuation of a pension interest which forms part of matrimonial or partnership property. Section 10(8) and the regulations made under it happen to provide a particularly detailed method of valuing pension interests, but it is still just a way at arriving at a value for an item forming part of the matrimonial or partnership property. Section 10(6) clearly allows the court to depart from equal sharing of the value of matrimonial or partnership property, if special circumstances dictate that this is justified. Perhaps one way of interpreting the comments in *Stewart* is that the decision is limited to the proposition that it is not open to use special circumstances to argue that *the basis of valuation* (i.e. the CETV itself) is unfair thus allowing unequal sharing. However, might there still be special circumstances in individual cases that allow the court to apply unequal sharing? How might this argument be developed?

As a preliminary matter, if unequal sharing is to be suggested, the case will need to be carefully pled. The *obiter* comments of the sheriff in *Miller v Miller*, 2000 Fam. L.R. 19 need to be kept in mind[60]:

"It might, in certain cases, be feasible for the pursuer to state the amount of the cash equivalent fund and then, by averment, set out why it does not provide a fair value."

However, the emphasis here might not be quite right—it is not necessarily the value produced by the CETV which is unfair. Rather, it

---

[60] At p.20.

might be better to argue that the circumstances (more particularly the *special circumstances*[61]) of the parties, or one of them, mean that the use of the CETV produces an unfair result in a particular case. A CETV can produce unfair results in two ways. First—and we might call this category *general unfairness*—the application of the CETV to particular types of scheme might produce unfair results. For example, in police, fire brigade and armed forces pensions where the normal retirement age is before the age of 60, actuaries suggest that the CETV is unfair because it makes assumptions which are not appropriate. Equally, the CETV may not take into account valuable discretionary benefits which are available under some schemes. However, this argument may be difficult to pursue. Legislation prescribes a method of valuation for pension schemes—why should whole categories of scheme be treated in a different way?[62]

However, there is a second way that special circumstances might apply. This time they would relate to the specific circumstances of individuals in a case, and we might categorise these as cases of *particular unfairness*. It may be more appropriate to argue for unequal division in these cases. For example, if the CETV for a party's pension is £100,000, but there is clear evidence that the individual is terminally ill and unlikely to live to take the pension, then there might be an argument for unequal sharing in the light of special circumstances.[63] Equally, apportionment of the pension to the period of the marriage or registration may produce unfair results in some particular circumstances.[64]

It might be argued that unfairnesses of the general category could more readily be corrected by legislation—parliament could, for example, introduce regulations to require armed forces pensions to be valued using different assumptions. Parliament has not done so, and that seems to strongly suggest that the CETV is prescriptive. Cases in the second category—particular unfairnesses—cannot easily be provided for by legislation because the circumstances creating the unfairness are much more idiosyncratic. It might be argued that these case-by-case unfairnesses are exactly what special circumstances are designed to correct.

Is it necessary to get a CETV in every case?

In practice, it is not difficult to obtain a CETV—the party with the **6–18** pension or their agent simply writes to the pension provider, and they will provide the valuation. However, in at least one case there was no CETV available to the court at the date of the proof, but the court still felt able to arrive at a value for the asset.[65] In another case, the court had before it a CETV brought down to a date other than the relevant date. Rather than delay a final decision by ordering a fresh CETV, the court employed a pragmatic approach and adjusted the valuation.[66]

---

[61] Within the meaning of s.10(6).

[62] Although for a contrary view see Harry Smith and Sandra Eden, "Fairness and the Division of Pension Rights on Divorce", 2001 Fam. L.B. 53.

[63] Having said this, pension sharing would allow the other party to achieve fair sharing without any real harm being done to the party with the pension. A particularly creative judge might even transfer the whole pension (ironically enough using special circumstances) to avoid the value of the pension being lost to the parties.

[64] See para.6–16.

[65] *Chaudry v Chaudry*, 2005 Fam. L.B. 73–7.

[66] *Webster v Webster*, 2003 G.W.D. 5–118.

State pension rights

6–19   The State Earnings Related Pension Scheme ("SERPS") is matrimonial and partnership property,[67] as are State Second Pension rights ("S2P"). SERPS and S2P rights can often be extremely valuable (particularly for older contracted-in employees) and must not be overlooked. Even parties in relatively low-paid employment will have SERPS rights and these should be valued.[68] SERPS may still have a value where an employee has contracted out.[69] Parties working between 1961 and 1975 may have acquired rights to graduated pension.[70]

Basic state retirement pension

6–20   It is thought that it is not appropriate to take the basic state pension into account when considering financial provision on divorce or dissolution.[71]

Armed forces pensions

6–21   Armed forces pension schemes are matrimonial and partnership property.[72]

Pensions in payment

6–22   Pensions in payment have a value which is matrimonial and partnership property.[73] It is interesting to note here that the value of the pension in payment will be calculated in accordance with the rules for producing a CETV[74] and for these purposes it will have a capital value. However, in the hands of the person receiving the pension, it can only produce income. It might be thought that the court could take into account this fact in considering whether an award was justified and reasonable having regard to the resources of the parties.[75] The matter was considered by the Court of Session in *Gribb v Gribb*, 1996 S.L.T. 719. In that case there were only two significant assets—the husband's pension (in payment) and a house. The court commented[76]:

> "Counsel for the defender's principal attack was based upon the assertion that the sheriff's order was unreasonable having regard to

---

[67] *Chaudry v Chaudry*, 2005 Fam.L.B. 73–7.

[68] See Harry Smith, "The Reality of Pension Sharing" (cited above).

[69] See Harry Smith, "The Reality of Pension Sharing" (cited above).

[70] For more information see John Buchanan, "The Treatment of Pension Rights on Divorce", J.L.S.S. April, 2006, p.31.

[71] See E.M.Clive, *The Law of Husband and Wife in Scotland*, 4th edn, at para 24.042; Green Paper on "The Treatment of Pension Rights on Divorce", Cm 3345 (1996), para.3.19.

[72] See e.g. *Thomson v Thomson*, 1991 S.C.L.R. 655 where the defender argued that by virtue of the Army Act 1955 (c.18) s.203, a pension could not be "attached", and in effect that was what the pursuer was trying to do through the financial orders sought in the divorce. The argument advanced was that a decree for capital payment would amount to a charge on the defender's pension. Sheriff Sischy rejected this argument.

[73] See *Gribb v Gribb*, 1996 S.L.T. 719.

[74] The Divorce etc. (Pensions) (Scotland) Regulations 2000, SI 2000/112. reg.3(2)(d).

[75] See s.8(2)(b).

[76] At pp.721–2.

the resources of the parties. That assertion was based upon the proposition that the defender's pension scheme should not be regarded as part of the capital of the parties. We are not persuaded that that approach is sound. In terms of s.10(5) of the Act of 1985, the rights of the parties under the defender's pension scheme are taken to form part of the matrimonial property. There was evidence before the sheriff, which was admitted, to the effect that the total value of the interests of both parties in the pension scheme was £100,800. We see no justification for concluding that that sum should be disregarded when attention is paid to the resources of the parties."

Pension Protection Fund

Compensation for losses suffered when pension funds collapse can be **6–23** paid to a member through the Pension Protection Fund.[77] The Pension Protection Fund is not itself a pension, but the proportion of any compensation referable to the period of the marriage or civil partnership up to the relevant date is matrimonial or partnership property.[78] However, this cannot be the subject of pension sharing or earmarking.[79] If pension fund assets are transferred into the Pension Protection Fund, then any pension lump sum orders under s.12A will be affected. Orders under s.12A(2) imposing requirements on the trustees or managers of an occupational pension scheme shall become requirements of the Pension Protection Fund itself.[80] Any orders under s.12A(3) requiring the person responsible for the pension arrangement to pay any part of the pension fund to the other party to the marriage or civil partnership are revoked.[81] If any part of the compensation due under the Pension Protection Fund relates to a period before the marriage or registration, then the compensation will be apportioned so that only the part referable to the period between the marriage or registration and the relevant date is to be included as matrimonial or partnership property.[82]

Earmarking and pension sharing

Pensions are different from many other assets because they will **6–24** generally be of little practical value to the parties until they retire. Even on retirement the member will not generally be able to take the whole of the CETV in cash—part of the value will be used to provide a regular income. In the early days of the Act, this lack of liquidity created a problem because pension interests could not be transferred from one party to the other. The party with the pension would retain a valuable asset, but would receive no tangible financial benefit from this for many years. The other spouse would be entitled to a balancing payment or transfer of other assets to offset the value. However, if there were no

---

[77] Established under the Pensions Act 2004.
[78] It is understood that the Pension Protection Fund will provide values.
[79] The Family Law (Scotland) Act 2006 s.17; 1985 Act s.10(5A).
[80] s.12A(7B) and (7C).
[81] s.12A(7A).
[82] s.10(5A).

other matrimonial assets available and no realistic means of raising finance, then offsetting might be impossible. Even the technique of deferring a capital payment until the member of the pension scheme retired was not ideal, since the member might die before retirement with the result that the pension would never be paid.

Amendments have been introduced to the Act to address this problem. There are now two useful types of orders available: (1) pension lump sum orders (more often referred to as earmarking orders)[83] which direct the pension trustees or managers to pay a sum to the spouse or civil partner of the scheme member on death or retirement;[84] and (2) pension sharing orders which can be implemented either through a qualifying agreement which takes effect on divorce or dissolution or by a court order.[85]

The issue of whether offsetting, pension sharing or earmarking should be used in any particular case is important. Expert advice will often be required.

Sharesave schemes

6–25 Sharesaves are schemes operated by some employers. The employees contribute money into an account, and have the right to buy shares from their employers with this money. Often the shares can be purchased at a preferential rate. In *Pressley v Pressley*, 2002 S.C.L.R 804 sharesaves were considered. The relevant facts were:

- The couple married in 1995.
- They separated in May 2000 (which was the relevant date).
- The wife had three sharesave schemes. She invested in these over several years, and then used the money accumulated within the scheme to buy shares.
- The first scheme ran from 1993 to 1998 when she bought 4,366 shares.
- The second scheme ran from 1994 to 1999 when she bought 1,430 shares.
- The third scheme ran from 1996 to 1999 when she bought 621 shares.

At first instance the sheriff held that none of the shares acquired through the first two schemes was matrimonial property, because the schemes were started before the marriage and only Mrs Pressley invested money in the schemes. On appeal, the sheriff principal reversed this decision holding that the shares were acquired during the marriage, and would appear clearly to fall within the definition of matrimonial property in s.10(4) of the Act. As the sheriff principal put it[86]:

"Section 10(4) of the Act provides, inter alia, that the matrimonial property means all the property belonging to the parties or either of

---

[83] s.12A.
[84] See paras 3–68 to 3–79.
[85] See paras 3–49 to 3–67.
[86] At p.810.

them at the relevant date which was acquired by them or him (otherwise than by way of gift or succession from a third party) during the marriage but before the relevant date. In his finding in fact 51 the sheriff records that at the close of the first sharesave account there was a credit balance of £6,900 with which the pursuer purchased 4,366 shares, and likewise he records in finding in fact 52 that at the close of the second sharesave account there was a credit balance of £2,700 . . . with which she purchased 1,430 shares . . . It is not in dispute that these acquisitions, in common with the acquisition of the 621 shares, were made during the marriage and before the relevant date so that, at first blush, it may be said that all the shares so acquired should have been treated as matrimonial property."

The important point is that the shares were matrimonial property because they were acquired during the marriage. The court went on to observe, however, that the provisions of the Act might allow unequal sharing of the shares.

Life policies

Section 10(5) of the Act makes specific provision about life policies: **6–26**

"The proportion of any rights or interests of either person . . . under a life policy or similar arrangement . . . referable to the period to which subsection 4(b) or (4A)(b) above refers[87] shall be taken to form part of the matrimonial property or partnership property."

There are different types of life policies. Some, such as whole of life policies, will have no value since they are designed to pay out only in the event of the death of the insured party. However, other policies—most notably endowment policies—will have a value which falls to be included in the pool of matrimonial or partnership property. There are two principal ways to value endowment policies.

   (a) *Surrender Value*—This is the value that the insurance company will pay to the policy holder for the surrender of the policy. The company will provide a surrender value on request.
   (b) *"Second Hand" Value*—Some businesses specialise in buying endowment policies from parties who no longer wish to continue paying premiums. In some cases, the prices offered will be higher than the surrender value, particularly if the policy has been running for a reasonable period of time.

Solicitors should bear in mind that the surrender or sale of an endowment policy may not be the best option available to parties from a financial perspective. It may be better to retain the policy until maturity. Agents should counsel clients to take appropriate financial advice before reaching a decision.

---

[87] That is, the period from the date of the marriage or registration to the relevant date.

The Act provides that it is the *proportion* of the rights or interests in the life policy (or similar scheme) referable to the period between the date of the marriage or registration and the relevant date which will be considered as matrimonial or partnership property.[88] So, if the policy was started before the marriage or registration only a proportion of the value of the asset will be matrimonial or partnership property. The remainder of the value will belong to the party who paid the premiums before the marriage or registration. The way in which this apportionment is carried out may be important in some cases. In *Tuke v Tuke*, 1998 Fam. L.B. 31–3 Sheriff Lothian was asked to consider the valuation of a life policy taken out by the husband before the marriage. The wife argued that the proportion of its value to be included as matrimonial property should be its value at the relevant date less the value at the date of the marriage. The husband argued that there should be a straightforward time-based apportionment. The sheriff preferred the wife's approach which he regarded as fair, equitable and simple.[89]

Businesses

General

6–27   Business interests can often be valuable assets. They are difficult to value and have been the subject of much litigation. There are various types of business interests including partnerships, sole traders and shareholdings in private companies. Different considerations may apply to each category. This section looks at some of the common questions which arise where one of the parties has a business interest.

Is the business interest matrimonial or partnership property?

6–28   The first issue for parties and their advisers to consider is whether the business interest is matrimonial or partnership property. If the business was purchased (or started) after the marriage or registration but before the relevant date, then it will be matrimonial or partnership property.[90] However, business interests may be excluded from the pool of matrimonial or partnership property because they were owned before the

---

[88] s.10(5).

[89] However, for a criticism of this decision see the commentary in the Family Law Bulletin cited above which points out that the sheriff's decision is contrary to the straight line apportionment advocated by Professor Thomson in *Family Law in Scotland* 3rd edn (Edinburgh: Butterworths, 1996), p.132, Dr Clive in *Husband and Wife*, 4th edn, p.452 and Dr Nichols in *The Family Law (Scotland) Act 1985*, 2nd edn (Edinburgh: W. Green, 1991), p.29. The commentary by Dr Nichols points out—"The method preferred by the sheriff ignores the fact that policies have little or no value in their early years because the premiums are applied to the whole administrative costs first. Later premiums can be allocated to investment only, because of front loading the charges. Also, some of the increase in value of the policy is due to the increase in value of the underlying investments at the date of the marriage." The commentary also points out that the decision also seems to be contrary to *Whittome v Whittome (No. 1)*, 1994 S.L.T. 114—an increase in value of non-matrimonial property is not matrimonial property. A straight line apportionment would also seem to be consistent with the statutory straight line apportionment for pensions. See para.6–16.

[90] See *McConnell v McConnell*, 1993 G.W.D. 34–2185.

marriage or civil partnership,[91] or because they were gifted to[92] or inherited by one party.[93] The position will not always be clear cut and some care is needed. Business interests often change their character over time. In some circumstances they may begin as non-matrimonial or non-partnership property, but may be "converted" into matrimonial or partnership property. A simple example would be a case where one party operated as a sole trader before the marriage, but then during the marriage took on a partner and altered the business to become a partnership. His interest in the new partnership is property acquired during the course of the marriage and would be matrimonial property.[94]

There are many ways that business interests can be restructured. The question of whether a business interest has been converted into matrimonial or partnership property in any given case may be rather tricky. A simple alteration in the par value of shares would not be enough. In *Whittome v Whittome (No.1)*, 1994 S.L.T. 114, shares of £1 in a non-matrimonial private company each became four 25p shares in a public company. This was held by Lord Osborne not to be sufficient restructuring to convert the shares into matrimonial property. Equally, a straightforward change from a private company to a public company would not convert the interest into matrimonial property.[95]

However, where the alteration to the business structure is more fundamental, the business interest may become converted. In *Latter v Latter*, 1990 S.L.T. 805 the wife sought a capital sum from the husband. At the relevant date the husband had shares in a private family company ("C"). The husband's holding in C was derived from shareholdings in five separate companies which had become subsidiaries of C following a reconstruction during the course of the marriage. The holdings in the five subsidiary companies were probably not matrimonial property[96] and the question was whether the restructuring meant that the shareholding in C was matrimonial property. The court held that it was; whatever the source of the holding, the new company was not the same item of property as the original shareholdings which had been gifted or inherited. Accordingly, C was part of the pool of matrimonial property. Lord Marnoch commented[97]:

"Next I come to deal with the subject of the defender's shareholding ... of 4,150 shares in [C]. These shares derived from a series of shareholdings in what are now five subsidiary companies and follow on an overall 'reconstruction' of all the companies which took place on 30th October 1970. [His Lordship goes on to recount the evidence and accepted that four of the original shareholdings were gifted to the husband and the fifth was purchased using funds gifted

<hr />

[91] *Whittome v Whittome (No. 1)*, 1994 S.L.T. 114; but contrast *Fulton v Fulton*, 1998 S.L.T. 1262.

[92] *Whittome v Whittome (No. 1)*, 1994 S.L.T. 114.

[93] *Wilson v Wilson*, 1999 S.L.T. 249.

[94] See *Sweeney v Sweeney*, 2003 S.L.T. 892.

[95] *Whittome v Whittome (No.1)*, 1994 S.L.T. 114.

[96] Four out of the five subsidiary share holdings had been inherited by the husband; the fifth had been purchased using funds gifted to him.

[97] At p.808.

to him] . . . I cannot accept [the husband's] counsel's submissions that any, let alone all, of the present shareholdings in [C] can be regarded as the same 'property' as the shares which were gifted prior to the reconstruction referred to above. While it is no doubt true for that for tax and other purposes the value of Mr Latter's shareholding following the reconstruction was calculated as being equivalent to the combined values of his earlier shareholdings, his proportionate interest in the underlying physical assets represented by the various shares undoubtedly altered at that time. For this reason alone I have little hesitation in reaching the view that the present shareholding falls within the pool of 'matrimonial property' within the meaning of the Act."

In *Latter v Latter*, there was a significant change in the underlying structure of the business. However, this differs from the situation where the business structure itself does not change, but the assets of the business alter over time. For example, in *Wilson v Wilson*, 1999 S.L.T. 249, at the relevant date the husband owned a valuable farming business. The business was held in a limited company. The problem for the wife was that the shareholdings themselves had either been held before the marriage, or had been inherited. On the face of it then, the shares were not matrimonial property, although much of their value had been built up during the marriage. The wife pursuer sought to argue that these should be included as part of matrimonial property. Her argument was that, but for the interposition of the company, the property acquired would clearly have been matrimonial property. Lord Marnoch commented[98]:

". . . in order that any of the foregoing property or assets could be included in the pool of 'matrimonial property' it was obvious that counsel for the pursuer had in some way to surmount the problem that the company was a separate legal persona and that the defender's shareholdings therein were excluded as having been either held prior to the marriage or subsequently inherited from the defender's father. In short counsel had to find some way of 'piercing the corporate veil'. In the event, he submitted that this could be done, first, because the defender and the company should be viewed as a 'single economic unit' and, secondly, and in any event, because the company should be seen as being merely a 'façade' concealing the true facts of ownership."[99]

---

[98] At p.252.

[99] Contrast this with Lord Marnoch's obiter comments in *Latter v Latter*, 1990 S.L.T. 805 at 808— ". . . I would regard it a very odd result of the legislation if I were forced to exclude from 'matrimonial property' a shareholding of which the present value is in large measure attributable to the defender's industry and effort during the marriage simply on the basis that, historically, the shares were gifted to him by his family some thirty years ago. The word 'property' is not defined in the legislation and plainly has a very wide connotation. It may be, therefore, that the word is open to construction depending on the nature of the property concerned. As regards incorporeal property it is difficult to see how the word can be meaningful unless related to value and, had I been driven to do so, I

The court rejected these arguments—the business had been incorporated for perfectly legitimate tax reasons and on the advice of accountants. In short, the company's property could not be equated with matrimonial property.

Can the value of "non-matrimonial/non-partnership" businesses be attacked?

As we have seen, business interests may not be matrimonial or **6–29** partnership property because they were acquired before the marriage or registration, or because they were gifted to or inherited by a party. In some cases this may give rise to a perceived unfairness. For example, the business may have been worth very little at the date of the marriage or registration (or at the time they were gifted or inherited). It may then increase substantially in value over the course of the marriage or civil partnership. Can the non-owner seek some credit through the provisions of the Act for this rise in value?

Section 9(1)(b) has been used in an attempt to circumvent the problem of growth in value of businesses. The argument here is not that the business has been converted into matrimonial or partnership property, but that the contributions of the non-owner to the growth in value of the business may have conferred an economic advantage on the owner. The arguments are considered at para.4–42.

It is also possible that, during the course of the marriage or civil partnership, the parties may have made loans to the business. If this is the case then the debt due to the parties will be matrimonial or partnership property—it is an asset created during the marriage or civil partnership, and the business will have an obligation to pay this back.[100]

Valuation of businesses

If the business is matrimonial or partnership property, then its value **6–30** will fall to be shared fairly between the parties in terms of s.9(1)(a) of the Act. If the business is to be sold following the divorce or dissolution, it may be possible for the court simply to make an order for sale with the proceeds to be divided between the parties (either equally or in some other proportion justified by the principles of the Act).[101]

However, if one party is to retain the business interest, the issue of how it is to be valued will arise. This is a complex matter. It is unusual for the value of a business "on paper" (i.e. in the accounts) to be a true

---

would have been prepared to hold that in relation to these shares the element of gift excluded by s.10(4) was restricted to their value as at the date of donation. I recognise the strained interpretation of the language of the statute which this would involve but any alternative view seems to me to carry with it the risk of great injustice and frustration of what appears to be the underlying objective of the legislation, namely an equitable division of the wealth which has accrued to the parties through their own efforts and savings during the course of their cohabitation." Whilst these comments seem at first glance to be sensible, they do not seem to be consistent with the wording of the Act. A better approach might be to recognise that businesses often grow partly due to the contribution of the non-owner spouse or civil partner, and to reflect this through s.9(1)(b). See paras 4–42 and 6–29.

[100] See *Cordiner v Cordiner*, 2003 G.W.D. 6–145.
[101] See *Jackson v Jackson*, 2000 S.C.L.R. 81.

reflection of the market value. There are various ways to value a business, and the different methods of valuation may produce quite different figures.[102] Different methods may be appropriate for different businesses. Usually an expert valuer should be instructed.

A fairly straightforward explanation of how the value of a business is to be arrived at is found in *Sweeney v Sweeney*, 2004 S.C. 372[103]:

> "As a matter of ordinary language 'the value' of [any] property which is realisable for money is the price which a hypothetical willing purchaser would pay, and the hypothetically willing seller receive from him, for that property on a hypothetical sale at the date in question."[104]

This still leaves considerable room for parties and experts to disagree about what the real value of the business is. There seem to be two main ways of valuing businesses, which might be termed the "assets basis" and the "future maintainable earnings basis".[105] The methods may produce substantial differences in valuation. In deciding which method is appropriate for any particular business, the court should look at the reality of the market for the business at the relevant date. A party seeking to rely on a particular mode of valuation should lead clear evidence both about why that method should be preferred, and about the actual valuation produced.[106] Each of the methods of valuation will now be considered in turn.

1. Assets basis

6–31 Broadly speaking, the assets basis of valuation involves valuing the underlying assets of the business and deducting any debts due. The debts which are to be deducted will generally be the debts currently payable. However, as discussed in more detail later, if it is appropriate to value the business on the assumption that it is to be wound up, it may be correct to take into account the hypothetical costs of sale, but it will not be appropriate to factor in hypothetical personal debts such as the notional capital gains tax which a party would need to pay on the disposal of their share in the business.[107]

The assets basis of valuation may be more appropriate if the prospect of future profit of a business is limited, or if there is a very limited market for the sale of the business (perhaps due to poor performance of

---

[102] See Joe Thomson, "Net Value of Matrimonial Property", S.L.G. 2002 70(6) 179–80.

[103] Opinion of the Court at p.381.

[104] In fact it might be more accurate to assume that there are least two hypothetically willing buyers so that there is an element of competition—see *Savage v Savage*, 1997 Fam. L.R. 132 at para.24–12.

[105] For a fairly exhaustive discussion of the methods of valuation see *McConnell v McConnell*, 1997 Fam. L.R. 97; see also *Bye v Bye*, 1998 Fam. L.R. 103.

[106] See *L v L*, 2003 G.W.D. 25–715; 2003 Fam. L.R. 101; *Kennedy v Kennedy*, 2000 G.W.D. 40–1491.

[107] See *Sweeney v Sweeney*, 2004 S.C. 372. However, in *Savage v Savage*, 1997 Fam. L.R. 132 notional capital gains tax was deducted in arriving at an assets value of a business. Although not specifically overruled by *Sweeney*, the decision must now be eyed with considerable caution.

the business sector).[108] In this context the prospects of the business should be analysed at the relevant date and not with the benefit of hindsight.[109] This method of valuation may also be appropriate if the nature of the business is such that it would not exist independently of the owner.[110]

The assets basis of valuation was used in *Mayor v Mayor*, 1995 S.L.T. 1097. Lord Marnoch considered the valuation of the husband's business. The court firstly valued the business's heritable property based on surveying evidence. It then turned its attention to the value of the remainder of the business. The value of the defender's capital account (under deduction of the value of the business premises which as outlined above were valued using surveying evidence) was £48,818—mainly made up of stock with a value of £45,000. However, the defender led evidence from a valuer to the effect that the stock was in reality only worth £10,000. The court accepted that the correct approach was to substitute the "real" value of the stock in arriving at the value for the business.[111]

If the assets value is used, care must still be taken over the way in which the assets are valued. One method of valuing the assets would be to consider their "break up" value. That is to say, the value the assets would realise if sold immediately. This will generally be a rather lower value than any basis of valuation which considers the value of the assets to the business as a going concern. In *Latter v Latter*, 1990 S.L.T. 805 Lord Marnoch took the view that, if the shares were to be valued on a "winding up" basis, it was appropriate to deduct the estimated costs of realisation of the shares. Again, the court is looking at a hypothetical situation and asking how much money the owner could have actually realised on a sale. In *Sweeney v Sweeney*, 2004 S.C. 372, the Inner House approved this approach, commenting that if (as in *Latter*) it was held appropriate to value a shareholding on the assumption that the company was being liquidated, then[112]:

> "It is inherent in such a valuation that the hypothetical purchaser of the shares would offer a price based on the assumption that the assets of the company would require to be realised and that any costs, including any corporation tax liability on a chargeable gain which would be incurred by the company in such an exercise, would require to be met. Thus in *Latter v Latter*, in a valuation of the defender's shareholding on the basis that the company would be liquidated, the costs of realisation were properly brought into account (p.809F) but the notional capital gains tax which the defender personally would incur on such realisation was properly not deducted (p.809G-H)."

However, a break up valuation will not always be appropriate and the court should temper its views with a degree of realism.[113] So, for

---

[108] See *McConnell v McConnell*, 1997 Fam. L.R. 97; *Savage v Savage*, 1997 Fam. L.R. 132; *Cordiner v Cordiner*, 2003 G.W.D. 6–145; *Brown v Brown*, 1998 Fam. L.R. 81.

[109] See *McConnell v McConnell*, 1997 Fam. L.R. 97 at para.19–52.

[110] *Bye v Bye*, 1998 Fam. L.R. 103 at para.103–31; *Brown v Brown*, 1998 Fam. L.R. 81.

[111] It is worth noting that in *Mayor* the evidence of the defender's valuer was not challenged. Parties should always consider instructing their own expert.

[112] At p.382.

[113] See *McConnell v McConnell*, 1997 Fam. L.R. 97 at para.24–12.

example, in *McKenzie v McKenzie*, 1991 S.L.T. 461, the pursuer had a small antiquarian bookselling business. The main asset of the business was its stock of books, which had been acquired over the years at a cost to the business of about £15,000. Evidence was led from a dealer who explained that, if she had been asked to make an offer for the stock of books at the relevant date, she would have offered £6,500. This was rather lower than the price paid by the pursuer for the stock, and was still lower than the price for which she could expect to sell the books if the business continued to operate as a going concern. Lord Prosser chose to value the books at their cost price. It ignored both the "break up" value of the books, and the possible profit that might be made on them in the future.

2. Future maintainable earnings basis

6–32   This method of valuation takes account of the fact that a business is being valued as a going concern.[114] If the method is to be used there has to be some realistic prospect of there being a market for the business if it were to be sold, and if there is no such market then the net assets basis of valuation will be preferred.[115] The future maintainable earnings basis of valuation involves assessing an annual maintainable profit and then applying a multiplier to this. The multiplier will depend on various factors for any given business. It may be appropriate to consider special factors in the valuation. The method was explained in some detail in *Crockett v Crockett*, 1992 S.C.L.R. 591 by Lord McCluskey[116]:

> "The best method, according to the evidence, and it is a very common one, is to arrive at an estimate of the future maintainable earnings, calculating and deriving that figure from the accounts of the business over a period of several years immediately preceding the date of valuation. That figure is an adjusted figure, to take account of any special, known considerations which can be seen to have had or to be likely to have an effect, upwards or downwards, upon the figures contained in or derived directly from the annual accounts for the periods preceding the valuation. Thus, and the accountants were agreed about this, one arrives at a reasonably dependable figure for future maintainable earnings. The next step is to evolve and apply a multiplier to that figure. There are various ways of doing this."

Often the figure for future maintainable earnings and the multiplier to be applied will be subject to a great deal of debate, and it will be for the court to assess the relative strengths of the arguments which will be brought to bear by expert witnesses for both sides. In theory there are methods of checking the valuation of a business as a going concern using future maintainable earnings. In *Crockett*, Lord McCluskey continued:

---

[114] There is a useful discussion about this method of valuation in *Sweeney v Sweeney*, 2003 S.L.T. 892 at pp.897–8.

[115] *Brown v Brown*, 1998 Fam. L.R. 81.

[116] At p.594.

"As the evidence of both accountants confirmed, it is common practice to attempt to check the valuation of a going concern by determining its net asset value. In this case, because the company never owned the premises, the business has not had any significant net asset value which could be used to check the primary valuation. In strict theory, a valuation arrived at by making a multiplication of future maintainable earnings ought to be able to be checked by comparing it with a figure comprising the net asset value and the value of 'goodwill'. In the present case, however, there is abundant evidence that by the relevant date the 'goodwill' value of a butcher's business such as this in Edinburgh was very small indeed. At the present time all the evidence demonstrates that the goodwill element has no real value at all . . . Accordingly there is no other reliable check upon the valuation of the business . . ."

Crockett stresses that certain factors can have an effect on the calculation of the figure for future maintainable earnings of the business. For example, if one of the parties to the marriage or civil partnership is a key member of the business, and their very presence enhances the value of the business, then it may be appropriate to discount the figure for future maintainable earnings. The argument is that, if the business was sold, that party will no longer be part of the business. Indeed, if the services of the party and key personnel are indispensable to the business, it may be very difficult to justify a future maintainable earnings valuation.[117] So, in *Crockett* the court recognised that the husband had effectively been the manager of the business for many years. Lord McCluskey commented:

"[The husband] was the brains of the business, the organiser and the overall supervisor. It may well be, and there was evidence to this effect which I accept, that the defender did not by any means spend the bulk of his time in the shop itself; but none the less, the defender's accountants argued any prospective purchaser would properly consider that he (the prospective purchaser) could not maintain the profits unless there was a manager for the business to take the place of the defender. If a manager had to be employed, a round figure for the cost of employing him, including his salary and the various other costs that go with employment, would fairly be put at a round figure of £20,000, which figure would therefore fall to be deducted from the future maintainable profits figure. Even if a prospective purchaser considered that he might personally supply the management services and so not need to engage and pay a manager, the value of these services would require to be taken into account, just as the cost of engaging an outside manager would be taken into account, because by providing the management services himself the purchaser would have to forego any opportunity to earn

---

[117] *Bye v Bye*, 1998 Fam. L.R. 103 at para.103–31; *Brown v Brown*, 1998 Fam. L.R. 81. See also *McConnell v McConnell*, 1997 Fam. L.R. 97 at paras 19–49 to 19–51—to value a business on the assumption that key personnel will remain for a number of years is not consistent with the terms of the Act. This is akin to valuing the business with the benefit of a hypothetical service contract and restrictive covenant.

money elsewhere; obviously the prospective purchaser might not want to manage the shop personally if he were not to be receiving for his actual labour in the shop a return approximately equal to that he could obtain by working in some paid job elsewhere. It appeared to me that this reasoning was entirely compelling."

So, certain hypothetical factors (like the hypothetical manager mentioned in the foregoing passage) may have a bearing on the net maintainable profit.[118] Equally, the decision in *Crockett* points out that, if a buyer would have to pay an increased rent on purchasing the business, then this could be taken into account in reducing the valuation of the business.

Goodwill

6–33   In some cases an important consideration will be whether the value of a business should be increased to reflect goodwill. There is no rule on the matter. In some cases it may be appropriate to take goodwill into account.[119] However, in others it has been left out of account.[120] If the future maintainable earnings basis of valuation is being used, it appears that any goodwill is actually included in the valuation; one method of checking such a valuation is to calculate the value of the business based on its net assets plus the value of goodwill.[121] Perhaps the most useful approach is to determine whether goodwill is actually of any value to the owner. If goodwill is readily realisable, then it may be appropriate to include it as a component of valuation.[122] However, if not then it should be excluded.[123]

Capital gains tax and business assets

6–34   The potential incidence of capital gains tax in relation to business assets can be important. The party retaining the business might point out that, if they sell the business, they may have to pay capital gains tax. This matter is discussed in detail at para.6–56.

Restrictions on the sale of the business interest

6–35   Sometimes business interests cannot be sold freely. For example, there may be restrictions in a partnership agreement stating that a partner cannot sell his interest to parties other than the existing partners. Equally, shares in private companies may not be readily marketable because the directors of the company may refuse to register a new shareholder. A minority interest in a private limited company may have a very limited market because of restrictions in the memorandum and articles. The owner of a minority interest in a partnership may be unable to force a sale of the business making it very difficult to realise their

---

[118] See also the comments in *Sweeney v Sweeney*, 2003 S.L.T. 892.
[119] See e.g. *Kennedy v Kennedy*, 2000 G.W.D. 40–1491.
[120] *Crockett v Crockett*, 1992 S.C.L.R. 591.
[121] See *Crockett v Crockett*, 1992 S.C.L.R. 591.
[122] See e.g. *Savage v Savage*, 1997 Fam. L.R. 132.
[123] *Rose v Rose*, 1998 S.L.T. (Sh Ct) 56.

interest. Should the court have regard to these restrictions when valuing the business interest?

The first point to make here is that, if a party wishes to argue that a value should be discounted, they will need to plead their case properly and lead evidence to establish the position. If they do not, the court is likely to value the holding without applying a discount. In *L v L*, 2003 Fam. L.R. 101 the husband held a 25 per cent holding in a company. The articles of association gave the directors power to reject any purchaser without giving reasons. The wife led evidence and argued that the shareholding should be valued as straightforward *pro rata* share of the total value of the company. The husband did not lead any evidence to support the application of a discount, nor was there any evidential basis for assessing an appropriate level for this. Lord Bonomy therefore accepted the wife's approach.

However, if evidence is led on this issue, the courts can sometimes be persuaded to grant a substantial discount in certain circumstances.[124] In *W v W*, 2004 Fam. L.R. 54 Lord Clarke allowed a 60 per cent discount in relation to the husband's minority shareholding. There were restrictions on the sale of the shares. In effect there was an extremely restricted market for the shares, and it was not even clear that the holding would be of interest to the other directors of the company.

However, a discount will not always be appropriate. The court has to look at the underlying reality in any situation. In *Latter v Latter*, 1990 S.L.T. 805 the husband was a minority shareholder. Strictly, he had no ability to force a sale of the company. This was important, because the husband's shareholding was much more valuable if it was valued on a winding-up basis. If the company was not wound up the shares would be worth very much less because they were subject to certain restrictions which would make them less attractive to a buyer. However, although the husband's shares by themselves were not enough to force the sale, the parties also held shares in trust for their son. If the two shareholdings were looked at as a voting unit, they were sufficient numerically to force a sale of the company. Lord Marnoch stated[125]:

> "The pursuer's accountant, Mr Crawford, took the view that as a practical matter the defender would vote his own and a comparable number of shares which he and his wife held in trust for their son Martin in favour of a winding up of the company thereby realising the value of its net assets. The defender's accountant, Miss Smart, on the other hand, opined that the shares should be valued as a minority shareholding in a going concern and subject to the very restrictive conditions on transfer contained in the articles. In my opinion, Mr Crawford's approach is to be preferred on this matter. It is perfectly true, as counsel for the defender pointed out, that Martin's interests would require to be considered separately— perhaps even to the extent of having an independent trustee appointed in place of his parents because of the possible conflict of interest. However, such a trustee could not be blind to the indirect

---

[124] See e.g. *Hodge v Hodge*, 2007 G.W.D. 13–269.
[125] At p.809.

effect on Martin of forcing his father to sell out at a figure which, on the evidence, was only about a third of that which he would receive on a winding up and unless, therefore, there were very cogent reasons to the contrary the inference I draw is that the trustee would vote in favour of the special resolution necessary to achieve that end."

This seems reasonable. The court is looking at a snapshot of the parties' wealth at the relevant date. What the court seems to be doing is posing the following question— "If the defender had been forced to realise his asset on the relevant date, what would he have received?" The court in *Latter* held that the reality would be that, in those circumstances, the defender could achieve the winding-up figure because it was likely that the shares held in trust would vote as a block to carry the special resolution necessary to realise a winding up.

Another case where the underlying reality was important was *Jackson v Jackson*, 2000 S.C.L.R. 81. Expert evidence was led to the effect that a discount might be appropriate on the parties' shareholdings in a private company. However, Lord Macfadyen felt that he did not need to consider these arguments because both parties accepted that, as a consequence of the divorce, the company would have to be sold as a going concern. In these circumstances the matter could be effectively dealt with simply by making an order for the sale of the business.

Debts due to the parties

6–36   If the parties are owed money, then the debt due to them will be matrimonial or partnership property provided that the obligation arose during the marriage or civil partnership and before the relevant date. However, it should be remembered that a debt may be worth less than its "book value" simply because there is a chance that the obligant will default. In these circumstances, it may be appropriate to discount the value of the debt if the prospects of recovery are less than certain. For example, in *Shipton v Shipton*, 1992 S.C.L.R. 23, the husband's business had a debt due to it which was shown as £37,000 in the business accounts. However, there was evidence that the debtor was in a precarious financial situation, and repayment of the loan in whole or in part seemed far from certain. In that case the sheriff took a "broad axe" approach and discounted the debt to £10,000.[126]

One or both parties may have lent money to a business operated by one of them. If this is the case then, if the loan was made after the marriage or registration but before the relevant date, the debt due by the business will be matrimonial or partnership property.[127]

Share options

6–37   Employers sometimes give share options to their employees. This gives the employee the right to take shares at some point in the future. These rights can be very valuable because the option price often turns

---

[126] It appears that in *Shipton* no evidence was led about the real value of the debt. A party seeking a discount in such circumstances would be well advised to carefully plead their position and back this up with evidence, perhaps from accountants or a debt factor.
[127] See *Cordiner v Cordiner*, 2003 G.W.D. 6–145.

out to be financially attractive. These options are almost certainly matrimonial or partnership property. They will require specialist valuation. Their value will depend on a number of factors including the price payable by the employee per share, the rules relating to transfer of the options, and the current and likely future performance of the employer. In some circumstances, the situation of the employee may be important. For example, if they intend to cease working for the employer, this may affect their right to take up the option.[128]

Redundancy payments

Claims for loss of employment after the relevant date

A redundancy payment received after the relevant date for loss of **6–38** employment after that date has been held not to be matrimonial property. In *Tyrrell v Tyrrell*, 1990 S.L.T. 406 the husband received a redundancy payment some years after the separation, but before the divorce. Lord Sutherland rejected the argument that this was matrimonial property, commenting[129]:

> "It was argued that as the sum was calculated under reference to the length of the defender's service with the company, he had acquired an assured right to part of it at least, built up during the cohabitation. This argument, in my opinion, misunderstands the position of a redundancy or severance payment. The payment is made not as compensation for loss of earnings, but as a payment for loss of employment. No contribution towards such a payment is made by the employee during his employment, nor has it ever been suggested that the possibility of a future redundancy payment having to be made has any bearing on the earnings of an employee during his employment. There can be no question of any part of the potential redundancy payment being vested in an employee during his employment as, of course, it only comes into effect on his dismissal . . . I am satisfied that it would be quite inappropriate to take into account a payment made to the defender some four years after the separation, in respect of an event which was not in contemplation at the time of the parties' separation."[130]

Claims for loss of employment before the relevant date

If the redundancy payment is made after marriage or registration, but **6–39** before the relevant date, the funds received will be matrimonial or partnership property. It may be possible to argue for a departure from equal sharing of the payment by suggesting that special circumstances apply in terms of s.10(6) although some care will be needed in advancing such an argument. In *Maclachlan v Maclachlan*, 1998 S.L.T. 693 the wife

---

[128] For a more detailed discussion of share options, and issues surrounding their valuation see Alan R. Barr, "Share Options: Are They Matrimonial Property?", 2000 Fam. L.B. 39–3.

[129] At p.408.

[130] See also *Smith v Smith*, 1989 S.L.T. 668 at p.671.

had been made redundant during the marriage but before the relevant date. She deposited the redundancy payment in a building society account. It was not disputed by either party that a redundancy payment during the marriage formed part of the matrimonial property. However, the pursuer wife argued that there should be a departure from equal sharing because the source of the funds constituted a special circumstance under s.10(6). The wife appears to have argued that the very fact that the funds in the account were derived from a redundancy payment was enough to establish special circumstances justifying unequal sharing. Lord Macfadyen held that this argument failed[131]:

> "It seems to me therefore that the mere fact that the source of the money in the Woolwich account was a redundancy payment received by the pursuer is by itself insufficient to amount to a special circumstance. Section 10(6)(b) identifies as a possible special circumstance the source of funds or assets used to acquire matrimonial property 'where the funds or assets were not derived from the income or efforts of the parties during the marriage'. For the defender it was submitted that a redundancy payment is derived from the efforts of the party who receives it . . . I am inclined to the view that that is correct. Since s.10(6) is not definitive of all possible special circumstances, it does not inevitably follow that [the funds from the redundancy payment] cannot be a special circumstance. I take the view, however, that since s.10(6)(b) specifically identifies as a special circumstance the source of funds when they are not derived from a party's efforts, the court should at least be slow to identify as a special circumstance the source of funds when they are so derived."

So, in general, the fact that funds are derived from a redundancy payment is not of itself special circumstances. The court will be unlikely to accept a special circumstances argument if the redundancy payment is made following a period of employment which falls entirely within the period from the date of marriage or registration until the relevant date. However, special circumstances might still be invoked if a redundancy payment is received during the marriage or civil partnership, but before the relevant date, and a large part of the payment is referable to a period of employment before the marriage or civil partnership.[132]

It is submitted that a claim for redundancy in respect of a loss of employment after the marriage or registration but before the relevant date is matrimonial or partnership property even where payment is not actually made until after the relevant date.[133]

Payments for leaving employment

6–40 Sometimes employers will pay a lump sum to an employee at the end of their period of employment. In *Gibson v Gibson*, 1990 G.W.D. 4–213, the husband received a payment when he left the army *after the relevant date*. Lord Clyde held that the payment was not matrimonial property.

---

[131] At p.697.

[132] It might also be possible to advance an economic advantage/disadvantage argument under s.9(1)(b).

[133] This seems to be a logical extension of the decisions relating to damages claims. See paras 6–41 to 6–42.

Personal injuries damages

Accidents during the marriage or partnership and before the relevant date

If one party is injured during the marriage or civil partnership but **6–41** before the relevant date, and they claim damages from a third party, questions may arise as to whether the damages are matrimonial or partnership property. If damages have already been paid by the relevant date, there will be no difficulty—the damages paid will form part of the pool of matrimonial or partnership property.[134] A more taxing question is how to deal with the personal injuries claim if it has not been settled at the relevant date. In *Skarpaas v Skarpaas*, 1993 S.L.T. 343, the Inner House held that the injured person's right to property (i.e. the right to claim damages) arises at the point that the accident occurs. It follows therefore that the other party is entitled to have that property included in any claim for financial provision. However, if the damages have not been paid by the relevant date, the value of the claim in the context of including it in the pool of matrimonial or partnership property, will be what someone would have paid for an assignation of the right to damages at the relevant date[135]:

> ". . . there is much to be said for the view that a claim of damages which is yet to be quantified and admitted will attract less if offered for sale on the market place than the amount awarded by the decree which is obtained at the end of the day. Common experience suggests that a discount will be insisted upon for the uncertainties inherent in the litigation, and the greater the uncertainty the larger the discount is likely to be."

The comments of Sheriff Principal Bennett at an earlier stage of the litigation are also useful[136]:

> "Section 10(4) of the [1985] Act provides that '"the matrimonial property" means all the property belonging to the parties or either of them at the relevant date which was acquired by them or him . . . (b) during the marriage but before the relevant date' . . . The solicitor for the defender argued that from the date of the accident the defender had an assignable claim to damages but that that claim had no value until it was either settled or decree was granted. There was a potential asset only, which might even turn out to be a liability in the event of the defender losing his action and becoming liable in expenses. At the relevant date there was only a possibility of damages which was not then capable of valuation. On this point I agree with the sheriff's reasoning when he holds that the claim itself was matrimonial property although not quantified until after the

---

[134] Although it is possible to envisage arguments for unequal division, particularly if a large portion of the claim is designed as compensation for loss of future earnings which would have been earned after the relevant date.

[135] Opinion of the Court at p.345.

[136] *Skarpaas v Skarpaas*, 1991 S.L.T. (Sh Ct) 15 at p.19.

relevant date. It cannot be said that prior to the relevant date the claim necessarily had no value at all, and no doubt a potential assignee after considering the available evidence would have been prepared to make him an offer for it."

The difficulty here is that there is no real market for assignations of claims of this nature.[137] It will therefore be difficult to assess a proper level of discount (or to lead evidence on this). However, it seems fair to argue that a reasonable discount against the maximum value of the claim should be applied to allow for the uncertainties of litigation.[138] The party seeking to discount the claim should be prepared to lead evidence on the appropriate level of discount.[139] It may be proper to deduct any expenses such as legal costs and compensation recovery payments.[140]

However, establishing a value for the claim for the purposes of division of matrimonial or partnership property is not the end of the story. It is not necessarily the case that the value of a claim for damages for personal injuries will always be split equally between the parties, even if it is part of the pool of matrimonial or partnership property. In *Skarpaas v Skarpaas* above, the sheriff at first instance held that, whilst the value of the claim was matrimonial property, there were special circumstances which justified unequal sharing. In particular he discounted the elements of the claim relating to solatium (arguing that this was personal to the injured party) and for loss of future earning capacity (because these represented loss of funds which the non-injured spouse would not have been entitled to following the breakdown of the marriage). Each case will turn on its own facts, but it seems clear that there may be strong arguments that a discount should be applied for awards of solatium (particularly where there will be an element of pain and suffering after the relevant date), and loss of future earnings or restriction of future employability. Sometimes damages cases will be settled without apportioning particular figures to each head of claim. In these circumstances the court will require to decide on an appropriate apportionment.[141]

Accidents before the marriage or registration

6–42   If a party is injured before the marriage or registration, it follows from the comments in *Skarpaas v Skarpaas* above that the claim itself is not matrimonial or partnership property (because the right to property arises at the time of the accident). However, if damages are paid after the marriage or registration but before the relevant date, whilst the claim itself is not matrimonial or partnership property, any money received and retained at the relevant date will be.[142]

---

[137] See *Carrol v Carrol*, 2003 Fam. L.R. 108.

[138] See *Carrol v Carrol*, 2003 Fam. L.R. 108; *Mackenzie v Middleton, Ross & Arnot*, 1983 S.L.T. 286.

[139] See *Skarpaas v Skarpaas*, 1993 S.L.T. 343 at p.345—if one side avers that the value to be attributed to the claim is the value actually awarded after the relevant date, and the other side does not challenge this in their pleadings by suggesting a discounted value, then there will be an inference that the value to be used is the non-discounted value.

[140] See *Carrol v Carrol*, 2003 Fam. L.R. 108.

[141] See *Carrol v Carrol*, 2003 Fam. L.R. 108.

[142] Although the source of funds and nature of the property might be special circumstances justifying unequal sharing—see s.10(6)(b) and (d). An economic advantage/disadvantage argument under s.9(1)(b) might be possible too.

Criminal injuries compensation

The issue of whether a claim for criminal injuries compensation is **6–43** matrimonial or partnership property will turn on the same arguments as outlined in the foregoing section relating to damages claims for personal injuries. The right to property will arise at the point of the incident, rather than at the point of payment. As with claims for personal injuries, there may be an argument for discounting if the award has not been made by the relevant date.[143] If the claim is matrimonial or partnership property, there may be arguments for unequal division of the value of the asset.[144]

Licences

Licences of many types may have a value. The value will be matri- **6–44** monial or partnership property.[145]

Farming subsidies

Payments under farming subsidies may be matrimonial or partnership **6–45** property, depending upon whether there is entitlement to payment at the relevant date.[146]

Property held in trust

Property held in trust by a spouse or civil partner for a third party is **6–46** not matrimonial or partnership property.[147] This will be the case even where the title to the property is held in the name (or partly in the name) of one of the parties to the marriage or civil partnership as an individual: if the reality is that (notwithstanding the terms of the title) the property is held in trust for a third party, then it will be excluded from the pool of matrimonial or partnership property.[148] However, if the trust is no more than a means of managing assets for the sole benefit of one of the parties, then the trust property may be held to belong to that party, and thus be included within the pool of matrimonial or partnership property.[149]

Sums due to the parties but not paid by the relevant date

A refund of income tax as a result of an overpayment made prior to **6–47** the relevant date has been held to be matrimonial property, even though the refund was not actually paid until after the relevant date.[150]

---

[143] *Skarpaas v Skarpaas*, above.
[144] See e.g. *McGuire v McGuire's C.B.*, 1991 S.L.T. (Sh Ct) 76. In the particular circumstances of this case the court declined to significantly depart from equal sharing, but the circumstances of the case are special, and the court seems to have had significant regard to the fact that the defender (who was incapax) would have received no significant benefit even if a higher award had been made in his favour. See para.7–38.
[145] See e.g. *Ogg v Ogg*, 2003 G.W.D. 10–281.
[146] *Simpson v Simpson*, 2007 S.L.T. (Sh Ct) 43 and the appeal judgement (unreported; Sheriff Principal Sir Stephen Young at Aberdeen, July 2, 2007 and discussed at 2007 Fam. L.B. 88–4).
[147] See *McHugh v McHugh*, 2001 Fam. L.R. 30.
[148] *Marshall v Marshall*, 2007 Fam. L.R. 48.
[149] *AB v CD*, 2007 Fam. L.R. 53.
[150] *MacRitchie v MacRitchie*, 1994 S.C.L.R. 348.

Generally, it is thought that if there is legal entitlement at the relevant date to a payment at some future point, then the sum due will be regarded as matrimonial or partnership property.[151]

Intellectual property

6–48   Intellectual property rights may be very valuable indeed and may form part of matrimonial or partnership property.[152]

Unusual assets

6–49   The categories of assets outlined in this chapter are not exhaustive. The terms "matrimonial property" and "partnership property" may include unusual assets which can sometimes be very valuable.[153] Where an unusual asset forms part of the matrimonial or partnership property, it will often be particularly important to engage an expert to value it. The case of *Ogg v Ogg*, 2003 G.W.D. 10–281 demonstrates that, because of the wide discretion of the courts at first instance, it is important to have that expert evidence available at the proof. The case involved the valuation of a fishing licence. There were several valuations available to the sheriff at first instance, and he ultimately opted to accept the highest available valuation as it was supported by an expert who had the broadest and most extensive experience of the market in fishing licences, which was a rapidly moving market. Indeed he was the only available witness who could truly be described as an expert.

Undisclosed assets

6–50   What happens if the court believes that a party has concealed assets, but there is no evidence of exactly what has been hidden? Can the court take these assets into account in some way? In *Latter v Latter*, 1990 S.L.T. 805, Lord Marnoch commented[154]:

> ". . . counsel for the pursuer submitted that the state of the evidence was such that I could and should infer the existence of undisclosed assets worth at least £100,000. Despite the difficulties inherent in such a submission I consider that in the particular circumstances of this case it is not without merit."

He then recounted the evidence tending to suggest the existence of such undisclosed assets, and then made a finding that these should be included in the value of matrimonial property. Of course, the party asserting that there are such undisclosed assets will need to lead evidence tending to suggest this at the proof.[155] It may be difficult to quantify exactly what assets have been concealed. However, provided

---

[151] See 2007 Fam. L.B. 4; *Simpson v Simpson*, 2007 S.L.T. (Sh Ct) 43 and the appeal judgement (unreported; Sheriff Principal Sir Stephen Young at Aberdeen, July 2, 2007 and discussed at 2007 Fam. L.B. 88–4).

[152] For a useful discussion see 2005 76 Fam. L.B. 2.

[153] See e.g. *Cay's Trustee, Noter* (2000) Fam. L.B. 47–5.

[154] At p.809.

[155] See *Toye v Toye*, 1992 S.C.L.R. 95.

that the court is persuaded that there has been concealment, it may still take the undisclosed assets into account even though the quantification is somewhat arbitrary.[156]

Matrimonial and partnership debts

"Net value"

Section 9(1)(a) makes it clear that it is the *net value* of the matri- **6–51** monial or partnership property which is to be shared between the parties. In turn, s.10(2) defines net value as follows:

> "Subject to subsection (3A) below,[157] the net value of the property shall be the value of the property at the relevant date after deduction of any debts incurred by one or both of the parties to the marriage or as the case may be of the partners—
>
> (a) before the marriage so far as they relate to the matrimonial property or before the registration of the partnership so far as they relate to the partnership property, and
> (b) during the marriage or the partnership, which are outstanding at that date."

It is worth stressing that debt incurred before the marriage or civil partnership is not to be deducted unless it relates to matrimonial or partnership property, and that it is only the debts outstanding at the relevant date which fall to be deducted in arriving at such net value. Debts which have been paid off prior to that date are not deducted. The court should take account of the factual position of liability for outstanding debt when selecting the orders used to effect financial provision.[158] It is possible that, after valuing all of the matrimonial or partnership property and deducting any debt, the result will be a negative figure. What is to happen in relation to the division of the debt? In *Hall v Hall*, 2001 G.W.D. 38–1429, the net value of the matrimonial property was in deficit to the tune of over £4,000. The sheriff made no order, but commented that the word "value" in s.10 could mean positive as well as negative value, and observed that it might be possible to make an order where there was no positive value to be divided.[159] Further, it would still be open to either party to seek an award under one of the principles set out in s.9(1)(b) to (e) which might be used to justify an award out of non-matrimonial or non-partnership property or out of income through a capital sum payable by instalments.[160] Section 9(1)(c) to (e) might also justify periodical allowance in some circumstances.

---

[156] *Lessani v Lessani*, 2007 Fam. L.R. 81 at para.21.

[157] See para.5–06.

[158] See *Lindsay v Lindsay* (Sh Ct) January 7, 2007, unreported; *Russell v Russell*, 2005 Fam. L.R. 96 unreported; and the discussion of these cases by Professor Joe Thomson, "Furthering Fairness?", 2007 S.L.G. 48.

[159] In fact, in *Hall* no order was made—both parties were working. It appears that the overall division of assets and debts was fair and no intervention was justified.

[160] See para.4–26.

Proving the debt

6–52   In many cases the amount of the debt can be readily established. However, a party seeking to establish that there is a debt which falls to be taken into account should aver and be in a position to prove this at court.[161] The onus is on the party claiming the debt exists to prove that this is the case.[162] In *Tahir v Tahir (No. 2)*, 1995 S.L.T. 451 the defender claimed that he had borrowed £5,000 from a third party and that none of the debt had been repaid. Lord Clyde considered that, on the evidence, he was not prepared to accept that any such loan was ever made.

Debts incurred before the relevant date but payable after

6–53   Some debts may be incurred before the relevant date, but may not be due for payment until after that date. These debts should still be deducted from the value of the matrimonial or partnership property at the relevant date. In *Buchan v Buchan*, 1992 S.C.L.R. 766, the husband was self-employed. He argued successfully that he was entitled to deduct from the value of the matrimonial property at the relevant date, his tax due on income up to that date. At that time income tax on the income in question was payable in arrears, and at the relevant date the husband had (a) a debt for tax which had already been assessed, and (b) a potential liability for income tax due on income up to the relevant date which had not yet been assessed. Sheriff McLernan commented[163]:

> "Now it is clear that a debt can still be a debt even if it is not immediately prestable. An obligation to pay the Collector of Taxes would seem to be clearly a debt . . ."

This seems fair; after all the couple both had the benefit of the income up to the relevant date, and that income presumably enhanced the value of the matrimonial property. The sheriff continued[164]:

> "That, of course, does not mean to say that all income is ipso facto matrimonial property, only that it may be. The significance of that is that if that income or asset is regarded as matrimonial property and is acquired with, as a necessary concomitant, an obligation to make a payment to the Inland Revenue, then that obligation to pay could be regarded as a debt in terms of section 10(2). While it was strongly argued that no sums were outstanding as at the date of separation by the defender and accordingly there was no sum due and therefore no debt, the fallacy of that argument seems to me that there is a false equation between the existence of the debt and the prestability of the debt. A debt does not become a non-debt simply because it is not immediately payable. It is still a debt even if the amount of the debt is not yet ascertained or quantified."[165]

---

[161] *Lessani v Lessani*, 2007 Fam. L.R. 81 at para.18.
[162] *Lessani v Lessani*, 2007 Fam. L.R. 81 at para.18.
[163] At p.766.
[164] At p.767.
[165] See also *McConnell v McConnell*, 1993 G.W.D. 34–2185 and 1995 G.W.D. 3–145 but contrast *McCormick v McCormick*, 1994 S.C.L.R. 958.

However, it should be carefully noted that the debt in *Buchan v Buchan* above had been incurred despite the fact that it had not been ascertained. In other words, there was a liability to pay the income tax, even though this had not been calculated. This is different from a situation where there is a contingent liability and the debt may only crystallise if certain events occur. The classic example is an obligation to pay capital gains tax which will only fall to be paid if a future event occurs such as the sale of the asset. Such a contingent liability will not be deducted in arriving at the net value of the matrimonial or partnership property.[166]

Accounting for debts repaid after the relevant date

If one party has paid off more of the matrimonial or partnership debt **6–54** since the relevant date, then they should be given credit for this in the ultimate division of property.[167] However, parties will need to establish that the payments were not part of their alimentary obligations.

Income tax

Buchan v Buchan, 1992 S.C.L.R. 766[168] holds that income tax due on **6–55** income earned up to the relevant date is a debt which falls to be deducted from the value of matrimonial or partnership property, even if the amount of the tax has not been assessed at the relevant date.[169]

Capital gains tax

The issue of capital gains tax is an important matter for high value **6–56** divorces and dissolutions. The essential point is this—a party may retain a valuable asset as part of the final settlement; however, if they were to dispose of that asset after the divorce or dissolution, it might attract substantial capital gains tax liability. Is that potential liability (often described as a "notional" liability) to be taken into account when assessing the net value of matrimonial or partnership property? In *Sweeney v Sweeney*, 2004 S.C. 372 it was held that there is to be no automatic deduction for notional capital gains tax. Within the pool of matrimonial property were shares in the husband's name. If they had been sold at the relevant date, the husband would have incurred a substantial liability for capital gains tax. When the case came before the Outer House[170] Lord Kingarth held that the incidence of notional capital gains tax should be taken into account in assessing the net value of the matrimonial property. The case was appealed, and the Inner House reversed the decision. In the Opinion of the Court delivered by Lord Hamilton, the Inner House explained that the value of the business interest should be reached in the following way[171]:

---

[166] See para.6–56.
[167] See e.g. *Cochran v Cochran*, 1992 G.W.D. 27–1579.
[168] See para.6–53.
[169] Interestingly, in *Smith v Smith*, 2001 G.W.D. 20–771, the husband was found to have £180,000 stored in the home which appears to have been money which the husband did not put through the books of his business. This was included as matrimonial property, and the wife received her share of this. It does not appear that the court took account of the husband's liability to pay income tax on the undeclared earnings.
[170] *Sweeney v Sweeney*, 2003 S.L.T. 892.
[171] At p.381.

"As a matter of ordinary language 'the value' of [any] property which is realisable for money is the price which a hypothetical willing purchaser would pay, and the hypothetically willing seller receive from him, for that property on a hypothetical sale at the date in question. It is not constituted by that price less any costs (including any liability to tax) which the hypothetical seller would incur in the event of such a sale. The circumstance that sec. 10 makes provision for a 'net value' of matrimonial property by deducting outstanding debts but makes no equivalent provision for the deduction of hypothetical liabilities tends to confirm that that ordinary usage is being employed."

The court approved the following comments of Lady Smith in *Coyle v Coyle*[172] when discussing the proposition that the value of matrimonial property should be reduced to take account of the incidence of hypothetical capital gains tax:

"Such an approach has, as Lord Marnoch said in *Latter*, no foundation in reality, it fails to take account of the fact that the asset might never be realised by the spouse who owns it, it fails to take account of the fact that even if the spouse does have to realise it, he or she will not have to pay the capital gains tax charge immediately, indeed, there may be scope for making a profit by investment of the proceeds of the asset before the tax has to be paid, and it fails to take account of the fact that whilst the owner of an asset might regard its value as its value after capital gains tax is paid [although that seems to be an odd way to express value], the recipient of the asset if it is transferred will regard its value as being its full value without taking account of tax. In short, I see no reason for depriving the word 'value' of its usual and ordinary meaning when assessing the value of matrimonial property. It would not be usual to refer to the 'value' of a house or any other investment as being its market value less whatever is anticipated will be the impact of selling it on a person's ultimate liability to the Inland Revenue in a particular tax year, whether in respect of capital gains, inheritance, or any other tax."

In *Sweeney*, the court approved of the approach taken in *Latter v Latter*, 1990 S.L.T. 805. In *Latter* the husband was held effectively to have had the power at the relevant date to force a winding up of the company. This was important because the value of his shareholding was worth a lot more on a winding up than if the shareholding had been sold as part of a holding in a going concern. Lord Marnoch held that, if the husband had been forced to realise the maximum value for his shares at the relevant date, he would have been able to force a winding up, so it was fair to value the shares on this assumption. However the court reasoned that, if it was adopting this view, it was also fair to deduct any reasonable costs that the company would bear in its winding up. A question arose as to

---

[172] *Coyle v Coyle*, 2004 Fam. L.R. 2.

whether notional capital gains tax should be deducted in this exercise. Lord Marnoch concluded that it should not:

". . . the parties were then divided on the question whether or not the notional capital gains tax on [the realisation of the company] should be deducted . . . However, in my opinion there is no reason why such notional tax should be deducted. In this connection I do not doubt that the reference to 'net value' in the 1985 Act presupposes a hypothetical realisation of the parties' wealth but it is just that, namely a hypothetical realisation, and accordingly I cannot see why one should have regard to a notional tax liability which is without foundation in reality."

This is not to say that the issue of capital gains tax in a given case will necessarily be entirely irrelevant. The comments in *Sweeney* at pp.382–3 are a reminder that, although notional capital gains tax is not to be deducted in arriving at the net value of matrimonial or partnership property, it may still be a matter of importance in deciding how that property is to be divided:

". . . the amount of any capital sum ordered to be paid does not depend exclusively on the valuation of matrimonial property at the relevant date but is tempered also by the statutory requirements for fair sharing of that property (including the incidence of any 'special circumstances') and for any award (when ultimately made) to be reasonable having regard to the resources of the parties."

In fact when the court later heard submissions on these factors, it found that in the particular circumstances of *Sweeney* there were no special circumstances allowing unequal division of the matrimonial property, but the argument remains open for consideration in other cases.[173] So, in the future there may still be room to argue in suitable circumstances that (a) the incidence of hypothetical capital gains tax might allow unequal division of matrimonial or partnership property, and (b) that the incidence affects the resources of the parties under s.8(2)(b).[174] It is not too difficult to envisage an argument along these lines, say, where one party does indeed need to realise the asset concerned shortly after the separation. No doubt other circumstances can be imagined.

Sweeney does not specifically overrule the decision in *Savage v Savage*, 1997 Fam. L.R. 132 where a partnership had been valued on the assets basis taking into account notional capital gains tax. However, such an approach now seems dangerous.

---

[173] See *Sweeney v Sweeney*, 2005 S.L.T. 1141 at p.1147— "We do not exclude the possibility that a contingent liability to capital gains tax might in some cases constitute special circumstances such as to justify a departure from the principle of equal sharing." The court also briefly considers the question of the effect of contingent CGT on the resources of the parties at p.1148. It is impossible to resist mentioning a delightful passage where the court magnanimously allowed Mr Sweeney to retain £100,000 in readily realisable form to deal with "the contingencies of life requiring ready funds". What are these contingencies? A pressing need to buy a Ferrari? An urgent round the world cruise?

[174] For an extremely useful discussion of the arguments see Joe Thomson, "Net Value of Matrimonial Property—Getting it Wrong", 2004 S.L.G. 72(2), pp.48–50.

Council house discounts

6–57   Tenants of public sector landlords often have a right to buy their property at a substantial discount. Most often the right to buy relates to council houses, but there are similar rights for other categories of public sector homes. If the purchaser re-sells the property within three years of acquiring it, then they require to repay the discount, or a proportion of it. What happens if a couple separate during the period that the discount is repayable? The issue now seems to have been resolved by comments in *Sweeney v Sweeney*, 2004 S.C. 372.[175] The potential clawback of a council house discount is not to be taken into account in arriving at the value of the former council house for the purposes of its inclusion in matrimonial or partnership property. In *Sweeney* the Inner House specifically approved the decision in *Stuart v Stuart (No.1)*, 2001 S.L.T. (Sh Ct) 20 where the sheriff principal commented[176]:

> "In my opinion the contingent liability to repay the discount is not to be regarded as a debt incurred by the parties or either of them which was outstanding at the relevant date. A contingent liability is one in which the existence of liability depends upon the occurrence of an uncertain future event, i.e. a contingency. If the contingency does not occur no obligation to repay arises. In this case the contingency in question did not occur on or before the relevant date. If it had done so the issue in this case would not have arisen; repayment would have been unavoidable. Since the contingency cannot have occurred on or before the relevant date and might never occur, it is not obvious that there is any basis for assuming that the contingency will occur at all, still less that it will occur, in this case, in the first year after the matrimonial home was purchased. There is certainly no factual basis for that assumption. The fact is that the contingency never occurred. There never was nor will be any liability to repay the discount in this case. What then is the justification for making an assumption which will confer the maximum advantage on one party and the maximum disadvantage on the other? There appears to be no such justification. That, in my view, is a further reason why the court should be slow to regard this contingent liability as a debt similar to a mortgage of which account must be taken in determining the net value of the matrimonial property. [The sheriff then refers to definitions of contingent debt found in two older cases[177]]. The pursuer and the defender are joint heritable proprietors of the matrimonial home. Prior to separation they both benefited from the discount which has been earned by their joint occupation and, to a limited extent, by the earlier occupation of that property by the defender as sole tenant. As joint proprietors either of them could have applied to the court for an order for sale of that property. If the property had been sold,

---

[175] See p.383.
[176] At p.24.
[177] *Re Sutherland, Dec'd* [1963] A.C. 235 at p.239; *Fleming v Yeaman* (1884) 9 App Cas 966 at p.976.

whether by order of court or not, each would have been entitled to one half of the net proceeds of sale. If the property were to have been sold on the date when divorce was granted no discount would have been repayable. Each would have received about £9,000 as a share of the net proceeds. It is not equitable to treat the pursuer as having no valuable interest in that property. That inequity is avoided if the foregoing reasoning is correct.

If the discount is not to be regarded as a debt incurred by the parties which was outstanding at the relevant date, the question arises as to how the risk that a discount will be repayable might be dealt with on divorce if the house is sold after the relevant date but during the period in which a proportion of the discount is repayable. That is a matter as to which the parties could reach agreement in terms of s.10(6)(a) of the 1995 Act. If they did, the terms of any such agreement could constitute a special circumstance which could justify an unequal sharing of the net value of the matrimonial property. If there was no such agreement, in making an order for financial provision, the court could order payment of a capital sum in stages which would enable money necessary to meet the obligation to repay to be retained until the contingency flew off either in part or in whole. It might be appropriate to make an award of interest in respect of such retained sums."

Non-matrimonial and non-partnership property

In order to be matrimonial or partnership property, property must **6–58** have been acquired by the parties (other than by way of gift or succession from a third party) either (a) before the marriage or registration for the use by them as a family home or as furniture or plenishings for such a home, or (b) during the marriage or partnership but before the relevant date. This means that some categories of property owned at the relevant date and/or the date of proof will not be matrimonial or partnership property. The value of these assets will not be available for division under s.9(1)(a). There are four categories.

(1) Gifts

Items or funds gifted to a spouse or partner by a third party are not **6–59** matrimonial or partnership property.[178] However, sometimes a gift may be a gift to the couple jointly.[179] Thus, whilst the gift may not be matrimonial or partnership property, it may still be joint property under normal rules of property law. Equally, one should always carefully consider whether the sum involved is actually repayable. If so, it is a loan and not a gift at all.[180]

---

[178] s.10(4) and (4A). See *Smith v Smith*, 1992 G.W.D. 23–1325.
[179] *Le Riche v Le Riche*, 2001 Fam. L.B. 51–8.
[180] *Le Riche v Le Riche*, 2001 Fam. L.B. 51–8.

(2) Inheritances

6–60   Inherited assets are not matrimonial or partnership property.[181] So, where the husband inherited shares in a farming partnership, the shares were not matrimonial property.[182] The onus will be on the party seeking to establish that the funds were inherited to prove that this is the case.[183]

(3) Property acquired before the marriage or registration

6–61   With two limited exceptions, property acquired by either party before the marriage or registration is not matrimonial or partnership property.[184] The first exception is that property acquired before the marriage or registration for use by the parties as a family home or as furniture or plenishings for that home will be classed as matrimonial or partnership property.[185] Secondly, life policies or pensions started before the marriage or registration will be matrimonial or partnership property, but only the proportion value referable to the period from marriage or registration up to the relevant date will be included.[186]

(4) Property acquired after the separation

6–62   Property acquired after the relevant date is not matrimonial or partnership property.[187] So, in *Porter v Porter*, 1988 G.W.D. 38–1570, the wife purchased a house after the separation using savings built up during the marriage. The house rose considerably in value between the date of purchase and the date of the proof. The husband argued that he should be entitled to a split of property which took into account the reversionary value of the wife's house at the date of the proof. Lord Cullen held very clearly that this was not a sound argument—the house bought after the separation was not matrimonial property. The fact that the wife had used savings which were matrimonial property to purchase the house was of no consequence. The value of the savings themselves would, of course, be taken into account. Property acquired after the relevant date will still be a resource of the parties to which the court may have regard in looking at *how* the matrimonial or partnership property is to be divided.

Conversion of non-matrimonial/non-partnership assets into matrimonial/ partnership property

6–63   Assets which are not matrimonial or partnership property may be realised or sold during the marriage or partnership. If the assets do not remain substantially in the same form throughout the period up to the

---

[181] s.10(4) and (4A).

[182] See *Wilson v Wilson*, 1999 S.L.T. 249.

[183] See *Wilson v Wilson*, 1999 S.L.T. 249, per Lord Marnoch at p.252—"In my opinion, so far as this case is concerned, it was the defender who should be seen as advancing the substantive or affirmative proposition that the funds in question were inherited, and I accordingly agree with counsel for the pursuer that the onus was on him to prove the averments in question and thus bring himself within the proviso to subs (4) of s10 of the 1985 Act."

[184] See e.g. *Wilson v Wilson*, 1999 S.L.T. 249—see para.6–28.

[185] See paras 6–06 and 6–11.

[186] s.10(5). There are similar provisions under s.10(5A) for compensation payable through the Pension Protection Fund.

[187] See e.g. *Petrie v Petrie*, 1988 S.C.L.R. 390.

relevant date, the value of the asset may become matrimonial or partnership property. For example, if a party is gifted a house, but sells this after marriage or registration but before the relevant date, and uses the funds to buy a new property, then that new property will be matrimonial or partnership property. Equally, if the non-matrimonial/non-partnership asset is cash then, in order remain excluded from the pool of matrimonial or partnership property, it must remain as cash. If funds are used to buy something prior to the relevant date, then the items acquired will be matrimonial or partnership property.[188] It is important to note that it does not matter whether the "new" asset is acquired in joint names or in the sole name of either party—if it is acquired during the marriage or partnership but before the relevant date, then it will be matrimonial or partnership property regardless of in whose name the asset is taken.[189]

The courts will take a pragmatic approach to the question of conversion. In *Latter v Latter*, 1990 S.L.T. 805, the wife's parents lodged money with her solicitors to use to purchase a house for her. An argument arose regarding whether the gift was the cash or the house. If the gift was actually the cash, then the house might be matrimonial property (because it had been acquired during the marriage). However, if the gift was the house then it would not be matrimonial property. Lord Marnoch decided that the house was not matrimonial property. He commented[190]:

> "[Parties] were divided on the question of whether the house did or did not constitute 'matrimonial property' in the first place. In this connection it is not, I think, disputed that the purchase price was gifted to the pursuer by her parents and/or grandparents and I accept the submission by counsel for the pursuer that on the evidence that purchase price was, in all probability, paid direct to Mrs Latter's solicitors. However the disposition narrates that, so far as the seller was concerned, the purchaser was Mrs Latter and Mrs Latter confirmed in evidence that the missives ran in her name. In that situation counsel for the defender submitted that the gift was one of cash and that therefore, on a strict reading of s.10(4) of the Act, the house itself was not excluded from the definition of 'matrimonial property'. As will appear later in this opinion I consider that it is indeed necessary to construe s.10(4) strictly and that the only 'property' excluded at that stage in the legislation is the actual subject matter of a gift or succession from a third party. I do not think that the alternative 'surrogatum' approach is either appropriate or practicable although clearly the source of funds used to acquire matrimonial property may be a 'special circumstance' for purposes of s.10(6)(b) of the Act. Nonetheless, with some hesitation I have reached the view that to draw a distinction as between a gift of the purchase price and a gift of the heritable property itself,

---

[188] *Davidson v Davidson*, 1994 S.L.T. 506; *Murley v Murley*, 1995 G.W.D. 31–1609.

[189] Although there may be an argument that the fact that the asset is not taken in joint names represents a special circumstance justifying unequal division. See para.7–06.

[190] At p.808.

simply because of the conveyancing techniques employed, would be over precise and that, accordingly, the house falls to be disregarded at this stage in the calculations."

If a non-matrimonial or non-partnership asset is converted into matrimonial or partnership property, it may still be possible to argue that special circumstances apply, justifying unequal division of the new assets acquired. The argument will be that the value of the new assets should be excluded or discounted because of the source of the funds.[191]

Increases in value of non-matrimonial/non-partnership property

6–64   Non-matrimonial or non-partnership property might grow substantially in value during the course of a marriage or civil partnership. Generally, rises in value of such assets will not be matrimonial or partnership property.[192] Provided the property remains in the same form as when it was acquired, gifted or inherited, then it is not matrimonial or partnership property no matter how much it grows in value. This may give rise to a perceived unfairness in certain circumstances. The unfairness may be particularly acute in relation to business assets, although often it may be possible to advance an argument under s.9(1)(b) if the non-owner has made contributions which have allowed the business to prosper.[193]

---

[191] Under s.10(6)(b). See paras 7–08 to 7–24.

[192] *Whittome v Whittome (No 1)*, 1994 S.L.T. 114 at pp.124–5; although see the contrary comments in *Latter v Latter*, 1990 S.L.T. 805 at 805 which Clive describes as "unsound" (*The Law of Husband and Wife in Scotland*, 4th edn, at para. 24.027). Another case which seems open to criticism is *Marshall v Marshall*, 2007 Fam. L.R. 48 where the husband was in partnership with his family before the marriage. His partnership account was therefore not matrimonial property. His wife made certain contributions which allowed the business to prosper. The court appears to use s.9(1)(b) to justify adding the increase in the value of the husband's capital account between the date of the marriage and the relevant date to the pool of matrimonial property. This reasoning seems muddled. The contributions might well justify an award under s.9(1)(b), but they do not in some way convert part of the value of the partnership account into matrimonial property. An award under s.9(1)(b) operates independently of the value of matrimonial property (and might be funded out of non-matrimonial property such as the business here). There is no need to draw the value of the business into the pool of matrimonial property.

[193] See para.4–42.

CHAPTER 7

SPECIAL CIRCUMSTANCES

INTRODUCTION

General comments

As discussed earlier, the most important of the s.9 principles is set out **7–01**
in s.9(1)(a) of the Family Law (Scotland) Act 1985 ("the Act") which
provides that the net value of the matrimonial or partnership property is
to be shared fairly between the parties. Section 10(1) provides that the
net value of the matrimonial or partnership property is taken to be
shared fairly when it is shared equally, or in such other proportions as
are justified by *special circumstances*. Section 10(6) expands on this and
states:

> "In subsection (1) above "special circumstances", without prejudice
> to the generality of the words, may include—
>
> (a) the terms of any agreement between the persons on the
>   ownership or division of any of the matrimonial property or
>   partnership property;
> (b) the source of the funds or the assets used to acquire any of the
>   matrimonial property or partnership property where those
>   funds or assets were not derived from the income or efforts of
>   the persons during the marriage or partnership;
> (c) any destruction, dissipation or alienation of property by either
>   person;
> (d) the nature of the family property or partnership property, the
>   use made of it (including use for business purposes or as a
>   family home) and the extent to which it is reasonable to expect
>   it to be realised or divided or used as security;
> (e) the actual or prospective liability for any expenses of valuation
>   or transfer of property in connection with the divorce or the
>   dissolution of the civil partnership."

It should be noted from the wording of this section that the five specific
examples of special circumstances set out in s.10(6)(a) to (e) are not
exhaustive. They are without prejudice to the generality of the words
"special circumstances". So, there are special circumstances other than
the five defined examples.[1] It is not possible to state hard and fast rules
in relation to special circumstances since so much is left to the discretion

---

[1] See paras 7–40 to 7–50.

of the courts.[2] However, it is possible to sketch out some broad guidelines.

At the outset of this discussion, it must be stressed that equal sharing is the norm. Section 10(1) is quite specific in stating that fair sharing will be equal sharing, unless special circumstances are established. The position is summarised by Lord Gill in *Adams v Adams (No.1)*, 1997 S.L.T. 144[3]:

> "The principle set out in s.9(1)(a) is that the net value of the matrimonial property should be shared 'fairly' between the parties. For this purpose, 'fairly' means 'equally' unless some other division is justified by special circumstances (s.10(1)), a number of which are specified in s.10(6)."

The analysis of Lord Clyde in *Jacques v Jacques (No.3)*, 1997 S.C. (H.L.) 20 is also useful[4]:

> "The final part of sec 10(1) requires the court to consider if there are any circumstances special to the case which justify a departure from the general course of an equal division. If the matter is approached by a consideration of evidence it could be analysed in terms of a presumption for equality in the absence of any special circumstances justifying otherwise. As matter of construction it is sufficient to understand that in the ordinary course an equal division will be fair but that where there are special circumstances some unequal division may be justified."

In fact, even if special circumstances exist, the court is not obliged to depart from equal sharing. Lord Clyde continued:

> "I find nothing in sec 10 which requires an unequal division whenever special circumstances are found . . . on a proper construction of the subsection it is not enough simply to identify some special circumstance in order to depart from an equal division. An unequal division must be justified by those circumstances. The court has the task of determining the proper apportionment where an unequal division is justified and that apportionment will be determined by what is justified by the special circumstances. But the earlier step of deciding whether any departure from equality should be made also involves the test of justification by the special circumstances."

The circumstances involved have to be "special"—the word is used in the Act and it is important. In any marriage or civil partnership, there will be many factors which might tend to suggest that there have been certain unfairnesses and imbalances, but in order to result in a deviation

---

[2] See para.7–02.
[3] At p.148.
[4] At p.25.

from equal sharing these have to be something *special*. In *Jacques v Jacques*, 1995 S.C. 327 the Inner House summarised and approved the conclusions of the sheriff at first instance regarding certain factors[5]:

> "His conclusion was that when account was taken of all the circumstances they could not be described as sufficiently special to justify a departure from the principle of equal sharing."

So, matters which are part of the normal give and take of a marriage or civil partnership will not be special circumstances. Further, it will be wasteful and expensive to argue that special circumstances exist where the value involved is modest.[6] Special circumstances can only be used to achieve a result which is fair to both parties,[7] and should not be used to achieve a result which is impractical.[8]

Special circumstances only have a bearing on the way that matrimonial or partnership property is to be split.[9] Special circumstances do not allow an award to be made which is independent of matrimonial or partnership property. This differs from awards under s.9(1)(b) to (e) which may be made even where there is little or no matrimonial or partnership property.[10]

Difficulties in special circumstances arguments

There are at least two major problems facing any party considering a **7–02** special circumstances argument. First, any analysis of special circumstances is complicated by the fact that, when reading reported cases, it is often difficult to determine exactly what weight is being given to a particular "special circumstance". This is because, in many cases, various competing parts of the Act are interacting.[11] The second problem—and it is a very significant one—is the very wide discretion of the court in these matters. Whether particular facts constitute "special circumstances" and the weight to be given to those circumstances are largely for the discretion of the court. Even the briefest examination of reported cases demonstrates that the courts have used special circumstances in a wide variety of ways. Sometimes the special circumstances have allowed the courts to look at different assets in the same case in different ways.[12] Sometimes the courts have used special circumstances to exclude discrete amounts or assets from matrimonial or partnership property.[13] In yet other cases the courts have used special circumstances in a broader way to allow the division of matrimonial or partnership property (or certain assets) in proportions other than 50/50.[14] In some cases the

---

[5] Opinion of the Court at p.332.
[6] See the comments regarding the furniture in *Latter v Latter*, 1990 S.L.T. 805.
[7] ss.10(1); *Cooper v Cooper*, 1989 S.C.L.R. 347; *McKenzie v McKenzie*, 1991 S.L.T. 461.
[8] *McKenzie v McKenzie*, 1991 S.L.T. 461; *Symon v Symon*, 1991 S.C.L.R. 414.
[9] ss.10(1).
[10] See para.4–26.
[11] See e.g. *Budge v Budge (No.1)*, 1990 S.L.T. 319; *Latter v Latter*, 1990 S.L.T. 805; *Davidson v Davidson*, 1994 S.L.T. 506; *Jackson v Jackson*, 2000 S.C.L.R. 81.
[12] See *Little v Little*, 1990 S.L.T. 785—see para.7–30.
[13] See e.g. *Phillip v Phillip*, 1988 S.C.L.R. 427; *Short v Short*, 1994 G.W.D. 21–1300; *Goldie v Goldie*, 1992 G.W.D. 21–1225.
[14] *Clark v Clark*, 1987 S.C.L.R. 517; *Sweeney v Sweeney*, 2003 S.L.T. 892.

courts have been strict in stating that evidence in quantifying the financial effect of special circumstances must be led,[15] but in others a much broader brush has been used.

All of this makes life difficult for solicitors. It is often impossible to give definitive advice to clients about the impact special circumstances will have on a case. A few tentative guidelines for solicitors might be advanced.

(a) Calculate the net value of the matrimonial or partnership property first.[16] Special circumstances do not change the way that the net value of the matrimonial or partnership property is to be determined. If special circumstances exist they simply give the court discretion to alter the division of the matrimonial or partnership property.[17]

(b) Try to assess the likely effect of a special circumstances argument by reference to similar reported cases. Whilst it will not be possible to establish with certainty the way that a court will exercise its discretion in any given case, it may be possible to establish a likely range of results.

(c) Consider carefully how to quantify the claim. What pleadings and evidence will be required?

(d) The client should be advised clearly about the discretionary nature of special circumstances arguments.

(e) It is important to consider whether the opponent has any reasonable "counter" arguments. Are there other principles of the Act or other special circumstances which tend to cancel out the effect of your special circumstances argument?

(f) The costs of arguing the matter must be considered. It will be counter-productive to win £2,000 in a hard fought special circumstances argument which costs £5,000 to pursue, perhaps because of extra legal costs and the need to employ expert witnesses.

(g) Think about non-economic disadvantages of pursuing the argument. Will it ruin goodwill on issues relating to the children? Will matters become unnecessarily protracted?

(h) Stand back, and check that the result which is sought is fair and reasonable.[18]

(i) Remember that all of these doubts will be weighing equally heavily on your opponent.[19]

Section 10(6)(a)—The Terms of any Agreement Between the Parties

General discussion

7–03   In terms of s.10(6)(a) special circumstances include:

---

[15] See e.g. *Jackson v Jackson*, 2000 S.C.L.R. 81.

[16] *Adams v Adams (No.1)*, 1997 S.L.T. 144.

[17] See *Lawson v Lawson*, 1996 S.L.T. (Sh Ct) 83; *Adams v Adams (No.1)*, 1997 S.L.T. 144.

[18] ss.8(2) and 10(1).

[19] Or at least they should be.

"the terms of any agreement between the persons on the ownership or division of any of the matrimonial property or partnership property;".

So, for example, if the parties agree that a particular asset is to belong to one of them, then the court can take account of this.[20] The parties might also agree that a particular asset is to be shared in unequal proportions. Of course, the terms of the agreement might state or imply that division of an asset is to be equal rather than unequal.[21] The parties might also agree that certain payments made by one party out of income should be taken into consideration in the final split of matrimonial or partnership property.[22] Strictly, the agreement of the parties is not definitive, as the over-arching requirement of s.10(1) is that property must be divided fairly. However, any clear agreement between the parties is likely to be highly persuasive.

Discussion of reported cases

There are not many reported cases dealing with this special circum- **7–04** stance. However, a few themes emerge from those cases which are reported.

Agreement or gift?

Sometimes a party may unilaterally give assets to the other party. The **7–05** question here is whether such an act is an "agreement" falling within the ambit of s.10(6)(a). In *Anderson v Anderson*, 1991 S.L.T. (Sh Ct) 11, the defender left the pursuer in 1987 after 20 years of marriage. When he left, he printed and signed a document in these terms:

"I sign everything over to my wife i.e. household contents money in bank, shares."

Two days later he rewrote the document in holograph form. The sheriff commented[23]:

"The primary issue between the parties is the legal effect of the two documents signed by the defender each narrating 'I sign everything over to my wife i.e. household contents money in bank, shares'. The evidence established that the first of these was signed by the defender on the date of separation . . . when he left the pursuer, and the second in holograph form [two days later], both of which he left with the pursuer and the pursuer accepted. It is averred in the defender's minute that the defender was pressurised into signing these documents by the pursuer "to mollify her following his departure from the former matrimonial home". The defender subsequently regretted his decision and makes his present claim.

---

[20] See e.g. *Toye v Toye*, 1992 S.C.L.R. 95; *Bateman v Bateman*, 1994 G.W.D. 38–2234.
[21] See e.g. *Jacques v Jacques*, 1997 S.C. (H.L.) 20.
[22] *Webster v Webster*, 1992 G.W.D. 25–1432.
[23] At p.12.

> Both parties gave evidence. While there was a dispute between
> them as to whether the pursuer had requested that the defender
> sign the first document, and I would prefer the pursuer's evidence
> that she did not, parties were agreed that the first document was
> printed and signed by the defender before he left and, once the
> pursuer had consulted her solicitor, he wrote out and signed the
> second document in proper holograph form. The evidence, includ-
> ing that of the defender, was equally clear that he was not
> pressurised in any way by the pursuer, that he was quite happy to do
> what he did at the time, that he signed for his own peace of mind,
> feeling guilty at leaving the pursuer to live with another woman and
> accepting that this departure was 'a bolt from the blue' to the
> pursuer. He was clear that at the time he did intend to make
> everything over to the pursuer, but changed his mind some two
> weeks later, having been advised and persuaded by friends that he
> had acted foolishly . . ."

The sheriff then rehearsed the arguments of the parties. He reached the
conclusion that, in the circumstances, the court was not dealing with an
agreement between the parties in terms of s.10(6)(a), but with a gift that
the defender made to the pursuer, which was legally enforceable. He
looked at pre-1985 Act authorities[24] which dealt with agreements
between parties after the divorce and indicated that he considered that
this line of authority applied not only to voluntary agreements between
parties, but also to gifts and other enforceable gratuitous alienations.[25]
Accordingly, the decision in *Anderson* is reached on general principles
relating to settlement rather that on an application of s.10(6)(a).
However, the sheriff went on to say[26]:

> "If, however, contrary to the view I have formed, the matter falls to
> be approached from the standpoint of an agreement between the
> parties, the result is in my view similar. Section 10(6)(a) of the 1985
> Act empowers me to take into account the terms of any agreement
> between the parties, and the terms of the documents signed by the
> defender are unequivocal and wholly destructive of the defender's
> present claim."

Purchase of property in joint names

7–06   In some cases, it has been argued that the fact that parties have taken
property in joint names is a factor reinforcing the statutory presumption
of equal sharing. Here, s.10(6)(a) is not being used to justify a departure
from equal sharing, but to demonstrate that the parties have agreed that
a particular asset should be shared equally. The argument is competent.

---

[24] *Elder v Elder*, 1985 S.L.T. 471; *Milne v Milne*, 1987 S.L.T. 45. Both cases contain a full
citation of authority on this matter.
[25] At p.13. However, it is important to keep in mind that *Anderson* deals with a
document disposing of *all* of the matrimonial assets, and accordingly it is effectively an
extra-judicial settlement ousting the jurisdiction of the court, so ss.10(6)(a) has no role to
play. See *Bremner v Bremner*, 2002 Fam. L.R. 140 at p.143 discussed below.
[26] At p.13.

In *Jacques v Jacques*, 1997 S.C. (H.L.) 20, title to the matrimonial home was in joint names and had been acquired using funds released from the sale of non-matrimonial property which had belonged to the husband before the marriage. In Lord Clyde's judgment he commented[27]:

> "Counsel argued that it was mistaken to have regard to the fact that by agreement the title to the property had been taken in joint names since an agreement was only relevant where it was an agreement to an unequal division and the illustration given at head (a)[28] was given as a special circumstance requiring departure from equality. I am not persuaded that head (a) is necessarily so limited since it refers to an agreement relating to 'any' of the matrimonial property, but in any event it is plainly proper to have regard to all the circumstances in deciding whether there are circumstances special to the case which justify an unequal division of the net value of the matrimonial property."

The foregoing argument may be particularly important if property is purchased in joint names using non-matrimonial or non-partnership funds. In circumstances where the parties have agreed to take title equally—so the argument goes—the court should avoid giving too much weight to other factors steering towards unequal sharing.[29] So, the purchase by the parties of property in joint names will sometimes be considered to be an agreement to share the property equally in terms of s.10(6)(a). On some occasions this might displace "source of funds" arguments[30] to the effect that the property should be divided unequally because it was acquired using non-matrimonial or non-partnership property of one party. In *Jackson v Jackson*, 2000 S.C.L.R. 81, the sale of the husband's business interest (which was not matrimonial property) had been used to buy shares in another company, with the husband and the wife taking a roughly equal number of shares. The new company was matrimonial property but there was a suggestion that the split of matrimonial property should be skewed in favour of the husband by applying s.10(6)(b) (source of funds). However, the court found that there were special circumstances under s.10(6)(a) which countered this. Lord Macfadyen commented[31]:

> "[The husband] chose to invest the sum realised from S.O.F.E.C. [i.e. his non-matrimonial business] in the purchase of a company, with the shares taken almost equally between him and the pursuer. I have already recorded that the defender said in evidence that that was done because he wished the pursuer to have the shares, and that I have accepted that evidence as a true reflection of his attitude

---

[27] At p.26.

[28] Of s.10(6).

[29] *Reynolds v Reynolds*, 1991 S.C.L.R. 175; *Wallis v Wallis*, 1992 S.L.T. 676 at p.680; *McCormick v McCormick*, 1994 G.W.D. 35–2078; *Jacques v Jacques*, 1995 S.L.T. 963 and 1997 S.L.T. 459.

[30] Under s.10(6)(b).

[31] At p.95.

at the time. I have also noted that that aspect of his evidence fitted with his expressed attitude to the S.O.F.E.C. stock, that he regarded it as belonging to them both because they were married. Section 10(6)(a) makes any agreement as to the division of matrimonial property a potential "special circumstance". Here I rely on the agreement (and, perhaps more importantly, on the underlying intention on the defender's part which it reflects) not in support of unequal division, but as countering the potential effect of other special circumstances and reinforcing the presumption in favour of equality."[32]

It certainly appears that the courts will more readily accept unequal sharing if title is not taken in joint names.[33] However, taking title in joint names is not a conclusive factor determining equal sharing. Sometimes other factors will have a role to play, and will justify a departure from equal sharing.[34]

Extra-judicial settlements and section 10(6)(a)

7–07   Section 10(6)(a) is designed to deal with circumstances where the parties have reached agreement about particular items of property, rather than where they reach agreement on the overall split of all of their matrimonial or partnership property after the separation. Usually, an overall deal will be reflected in a minute of agreement between the parties or through a joint minute presented to the court. In these circumstances, if there has been offer and acceptance, the agreement will be enforceable according to normal contractual principles, and s.10(6)(a) will have no role to play.[35] In *Bremner v Bremner*, 2002 Fam. L.R. 140, Sheriff Cusine discussed the matter[36]:

> "It is also true that under s.10(6) of the Family Law (Scotland) Act 1985, the court may look at an agreement to determine whether there should be an unequal division of matrimonial property. That agreement is, however, radically different from an extrajudicial agreement to settle the whole action. In my opinion, s.10(6)(a) envisages that there is an agreement in relation to some, but not all, of the matrimonial property and the court's role is to consider what effect that agreement should have on the distribution of the remaining assets. It is not to look into the agreement itself, unless it is argued that there are circumstances which make the agreement subject to challenge."

---

[32] See also *Jacques v Jacques*, 1997 S.C. (H.L.) 20 at p.25.

[33] See *R v R*, 2000 Fam. L.R. 43 (particularly the commentary to the report).

[34] *Kerrigan v Kerrigan*, 1988 S.C.L.R. 603; *Farrell v Farrell*, 1990 S.C.L.R. 717; *Peacock v Peacock*, 1994 S.L.T. 40.

[35] Although in certain limited circumstances the agreement may be challenged under s.16.

[36] At p.143.

SECTION 10(6)(b)—THE SOURCE OF FUNDS OR ASSETS

General discussion

Section 10(6)(b) of the 1985 Act provides that one of the special **7–08** circumstances which may justify unequal division of matrimonial or partnership property is:

> "the source of the funds or assets used to acquire any of the matrimonial property or partnership property where those funds or assets were not derived from the income or efforts of the persons during the marriage or partnership;"

This is an important provision. The definitions of matrimonial and partnership property set out in s.10(4) and (4A) of the Act have the result that (with the exception of gifted and inherited property) property owned by the couple at the relevant date and acquired by them during the period between the date of the marriage or registration and the relevant date, will be matrimonial or partnership property. Such property will be matrimonial or partnership property even if the asset was acquired using assets which were non-matrimonial or non-partnership property of one of the parties. So, for example, if a spouse inherits money (non-matrimonial property) and then buys a house with it during the marriage and before the relevant date, the house is matrimonial property. This will be the case whether the house is in joint names of the parties or in the sole name of one of them. The act of acquisition converts the property into matrimonial property and it will fall to be shared fairly between the parties in terms of s.9(1)(a). The position is summarised in *Davidson v Davidson*, 1994 S.L.T. 506 (an Outer House decision) where the wife had given two sums out of her own non-matrimonial property to the husband during the marriage—£10,000 to acquire equipment for his business and £1,500 to buy a car. Lord Maclean said[37]:

> ". . . it must be determined what constitutes the matrimonial property of the parties . . . As I read s.10(4) together with s.10(6)(b) of the Act, any property acquired by the parties during the marriage but before separation is matrimonial property even if it has been purchased with funds which one of the parties has acquired by way of gift or succession. The funds themselves before their application in acquiring the property, would not, according to the terms of s.10(4), be matrimonial property."

Section 10(6)(b) allows the courts to recognise that some matrimonial or partnership property may have been acquired using non-matrimonial or non-partnership assets or funds. The courts can use this as a special circumstance to justify unequal division.

---

[37] At p.508.

Some general principles

7–09   Like so much in the Act, much is left to the discretion of the court at first instance, and it is difficult to give more than broad guidelines. However, there seem to be some general themes in the way that s.10(6)(b) has been applied.

Shorter "audit trails" improve section 10(6)(b) arguments

7–10   If parties seek to rely on this special circumstance, they should ensure that their pleadings are clear and specific regarding the source of the funds. In particular, it is important to present a clear "audit trail" to the court, linking the source of the funds to the matrimonial or partnership property. The more that the funds become intermixed with other matrimonial or partnership property, the more difficult it will be to succeed with a source of funds argument. So, it will generally be easier to establish special circumstances if the marriage or civil partnership is brief and there has been little inter-mixing of funds,[38] than it will be in cases where the court has to trace the source of funds back over many years.[39] Similarly, if the conversion of non-matrimonial or non-partnership property into matrimonial or partnership property took place a short time before the separation, then it is more likely that the court will use s.10(6)(b) to justify non-equal division.[40]

Purchase of property in joint names is detrimental to section 10(6)(b) arguments

7–11   It will be more difficult to successfully advance a s.10(6)(b) argument if the property acquired with the non-matrimonial or non-partnership property is in joint names of the parties. This is by no means a hard and fast rule however, and much will depend on the reasons for taking the property in joint names. What may be happening is that the source of funds argument under s.10(6)(b) is counteracted by an argument under s.10(6)(a) to the effect that the parties have made an implicit or explicit agreement to share the property equally.[41] The other side of this coin is that it will be easier to make a source of funds argument if the parties reflect the non-matrimonial or non-partnership funds in some way, perhaps by taking title to property acquired using the funds in the sole name of the party introducing the funds, or perhaps by taking title in unequal shares.[42]

---

[38] See *Kerrigan v Kerrigan*, 1988 S.C.L.R. 603; *Mukhtar v Mukhtar*, 2002 Fam. L.B. 60–7; *White v White*, 1992 S.C.L.R. 769; but contrast *Phillip v Phillip*, 1988 S.C.L.R. 427 where a s.10(6)(b) argument was used successfully in a longer marriage, but note that there had been no intermixing of the relevant asset with other matrimonial property in this case— although the marriage was long, the "audit trail" was short.

[39] See *McCormick v McCormick*, 1994 G.W.D. 35–2078; *Moffat v Moffat*, 2006 Fam. L.B. 82–5.

[40] See *White v White*, 1992 S.C.L.R. 769 quoted at length below.

[41] See para.7–06 and *Jacques v Jacques*, 1997 S.C.(H.L.) 20; see also *R v R*, 2000 Fam. L.R. 43.

[42] See the comments of Sheriff Lothian in *Le Riche v Le Riche*, 2001 Fam. L.B. 51–8.

The application of section 10(6)(b) arguments to family homes may be more difficult

Several decisions suggest that a source of funds argument is less likely **7–12** to succeed where the non-matrimonial or non-partnership funds have been used to acquire a family home. In *Cunningham v Cunningham*, 2001 Fam. L.R. 12[43] the husband inherited a substantial sum of money. He used £100,000 of the inheritance together with the proceeds of the sale of the existing family home to buy a new family home. He also used £70,000 of the inherited money to buy a holiday home. Title to the new family home was taken in joint names, but title to the holiday home was taken solely in the name of the husband. Lord Macfadyen awarded financial provision on the basis of equal shares of the family home, but no part of the holiday home. He commented:

> "Money used to purchase the matrimonial home is, in my view, devoted in a particularly clear way to matrimonial purposes, and the source of the funds so used is in my view less important than it would be in the case of other types of matrimonial property. In my view the whole value of the former matrimonial home ought to be treated as equally divisible, notwithstanding the fact that its purchase was financed in part from funds derived by inheritance . . ."

However this is not a firm rule and much will depend on the circumstances of any given case. In *White v White*, 1992 S.C.L.R. 769 there had been a brief marriage and title to the matrimonial home had been taken in the sole name of the husband. A source of funds argument under s.10(6)(b) was accepted.[44]

Avoid using the argument for low value items

It would be difficult, time-consuming and expensive to try to trace **7–13** every non-matrimonial or non-partnership asset through the marriage or partnership in an effort to take advantage of the source of funds argument.[45] The argument should be limited to situations where there have been substantial funds or assets introduced into the marriage or partnership from non-matrimonial or non-partnership sources.

Plead quantum as accurately as possible

Care should be taken by advisers to establish as accurately as possible **7–14** the quantum of the source funds. In *Jackson v Jackson*, 2000 S.C.L.R. 81, the court accepted that the source of the funds used to acquire a substantial part of the matrimonial property came from the sale of the husband's interest in a business. The value of that business had been built up to a significant extent by the efforts of the husband before the

---

[43] See also *Le Riche v Le Riche*, 2001 Fam. L.B. 51–8.
[44] See also *Phillip v Phillip*, 1988 S.C.L.R. 427; *Clark v Clark*, 1987 S.C.L.R. 517; *Langlands v Baron*, 2006 Fam. L.B. 84–6.
[45] See the comments about furniture owned before the marriage in *Latter v Latter*, 1990 S.L.T. 805.

marriage. However, Lord Macfadyen decided that the evidence did not support a departure from equal sharing[46]:

> "In my opinion, the evidence did not disclose special circumstances which displace the presumption that equal sharing of the value of the matrimonial property is fair . . . I accept that to some extent those funds may be regarded as not 'derived from the . . . efforts of the parties during the marriage' (s.10(6)(b)). It does not seem to me, however, that the evidence very clearly established to what extent those funds were, and to what extent they were not, so derived."[47]

Consider the relationship of section 10(6)(b) with other parts of the Act

7–15   A source of funds argument will not always be argued in isolation. In most cases other principles of the Act will also be operating. In looking at decided cases this can make it difficult to determine the weighting which the court has placed on the source of funds argument.[48] Sometimes there may be competing special circumstances for both sides which will tend to cancel each other out.[49] For example, in *Budge v Budge (No.1)*, 1990 S.L.T. 319, Lord Cameron of Lochbroom noted that a croft and croft house (which formed part of the matrimonial property) was purchased using funds derived from the sale of a cottage which belonged to the defender before the marriage. However, against this was balanced the fact that the pursuer had expended time and effort on maintaining the croft and improving the house, which meant that the defender had derived some economic advantage from her efforts.

Some applications of section 10(6)(b)

7–16   In this section some ways in which s.10(6)(b) has been applied in various circumstances are examined.

Property owned before the marriage or partnership

7–17   Often one party may bring more assets into the marriage or partnership than the other. Those assets may be used to acquire matrimonial or partnership property. Section 10(6)(b) has been used to justify unequal division in favour of the party who introduced the funds.[50]

White v White, 1992 S.C.L.R. 769 was a case where the couple had lived together as man and wife for only a very brief period before they separated. Shortly before the marriage the husband bought a house and title was taken in his sole name. The house was matrimonial property. The funds for the purchase were entirely provided by the husband from a loan which he obtained. The couple were married and co-habiting for

---

[46] At p.94.
[47] In *Jackson* there were also certain other special circumstances which counterbalanced s.10(6)(b).
[48] See e.g. *Jesner v Jesner*, 1992 S.L.T. 999.
[49] See *Latter v Latter*, 1990 S.L.T. 805.
[50] In addition to the cases discussed below, see also *Budge v Budge (No.1)*, 1990 S.L.T. 319.

only about six weeks before the husband left the wife. The sheriff found that the wife was not entitled to any financial provision commenting[51]:

"In my opinion, special circumstances existed. In the first place, I am entitled to take into account the source of the funds provided for the purchase of [the matrimonial home], by virtue of section 10(6)(b) of the 1985 Act.. . . The defender contributed nothing to the purchase of the matrimonial home, the funds being provided by the pursuer and a loan obtained by the pursuer from The Royal Bank of Scotland plc. The defender may well be embarrassed or even humiliated by the conduct she feels she has suffered at the hands of the pursuer and entered into a marriage which was clearly a mistake, but this is no reason on its own entitling the defender to an equal share or indeed any share of the value of the matrimonial home. In the special circumstances prevailing, the defender is not entitled to any capital sum."

In *Jesner v Jesner*, 1992 S.L.T. 999, a farm purchased during the marriage and before the relevant date was acquired using the proceeds of sale of a house which was not matrimonial property, and other matrimonial property was purchased using money which had been put in trust for the defender. Lord Osborne took the view that these were circumstances allowing an unequal division in terms of s.10(6)(b).

In *Phillip v Phillip*, 1988 S.C.L.R. 427 the couple had been married for 24 years before they separated. They had purchased a property together for £16,500 and about a quarter of the price had been funded from non-matrimonial property of the husband. The sheriff used s.10(6)(b) to justify unequal division, awarding the husband £4,000 "credit" in the division of matrimonial property. It is interesting to note that by the date of the proof the property had nearly trebled in value, being worth about £45,000. In spite of this, the husband was simply reimbursed for the capital which he had introduced. He was not awarded 25 per cent of the equity in the property, nor was he awarded interest on the funds.

There was an unusual use of s.10(6)(b) in *Cordiner v Cordiner*, 2003 G.W.D. 6–145.[52] In that case, at the date of the marriage, the husband had various investments worth about £75,000 and a house worth £32,000. These assets were sold during the marriage. The sheriff approached the matter by deducting the value of the husband's capital at the date of the marriage from the pool of matrimonial property. The court justified this in terms of s.10(6)(b). The sheriff principal refused to interfere on appeal. This case has been the subject of criticism.[53] It does appear to be a rather blunt way of using s.10(6)(b). If the husband's assets remained in his name at the relevant date they would not be matrimonial property anyway, and insofar as the assets had been realised and used during the marriage, the decision does not take account of the complex financial reality that must apply in any such case. For example, surely the decision

---

[51] At p.771.

[52] Also at 2003 Fam. L.R. 39.

[53] For a particularly useful discussion of the case see Joe Thomson, "Non-Matrimonial Property: A Recurring Problem", 2004 S.L.G. 72(5) at pp.139–40.

would not have been just if all of the assets had been realised and then spent on an expensive round the world trip for the couple?

It seems that an in-depth analysis of each and every asset which the parties owned before the marriage or partnership is not to be encouraged. In *Latter v Latter*, 1990 S.L.T. 805[54] Lord Marnoch looked at a number of special circumstances arguments including an argument under s.10(6)(b). The wife argued that no account should be taken of the value of the couple's furniture at the relevant date insofar as it replaced furniture originally donated to the parties by the pursuer's parents. Lord Marnoch felt that there was "some force" in this argument, although the value of the original furniture was so small that it would be neither profitable nor even practicable to enter into detail on this matter.[55]

Inheritances

7–18   The cases of *Cunningham v Cunningham*, 2001 Fam. L.R. 12; and *Le Riche v Le Riche*, 2001 Fam. L.B. 51–8 involved inheritances.[56]

Gifts

7–19   The courts have placed reliance on this provision in circumstances where matrimonial property has been acquired using money or property gifted by the family of one party.[57] In *Buczynska v Buczynski*, 1989 S.L.T. 558,[58] the pursuer's mother had owned a house which she sold, and then used the proceeds to buy a flat in the sole name of the pursuer. It was held that, in fact, the purchase of the flat represented a gift and accordingly the value of the flat did not form part of the matrimonial property at all (under s.10(4)). However, the Lord Ordinary took the view that, even if he was wrong about the flat being a gift, it would fall to be shared unequally using s.10(6)(b).

In *Shipton v Shipton*, 1992 S.C.L.R. 23, during the course of the marriage the husband's father provided £4,800 to buy a plot of ground upon which the parties built a house which became the matrimonial home. It was not clear whether these funds were a gift or a loan, but the sheriff took the view that it did not matter—the funds were not to be considered as part of the matrimonial property.[59]

In *Latter v Latter*, 1990 S.L.T. 805, the husband had been gifted shares in a family company. However, during the marriage the family business had gone through a reconstruction, with the result that the husband's shareholding at the relevant date was not the same "property" which had

---

[54] At p.810.

[55] In the event the court appears to have "lumped" this special circumstances with other matters in order to weight the financial award in favour of the wife—see p.810.

[56] See also *Robertson v Robertson (No.1)*, 2000 Fam. L.R. 43.

[57] In addition to the cases mentioned below, see also *Russell v Russell*, 1977 S.L.T. (Notes) 13; *Kerrigan v Kerrigan*, 1988 S.C.L.R. 603; *Maclean v Maclean*, 1996 G.W.D. 22–1278; *Robertson v Robertson (No.1)*, 2000 Fam. L.R. 43.

[58] Outer House, Lord Morton of Shuna.

[59] In fact, the reasoning here seems to be odd—the funds were invested in land which certainly *was* matrimonial property. Although the court states at p.26 that the funds introduced by the father were not matrimonial property, what really seems to be happening is that the value of that gift is being discounted from the matrimonial property using s.10(6)(b).

been gifted to him. The shareholding at the relevant date was therefore matrimonial property. However, Lord Marnoch held that the value of the shareholding should be shared unequally because of the source of the shareholding.

There was an interesting application of s.10(6)(b) in *Clark v Clark*, 1987 S.C.L.R. 517. At the date of the proof, virtually the only matrimonial property was the equity in the matrimonial home. The house was in joint names of the parties. It was bought for a price of £14,000 and this had been funded using (a) £6,500 from the pursuer's mother, (b) £5,000 of the pursuer's own non-matrimonial funds, and (c) £2,500 from joint funds of the parties. By the time of the proof the house had grown in value to £40,000. The sum introduced by the mother had been secured by a standard security, so when this figure and likely sale expenses were deducted from the value of the property, it left a net value of about £32,000. Lord McCluskey felt that a number of factors had to be looked at in assessing how the value should be divided and awarded division 60/40 in favour of the pursuer. One interesting aspect of this case is that the funds of £6,500 introduced by the pursuer's mother were secured, and the figure of £6,500 was deducted from the value in the house in arriving at the net value of the property at the relevant date. Accordingly, the mother was to get her money back, but even so, the fact that the house had been purchased using her money, was a factor justifying unequal division of the equity.

Damages for personal injuries

In *Petrie v Petrie*, 1988 S.C.L.R. 390, Sheriff Risk dealt with a case **7–20** where the only substantial asset was a claim for damages for personal injuries arising from an accident before the marriage. In the event, the court held that it was not matrimonial property, but stated that, if it was wrong about this, and the claim was matrimonial property, then having regard to the special circumstances set out in s.10(6)(b)[60] it would probably have discounted the wife's share to a very great extent, if not entirely.

Redundancy payments

In *Maclachlan v Maclachlan*, 1998 S.L.T. 693, the pursuer had **7–21** received a large redundancy payment. This was matrimonial property as it had been received during the marriage. The pursuer argued that the fact that the money had been paid under a redundancy payment was itself sufficient to allow s.10(6)(b) to come into play. Lord Macfadyen rejected this[61]:

"It seems to me therefore that the mere fact that the source of the money . . . was a redundancy payment received by the pursuer is by itself insufficient to amount to a special circumstance. Section 10(6)(b) identifies as a possible special circumstance the source of funds or assets used to acquire matrimonial property 'where the

---

[60] And also s.10(6)(d).
[61] At p.697.

funds or assets were not derived from the income or efforts of the parties during the marriage.' For the defender it was submitted that a redundancy payment is derived from the efforts of the party who receives it . . . I am inclined to the view that that is correct."

So, the fact that the source of money is a redundancy payment is not a special circumstance. However, it still seems open to argue that, if the redundancy payment had been made as a result of a long period of employment *before* the marriage or registration, s.10(6)(b) might be used to justify unequal division.

Local authority discounts

7–22   Tenants of local authorities and certain other landlords have the right in certain circumstances to purchase the property which they lease at a discount. If the right to that discount is substantially acquired as a result of the tenancy of only one of the parties started long before the marriage or civil partnership, can that party successfully argue for unequal sharing in terms of s.10(6)(b)? The matter was explored in *Lawson v Lawson*, 1996 S.L.T. (Sh Ct) 83. The only matrimonial property was the house which the husband had purchased from the local authority. The purchase took place only nine days before the marriage at a discounted price of £11,960, the market value at that stage being £25,500. The husband obtained a mortgage of £15,000. The parties separated just over a year after the marriage and the purchase of the house. By the time of the separation the market value of the house was £29,000. At the time of the separation 60 per cent of the discount would have been repayable to the council if the house had been sold. After proof the sheriff assessed the value of the house at the relevant date as £14,000 (ie £29,000 less £15,000) and a capital sum was awarded to the wife. The husband appealed. One of the arguments advanced by the husband was that there had been a special circumstance in terms of s.10(6)(b) in that he had contributed a special and personal asset to the purchase of the matrimonial home in the form of his entitlement to the discount. Sheriff Principal Nicholson rejected this argument[62]:

> "So far as this submission is concerned, I have come to the conclusion that it is not soundly founded. In the first place, the reference to 'special circumstances' in s.10(1) does not qualify the way in which the net value of matrimonial property is to be determined. It simply introduces a factor of which account may be taken when a court is determining the division of matrimonial property of which the net value has already been determined. In the second place, I am not persuaded that an entitlement to a discount on the purchase price of a house is an asset within the meaning of s.10(6)(b). Neither 'assets' nor 'funds' are defined in the 1985 Act, but in my opinion they are both terms which must be taken as denoting some form of economic wealth which is realisable and useable for any purpose. In my opinion an entitlement to a discount on the purchase of a particular thing is not an asset in that sense."[63]

---

[62] At p.85.
[63] For a more detailed discussion on council house discounts in the light of *Sweeney v Sweeney*, see para.6–57.

Laying the foundations of a business

Sometimes a business will be started by one party before the marriage **7–23** or registration. If the business remains constituted in the same way throughout the marriage or partnership, it is likely that it will be excluded from matrimonial or partnership property (since it was in existence before the marriage or partnership). However, if the way that the business is constituted changes during the marriage or civil partnership and before the relevant date (e.g. by a sole trader becoming incorporated, or by a company substantially restructuring) it is possible that the business will become matrimonial or partnership property since the new entity was created after the marriage or registration but before separation.[64] In these circumstances, if the business is held to be matrimonial or partnership property at the relevant date, the party who built up the business before the marriage or registration may argue that their efforts and capital put into the business beforehand should be taken into account in terms of s.10(6)(b).[65]

In *Sweeney v Sweeney*, 2003 S.L.T. 892,[66] the husband operated a business as a sole trader before the marriage. That business would not have been matrimonial property, but the husband's business interests changed during the marriage—he ceased to be a sole trader and took interests in a partnership and three limited companies. The s.10(6)(b) argument is summarised by Lord Kingarth[67]:

> ". . . counsel founded on the development of the Sweeney business by the defender operating as a sole trader between January 1973 and October 1981, the date of the marriage. Although, as I understood it, he accepted that the expansion of the business thereafter, and indeed the partnership and the three companies, fell properly to be regarded as matrimonial property, he submitted that there should be proper recognition of the special circumstance that by the date of the marriage, largely due to the efforts of the defender himself, the business was to a very large degree 'up and running', and that the subsequent successful expansion of that business could be regarded as significantly founded upon that base. I was invited in particular, to have regard to s.10(6)(b) of the 1985 Act which provides that 'special circumstances . . . may include . . . the source of funds or assets used to acquire any of the matrimonial property where those funds or assets were not derived from the income or efforts of the parties during the marriage'. He accepted that it was not easy to fit his argument precisely to those words but the Act merely provided examples of special circumstances, and the argument, he submitted was plainly based on similar principles."

Notice that the argument here may not be exactly within the terms of s.10(6)(b), although it appears to be something very like it—the laying of

---

[64] See para.6–28.

[65] See *Crockett v Crockett*, 1992 S.C.L.R. 591.

[66] *Sweeney v Sweeney* was appealed, but this part of the decision was not challenged—see *Sweeney v Sweeney*, 2005 S.L.T. 1141 at p.1143.

[67] At p.900.

the foundations of a successful business is not the same as introducing assets or funds to the marriage or partnership, but nevertheless one party has (by their sole effort) provided a firm base to allow a business to grow and flourish during the marriage or civil partnership. The list of special circumstances is not exhaustive—there are other types of "special circumstance" which lie outwith the particular types set out in paras (a)–(e) of s.10(6). In *Sweeney*, the court recognised the husband's contribution in building the business up before the marriage (although to a rather limited extent) and shared the value of the businesses 52 per cent to the husband and 48 per cent to the wife.

One practical problem which may arise in relation to this type of argument is how to establish what value to ascribe to the business at the point it becomes matrimonial or partnership property. Failure to lead evidence on this point may make it difficult for the court to share the value of the business unequally.[68]

Increases in value after the relevant date

7–24 There is a line of authority which holds that an increase in value of an item of property after the relevant date is not a special circumstance to be taken into account.[69] These arguments will now be of less importance in many circumstances as a result of the introduction of s.10(3A) of the Act.[70]

SECTION 10(6)(c)—DESTRUCTION, DISSIPATION OR ALIENATION

General comments

7–25 Section 10(6)(c) of the 1985 Act provides that one of the special circumstances which may permit unequal division of matrimonial or partnership property is:

"any destruction, dissipation or alienation of property by either person;".

This provision is linked closely with the provisions of s.11(7)(a) under which the court may take into account the conduct of a party if it has adversely affected the financial resources of the parties which are relevant to the decision of the court in a claim for financial provision. The wording in both sections is clear. They are both aimed at actions which affect *finances*.

Some themes

7–26 There are not many reported decisions relating to this provision. Nevertheless there are a few broad themes which have arisen in such reports as there are.

---

[68] See *Jackson v Jackson*, 2000 S.C.L.R. 81.
[69] See *Buczynska v Buczynski*, 1989 S.L.T. 558; *Wallis v Wallis*, 1993 S.L.T. 1348; *Dible v Dible*, 1997 S.L.T. 787.
[70] See para.5–06.

Deliberate actions will help a section 10(6)(c) argument

The courts will more readily accept that deliberate actions which **7–27** destroy, dissipate or alienate will allow unequal division using s.10(6)(c), as compared to circumstances where the loss is not deliberate. An example of deliberate dissipation can be found in *Short v Short*, 1994 G.W.D. 21–1300 where the wife, without the knowledge of her husband, took on a number of loans secured over the matrimonial home. In some of the loan applications she forged her husband's signature. She dissipated the funds and this was taken into account by the sheriff. Similarly in *Goldie v Goldie*, 1992 G.W.D. 21–1225, the husband had dissipated £2,000 from a loan obtained for his own benefit, and this was taken into account in division of the matrimonial property. However, contrast these cases with the decision in *Russell v Russell*, 1996 Fam. L.B. 21–5, where the wife had reduced resources by travelling to Turkey, giving up her job and losing money. It was held that losses arising from bad luck or judgement in business did not amount to dissipation of assets.[71]

Positive actions rather than passive failures improve a section 10(6)(c) argument

In one case failure to pay mortgage payments was held not to amount **7–28** to dissipation of assets. In *Park v Park*, 1988 S.C.L.R. 584 the husband's failure to make these payments resulted in a build-up of arrears, and the house was eventually repossessed by the heritable creditors. The property was sold by the creditors at a loss. Sheriff Kelbie dealt with this argument[72]:

> "[The agent for the pursuer] complained that the defender's failure to meet the mortgage payments had been a deliberate decision by the defender which had resulted in the loss of an important part of the matrimonial property. She sought an award of additional capital sum to the pursuer, referring to section 10(6)(c) of the 1985 Act which provides that 'special circumstances' may include any 'destruction, dissipation or alienation of property by either party'. She did accept that the defender's fault lay in not paying the building society, which had then taken action. That could not amount to destruction or alienation of property. She maintained it did amount to dissipation.
>
> In my view 'dissipation' in this context means a wasting or squandering of property and any dissipation by a party, as in the case of destruction or alienation of property, requires some definite action by the party to bring it about. A passive failure to take definite steps to prevent destruction, dissipation or alienation is not sufficient. The defender's failure to make payments to the building society does not amount to dissipation of the property. Section

---

[71] See also *Short v Short*, 1994 G.W.D. 21–1300.
[72] At p.587; See also *Cunniff v Cunniff*, 1999 S.L.T. 992; *Buchan v Buchan*, 2001 Fam. L.R. 48 at para.7–55 where it was held that for dissipation to be established, there has to be an element of deliberate and positively wanton conduct.

10(6)(c) does not, accordingly, apply to this case. Even if it could be said that it did, I would not be in a position to make any award in respect of that matter to the pursuer. The property was joint property and the obligation to make payments was a joint obligation. While it is true that the defender was in a better position to make payments than the pursuer, she could have taken steps to insure payment of the loan if she thought it appropriate. She did not do so. In any event, house prices in Aberdeen have notoriously fallen and in the end of the day, the value of the house is what it can be sold for. This house was sold for less than the value of the mortgage and, in these circumstances, it is not clear that the defender's decision not to make the payments was unwise. Lastly, the fact is that nothing was put before me which would indicate what better position the pursuer might have been in in relation to the property if the defender had made the payments to the building society. In these circumstances, I feel unable to make any additional award of capital sum on the basis of the pursuer's agent's argument in terms of section 10(6)(c)."[73]

Quantum

7–29   If the court finds that there should be unequal division because of the application of s.10(6)(c), the financial adjustment to be applied is within the discretion of the court. The courts have tended to look at the value of the property destroyed, dissipated or alienated. So, where a party burdened the house with additional debt for their own benefit, the amount of the loan was deducted in calculating their share of matrimonial property,[74] and when a party borrowed £2,000 and used the funds for himself, his share of matrimonial property was reduced by this amount.[75]

SECTION 10(6)(d)—THE NATURE AND USE OF PROPERTY

General comments

7–30   Under s.10(6)(d), one of the special circumstances which can be used to justify unequal division of matrimonial or partnership property is:

"the nature of the family property or partnership property, the use made of it (including use for business purposes or as a family home) and the extent to which it is reasonable to expect it to be realised or divided or used as security;".

This provision seems mainly to have been relied upon in two situations. First, where one party wishes to retain the family home and continue to use it as a home for children; and secondly, where much of the

---

[73] See also, however, *Gray v Gray*, 2001 Fam. L.B. 52–5 and *Gray v Gray*, 2001 G.W.D. 21–811.
[74] *Short v Short*, 1994 G.W.D. 21–1300.
[75] *Goldie v Goldie*, 1992 G.W.D. 21–1225.

matrimonial or partnership property is locked up in an asset which it would be unfair or impossible to ask a party to realise. The second situation formerly arose most often in relation to pensions, but since the introduction of pension sharing and pension lump sum orders, this use of the argument is less important. Having said this, there may be other types of property (such as farming or crofting businesses) which are difficult to realise and where the argument will still apply. However, if there are other assets which can be readily realised then it will often be the case that these can be transferred to the other party thus allowing equal sharing.[76] Even where assets are not readily realisable, there may well be other techniques which the court can deploy to ensure equal sharing. These include payment of a capital sum by instalments[77]; deferred payments (perhaps with interest to be added to account for late payment)[78]; pension sharing and earmarking; and periodical allowances. A party who is faced with a s.10(6)(d) claim would be well-advised to draw these alternatives to the attention of the court.

Section 10(6)(d) allows the court to treat different items of property in different ways, according to the property's nature and use. There is a rather extreme example of this in *Little v Little*, 1990 S.L.T. 785. At first instance, the Lord Ordinary did not value the total matrimonial property at the relevant date. Instead he separated the matrimonial property into three categories and treated each differently for the purpose of financial provision. The categories were: (1) property which he left undisturbed and out of account altogether on the basis that it would be unreasonable to disturb the existing situation—in this category were timeshare interests and motor cars; (2) the matrimonial home which was in the defender's name, but which was occupied by the pursuer—the Lord Ordinary awarded a one half share of this item to the pursuer; and (3) the remaining property which was valued at the date of separation, and which was split equally between the parties. On appeal to the Inner House it was argued that this was not a proper approach—the proper approach was to value the matrimonial property at the relevant date, and then decide how this value was to be divided using the principles of the 1985 Act. The appeal was dismissed, and the court used s.10(6)(d) to justify the approach taken by the Lord Ordinary in looking at different types of matrimonial property in different ways.[79] In the appeal judgement Lord President Hope commented[80]:

"The significance of s.10(6)(d) is that the court can in its discretion take account of the nature or use of individual items of matrimonial property in whatever way it thinks fit, so it can if it thinks appropriate refrain from valuing a property if to do so will have no practical result. Moreover, since s.10(1) permits the net value of the matrimonial property to be shared, if not equally, in such other

---

[76] *McConnell v McConnell (No.2)*, 1997 Fam. L.R. 108; *Little v Little*, 1990 S.L.T. 785.
[77] *Johnstone v Johnstone*, 1990 S.L.T. (Sh Ct) 79; *McEwan v McEwan*, 1995 G.W.D. 31–1610; *Buckle v Buckle*, 1995 S.C.L.R. 590.
[78] *Gulline v Gulline*, 1992 S.L.T. (Sh Ct) 71; *Bannon v Bannon*, 1993 S.L.T. 999.
[79] It is interesting to note that the Lord Ordinary did not refer to s.10(6)(d) in terms.
[80] At p.792.

proportions as are justified by special circumstances, the discretion extends to treating some items of matrimonial property differently from others according to their nature or the use to which they are put. I see no conflict between what the Lord Ordinary decided was appropriate in regard to the parties' motor cars, for example, which he left out of account altogether because of their nature and their use, and what s.10(1) requires. Nor can I see any such conflict in the case of his treatment of the matrimonial home, which as it happens is one of the clearest examples of a particular item of matrimonial property for which special arrangements may be justified."

Lord Dunpark commented[81]:

"Counsel submitted that the Lord Ordinary was not entitled to cancel out the cars which each party owned because the value of the pursuer's car at the relevant date was less than that of the defender's. In my opinion the Lord Ordinary, in the exercise of his discretion in terms of s.10(6)(d), was entitled to regard the cars as required for the practice of their professions and to ignore the difference in values."

Although *Little v Little* is authority for the proposition that the court has a discretion to treat property in a variety of ways (including leaving it out of account), this does not appear to be the way that the courts have generally approached matters. Again and again reported cases tend to establish the value of all of the matrimonial property (rather than choosing to leave some out of account altogether) before applying the principles of the Act to the division of this property.

Section 10(6)(d) and the family home

7–31   Section 10(6)(d) is often relied upon in circumstances where the parties own a house which is the family home of the children, and where one party wishes to continue to occupy the house with the children. It might be reasonable that the house should be transferred to the party with whom the children are to reside, but sometimes that party will simply not be able to afford to do so if equal sharing of matrimonial or partnership property is to be employed. Section 10(6)(d) can be used to argue that the court should depart from equal sharing by ordering the transfer of the house to the party who is the main carer for the children.[82]

When examining a request under s.10(6)(d) for the transfer of the family home and a departure from equal sharing, it appears that three inter-related questions need to be asked: (1) is the order necessary?; (2) is the order fair and reasonable for both parties?; and (3) is the order practical? The remainder of this section looks at each of these three questions in turn.

---

[81] At p.790.
[82] See *Muir v Muir*, 1993 G.W.D. 21–1297 and 1993 G.W.D. 39–2593; *Peacock v Peacock*, 1994 S.L.T. 40; *McCormick v McCormick*, 1994 G.W.D. 35–2078; *Murphy v Murphy*, 1993 G.W.D. 3–156.

1. Is the order necessary?

If s.10(6)(d) is employed to argue for a departure from equal sharing **7–32** through the transfer of the family home, the first question is whether the order is necessary. To put this another way—is there some compelling reason for the transfer? The argument will be at its strongest if (a) there are children (particularly young children) whose lives will be substantially disrupted if the family home is sold, and (b) the party seeking the transfer has no other means of securing reasonably suitable accommodation.[83] So, in *Murphy v Murphy*, 1996 S.L.T. (Sh Ct) 91, where it was held that a house was necessary for the welfare of the child, and there were special circumstances allowing a departure from equal sharing, Sheriff Bell commented[84]:

"While fair sharing is in the first instance equal sharing of the net value, the court can of course depart from this principle if other proportions are justified by special circumstances.

I consider that I am justified in departing from this principle. The special circumstances which I have taken account of are (1) the fact that the pursuer has custody of the child . . .; (2) that the house is, in my opinion, necessary for the welfare of the pursuer and the child, as well as one of the older children who also lives there; (3) that it is not necessary to sell the house to allow the parties to have alternative accommodation, as the defender has somewhere else to live; (4) that the pursuer will receive no benefit from the pension rights after divorce and will receive no other payment from the defender. In these circumstances, I have reached the view that the net value of the matrimonial property can be shared fairly between the parties if I were to make an order for the transfer by the defender to the pursuer of the defender's one half share in the reversionary interest in the home. That would be without any further payment by the defender to the pursuer and without any counterbalancing payment by the pursuer to the defender."

Notice the emphasis on the fact that the house is necessary for the welfare of the children. Similarly, in *Muir v Muir*, 1993 G.W.D. 21–1297 and 1993 G.W.D. 39–2593, it was held that a transfer of the former matrimonial home in favour of the wife was appropriate—she had no other accommodation and if the net value of the matrimonial property was split equally, she would be unable to afford anywhere else.

In *Peacock v Peacock*, 1993 S.C. 88, at first instance the wife had craved an order transferring the husband's interest in the former matrimonial home to her. The sheriff granted this order. There was an unsuccessful appeal to the sheriff principal and the husband appealed to the Court of Session, contending that there were no grounds to depart from equal sharing. The Inner House seems to stress that the issue of the order's *necessity* is important in the following passage[85]:

---

[83] See e.g. *Cooper v Cooper*, 1989 S.C.L.R. 347 discussed at para.7–33.
[84] At pp.93–4.
[85] At p.94.

". . . having regard to the terms of sec.10(6)(d) we are of opinion that the sheriff in his discretion was entitled to reach the view that the net value of the matrimonial property should be taken to be shared fairly between the parties even though the division was not an equal one. He was entitled to conclude that there were special circumstances justifying an order for the transfer by the defender to the pursuer of the defender's one-half share in the reversionary interest in the home. The fact that the pursuer had custody of the two children and that the house was necessary for their welfare, the fact that the defender was not in a position to contribute to the support of the children, the fact that there were only two items of matrimonial property, the fact that the house did not have to be sold to allow the parties to purchase alternative accommodation, and the fact that the defender was to receive an assignation of the pursuer's whole right and interest in the life assurance policy all combine to warrant the conclusion that there were special circumstances justifying the division of the matrimonial property to which the sheriff gave effect."

The Inner house held that in all these circumstances there was sufficient material to allow the court to hold that the house was necessary for the welfare of the children because there would be disruption to them if they had to move out of the family home.

If the children are young, vulnerable or at an important stage of their education then the argument for a transfer may be stronger.[86] So, it will be much harder to establish special circumstances if there are no young children in the house who would be disadvantaged by disruption.[87] However, there is no definitive rule on the matter and each case will be considered on its merits. In *Trotter v Trotter*, 2001 S.L.T. (Sh Ct) 42 Sheriff Principal Nicholson commented[88]:

". . . it was also submitted that the sheriff erred in law in holding that a child who is over 16, who is not in full time education but who is in full time employment, and who lives with the pursuer, can give rise to a special circumstance justifying departure from the principle of equal sharing . . . In support of his submissions in relation to the consideration to be given to the children of the marriage living with the pursuer the solicitor advocate for the defender referred to [the undernoted cases[89]]. I have to say at once, however, that none of the foregoing cases gives any support to the grounds of appeal actually advanced on behalf of the defender,

---

[86] See *Christie v Christie*, 2004 S.L.T. (Sh Ct) 95.

[87] See *Quinn v Quinn*, 2003 S.L.T. (Sh Ct) 5; *Webster v Webster*, 2003 G.W.D. 5–118 (where a transfer would have resulted in the wife receiving funds out of all proportion with what she was due on an equal sharing).

[88] At pp.45–6.

[89] *Cooper v Cooper*, 1989 S.C.L.R. 347; *Farrell v Farrell*, 1990 S.C.L.R. 717; *Muir v Muir*, 1993 G.W.D. 21–1297 and 1994 S.C.L.R. 178; *Peacock v Peacock*, 1994 S.L.T. 40 and 1993 S.C. 88; *McCormick v McCormick*, 1994 S.C.L.R. 958; *Murphy v Murphy*, 1996 S.L.T. (Sh Ct) 91; *Main v Main*, 1990 S.C.L.R. 165; *Cunniff v Cunniff*, 1999 S.C. 537 and 1999 S.L.T. 992.

namely that the sheriff had erred in law in having regard to the situation of the two children of the marriage who, at the time of the proof, were aged 16 and 18 respectively. It is clear from the cases referred to that the position of the children of any age may lawfully be taken into account by a court which is considering the distribution of matrimonial property, and it does not become unlawful to do so simply on account of the fact that the children in a particular case are of, or above, the age of 16. It is plain, of course, that the weight to be attached to the position of children residing in the matrimonial home with one parent will probably be greater when those children are young, and therefore unable to make arrangements for their own residence and welfare. But nothing in the cases to which I was referred suggests that it is improper to have regard to the position of children who are older. In such cases, of course, much will depend on the actual ages of the children concerned, and on their particular circumstances."

Another issue which has a bearing on whether the order is necessary is the question of whether the house is simply too big for the reasonable needs of the family. If it is, and there is suitable alternative accommodation available for the party with whom the children regularly reside, it will be more difficult to argue that the transfer is necessary to achieve a fair result.[90] In fact, in some circumstances it can be argued that it is positively in the best interests of the family to sell the existing property and move to one which is less expensive and easier to maintain.[91] So, in the case of *Thom v Thom*, 1990 S.C.L.R. 800, after the separation the wife was residing in an eight-bedroom hotel with the child of the marriage. For present purposes there are important comments towards the end of Lord McCluskey's judgement[92]:

". . . it is plain that the sensible thing appears to be to dispose of this hotel. It is unfortunate that that may mean in the next few weeks or months that the pursuer will lose her present home, but an eight-bedroomed hotel is not, on the face of it, the most suitable accommodation for her and the child."

If the family home is already in joint names, one might ask why the court need disturb the status quo at all; after all the value of the property is already shared equally. The answer is that the party entitled to the transfer order will often need the security of outright ownership. In *Trotter v Trotter*, 2001 S.L.T. (Sh Ct) 42 the sheriff principal noted[93]:

". . . the sheriff then went on to consider the possibility that, if there were to be no transfer of the matrimonial home to the pursuer, albeit that that resulted in unequal sharing, the pursuer might then

---

[90] See the comments in *Christie v Christie*, 2004 S.L.T. (Sh Ct) 95 at 100; see also *MacDonald v MacDonald*, 1991 G.W.D. 31–1866.

[91] See *Adams v Adams (No.1)*, 1997 S.L.T.144 at p.146.

[92] At p.802.

[93] At p.45.

be at risk of an action of division and sale at the instance of the defender. The sheriff concluded that that would put the pursuer in a very vulnerable position; and she considered that that was a further element amounting to a special circumstance under s.10(6)(d) of the 1985 Act."

The precarious position of the party in occupation was stressed in *Farrell v Farrell*, 1990 S.C.L.R. 717, where the wife pursuer sought the outright transfer of the defender's interest in the family home and a capital sum payment. The sheriff noted that, on the facts, if no order was made (leaving the house in joint names) then the property could be subject to an action of division and sale.[94] The sheriff said[95]:

"It seems to me that it would be very unfair to make no orders at all; that would leave the pursuer in a highly vulnerable position in which she would (at the whim of the defender) lose her home and much of the benefit of her investment. Any action of division and sale taken after divorce would result in further expense to the pursuer . . . By contrast, the defender stands to pocket a proportion of the net free proceeds of the sale of an asset to the purchase of which he has contributed very little. That would seem to be a manifestly inequitable outcome in the peculiar circumstances of this case."

Of course, in many cases there will be the further practical consideration that the party who is not in occupation of the house will be unlikely to want or be in a position to retain a mortgage commitment over the property.

2.   Is the order fair and reasonable?

7–33   Special circumstances may only be deployed to achieve a result which is *fair*.[96] Further, the court can only make orders which are reasonable having regard to the resources of the parties.[97] Often, the family home will be the parties' most valuable asset. Even if its transfer to one of the parties is desirable, this will not necessarily achieve a fair result, or one which is reasonable having regard to the resources of the parties. For example, in *McKenzie v McKenzie*, 1991 S.L.T. 461 Lord Prosser considered a case where the wife continued to reside in the family home with the son of the parties at the date of the proof. She sought an order for the transfer of her husband's interest in the property to her. There was substantial equity in the property, and it was conceded that an order of this nature would result in a significant departure from equal sharing. Lord Prosser said[98]:

"The [wife's] suggestion has the attraction of simplicity, but I am not persuaded that it would be at all fair to the defender."

---

[94] Although see *Milne v Milne*, 1994 G.W.D. 11–666.
[95] At p.726.
[96] s.10(1); see also the comments on *Cooper v Cooper* below.
[97] s.8(2)(b).
[98] At p.463.

Even if it is the case that it is appropriate to grant a transfer of the house from one party to the other, the court has to look at whether other orders of one sort or another may be employed to avoid unfairness. Although these balancing orders might not achieve equal division of matrimonial or partnership property, they might soften the blow for the party who does not retain the family home.[99] In *Cooper v Cooper*, 1989 S.C.L.R. 347, Sheriff Principal Ireland considered a situation where the main matrimonial asset was the matrimonial home. It was in joint names, and the equity in the house was about £13,500. The sheriff at first instance noted that the pursuer continued to reside in the house with the three children of the marriage, and held that because of the special circumstances found in s.10(6)(d) unequal sharing was justified. He ordered a transfer of the house to the pursuer. On appeal, Sheriff Principal Ireland commented[100]:

"The fact that the house is required as a home for the pursuer and the children, and cannot be sold without making them homeless, is a circumstance making it unreasonable to expect the house to be realised, and therefore section 10(6)(d) applies. The sheriff has therefore ordered the defender to transfer to the pursuer his half share in the house. The defender's solicitor argued that this was unfair to the defender, who has no income of his own and no prospect of earning any. The need for the pursuer to provide a home for the children would cease to be a legal obligation in about two years, when the youngest child attains the age of sixteen. The sheriff should have ordered the house to be sold, at least when that happened, or alternatively made an order for the payment of the defender's share by instalments.

In my opinion, the sheriff was justified in the order which he made. This is not a case in which the defender has got nothing at all out of the matrimonial property. He has already had £2,700 and he has also been found entitled to the items of property set out in the sheriff's interlocutor. No separate valuation seems to have been made of these, but they are not insubstantial, and the figure of £2,000 suggested by the pursuer's solicitor does not seem to be too wide of the mark. In addition he has been relieved not only of the future mortgage payments on the house, but also of his liability to repay the loan from the pursuer's parents. There is thus a closer approach to equal division than might appear from the figures relating to the house alone. Moreover, even to the extent that the sheriff's division favours the pursuer rather than the defender, there was material on which the sheriff was entitled to exercise his discretion in this way."

It is worth noting that this passage continually emphasises that the court regards the result as fair and the court is at pains to point out that the sums retained by the husband are not insubstantial. In this context, the

---

[99] In addition to the cases discussed below see also *MacDonald v MacDonald*, 1991 G.W.D. 31–1866.
[100] p.348.

decision in *Muir v Muir*, 1993 G.W.D. 21–1297 and 1993 G.W.D. 39–2593 is interesting. In that case it was held that there were special circumstances in terms of s.10(6)(d), and the transfer of the former matrimonial home to the wife was ordered—she had no other accommodation and if the net value of the matrimonial property was split equally, she would be unable to afford anywhere else. In addition she had been trying to repay joint debts on her own and the net value of the matrimonial home was relatively low. For current purposes it is worth noting the observation in the decision that it was probably appropriate to make a small counterbalancing award to the husband of a capital sum to prevent a situation arising where the wife obtained the whole of the matrimonial property, although the court could not competently do so in the absence of a crave.[101]

In *Murley v Murley*, 1995 S.C.L.R. 1138, the Lord MacLean employed an interesting device to achieve fairness. He was convinced that the house should be retained for the benefit of the wife and family, but was concerned about the imbalance that this would create for the husband. He tackled this by ordering the wife to grant a standard security over the house in favour of the husband ordering payment of a specified sum on sale of the property, or when the younger child of the parties reached 18, whichever was the earlier. It does seem that flexible orders like this are a sensible application of the Act. The court was recognising that the house was needed for the young family, but put checks and balances in place to try to achieve overall financial fairness.[102]

3. Is the order practical?

7–34   The court must carefully consider whether the order sought is practical. It may be desirable to transfer the family home to one party, but if that party cannot reasonably afford to finance the mortgage payments and/or the running costs of the property, then the order will not be appropriate.[103] In *McKenzie v McKenzie*, 1991 S.L.T. 461 Lord Prosser commented[104]:

> "Moreover, it does not seem to me that the proposal produces a practicable solution, enabling the pursuer to remain in the matrimonial home. As I have indicated, her income amounts to less than £6,000 per annum. If the proposal were put into effect, she would require not merely to live on that income, but to meet the mortgage and insurance payments in relation to the house. These payments amount to some £300 per month. In my opinion, if this course were adopted, it would immediately or rapidly become necessary to sell

---

[101] Practitioners who are faced with an opponent seeking transfer of the family home beware! Do not rely on an all or nothing strategy. Consider what is to happen if the opponent is granted the property transfer. In particular, what counter-balancing orders can be craved to soften the blow and achieve a fairer result?

[102] See also *C v C*, 2007 G.W.D. 08–145 where the court ordered the transfer of the house to the wife, but also ordered a deferred payment by the wife to the husband, to be paid at a point where she was likely to be more financially secure.

[103] In addition to the cases quoted below, see also *Murphy v Murphy*, 1996 S.L.T. (Sh Ct) 91.

[104] At p.463.

the house. In my opinion, an order for transfer is not a solution, and sale of the house is going to be necessary if fairness is to be achieved."

Similarly, the comments of Sheriff Russell in *Symon v Symon*, 1991 S.C.L.R. 414 are pertinent[105]:

"The . . . matrimonial home is the only significant capital asset of the parties. It is financially necessary for the house to be sold as there is no other way in which either the pursuer or the defender could reasonably be able to afford the mortgage . . . having regard to their respective means."

This makes perfect sense. A party should not be allowed to use s.10(6)(d) to obtain transfer of the home (and an unequal sharing of matrimonial or partnership property) if they cannot afford to keep it. All that will happen in those circumstances is that the house will be sold after the order is made with the party who retained the family home obtaining a windfall.[106]

Section 10(6)(d) and other assets

In this section there is an examination of how s.10(6)(d) has been **7–35** applied to various assets other than the family home.

Businesses

The argument here will be at its strongest where much of the **7–36** matrimonial or partnership property is locked up in a business which one party needs to earn their living. It may be unreasonable to order that the business is sold, thereby depriving one party of their normal livelihood. So, in *Budge v Budge (No.1)*, 1990 S.L.T. 319, the husband argued that regard should be had to s.10(6)(d) because his croft and the croft house provided his source of income and also his only home—the court should not make an order which would force him to leave. The court was persuaded that s.10(6)(d) (along with other factors) allowed a departure from equal sharing. In *Davidson v Davidson*, 1994 S.L.T. 506, Lord Maclean heard (in a case which balances many competing principles of the Act)[107] that the parties had married in 1988 and split in 1991. The parties bought a farm in 1989 which the wife farmed, and this was the only item of matrimonial property at the relevant date. The farm was used solely by the wife for business purposes and that was considered to be a special circumstance justifying unequal division.

It is not enough, however, to argue that business assets in themselves are difficult to realise. The value of the business assets has to be looked

---

[105] See p.414.
[106] Of course the reality here is that there is no easy way to prevent the party who retains the home after divorce or dissolution from selling the asset after an order is made. That is why it is important for the court to be absolutely satisfied that there are compelling reasons for that party to retain the particular asset.
[107] The case is "a fairly extreme case and . . . an unusual one"—see p.508.

at in the context of the whole financial position of the parties. If there are other substantial assets available then these can be transferred to the party who is not retaining the business allowing equal sharing without any unfairness. So, in *McConnell v McConnell (No.2)*, 1997 Fam. L.R. 108, the matrimonial property included substantial loans made by the husband to his company and also his shareholding in that company. Although these would have been difficult to realise, there were other readily realisable assets available to transfer to the wife. Accordingly, there were no special circumstances which required the value of the loans and the shareholding to be discounted.[108]

If the value of a business falls between the relevant date and the date of the proof it may be that s.10(6)(d) will have a bearing in an argument that the value of the business should be discounted in the final division of matrimonial or partnership property.[109]

Pensions

7–37   Section 10(6)(d) arguments were sometimes used to argue that the value of a pension should be discounted to take account of the fact that the asset was not readily realisable.[110] The argument is less important because there are now techniques available to the court to share and split virtually all types of pension assets.[111] However, the reported cases may still have some relevance in circumstances where it is argued that the value of an asset should be discounted under s.10(6)(d) because it is difficult to realise. They may also be useful in circumstances where a party refuses to contemplate pension sharing or earmarking.

Damages awards and criminal injuries compensation

7–38   The question of whether damages awards and awards of criminal injuries compensation are matrimonial or partnership property is examined at paras 6–41 to 6–43. If such an award is matrimonial or partnership property, then it may be possible to argue that some elements of the claim should be discounted using s.10(6)(d) because they are personal to the injured party. In particular, claims for solatium and loss of future earnings have been placed in this category. In *Skarpaas v Skarpaas*, 1991 S.L.T. (Sh Ct) 15,[112] the sheriff at first instance considered whether an award of compensation for injuries was to be equally divided between the parties. He commented[113]:

"... I consider that I should pay heed to the terms of s.10(6)(d) and have regard to 'the nature of the matrimonial property'. It was submitted that I was not entitled to look at what the defender's compensation was awarded for. In my opinion this submission is ill

---

[108] See also *Little v Little*, 1990 S.L.T. 785.
[109] See *Crockett v Crockett*, 1992 S.C.L.R. 591.
[110] See e.g. *Stephen v Stephen*, 1995 S.C.L.R. 175; *Bannon v Bannon*, 1993 S.L.T. 999; *Crosbie v Crosbie*, 1996 S.L.T. (Sh Ct) 86; *MacQueen v MacQueen*, 1992 G.W.D. 28–1653; *Fleming v Fleming*, 1993 G.W.D. 9–620.
[111] See paras 3–49 to 3–80.
[112] See also 1993 S.L.T. 343; and *Carrol v Carrol*, 2003 Fam. L.R. 108.
[113] At p.18.

founded. I agree with the remarks of Sheriff Risk in *Petrie v Petrie*, 1988 S.C.L.R. 390 at p.393 when he described a case where the only substantial capital asset was a husband's compensation payment as a 'very special case'. Sheriff Risk went on to say that, had he had to decide the matter, he would probably have discounted the wife's share to a very great extent, if not entirely. While I have no doubt that such a comment was justified in the circumstances of *Petrie*, I do not consider that in the present case such a large discount should be applied. I am prepared, however, to accept that there should be some discount in respect of the part of the award representing solatium and loss of future earning capacity. Solatium is essentially personal to the defender. Compensation for loss of future earning capacity represents funds to which the pursuer would not normally have had access following the dissolution of the marriage. I am therefore prepared to discount these sums . . . I consider that the proper way to do this is to deduct these sums from the net value of the matrimonial property . . .''[114]

However, the question of whether a discount will be applied in any given case is discretionary. In *McGuire v McGuire's CB*, 1991 S.L.T. (Sh.Ct.) 76 the wife sought a capital sum in relation to a criminal injuries compensation award made to her husband. He had received a severe head injury and required permanent residential care. Sheriff Henderson looked at the nature of the award[115]:

". . . special circumstances may include 'the nature of the matrimonial property, the use made of it and the extent to which it is reasonable to expect it to be realised or divided'. Its nature would clearly refer to the element of solatium and while this is an appropriate and proper consideration in certain cases, it is by no means the only consideration and the circumstances may be such that only slight if any significance has to be attached to its nature."

The sheriff went on to recount the particular facts of this case, which included the fact that the defender's tragic circumstances meant he would need residential care for the rest of his life, and that whatever capital he received from the divorce, his position was secure because he was in receipt of public funds to provide for his care costs. In these circumstances the court chose to exercise its discretion in relation to the nature of the award by paying "fairly slight regard" to s.10(6)(d), and awarded the wife about one half of the criminal injuries compensation.

SECTION 10(6)(e)—LIABILITY FOR EXPENSES OF VALUATION OR TRANSFER

General comments

Section 10(6)(e) states that one of the special circumstances which **7–39** allows the court to depart from equal sharing is:

---

[114] See also *Carrol v Carrol*, 2003 Fam. L.R. 108.
[115] At p.78.

> "the actual or prospective liability for any expenses of valuation or transfer of property in connection with the divorce or the dissolution of the civil partnership."

If one party has to bear more expense than the other in transferring assets or having them valued, then the courts can use this as a special circumstance justifying unequal division. The section seems to be rarely used,[116] and it may be that it could be employed a little more often. Most agents will have encountered cases where one of the parties refuses to incur valuation costs, putting the responsibility for these onto the party who wants to make progress. This provision could be used to prevent unfairness in such cases.

OTHER SPECIAL CIRCUMSTANCES

General comments

7–40   Section 10(6) states that the five specific examples of special circumstances set out in paragraphs (a)–(e) are without prejudice to the generality of the words. This means that there are categories of special circumstance which lie outwith the defined examples, and if these can be identified in a case they may justify unequal sharing of matrimonial or partnership property. The position is neatly summed up by Lord McCluskey in *Cunniff v Cunniff*, 1999 S.L.T. 992[117]:

> "It is important to note that, although 'special circumstances' may include the examples specified as (a) to (e), that provision as to inclusion is 'without prejudice to the generality of the words'. It is clear that the court of first instance is not obliged to ignore relevant and material circumstances just because they are not specified in the five particular paragraphs, but must take account of any material circumstances special to the case."

Some examples

7–41   In this section some situations are examined where it has been argued that there are special circumstances outwith the defined examples in paras (a) to (e) of s.10(6).

Short marriages/civil partnerships

7–42   In several cases involving short marriages, the courts have held that the brevity of the marital relationship was a special circumstance justifying a departure from equal division. For example, in *Kerrigan v Kerrigan*, 1988 S.C.L.R. 603, Sheriff Evans pointed out that the words "special circumstances" were general and decided that the fact that the marriage was "very brief indeed" (the couple had been married and co-

---

[116] There is a brief discussion in *Farrell v Farrell*, 1990 S.C.L.R. 717.
[117] At p.994; see also e.g. *Jacques v Jacques*, 1997 S.L.T 459 at pp.460–1; *Lessani v Lessani*, 2007 Fam. L.R. 81.

habiting for only about a year) was a special circumstance allowing him to depart from equal sharing. The couple had bought a house shortly before the marriage, using a mortgage and £10,000 provided by the pursuer's mother. Throughout the short marriage the pursuer had paid the mortgage. In the circumstances the sheriff ordered the transfer of the defender's share of the property to the pursuer.

In *White v White*, 1992 S.C.L.R. 769, the couple had been married for an even shorter period before they separated—the couple were married and co-habiting for only about six weeks. The husband had bought a house shortly before the marriage, taking title in his sole name. The funds for the purchase came entirely from the husband's savings and a loan obtained by him. The house was matrimonial property, but the court decided that the very short duration of the marriage was a special circumstance allowing a departure from equal sharing. Sheriff Gilmour commented[118]:

"... the general definition of 'special circumstances' contained in section 10(6) of the Act does not prohibit me from taking into account the very brief practical period of this marriage, which effectively lasted from 1st January 1991 to 15th February 1991,[119] when the defender left the matrimonial home."

Increases in the value of assets after the separation

An increase in the value of an asset after the date of separation is not **7–43** in itself a special circumstance.[120]

Unequal contribution to joint expenses after separation

Sometimes, after separation, one party will pay more than the other **7–44** towards various joint expenses—most commonly the mortgage payments and other household expenses. Sometimes this may be interpreted as special circumstances justifying unequal division. Care will need to be taken, however, as in many cases the payments may be regarded by the court as alimentary in nature, and in those cases it may be that no unfairness arises. *Farrell v Farrell*, 1990 S.C.L.R. 717 is a case where the argument was accepted. The family home was in joint names of the parties and was subject to a mortgage. After separation the wife voluntarily undertook the mortgage payments. On divorce she successfully sought a departure from equal sharing.[121]

Loss of property

Sometimes one party may claim that they have lost an item of **7–45** property, or that it has been destroyed. This type of suspicious loss can be a special circumstance. In *Jesner v Jesner*, 1992 S.L.T. 999, evidence

---

[118] At p.771.

[119] One imagines it may not have been the best ever Valentine's Day.

[120] *Wallis v Wallis*, 1992 S.L.T. 676; *Buczynska v Buczynski*, 1989 S.L.T. 558; *Welsh v Welsh*, 1994 S.L.T. 828.

[121] A little care should be taken in relation to this decision. It is difficult to know what weight the sheriff has attached to these "other" special circumstances because there also appears to be quite a significant s.10(6)(d) argument operating; see also *Bateman v Bateman*, 1994 G.W.D. 2234.

established that the husband had put certain items into storage. Whilst in storage these items had either been lost or destroyed. The husband had submitted an insurance claim but the parties were agreed that this was unlikely to have any financial value. Lord Osborne (using rather loaded language) held that[122]:

> ". . . the defender's having contrived to lose the furnishings of the matrimonial home for all practical purposes must be regarded also as 'special circumstances'."

Recognition of greater financial input

7–46   This argument overlaps with the principle set out in s.9(1)(b) under which the court is to take fair account of any economic advantage derived by either person from contributions of the other, and of any economic disadvantage suffered by either person in the interests of the other person or the family. In some marriages or civil partnerships, a party might argue that they contributed much more in financial terms to the accumulation of matrimonial or partnership property. In many cases this will be part of the normal give and take in a marriage or civil partnership, perhaps with one party bringing in most of the money, and the other devoting more time to the children. If there is this give and take, the courts are unlikely to be sympathetic to an unequal division of matrimonial or partnership property in favour of the party who has been earning the money.[123] Often there will be other balancing factors which will need to be looked at carefully before a "special circumstances" argument can succeed here.[124]

However, it is possible to envisage a marriage or civil partnership (perhaps where there are no children) where one party works very hard whilst the other is lazy and does not make any significant contribution to the household purse. *Little v Little*, 1990 S.L.T. 785 gives a glimmer of hope to industrious parties. Lord Dunpark commented[125]:

> "The object of this Act is to produce a *fair* division of the matrimonial property. [The Lord President then quoted from s.10(1)] In s.10(6) special circumstances include specified circumstances 'without prejudice to the generality of the words'. In my opinion in a case of this nature, where both parties were earning during the consortium, an equal division of the total net value would not necessarily be fair, for the defender was contributing to the matrimonial property more than the pursuer could do. Section 9(1) does not require a judge to divide the total net value equally, but fairly."

Unusual needs of a party

7–47   In *Collins v Collins*, 1997 Fam. L.R. 50 the husband suffered from multiple sclerosis. At the relevant date he was still relatively mobile and

---

[122] At p.1000.
[123] Quite the opposite in fact—s.9(1)(b) will often allow the non-earning party to argue that they have been economically disadvantaged by e.g. giving up earning potential.
[124] See e.g. *Welsh v Welsh*, 1994 S.L.T. 828.
[125] At p.792.

did not require nursing care, but by the time the case came to proof he was confined to a wheelchair, required nursing care seven days a week, and was dependent on state benefits. Quite some years after the separation he raised an action of divorce and sought the transfer of the family home to him. The property transfer order was granted in spite of the fact that there was a substantial departure from equal sharing. Sheriff Smith pointed out that the circumstances of this case are highly unusual[126]:

". . . in this divorce the circumstances are more extraordinary than merely special. The house is the pursuer's only link to normality in his life and will remain so throughout his life. Anything which would disturb that would be cruel. Further, that link requires to be bulwarked by the pursuer knowing he has total security in his home and that can now be achieved only if he is the sole owner."

However, it is worth noting that, even in these highly specialised circumstances, the court softened the financial effect of the property transfer order by awarding a capital sum to the wife with payment deferred until death of the husband. The payment was secured over the property.

Laying the foundations of a business

A business started by one party before the marriage or registration **7–48** may become converted to matrimonial or partnership property if the business structure changes after the marriage or registration.[127] In these circumstances, the party who started the business may argue that their efforts and capital put into the business before the marriage or registration should be taken into account as a special circumstance.[128]

Lack of candour about resources

If the court considers that one of the parties has failed to fully disclose **7–49** their assets, this may be a special circumstance allowing unequal sharing in favour of the other party.[129]

Conduct

In certain circumstances, the court may be entitled to take conduct of **7–50** the parties into account in making its award of financial provision.[130] If conduct is to be taken into account, one way of doing so is to classify it as a special circumstance justifying unequal division of matrimonial or partnership property.[131]

---

[126] At para.10–12.
[127] See para.6–28.
[128] The argument here is closely linked to ss.10(6)(b). See the more detailed discussion on *Sweeney v Sweeney*, 2003 S.L.T. 892 at para.7–23.
[129] *Lessani v Lessani*, 2007 Fam. L.R. 81 at para.21; *Burchell v Burchell*, 1997 Fam. L.R. 137.
[130] See paras 4–12 to 4–14.
[131] See the discussion of *Bremner v Bremner*, 2000 S.C.L.R. 912, see para.4–13.

INTERIM ALIMENT

Scope of this chapter

8–01   This chapter deals only with interim aliment in relation to spouses in actions of divorce and civil partners in actions for dissolution. It does not deal with actions of aliment for spouses or civil partners nor does it deal with aliment of children.[1]

General comments

8–02   In an action of divorce or dissolution, interim aliment can provide short-term financial support for a party who needs this until the disposal of the case, at which point longer-term financial provision will be made. An obligation of aliment is owed inter alia by each spouse to the other and by each civil partner to the other.[2] A claim for interim aliment is competent inter alia in an action of divorce or dissolution.[3] Further, if one party raises an action for declarator of nullity, denying the existence of the marriage or civil partnership, it is competent for that party to claim interim aliment.[4]

In an action of divorce or dissolution, an application for interim aliment is made by motion.[5] The application for interim aliment may be made at the earliest point in the action, even before defences have been lodged,[6] or before eligibility for legal aid has been determined.[7] An award of interim aliment is to consist of periodical payments which will subsist only until disposal of the action in which the award is made, or until such earlier date as the court may specify.[8] If decree of divorce or

---

[1] For an excellent discussion of these matters see E.M. Clive, *The Law of Husband and Wife in Scotland*, 4th edn, Chs 12 and 25.

[2] s.1(1).

[3] s.6(1)(b) and (c).

[4] s.17(2).

[5] O.C.R. r.33.50.

[6] *Fyffe v Fyffe*, 1954 S.C. 1; *Currie v Currie* (1833) 12 S. 171—". . . there was no incompetency in applying for an award of interim aliment at the earliest stage of the cause . . .*"; *Pirrie v Pirrie* (1903) 10 S.L.T. 598; *Johnston v Johnston* 1916 2 S.L.T. 191.

[7] *Fyffe v Fyffe*, 1954 S.C. 1.

[8] s.6(3). Although, in this context the action will not be regarded as disposed of until all claims for financial provision have been determined. So, if the court reserves its decision on financial matters under s.12(1)(b) until a date after the date of decree, the obligation to provide aliment will subsist until the financial orders have been disposed of. The matter was considered in *Neill v Neill*, 1987 S.L.T. (Sh Ct) 143 where decree of divorce was granted and the cause was continued for determination of certain orders for financial provision. Prior to the proof on those matters, the defender lodged a motion for interim

dissolution is granted, but one party appeals an award of financial provision, an award of interim aliment may subsist pending the appeal being heard.[9]

In order to establish a case for interim aliment (and in order to defend such a claim) the parties must place before the court information about their resources.[10] The court will base its decision on such information as is available and upon ex parte statements.[11] Often the information available will be incomplete. The sheriff should make his decision on the basis of the information actually available at the hearing and, in the absence of conflicting material, should not speculate that the information produced does not present matters accurately.[12] It will not be possible at a hearing on interim aliment to assess every detail of the parties' finances.[13] If there is a dispute about material matters, the court will need adequate information upon which to resolve that dispute, and should not base its decision simply on suspicion.[14] The court should deal with matters on an interim basis, assessing the need for interim aliment based on the current needs and resources of the parties, and should not base its decision on assumptions about the long-term disposal of the case.[15]

Interim awards of aliment are often required quickly to protect a party who is in need of income. This means that there will often be pressure on the court to make an early decision, generally without all of the information which it would have available in the final disposal of a case. However, once an interim award has been made, it will be difficult to appeal the decision for two reasons. First, appeal is competent only with leave;[16] and secondly, the quantum of the award is within the discretion of the sheriff and will be difficult to alter on appeal.[17] Accordingly, the initial hearing on interim aliment may be very important, and the initial order may regulate matters for quite some time. For these reasons, it is crucial that the parties involved prepare as fully as possible for the motion for interim aliment. Full details of income, outgoings, resources and all other relevant factors should be available, and any appropriate vouching should be produced to the court. Expenses will tend to follow success, but it may be difficult to obtain certification for employment of counsel in cases involving interim aliment.[18]

---

aliment. This was opposed on the basis that the parties were no longer husband and wife, and (so the argument went) an obligation of aliment no longer subsisted. On appeal, however, the sheriff principal held that the action remained "an action of divorce" until all of the financial aspects of the case had been dealt with and accordingly a claim for interim aliment was competent.

[9] *Lessani v Lessani*, 2007 Fam. L.R. 81; s.6(3); *De La Motte v Jardine* (1789) Mor 447.

[10] See e.g. *Fyffe v Fyffe*, 1953 (Notes) 70; *B v B*, 1999 Fam. L.R. 74; see also 1996 Fam. L.B. 19–5.

[11] *Adams v Adams*, 2002 S.C.L.R. 379.

[12] *Welikanna v Welikanna*, 2000 G.W.D. 23–890.

[13] *B v B*, 1999 Fam. L.R. 74 at para.74–11.

[14] *Adams v Adams*, 2002 S.C.L.R. 379; *Welikanna v Welikanna*, 2000 G.W.D. 23–890.

[15] *G v G*, 2002 Fam. L.R. 120.

[16] See para.8–09.

[17] See *Nicol v Nicol*, 2001 G.W.D. 23–865; although remember that an application for variation is always available. See para.8–10.

[18] *Welikanna v Welikanna*, 2000 G.W.D. 23–890.

Discretionary nature of interim aliment

8–03 The question of whether to award interim aliment in any given case is a matter for the discretion of the court.[19] The only guidance given in the Act is that the court may award the sum claimed or any lesser sum or may refuse to make the award.[20] The extent of this discretion was stressed in *Begg v Begg*, 1987 S.C.L.R. 704 where Sheriff Principal Gillies commented as follows[21]:

> "It is trite law that awards of interim aliment are very much within the discretion of the sheriff, and it is, I think, clear that the provisions of section 6(2) of the Family Law (Scotland) Act 1985 do not innovate on the law. Accordingly, in the ordinary case, before I can interfere with an award made by the sheriff, I must be satisfied that he has erred in law, or that he has failed to notice a relevant factor, or that he has arrived at a wholly unreasonable decision."

Criteria

Criteria generally

8–04 It is difficult to know in precise terms what the test for interim aliment is. It is not defined in the Act. Interim aliment under s.6 replaces the old aliment *pendente lite*, in terms of which the test was need of the claimant, with this being assessed with reference to the means of the other party, and the standard of living of the parties when they co-habited. It has been suggested that this remains the test,[22] and this seems correct.[23] In *Donaldson v Donaldson*[24] the sheriff agreed, commenting:

> "The basis for an award of interim aliment is the relief of need taking into account the current standard of living enjoyed by the spouses during the cohabitation and other circumstances of the case so far as known. (See Clive on *Husband and Wife*, 4th edition page 173). Other circumstances would obviously include the financial positions of the parties."

Relevance of the section 4 criteria

8–05 Section 4 of the Family Law (Scotland) Act 1985 ("the Act") lays down certain criteria for the court in relation to final (as opposed to interim) awards of aliment. It should be noted that these criteria do not specifically apply to claims for interim aliment, but they do have some relevance in such claims. Section 4 provides in relation to an award of aliment that the court shall have regard: (a) to the needs and resources

---

[19] See e.g. *Currie v Currie* (1833) 12 S. 171; *Johnston v Johnston*, 1916 2 S.L.T. 191.

[20] s.6(2). Note that there is no power to increase the sum claimed.

[21] At p.705.

[22] See e.g. the commentary to *Bisset v Bisset*, 1993 S.C.L.R. 284.

[23] See e.g. *Johnson v Johnson*, (Sh Ct), November 5, 2003 unreported but discussed at 2004 Fam. L.B. 67–6 and available on the Scottish Courts Administration website—"I did however consider that the Pursuer had a genuine need for herself and her child."

[24] 2005 G.W.D. 71, a decision of Sheriff Cusine at Aberdeen, February 2005—full report available on the Scottish Courts Administration website.

of the parties; (b) to the earning capacities of the parties; and (c) generally to all the circumstances of the case.[25] In *McGeachie v McGeachie*, 1989 S.C.L.R. 99, Sheriff Principal Caplan considered a motion for interim aliment. He held that while s.4 does not apply to interim aliment, nevertheless the criteria set out there are consistent with pre-existing law and practice, commenting[26]:

> "While it is true that the criteria set out in section 4 of the 1985 Act do not by virtue of the Act apply to interim aliment awards, it seems to me that these criteria are consistent with pre-existing law and practice in relation to the determination of interim aliment and that therefore the sheriff has not erred in declaring that these are factors to be taken into account. I consider it to be indisputable that needs, earning capacity and general circumstances are all proper elements to consider when awarding interim aliment. An award of interim aliment which was totally beyond the capacity of the obligant party to pay would be pointless."

Section 4 considerations have been considered relevant in other cases involving claims for interim aliment,[27] and the three criteria set out in s.4(1) seem a reasonable place to begin when considering any such claim. The remainder of this section considers each of these in turn.

(a) Needs and resources

A party's needs includes present and foreseeable needs,[28] and will **8–06** generally include essentials such as accommodation costs, clothing, food, medical costs and travel costs. However, the definition of "need" is a relative one, and to some extent will be assessed with reference to the standard of living previously enjoyed by the party seeking the award.[29] Accordingly, "needs" in some circumstances might include costs for matters which are not strictly essential such as holidays, entertainment, school fees and the like.

Section 27(1) defines "resources" as "present and foreseeable resources". The term will generally encompass income from whatever source, earned or unearned. Under s.20 the court may order either party to provide details of their resources.[30] Emoluments such as company cars

---

[25] s.4(1). In having regard to para.(c) the court (in terms of s.4(3)) may, if it thinks fit, take account of any support, financial or otherwise, given by the defender to any person whom he maintains as a dependant in his household, whether or not the defender owes an obligation of aliment to that person; and shall not take account of any conduct of a party unless it would be manifestly inequitable to leave it out of account.

[26] At p.100.

[27] *Johnson v Johnson* (Sh Ct), November 5, 2003 unreported but available on the Scottish Courts Administration website; *Adams v Adams*, 2002 S.C.L.R. 379.

[28] s.27(1).

[29] See e.g. *B v B*, 1999 Fam. L.R. 74 at para.74–04; *Fyfe v Fyfe*, 1970 S.L.T. (Notes) 25.

[30] Although if the motion is made an early stage it might be refused as premature—see *Fernandes v Fernandes, The Scotsman*, July 2, 2003, *http://thescotsman.scotsman.com/ViewArticle.aspx?articleid=2440346* [accessed January 11, 2008]. Perhaps the family motto of Mr Fernandes—"Two rams cannot drink from the same bucket."—might be seen as a useful reminder that the resources of the parties are a relevant consideration in a claim for interim aliment.

or rent-free accommodation may be resources in certain circumstances, and may be particularly relevant if they increase the free income available to meet a claim for interim aliment.[31] If the defender is already paying bills and outgoings for the family, or is paying child support, these will be relevant matters.[32] Where a self-employed party's business is earning substantial profits but they choose to draw only a relatively small amount, the court may be justified in assessing their resources based on the profits rather than the drawings.[33] The impact of taxation on parties may be a relevant consideration in assessing resources,[34] but it may be impractical and undesirable for the courts to engage in detailed inquiry into complex tax treatment when assessing interim aliment.[35]

The earnings of a cohabitee of the person against whom payment is sought may be relevant, but only to a limited degree. In *Munro v Munro*, 1986 S.L.T. 72, the Outer House dealt with a case where the wife sought interim aliment against her husband. The husband claimed deductions from his salary should be taken into account before aliment was fixed. These included provisions for a home which he shared with another person. That cohabitee had an income of her own. It was held that the cohabitee's salary was a relevant factor in assessing the husband's outlays when determining the amount of aliment which he could afford to pay to the wife. The Lord Ordinary (Lord Mackay of Clashfern) commented[36]:

> "I was informed by counsel for the pursuer that the defender was living with another woman who was in employment. The defender's counsel submitted that her financial position was irrelevant to the circumstances, since it was the defender and not the other lady who has responsibility for the aliment of the pursuer and the children. Naturally I accept that it is for the defender to shoulder the responsibility of aliment for the pursuer and the children, but where he claims deductions from his salary to be taken into account before such aliment is fixed which include provisions for a home which he shares with another person with an income, I consider this is a factor which has to be taken into account in considering to what extent his outlays fall to be considered in relation to the amount of aliment which the defender should be ordered to pay."

Notice that the judgment suggests that, in assessing claims for interim aliment, it is not simply the case that the income of the cohabitee is aggregated with that of the party who is being asked to pay. Rather, the income of the cohabitee is relevant in assessing how much of the income of the party against whom interim aliment is sought needs to be devoted to the outlays for his or her new household.[37]

---

[31] *Semple v Semple*, 1995 S.C.L.R. 569.
[32] *B v B*, 1999 Fam. L.R. 74.
[33] *B v B*, 1999 Fam. L.R. 74.
[34] See e.g. *Wiseman v Wiseman*, 1989 S.C.L.R. 757; *Begg v Begg*, 1987 S.C.L.R. 704.
[35] *MacInnes v MacInnes*, 1993 S.L.T. 1108; *Gray v Gray*, 1968 S.C. 185; *Thomson v Thomson*, 1943 S.C. 154.
[36] At p.73.
[37] See also *Henderson v Henderson*, 1991 G.W.D. 31–1864.

(b)   Earning capacities of the parties

A party who has the capacity to be in full-time employment (provided **8–07** that such employment is available) cannot elect to be unemployed simply to improve their position in relation to a claim for interim aliment.[38] However, in *Adams v Adams*, 2002 S.C.L.R. 379, it was emphasised that there is a need for some caution in circumstances where a court is asked to take an earning capacity into account where that capacity is not actually being realised[39]:

> "In my opinion, however, the solicitor for the appellant was well founded in her submissions that, while the defender may have a capacity to earn, that capacity has not been realised in fact. In the course of the appeal I never received a satisfactory response from the solicitor for the pursuer as to how a capacity to earn can provide the resources to meet a claim for interim aliment if that capacity is not realised in fact. Of course a party may have a capacity for work but makes no effort to seek work. In this case, however, there was no suggestion made to the sheriff nor in the appeal that the defender had not genuinely been unable to secure employment. I accept of course that the pursuer contended that the defender was still working . . . but, on the basis of the information presented to him, the sheriff has not resolved and probably could not satisfactorily resolve that dispute. That is not to say, however, that there is no suspicion about the defender's position, but suspicion is in my view an inadequate basis upon which to proceed."

(c)   Generally all the circumstances of the case

Under s.4(1)(c) the court may take into account "generally all the **8–08** circumstances of the case". Clearly the court's discretion is wide. These circumstances might include any support, financial or otherwise, given by the defender to any person whom he maintains as a dependant in his household, whether or not the defender owes an obligation of aliment to that person.[40] However, the court is not to take account of any conduct of a party, unless it would be manifestly inequitable to leave it out of account.[41]

One important matter which the court may have to consider is a situation where the party seeking aliment is co-habiting with a third party. Even where the new relationship has very limited collective means, it may be difficult to successfully claim interim aliment in these circumstances. In *Brunton v Brunton*, 1986 S.L.T. 49, the court considered a situation where the pursuer was living with a new partner. Lord Allanbridge commented[42]:

---

[38] *Johnson v Johnson* (Sh Ct), November 5, 2003, unreported but available on the Scottish Courts Administration website—the husband had been in well-paid employment earning about £2,500 per month, but claimed at the hearing on interim aliment not to be working. However, he produced no satisfactory evidence to vouch for this. In these circumstances the court was entitled to take into account earning capacity of £2,500 per month in assessing interim aliment.

[39] Sheriff Principal Dunlop at p.381.

[40] s.4(3)(a).

[41] s.4(3)(b); see e.g. *Walker v Walker*, 1991 S.L.T. 649; *Donnelly v Donnelly*, 1959 S.C. 97.

[42] At p.50.

"Counsel for the pursuer said she admitted she was living with another man but submitted that, as both she and her paramour were unemployed, she was still entitled to aliment from her husband. Counsel for the defender stated that the wife and the other man were both assessed by the social security authorities as living together and were receiving support from public funds on that basis and argued that the wife was therefore not entitled to any aliment at present.

I reduced the aliment payable by the husband to nil in the special circumstances of this case. I took the view that a husband should not be expected to support his wife when she was actually living with another man, albeit that man was unemployed and unable to support her directly. Whilst the court will normally take into account the standard of living enjoyed by spouses during cohabitation this case was unusual in that the wife admitted she was living with another man and that both were being supported by public funds on such a basis. Any aliment paid by the husband would in effect be supporting not only his wife but also the man with whom she was living."[43]

Appeal

8–09   Appeal is only competent with leave.[44] As the level of interim aliment is within the discretion of the court, an appellate court can only interfere with the decision if the judge at first instance: (a) has erred in law; (b) has failed to note a relevant factor; or (c) has arrived at a wholly unreasonable decision. Accordingly, it may be rather hard to persuade the appellate court to interfere with an award of interim aliment.[45] However, if the court is misinformed about a material matter (or fails to take into account such a matter), then the chances of a successful appeal are enhanced.[46]

Variation

8–10   Section 6(4) provides that any interim award may itself be subsequently varied or recalled by a further order of the court. An application for variation is made by motion.[47] Final decrees for aliment may only be varied if there is a material change in circumstances.[48] However, a material change in circumstances is not required (although it may well be highly relevant) to allow variation of awards of interim aliment; all that is needed is that there is sufficient reason for a variation. The justification for this seems to be that a final decree for aliment will only have been reached after full enquiry into the facts, and accordingly it is

---

[43] Although see e.g. *Kavanagh v Kavanagh*, 1989 S.L.T. 134, a case involving periodical allowance rather than interim aliment.
[44] See e.g. *Rixson v Rixson*, 1990 S.L.T. (Sh Ct) 5; *Hulme v Hulme*, 1990 S.L.T. (Sh Ct) 25; *Dickson v Dickson*, 1990 S.L.T. (Sh Ct) 80; *Richardson v Richardson*, 1991 S.L.T. (Sh Ct) 7.
[45] e.g. *Nicol v Nicol*, 2001 G.W.D. 23–865.
[46] *Wiseman v Wiseman*, 1989 S.C.L.R. 757.
[47] O.C.R. r.33.50.
[48] s.5(1).

reasonable to limit variation to circumstances where there has been a material change in those facts. However, interim orders will often have been reached on the basis of less comprehensive information, and should be more readily open to review.[49] Interim awards of aliment cannot be varied retrospectively.[50]

---

[49] *Bisset v Bisset*, 1993 S.C.L.R. 284.
[50] *McColl v McColl*, 1993 S.C. 276; *Adamson v Adamson*, 1996 S.L.T. 427; *Kirk v Kirk*, 2003 Fam. L.R. 50.

Chapter 9

MISCELLANEOUS MATTERS

Section 20—Orders for Provision of Details of Resources

General comments

9–01   Section 20 of the Act provides:

> "In an action—
>
> (a) for aliment;
> (b) which includes a claim for an order for financial provision; or
> (c) which includes a claim for interim aliment,
>
> the court may order either party to provide details of his resources or those relating to a child or incapax on whose behalf he is acting."

One of the biggest problems facing practitioners in a contentious action for financial provision or aliment is obtaining full disclosure of the opponent's resources. Section 20 is designed to allow a party to obtain information about those resources. In this context the term "resources" is defined by the Act as meaning present and foreseeable resources.[1] In addition to using s.20 orders, parties may also use the more traditional approach of seeking commission and diligence for the recovery of documents.[2]

Some procedural comments

9–02   The party seeking a s.20 order does not need to aver that the other party has concealed assets, and in particular the rules on averments required in a motion for recovery through commission and diligence do not apply.[3] It is enough that there is reason to suppose that there has not been full disclosure.[4]

The motion may be made at an early stage in the case, but if it is made too early it may be refused as premature.[5] It appears that a s.20 motion

---

[1] s.27(1).

[2] See e.g. *Douglas v Douglas*, 1966 S.L.T. (Notes) 43.

[3] *Lawrence v Lawrence*, 1992 S.C.L.R. 199.

[4] *Lawrence v Lawrence*, 1992 S.C.L.R. 199. Indeed the sheriff principal in that case comments that technically it may be possible to make a s.20 order even if there is no suggestion that assets have been concealed.

[5] See the rather colourful report on *Fernandes v Fernandes*, *The Scotsman*, July 2, 2003, *http://thescotsman.scotsman.com/ViewArticle.aspx?articleid=2440346* [accessed January 11, 2008].

can be made very late in the day—even during the proof to bring matters before the court which are not on record,[6] although presumably there would have to be good reason for leaving matters so late.

If a s.20 order is granted, the obligation is to supply details of all resources, and a failure to do so will be a contempt of court.[7] The obligation is to provide details of the resources together with an estimate of their value.[8] The court can seek clarification on certain issues, but is not entitled to insist on vouching of the value of the resources.[9] If there is a dispute about the value of an asset, the parties will require to establish their position in evidence in the normal way,[10] and it will be for the party seeking financial provision to formulate and prove their entitlement.[11] The following passage from Sheriff Principal Maguire in *Nelson v Nelson*, 1993 S.C.L.R. 149 illustrates the obligations imposed by, and the limitations of, s.20[12]:

> "The case turns upon the interpretation of section 20. That section empowers the court to order either party to provide details of his resources. If the party so ordered fails to provide details of his present or foreseeable resources (section 27 of the Act), he will be in contempt of an order of court. The Act does not give the court power to conduct an inquiry as to the extent of the disclosure. The obligation is upon the party ordered. At the same time, I consider that the court is entitled to seek clarification of matters in any list of resources. If a party, for example, were to say simply that he had a house, without disclosing its whereabouts or putting any value on it, the court would in my view be entitled to say that was not disclosing details of the resources. I am not convinced, however, that the court, using its powers under section 20, could insist on a party producing vouched evidence of the valuation of the house. The exact valuation of an asset is always open to argument and it would be for each party to seek to convince the court of the proper valuation. In the present case, therefore, I consider that the sheriff went too far in seeking documents vouching the net value of the house. In any event, the defender had in his pleadings supplied a figure for the value of the house. So far as the value of the motor-car is concerned, I consider that fulfilling his obligation under section 20 would require the defender to provide a figure for the value of the vehicle."

---

[6] *MacQueen v MacQueen*, 1992 G.W.D. 28–1653.

[7] *Nelson v Nelson*, 1992 S.C.L.R. 149. Repeated failure to disclose assets may justify a decision to allow the action to proceed as undefended by way of affidavit evidence—see *Fairbairn v Fairbairn*, 2003 Fam. L.B. 64–2.

[8] *Nelson v Nelson*, 1992 S.C.L.R. 149.

[9] *Nelson v Nelson*, 1992 S.C.L.R. 149; although it will always be open to a party to apply for an incidental order for valuation of the asset using s.14(2)(b); see *Williamson v Williamson*, 1989 S.L.T. 866 at p.867.

[10] *Nelson v Nelson*, 1993 S.C.L.R. 149.

[11] *Williamson v Williamson*, 1989 S.L.T. 866 at p.867.

[12] At p.150.

COURT EXPENSES

9–03 Normally, expenses follow success in court actions. However, this rule is not applied in its full rigour in family actions.[13] In any event, it is often difficult to determine in these actions that one party has been wholly successful.[14] Generally a formal minute of tender is not thought to be appropriate in family actions, but nevertheless offers to settle the financial aspects of a case may be important in establishing liability for expenses.[15] A party who succeeds in obtaining an award which is only modestly higher than a sum offered judicially or extra-judicially will not necessarily obtain an award of expenses against the other party. Where both parties co-operate in making full and frank disclosure of matters to the court, and seek to narrow the points at issue between them, then often the result will be no award of expenses to or by either party.[16] However, on the other hand, if one party takes the other to proof on issues on which he is unsuccessful to the extent of failing to secure an award significantly greater than an offer which has been made by the other party, then the expense caused to the other party may well be recoverable.[17] In some cases, failure to settle a case on generous terms may constitute conduct of which the court is entitled to take account in making its order for financial provision.[18]

ANTI-AVOIDANCE MEASURES

9–04 Section 18 allows the court to set aside transfers of, and transactions involving, property if it is satisfied that the purpose was to defeat claims for financial provision. The court also has power to interdict such conduct. An application for an order is made by a crave in the initial writ or defences,[19] unless the application is made after final decree, when it is made by minute in the original process.[20]

Section 18 provides:

> "(1) Where a claim has been made (whether before or after the commencement of this Act), being—
>
> (a) an action for aliment,
> (b) a claim for an order for financial provision, or
> (c) an application for variation or recall of a decree in such an action or of an order for financial provision,
>
> the person making the claim may, not later than one year from the date of the disposal of the claim, apply to the court for an order—

---

[13] *Little v Little*, 1990 S.L.T. 785.
[14] *Cameron v Cameron*, 2002 S.C.L.R. 313.
[15] *Cameron v Cameron*, 2002 S.C.L.R. 313.
[16] *Sweeney v Sweeney (No.3)*, 2007 Fam. L.R. 12.
[17] *Adams v Adams (No.2)*, 1997 S.L.T. 150; *Sweeney v Sweeney (No.3)*, 2007 Fam. L.R. 12.
[18] *Collins v Collins*, 1997 Fam. L.R. 50.
[19] O.C.R. r.33.48. Appropriate craves, averments and pleas-in-law should be included— O.C.R. r.33.53(1).
[20] An application for such an order is made by minute in the original process—O.C.R. r.33.53

(i) setting aside or varying any transfer of, or transaction involving, property effected by the other person not more than 5 years before the date of the making of the claim; or

(ii) interdicting the other person from effecting any such transfer or transaction.

(2) Subject to subsection (3) below, on an application under subsection (1) above for an order the court may, if it is satisfied that the transfer or transaction had the effect of, or is likely to have the effect of, defeating in whole or in part any claim referred to in subsection (1) above, make the order applied for or such other order as it thinks fit.

(3) An order under subsection (2) above shall not prejudice any rights of a third party in or to the property where that third party—

(a) has in good faith acquired the property or any of it or any rights in relation to it for value; or

(b) derives title to such property or rights from any person who has done so.

(4) Where the court makes an order under subsection (2) above, it may include in the order such terms and conditions as it thinks fit and may make any ancillary order which it considers expedient to ensure that the order is effective."

SECTION 16—ORDERS SETTING ASIDE OR VARYING SEPARATION AGREEMENTS

Introduction

If parties enter into a separation agreement dealing with financial **9–05** provision on divorce or dissolution, the court will not normally interfere with this. However, s.16 allows the court to vary or set aside such an agreement (or terms within it) in three fairly narrow situations. Two of these relate to the power of the court to set aside or vary terms relating to a periodical allowance in certain circumstances and these are discussed elsewhere.[21]

However, there is a more general power available to the court in terms of s.16(1)(b). Under this provision, the court may set aside or vary the agreement or any term of it where the agreement was not fair and reasonable at the time it was entered into. This allows the court to interfere with the terms of an agreement in circumstances which fall short of common law powers to reduce a contract on the grounds of error, fraud, force or fear.[22] Section 16(1)(b) gives the court power to correct injustices between the parties. It is implicit in the wording of s.16(1)(b) that it is designed to redress injustices arising at the point that the agreement was entered into. It cannot be used to vary or set aside terms because of events arising after the agreement is made which a

---

[21] See paras 3–47 to 3–48.
[22] *McAfee v McAfee*, 1990 S.C.L.R. 805.

party perceives as giving rise to an injustice.[23] An application for an order is made by a crave in the initial writ or defences,[24] unless the application is made after final decree when it is made by minute in the original process.[25]

When can the court make a section 16(1)(b) order?

9–06   If the agreement does not contain a term relating to pension sharing, the court may make a s.16(1)(b) order on granting decree of divorce or dissolution, or within such time as the court may specify on granting of such decree.[26] If the agreement does contain a provision relating to pension sharing, then (i) where the order sets aside the agreement or sets aside or varies the terms relating to pension sharing, on granting of decree of divorce or dissolution, and (ii) where the order sets aside or varies any other term of the agreement, on granting decree of divorce or dissolution, or within such time as the court may specify on granting of such decree.[27]

What types of agreement can be set aside or varied?

9–07   Separation agreements entered into between the parties may be set aside or varied.[28] Joint minutes between the parties to a court action may be set aside or varied provided that decree in terms thereof has not yet been pronounced.[29] An agreement constituted by acceptance of a tender may also be challenged.[30]

Relevant factors

9–08   The court should recognise that the parties are husband and wife, and should not analyse matters as if the parties had entered into a commercial contract.[31] The court should look at all the circumstances prior to and at the time that the agreement was entered which were relevant to its negotiation and signing. It should then seek to determine whether there was an unfair or unconscionable advantage taken of some factor or relationship between the parties. If this is the case, the court may be able to hold that one party did not truly enter into the agreement as a free agent, and that the agreement (or some term within it) was not therefore fair and reasonable at the time it was entered into.[32] The best summary of the principles to be applied by the court in approaching challenges to separation agreements under s.16(1)(b) can be found in *Gillon v Gillon (No.3)*, 1995 S.L.T. 678 where Lord Weir explained that the court should take the following approach[33]:

---

[23] *Anderson v Anderson*, 1989 S.C.L.R. 475. See also the discussion of *Jongejan v Jongejan*, 1993 S.L.T. 595 at 1993 Fam. L.B. 4–6.
[24] O.C.R. r.33.48.
[25] O.C.R. r.33.52.
[26] s.16(2)(b).
[27] s.16(2)(c).
[28] See e.g. *McAfee v McAfee*, 1990 S.C.L.R. 805.
[29] *Jongejan v Jongejan*, 1993 S.L.T. 599.
[30] *Young v Young (No.2)*, 1991 S.L.T. 869.
[31] The purpose of ss.16(1)(b) is different from the purpose of the Unfair Contract Terms Act 1977, and authorities relating to the 1977 Act will not be useful in s.16(1)(b) arguments. See the discussion of *Gillon v Gillon* at 1993 Fam. L.B 2–4.
[32] *McAfee v McAfee*, 1990 S.C.L.R. 805.
[33] He deduced these principles from an analysis of the cases of *Edgar v Edgar* [1980] 1 W.L.R. 1410, [1980] 3 All E.R. 887; *McAfee v McAfee*, 1990 S.C.L.R. 805 and *Gillon v Gillon (No.1)*, 1994 S.L.T. 978.

"(1) It is necessary to examine the agreement from the point of view of both fairness and reasonableness. (2) Such examination must relate to all the relevant circumstances leading up to and prevailing at the time of the execution of the agreement, including amongst other things the nature and quality of any legal advice given to either party. (3) Evidence that some unfair advantage was taken by one party of the other by reason of circumstances prevailing at the time of negotiations may have a cogent bearing on the determination of the issue. (4) The court should not be unduly ready to overturn agreements validly entered into. (5) The fact that it transpires that an agreement has led to an unequal and possibly a very unequal division of assets does not by itself necessarily give rise to any inference of unfairness and unreasonableness."

The fact that a party is legally represented (or indeed legally qualified themselves) may be important but it does not bar them from challenging the agreement.[34] If a party receives poor legal advice, this might be a relevant factor in allowing a successful challenge.[35] However, if a party enters into a separation agreement, albeit in disadvantageous terms, having received sound legal advice about material matters it will be difficult to challenge the agreement.[36] If a party is given clear warnings that they should take independent advice about an agreement but declines to do so, it will be more difficult for them to challenge its terms.[37] The fact that a party signed an irrevocable mandate to her agents instructing them to accept a tender on her behalf did not preclude her from challenging the agreement set up by the acceptance of the tender. Of course, the circumstances under which those instructions were given might be relevant matters having a bearing on whether the agreement was fair and reasonable at the time it was entered into.[38]

Other circumstances which might allow a successful challenge include: where one party applies undue and unreasonable pressure on the other;[39] where one party exploits a dominant business position to their unreasonable advantage;[40] or where one party's judgement is clouded due to ill health, poor mental health or stress.[41]

Where parties enter into an agreement without any awareness of the significance of material matters such as the value of pension rights, they may have grounds to challenge an agreement.[42] Similarly, if one party does not declare a significant asset to the other (such as pension rights) then, provided the value of the asset is material, this may give grounds for varying or setting aside the agreement.[43] However, if the parties are aware of a potential claim on pension rights but choose not to have

---

[34] *McAfee v McAfee*, 1990 S.C.L.R. 805.
[35] *Short v Short*, 1994 G.W.D. 1300.
[36] See e.g. *Gillon v Gillon (No.3)*, 1995 S.L.T. 678.
[37] *Inglis v Inglis*, 1999 S.L.T. (Sh Ct) 59.
[38] *Young v Young (No.2)*, 1991 S.L.T. 869.
[39] *McAfee v McAfee*, 1990 S.C.L.R. 805.
[40] *McAfee v McAfee*, 1990 S.C.L.R. 805.
[41] *McAfee v McAfee*, 1990 S.C.L.R. 805; *Short v Short*, 1994 G.W.D. 1300.
[42] *Worth v Worth*, 1994 S.L.T. (Sh Ct) 54.
[43] *McKay v McKay*, 2006 Fam. L.R. 78.

those rights valued, then it will be difficult to maintain this argument, particularly if the agreement secures other beneficial results for them (such as securing the other party's departure from the matrimonial home).[44] It is not enough to approach the agreement with hindsight and argue that it was unreasonable because it was financially disadvantageous to one party. If parties choose freely to enter into an agreement when they have not obtained full valuations of some assets, it will be difficult for them to argue that the agreement should be set aside; after all the parties may quite legitimately have chosen this course of action to avoid the expense and delay of obtaining valuations.[45] If a party is given clear advice about the pros and cons of an agreement then it will be difficult for them to argue that the agreement was unfair or unreasonable.[46]

---

[44] *Inglis v Inglis*, 1999 S.L.T. (Sh Ct) 59.
[45] *Gillon v Gillon (No.3)*, 1995 S.L.T. 678 at p.681.
[46] *Gillon v Gillon (No.3)*, 1995 S.L.T. 678 at p.681.

FINANCIAL PROVISION CHECKLIST

1. Preliminary matters

(a) Consider alternative dispute resolution (e.g. mediation, collaborative family law) [para.1–03].

(b) Establish client's priorities [para.4–10].

(c) Is interim aliment required? [paras 8–02 to 8–08].

(d) Are there any existing separation agreements? If so, are there grounds for setting aside or variation? [para.9–05].

2. Establish relevant date

(a) What was the final date of separation?

(b) Are there any arguments that the parties were not co-habiting although they were living under the same roof? [para.5–04].

(c) Were there any periods of reconciliation before the final split? If so what effect do they have? [para.5–05].

(d) Remember that property subject to a transfer order will generally be valued at the date of transfer not the relevant date [para.5–06].

3. Establish matrimonial/partnership property

(a) Prepare a schedule of assets and debts [para.4–05].

(b) Ascertain matrimonial/partnership property at the relevant date [para.6–01].

(c) Ascertain any debts to be taken into account [paras 6–51 to 6–57].

(d) Remember that the term "property" is a broad one [para.6–49].

(e) Was any heritable property (and its contents)acquired before marriage/registration acquired for use as a family home? [paras 6–06 and 6–11].

(f) Make necessary enquiries with financial institutions etc. [para.4–03].

(g) Make necessary enquiries with the opponent [para.4–03].

(h) Establish employment histories for both parties and consider likely pension rights [para.6–14].

(i) Do not forget SERPS [para.6–19].

(j) Are there any sums due to the parties but not yet paid at the relevant date (e.g. damages claims, tax repayments etc.)? [para.6–47].

(k) Are any assets apparently in the name of the parties actually held in trust for third parties? [para.6–46].

(l) Is discovery of assets required if the opponent is obstructive? [para.9–01].

4. Consider gifts/inheritances/property owned before marriage or registration

   (a) Did either party receive substantial gifts or inheritances during the marriage/civil partnership? [para.6–01].

   (b) Did either party have substantial assets of their own before the marriage or civil partnership? [para.6–01].

   (c) Is there an argument that such property has become "converted" into matrimonial/patnership property? [para.6–63].

   (d) If there has been "conversion" does a s.10(6)(b)(source of funds) or a s.9(1)(b)argument have merit? [para.6–63].

   (e) Pay particular attention to business interests [para.6–28].

5. Value matrimonial/partnership property

   (a) Initially value all property and debts at the relevant date [para.6–02].

   (b) Consider employing experts to value unusual/difficult assets [para.6–49].

   (c) Obtain CETVs for all pension interests (including SERPS) [para.6–15].

   (d) Ensure values of pension interests and life policies are properly apportioned [paras 6–16 and 6–26].

   (e) Should the value of certain business interests be discounted? [para.6–35].

   (f) Bear in mind that property which is to be transferred will need to be re-valued [para.5–06].

   (g) Consider whether there are any special circumstances arguments relating to any particular assets (paying particular attention to valuable assets) [para.7–02].

6. Consider the effect of equal sharing

   (a) Remember that there is a presumption for equal sharing of matrimonial and partnership property [paras 4–03 to 4–06].

7. Consider possible special circumstances

   (a) Are the circumstances "special"? [para.7–01].

   (b) Try to quantify the argument [para.7–02].

   (c) Does the argument fall within the five examples of "special circumstances", namely—

      a. the terms of any agreement [paras 7–03 to 7–07];

      b. the source of funds or assets [paras 7–08 to 7–24];

      c. destruction, dissipation or alienation of property [paras 7–25 to 7–29];

      d. the nature of any property [paras 7–30 to 7–38];

      e. liability for certain expenses [para.7–39].

   (d) Remember that the five examples are not exclusive—there are other "special circumstances" lying outwith these categories [paras 7–40 to 7–41].

8. Consider section 9(1)(b)—economic advantage/disadvantage

   (a) Consider advantages and disadvantages before and during the marriage/civil partnership [paras 4–21 to 4–23].

(b) Remember "contributions" must have an economic effect [para.4–24].
(c) Weigh up advantages and disadvantages of both parties [para.4–25].
(d) Try to quantify the argument [paras 4–27 to 4–31].
(e) Some (but by no means all) s.9(b) arguments are:

- Interruption of career in the interests of the family [paras 4–33 to 4–36];
- Exclusive enjoyment of assets following separation [para.4–37];
- Expenditure on the family after the separation [para.4–38];
- Payment of mortgage/other expenses after separation [paras 4–39 to 4–40];
- Improvements to property belonging to the other party [para.4–41];
- Contributions to businesses owned by the other party [para.4–42];
- Conduct [para.4–44].

9. Consider section 9(1)(c)—economic burden of childcare

(a) Should an enhanced "one off" order or periodical allowance be sought [para.4–53].
(b) Consider the age of the children [para.4–54].
(c) Try to quantify the argument [para.4–59].
(d) Consider the relationship with child support [paras 4–60 to 4–67].
(e) Analyse reported cases [paras 4–50 to 4–67].

10. Consider section 9(1)(d)—adjustment to loss of support

(a) Should an enhanced "one off" order or periodical allowance be sought [para.4–70].
(b) Remember the three-year time limit [para.4–71].
(c) Consider what "adjustment" is required—are there other resources which already allow adjustment? [paras 4–72 to 4–74].
(d) Consider the level of support available before divorce or dissolution [para.4–75].
(e) Analyse reported cases [para.4–77].

11. Consider section 9(1)(e)—serious financial hardship

(a) Should an enhanced "one off" order or periodical allowance be sought [para.4–80].
(b) What other resources will be available to alleviate hardship? [para.4–81].
(c) What period of award should be sought? [para.4–82].
(d) What level of support was available before divorce or dissolution? [para.4–83].
(e) Does the hardship arise *as a result of divorce or dissolution*? [para.4–84].
(f) Analyse reported cases [para.4–86].

12. Which section 8 orders might achieve the desired result?

(a) Consider what combination of s.8 orders is required to achieve the client's aspirations [paras 4–10 and 4–20].
(b) Keep in mind the "clean break" principle [para.3–34].
(c) If a transfer of property is sought, the property should be valued at the date of transfer, not the relevant date [para.5–06].
(d) If pension sharing or earmarking is sought consider the potential pitfalls and engage an expert [paras 3–57 and 3–79].

13. Consider resources as the case progresses

(a) Any orders sought must be reasonable having regard to the resources of the parties at the time the order is made [paras 3–02 to 3–08].
(b) Consider significant changes in resources of both parties since the date of separation [paras 3–02 to 3–08].

14. Conduct

(a) Has there been any "financially adverse" conduct? [paras 4–12 to 4–13].
(b) If s.9(1)(d) or (e) apply, would it be manifestly inequitable to leave conduct out of account? [para.4–14].

15. Valuation of assets to be transferred

(a) If any assets are to be transferred from one party to the other, value these at the date of transfer in accordance with s.10(3A) [para.5–06].

INDEX